THE MYSTICISM OF PAUL THE APOSTLE

THE MYSTICISM
OF
PAUL THE APOSTLE

ALBERT SCHWEITZER

WITH A PREFATORY NOTE BY

F. C. BURKITT, D.D.
LATE PROFESSOR OF DIVINITY, UNIVERSITY OF CAMBRIDGE

THE SEABURY PRESS • NEW YORK

First *Seabury Paperback* Edition Published 1968
Second Printing

Copyright 1931 by Albert Schweitzer
Library of Congress Catalog Card Number: 68-28707
607-868-C-5
Translated from the German (*Die Mystik des Apostels Paulus*)
by William Montgomery, B.D.
Published in England by A. and C. Black, Limited
Printed in the United States of America
ISBN 0-8164-2049-1

PREFATORY NOTE

M Y regretted friend William Montgomery, who translated this book, died quite suddenly in October, 1930, at the early age of 59, just after finishing his translation. His name was familiar to English-speaking readers of theological literature by his work on St. Augustine—he was co-editor of the 'Confessions' in the Cambridge Patristic Series—but still more as the translator of Dr. Schweitzer's great book, called in German Von Reimarus zu Wrede, *but in English "The Quest of the Historical Jesus".[1] He was also the translator of Schweitzer's Ge-schichte der paulinischen Forschung, called in English "Paul and his Interpreters" (1912), as noted in this volume on p. 17.*

Montgomery was an admirable translator of German theological literature, and had he lived to superintend the printing of the present work it would, I am sure, have been as excellent a translation as "The Quest of the Historical Jesus", allowance being made for the difference of the subject-matter. Unfortunately what he left was a rather illegible draft, not fully revised, and some one acquainted not only with German but also with theological research was needed to see it through the press, and add Indices and a translation of the Author's Preface. For the Indices I am indebted to the careful and intelligent co-operation of Mrs. A. H. Quiggin, of Cambridge, who also detected a certain number of errata which had escaped both me and the printers.

After having read this work through several times in the course of correcting the proofs it is perhaps not inappropriate for me to say a few words about the book itself. Dr. Schweitzer's own Preface explains very well his aims and his main conclusions, but I feel that the present-day English attitude to St. Paul is somewhat different from that current in Germany, a fact which makes any Continental book on the Apostle of the Gentiles hard reading, however well it may be expressed and however idiomatically it may be translated. With the decay of the popularity of 'Evangelical' doctrine Paul has gone out of favour, and

---

[1] *Published by A. and C. Black, London, 1910: the 2nd German edition, so often referred to in this volume (e.g. p. 57), is called* Geschichte der Leben-Jesu-Forschung.

his letters are much too little studied by modern Englishmen. Further, there is an idea widely current that Paul put 'dogma' into the original Gospel, and that he thereby spoilt it. What the original Gospel was is not enough understood, notwithstanding the wide use nowadays of the term 'eschatological'. We are still, as a nation, too much under the influence of Reformation theology (and the reaction from it) to apprehend the nature of the Church of the second and immediately succeeding centuries, or properly to realize the difficulties inherent in turning the hope of the coming of the Kingdom of God, set forth in a form appropriate to Jews in the first century, into a religious faith appropriate for Gentiles who lived in the days of Marcus Aurelius and Commodus. If Christianity was to survive at all it needed to evolve into such a form. If Christianity is to renew its youth in this our changing age it can only do so through Christians learning to understand the inner developments of Christianity in former ages, even though these developments do not directly satisfy our present religious needs.

Of these developments incomparably the most important and significant is that represented by St. Paul: it is the step, as it might be called, between Jesus Christ and Ignatius of Antioch. Paul was a product of his time, and his religious view was deeply conditioned by his unique environment. Dr. Schweitzer asks us to consider it again, and in detail, from a point of view which is neither that of the late Bishop Lightfoot nor of Lightfoot's adversaries. It is the problem of how the Evangel of Jesus survived as the Catholic Church.

F. C. BURKITT

CAMBRIDGE,
July, 1931

AUTHOR'S PREFACE

THE chapter which was to have served as the Introduction to "The Mysticism of Paul the Apostle" grew into a book and appeared in 1911 under the title *Geschichte der paulinischen Forschung* (in English, "Paul and his Interpreters, a Critical History", trans. by W. Montgomery, 1912). "The Mysticism of Paul the Apostle", the first draft of which goes back to the year 1906, was to have followed immediately. Illness and the work of preparing the second enlarged edition of the *Geschichte der Leben-Jesu-Forschung* (= "Quest of the Historical Jesus," 1910) made it impossible for me to get the MS. of the present work ready for press before my first visit to Africa in 1913, an event which could not be further delayed. During my first leave in Europe I was fully occupied with my two volumes on the Philosophy of Civilization, so that it was not till the end of 1927, during my second return to Europe, that I was able again to take in hand "The Mysticism of Paul", and give the MS. its final form during that two-years' visit. It is to this delay I owe it that my conception of the teaching of Paul was forced, in the course of comparison with the works of Reitzenstein, Bousset, Deissmann, and others, to attain to fuller inward lucidity and to be based on wider foundations than would otherwise have been the case.

Since I have aimed only at an exposition of Paul's view of things I had to give up attempting to go into contemporary literature about Paul as fully as I would have liked, and to exhibit what I have learnt from it only in single details. Moreover, in the second edition of my *Geschichte der paulinischen Forschung*, for which I hope soon to find time, I have to express my opinion on the works which have appeared since 1911.

How much I owe to Hans Lietzmann, to Martin Dibelius, and to other recent commentators on Paul, can be seen from many details in this book. And what enduring value, on the other hand, still remains in the detailed analyses to be found in the works of H. J Holtzmann, P. W. Schmiedel, and other exponents of the older school, I have again and again experienced.

vii

With this exposition of the teaching of Paul I bring the theological work I have hitherto undertaken to a kind of conclusion. When still a student I conceived the plan of explaining the evolution of thought in the first generation of Christianity on the basis of the axiom, which to me seems incontrovertible, that the Preaching of the Kingdom of God by Jesus was in itself eschatological, and that it was so understood by those who heard it. My studies on the problem of the historic origins of the Eucharist, on the 'mystery' of Jesus' Messiahship and Suffering, on the course of modern investigation of the Life of Jesus and that of the teaching of Paul, all turn about the two questions—whether besides the eschatological interpretation of the Preaching of Jesus there was any room for another, and how the original completely eschatological faith of Christians fared in the course of the substitution of the Hellenistic for the eschatological way of thinking.

The History of Dogma as formerly set forth made its solution of the problem presented by the Hellenization of Christianity easier by assuming in Jesus the presence of uneschatological as well as eschatological ideas, and by expounding the teaching of Paul as partly eschatological, partly Hellenistic. By the aid of general religious concepts, and of Hellenistic concepts which were assumed to have been present in Christianity from the beginning, the total Hellenization, which came to pass in the Asia Minor theology of the beginning of the second century, was represented as something already well prepared for.

But in reality the need was to explain how the purely eschatological belief had developed-into the Hellenistic one. The problem of the Hellenization of Christianity, so stated, turns round the question of Paul. Instead of the untenable notion that Paul had combined eschatological and Hellenistic ways of thinking we must now consider either a purely eschatological or a purely Hellenistic explanation of his teaching. I take the former alternative throughout. It assumes the complete agreement of the teaching of Paul with that of Jesus. The Hellenization of Christianity does not come in with Paul, but only after him.

The problem of the Hellenization of Christianity is also occupied with the questions why Ignatius and the representatives of the Asia Minor theology of the second century were unable to make their own the primitive-Christian teaching they found already existing, and in what way they translated and transformed it into Hellenistic

teaching. The very simple answer is that the fading of the eschatological Hope quite naturally brought them to comprehend their
faith afresh in terms of current Hellenistic concepts. This was made
possible for them, because they were familiar with Paul's mystical
doctrine of Being-in-Christ. They took this over, at the same time
substituting a Hellenistic rationale for the eschatological rationale
of it, which had become no longer intelligible to them. So in a most
natural way the evolution from Jesus by way of Paul to Ignatius is
explained. Paul was not the Hellenizer of Christianity. But in his
eschatological mysticism of the Being-in-Christ he gave it a form in
which it could be Hellenized.

In this way I believe I have shown that the recognition of the
eschatological character of the Preaching of Jesus and of the Teaching of Paul, though it may pose the question of the Hellenization of
Christianity in a more abrupt way than formerly, yet at the same
time leads to a much simpler solution of the difficulty.

It was of great importance for me to demonstrate the connection
of the eschatological ideas of Paul with those of 'Late-Judaism', and
to trace their roots back into the time of the Prophets both after
and before the Exile. For this undertaking it was of great advantage to me that Professor Gerhard Kittel of Tübingen and his
assistant Dr. Karl Heinrich Rengstorf were kind enough to take
the trouble to read my MS. and make comments upon it. Their
knowledge of Late-Judaism and of Rabbinics put me in a position
to draw many lines firmer and clearer than would have been otherwise possible to me. For the improvement that my work attained
through their scholarship I owe them heartfelt thanks.

My methods have remained old-fashioned, in that I aim at setting
forth the ideas of Paul in their historically conditioned form. I
believe that the mingling of our ways of regarding religion with
those of former ●istorical periods, which is now so much practised,
often with dazzling cleverness, is of no use as an aid to historical
comprehension, and of not much use in the end for our religious
life. The investigation of historical truth in itself I regard as the
ideal for which scientific theology has to strive. I still hold fast to
the opinion that the permanent spiritual importance that the religious thought of the Past has for ours makes itself most strongly
felt when we come into touch with that form of piety as it really
existed, not as we make the best of it for ourselves. A Christianity
which does not dare to use historical truth for the service of what

is spiritual is not sound within, even if it appear to be strong. Reverence for truth, as something that must be a factor in our faith if it is not to degenerate into superstition, includes in itself respect for historical truth.

Just because Paul's mystical doctrine of Christ has more to say to us when it speaks to us in the fire of its primitive-Christian, eschatological, manner of thought than when it is paraphrased into the language of modern orthodoxy or modern unorthodoxy, I believe I am serving in this work the cause not only of sound learning but also of religious needs. It is in this conviction that I have worked.

For valuable help in correction for the press I have to thank my fellow-workers the Rev. Karl Leyrer of Stuttgart, Dr. K. H. Rengstorf of Tübingen, and my wife.

The preparation of the Indices was the work of Mr. Liemar Hennig in collaboration with Dr. Rengstorf, as my journey to Africa left me no time to do it. For this work I thank him heartily.

ALBERT SCHWEITZER

On the Ogowe steamer on the way to Lambaréné,
    St. Stephen's Day, 1929

CONTENTS

xi

CONTENTS

THE MYSTICISM OF PAUL THE APOSTLE

THE MYSTICISM OF ST. PAUL

CHAPTER I

THE DISTINCTIVE CHARACTER OF PAULINE MYSTICISM

WHEN we say that Paul is a mystic, what do we mean by mysticism?
We are always in presence of mysticism when we find a human
being looking upon the division between earthly and super-earthly,
temporal and eternal, as transcended, and feeling himself, while still
externally amid the earthly and temporal, to belong to the super-
earthly and eternal.

Mysticism may be either primitive or developed. Primitive mysticism has not yet risen to a conception of the universal, and is still
confined to naïve views of earthly and super-earthly, temporal and
eternal. The entry into the super-earthly and eternal takes place by
means of a 'mystery', a magical act. By means of this the participant enters into communion with a divine being in such a way that
he shares the latter's supernatural mode of existence. This view of
a union with the divinity, brought about by efficacious ceremonies,
is found even in quite primitive religions. The most fundamental
significance of the sacrificial feast is, no doubt, that by this meal the
partaker becomes in some way one with the divinity.

In a more developed form magical mysticism is found in the
oriental and Greek mystery-religions at the beginning of our era.
In the cults of Attis, Osiris, and Mithras, as well as in the Eleu-
sinian Mysteries in their later more profound form, the believer
attains, by means of an initiation, union with the divinity, and
thereby becomes a partaker in the immortality for which he yearns.
Through these sacraments he ceases to be a natural man and is
born again into a higher state of being.

But when the conception of the universal is reached and a man
reflects upon his relation to the totality of being and to Being in
itself, the resultant mysticism becomes widened, deepened, and
purified. The entrance into the super-earthly and eternal then takes

place through an act of thinking. In this act the conscious personality raises itself above that illusion of the senses which makes him
regard himself as in bondage in the present life to the earthly and
temporal. It attains the power to distinguish between appearance
and reality and is able to conceive the material as a mode of manifestation of the Spiritual. It has sight of the Eternal in the Transient.
Recognising the unity of all things in God, in Being as such, it
passes beyond the unquiet flux of becoming and disintegration into
the peace of timeless being, and is conscious of itself as being in
God, and in every moment eternal.

This intellectual mysticism is a common possession of humanity.
Whenever thought makes the ultimate effort to conceive the relation of the personality to the universal, this mysticism comes into
existence. It is found among the Brahmans and in Buddha, in
Platonism, in Stoicism, in Spinoza, Schopenhauer, and Hegel.

Even into Christianity, naïvely dualistic as it is, distinguishing
strictly between the present and the future, the here and the hereafter, this mysticism penetrates. Not indeed unopposed; but whenever in the great thinkers or under the influence of great movements
of thought Christianity endeavours to attain to clarity regarding
the relation of God and the world, it cannot help opening the door
to mysticism. Mysticism finds expression in the Hellenistic theology of Ignatius and the Johannine Gospel, in the writings of
Augustine and in those attributed to Dionysius the Areopagite; it is
found in Hugo of St. Victor and other scholastics, in Francis of
Assisi, in Meister Eckart, in Suso, in Tauler and the other fathers
of the German theological mysticism; it speaks in the language of
Jakob Boehme and other mystical heretics of Protestantism; there
is mysticism in the hymns of Tersteegen, Angelus Silesius, and
Novalis; and in the writings of Schleiermacher mysticism seeks to
express itself in the language of the Church.[1]

The type of intellectual mysticism differs according to place and
time. Among the Brahmans and in Buddhism it is found in its most
abstract form. The mystic thinks of his existence under the pure
indifferentiated conception of being, and sinks himself therein.
Jakob Boehme is the herald of an imaginative mysticism. In the
Christian mysticism of Meister Eckart and his followers the con-

---

[1] An all too brief sketch—in many respects open to criticism—of Mysticism
is to be found in Ed. LEHMANN, *Mystik in Heidentum und Christentum* (Leipzig,
3rd ed., 1923, 144 pp.).

ception is of being in the living God, as is also the case with the mysticism of Hindu pietism, which endeavours to get beyond the cold Brahmanic mysticism. Whatever colouring it may take on, however, what intellectual mysticism is concerned with is Being in its ultimate reality.

Of what precise kind then is the mysticism of Paul?

It occupies a unique position between primitive and intellectual mysticism. The religious conceptions of the Apostle stand high above those of primitive mysticism. This being so, it might have been expected that his mysticism would have to do with the unity of man with God as the ultimate ground of being. But this is not the case. Paul never speaks of being one with God or being in God. He does indeed assert the divine sonship of believers. But, strangely enough, he does not conceive of sonship to God as an immediate mystical relation to God, but as mediated and effected by means of the mystical union with Christ.

Thus, higher and lower mysticism here interpenetrate. In Paul there is no God-mysticism; only a Christ-mysticism by means of which man comes into relation to God. The fundamental thought of Pauline mysticism runs thus: I am in Christ; in Him I know myself as a being who is raised above this sensuous, sinful, and transient world and already belongs to the transcendent; in Him I am assured of resurrection; in Him I am a Child of God.

Another distinctive characteristic of this mysticism is that being in Christ is conceived as a having died and risen again with Him, in consequence of which the participant has been freed from sin and from the Law, possesses the Spirit of Christ, and is assured of resurrection.

This 'being-in-Christ' is the prime enigma of the Pauline teaching: once grasped it gives the clue to the whole.

UTTERANCES OF PAULINE MYSTICISM

Gal. ii. 19-20: "Through the law I have died to the law that I might live unto God: I have been crucified with Christ. I live no longer as I myself; Christ lives in me."

Gal. iii. 26-28: "You all are sons of God through (the) faith in Jesus Christ. As many of you as were baptized unto Christ have clothed yourselves in Christ. In Him is neither Jew nor Greek, neither bondman nor freeman, neither male nor female; yet are all one (masculine) in Christ Jesus."

Gal. iv. 6: "Because you are sons, God has sent forth the Spirit of His Son unto our hearts, who there cries Abba, Father."

Gal. v. 24-25: "Those who belong to Christ have crucified the flesh with its passions and lusts. If we live by the Spirit let us also walk in the Spirit."

Gal. vi. 14: "But let it not befall me to boast except in the cross of our Lord Jesus Christ, through which the world has been crucified to me and I to the world."

2 Cor. v. 17: "So that, if any man is in Christ he is a new creation; the old (neuter) has passed away; nay, has become new."

Rom. vi. 10-11: "The death that Christ died is a death unto sin once for all; the life that He lives, He lives for God. Even so, count yourselves dead for sin (sic) but alive for God in Christ Jesus."

Rom. vii. 4: "Similarly, my brethren, you have been made dead so far as the law is concerned through the body of Christ, in order that you may belong to another, namely to Him who was awakened from the dead, in order that we may bear fruit for God."

Rom. viii. 1-2: "There is therefore now no condemnation for those who are in Christ Jesus. For the law of the Spirit of life in Christ Jesus has made you free from the law of sin and of death."

Rom. viii. 9-11: "For you are not in the flesh but in the Spirit, if it be so that the Spirit of God is dwelling in you; and if any have not the Spirit of Christ he is none of His. But if Christ is in you, then the body indeed is dead because of sin, but the spirit is life because of righteousness. But if the Spirit which awakened Jesus from the dead dwells in you, then He who awakened Christ Jesus from the dead will also make your mortal bodies to live through His Spirit which dwells in you."

Rom. xii. 4-5: "For, as we in one body have many members and the members all have their different functions, so we, many as we are, are one body in Christ, though in relation to one another we are (various) members."

Phil. iii. 1-11: "That I may win Christ and be found in Him not having my own righteousness, the righteousness of the law, but the righteousness which is by faith in Christ, the righteousness (which comes) from God on the ground of faith; to know Him and the power of His resurrection and the fellowship of His sufferings, being conformed to His death, if anywise I might attain to the resurrection from the dead."

.   .   .   .   .   .

The most obvious and natural thing, from our point of view, would have been that Paul should have developed on mystical lines that conception of sonship to God which Christ proclaimed and which was current in early Christianity. He, however, leaves that as he found it, and works out in addition to it the mystical conception of being-in-Christ, as though sonship to God needed for its foundation the being-in-Christ. Paul is the only Christian thinker who knows only Christ-mysticism, unaccompanied by God-mysticism. In the Johannine theology both appear alongside of one another and intermingled with each other. The Johannine Logos-Christ speaks both of a being-in-him and a being-in-God, and represents the being-in-God as mediated by the being-in-Christ. From that point onwards Christ-mysticism and God-mysticism interpenetrate.

What makes it more remarkable that the direct mystical relations of the believer to God should find no place in Paul's manner of thought, is that in his statements about the believer's possession of the Spirit he does not make any clear distinction between the Spirit of God and the Spirit of Christ. Passages in which he describes those who are in Christ as possessing the Spirit of Christ alternate with those in which he reminds them that they have the Spirit of God.

Rom. viii. 9: "You are not in the flesh but in the spirit, if so be that the spirit of God dwells in you; but he who has not the Spirit of Christ is none of His."

Gal. iv. 6: "But because you are sons, God has sent forth the Spirit of His Son into our hearts, who there cries Abba, Father."

Although he so unhesitatingly equates the possession of the Spirit of Christ with the possession of the Spirit of God, Paul nevertheless never makes the being-in-Christ into a being-in-God. That he never does this apparently so obvious thing is so remarkable that all accounts of his teaching are inclined simply to overlook this absence of a God-mysticism, or at any rate not to realise the significance of its absence. Although in the Epistles there is never any mention of the believer's being in God, it is constantly assumed that Paul's Christ-mysticism does ultimately run out into a God-mysticism.

Even Wilhelm Bousset, the only writer to whom this absence of a God-mysticism has given pause, does not go further into the problem, but contents himself with the inference from the presence of God-mysticism in the Johannine writings "that in the course of the history of Christianity God-mysticism developed out of Christ-mysticism."[1]

[1] Wilhelm BOUSSET, *Kyrios Christos: Geschichte des Christusglaubens von den Anfängen des Christentums bis Irenaeus.* Göttingen, 1913: 474 pp.; 2nd ed., 1921. For Christ-mysticism and God-mysticism see 2nd ed. pp. 119 ff., 163 ff., 177 ff.

One thing which made it easy to overlook the absence of God-mysticism in Paul is the fact that, according to the Acts of the Apostles, Paul did in his speech on the Areopagus in Athens proclaim a mysticism of being-in-God. The absence of statements about being in God in the Paul of the Letters is accordingly regarded as something accidental and without significance, since after all the Paul of Acts expressly says of God "in Him we live and move and have our being" (Acts xvii. 28). On the strength of this passage from Acts Adolf Deissmann, for example, thinks himself justified in assuming in Paul a mysticism of being-in-God which has its roots in pre-Christian Jewish thought. This forms an inner core to which the Christ-mysticism which arose out of the experience on the road to Damascus forms an outer envelope.[1]

But was the Areopagus utterance really Paul's? There are weighty objections to this assumption, which make it probable that the speech to the Athenians is to be ascribed solely to the writer of the Acts. It was of course the general practice of the historians of antiquity to compose speeches such as seemed to them appropriate to a particular person and occasion, and represent them as spoken by the person in question. This custom the author of the Acts had no scruples in adopting. His purpose was to exhibit a Paul at Athens who to the Greeks had become a Greek.[2]

That the speech is unhistorical is at once betrayed by the fact that Paul takes for his starting-point an inscription dedicating an Athenian altar "to an unknown God." There can never have been such an inscription. There is evidence in current literature only for altars to 'unknown Gods' in the plural, not to *an* Unknown God in the singular.

We have in fact notices of three such altars. One stood on the road from Phaleron to Athens (Pausanias, i. 1, 4), another at Olympia (Pausanias, v. 14, 8), another at Athens (Philostratus, *Vita Apollonii*, 6, 3). It is possible that, in addition to these known to us from literary evidence of the second and third centuries A.D., an actual altar has come down to us. In the excavations at Pergamon there was found in the autumn of 1909 in the *temenos* of Demeter an altar inscription which

---

[1] Adolf DEISSMANN, *Paulus*, 2nd ed. Tübingen, 1925: 292 pp.; p. 116, 1st ed., 1911. English trans., *St. Paul: A Study in Social and Religious History*, 1912.

[2] On the question of the Areopagus speech see Eduard NORDEN, *Agnostos Theos* (Leipzig, 1913: 410 pp.), p. 1-140. Norden sees in the speech a creation of the author of Acts, a view which had been taken earlier by Eduard REUSS, H. J. HOLTZMANN, and the representatives of the older criticism generally.

states that the torch-bearer Kapit(on) dedicates the altar to θεοῖς ἀγν ...
It is possible that the mutilated word should be restored as ἀγνώστοις
(unknown).

As early as the Church Father Jerome we find it remarked that the
altar referred to in Acts could only have been dedicated to unknown
gods in the plural, not to a single God. According to Jerome the inscription is said to have run: "To the gods of Asia and Europe and
Africa, gods unknown and foreign" (*Diis Asiae et Europae et Africae,
diis ignotis et peregrinis*).[1]

Who was it then who made this 'unknown gods' into 'an unknown
god'? Jerome thinks that Paul himself altered and corrected the inscription in order to serve the purpose of his sermon in favour of monotheism, and a similar view is taken by some modern expositors who
wish to preserve the authenticity of the speech on the Areopagus, or,
alternatively, they suggest that Paul inadvertently read the singular instead of the plural. Many commentators also fall back on the assumption
that there actually was at Athens, in addition to the altar "to unknown
gods," another "to an unknown God." But in point of fact it is impossible to suppose that in the presence of people who had the altar
daily before their eyes Paul could have taken liberties with the inscription. Besides, an altar to 'unknown gods' would have been more likely
to inspire him to a flaming invective against polytheism rather than to
a eulogy of monotheism.

We may assume therefore that it was the author of Acts who
transposed the inscription from the plural to the singular, in order
to provide Paul with a starting-point for his discourse on monotheism. Such alterations of traditions and citations were practised
without scruple by the religious propaganda of antiquity in its
literary forms.

The remainder of the discourse on the Areopagus belongs to
Paul as little as the beginning. The God-mysticism of the quotation "In him we live and move and have our being" is Stoic, and
the quotation "For we are also His offspring" is from Aratus
(*Phaenomena*, 5), who like Paul was a native of Cilicia.

Even the connection in which these mystical sayings are introduced is open to objection. The discourse is directed to proving the

---

[1] HIERON. *Ad Titum* i. 12. In this passage Jerome is commenting on the line
of Epimenides cited in *Tit.* i. 12, "The Cretans are ever liars, beasts of prey, slow
bellies," and incidentally remarks that Paul, whom he assumed to be the author
of the Epistle to Titus, quotes a Greek poet (Aratus) in the speech on the
Areopagus, and even refers to the inscription on an Athenian altar.

folly of polytheism and idolatry, to call the hearers to repentance and announce the coming of Christ as the Judge of the World. For this purpose it was not necessary to carry the thought up into the heights of mysticism from which it has immediately to descend again. Finally, the mysticism is an unmotived addition; it serves as an artfully contrived modulation in an otherwise simple theme.

How very differently the mystical utterances are motived in the Pauline Epistles! In these the doctrine of the being-in-Christ claims its place in the train of thought as the argument of arguments and dominates the logic of the whole passage. Mysticism is here handled by a thinker; in the Areopagus discourse of Acts it is a literary device. In order to be a Greek to the Greeks, Paul must for a moment move in the realms of the Stoic pantheistic mysticism and appeal to a well-known literary passage. The soaring rocket of the altar dedication is followed up by this impressive set-piece.

The discourse on the Areopagus has its place in our hearts because it proclaims the being-in-God mysticism which our own religious sense craves, and which is nowhere else in the New Testament expressed in so direct a fashion. Our modern thought is conscious of a need to conceive of ourselves and all nature with us as being in God, and for that reason we find it very difficult to give up the idea that Paul himself expressed this thought in the Areopagus discourse.

.   .   .   .   .   .

In the phrase "In Him we live and move and have our being: we are His offspring," that which is expressed is the Stoic pantheistic Mysticism. It implies a way of looking at life in which the conception of the divine is immanent. God is conceived as the essence of all the forces at work in nature. Accordingly all that is is 'in God.' In man as capable of thought this fact becomes an object of consciousness.

Where this direct relation between God and nature is not assumed, even the primitive mysticism of being-in-God is unthinkable. But Paul is far removed from the *Deus sive natura.* His world-view is not one of an immanent but of a transcendent God. The Stoic idea of a natural and unmediated being-in-God, had he ever encountered it and directed his thought to it, would necessarily have appeared to him as folly and presumption.

So far removed was he from the Stoic presuppositions that even the general conception of man which is presupposed in the Areopagus discourse is for him unthinkable. The possibility that man, as man and universally, stands in close relation to God lies outside his horizon. For him there is no homogeneous humanity, but only various categories of men.

For, in the first place, his thought is dominated by the idea of predestination. A mighty cleavage cuts humanity asunder. Not man as such, but only the man who is elected thereto, can enter into relation with God. The glorious words of Rom. viii. 28: "We know that for those who love God He makes all things work together for good," are followed by the dreadful limitation "namely those who are called according to His purpose."

But even apart from Predestination men do not all stand for Paul upon the same level. The distinctions of male and female, Jew and Greek, are not for him distinctions of sex and race only, but also gradations of nearness to God. That this is true as regards Jew and Gentile stands, for Jewish presuppositions, unquestionable. But also the surprising fact that the man stands nearer to God than the woman is made known to us by the curious arguments by which Paul supports his precept that in praying women must cover their heads, while men, on the contrary, must uncover theirs.

1 Cor. xi. 7-11: "The man has no need to cover his head, for he is the image and reflection of God, the wife is the reflection of the man; for the man was not made for the sake of the woman, but the woman for the man. Therefore the woman must have a covering (ἐξουσία) upon her head because of the angels."

According to G. KITTEL (*Arbeiten zur Religionsgeschichte des Urchristentums*, vol. i. pt. 3 (Leipzig, 1920), pp. 17-31, *Die Macht auf dem Haupte*, "power on the head").

"The signification 'covering' (*i.e.* veil) has come to attach itself to the Greek word ἐξουσία, 'power', owing to the fact that there were in Semitic two roots *šlṭ*, one of which meant to 'surround' and the other to 'rule'. Paul, having no knowledge of the former meaning, mistakenly translated the Rabbinic *shalṭonayya* by ἐξουσία 'power'."

That women should cover their hair is, according to Kittel, a general practice inspired by modesty. In order not to give offence to their guardian angels who are round about them they must therefore wear a veil upon their heads. The interpretation starts from the story of the seduction of the daughters of men by the angels

(Gen. vi. 1-4), and represents the women as wearing their hair covered to avoid arousing the lust of these angels. This reason is also cited by Tertullian in his tractate *De Virginibus Velandis*, in which he refers to the present passage (Tert. *De Virg. Vel.* 7). In any case the veiling of the head, during divine service, which Paul here enjoins on the Greek women, was a custom to which he was accustomed among the Jews.

That woman was not immediately created by God but mediately out of the substance of the man is, according to Paul, the reason for her inferiority. He assumes a hierarchic gradation, God—Christ—Man—Woman.

1 Cor. xi. 3: "I would have you know that every man's Head is Christ, the head of the woman is the man, and the Head of Christ is God."

This difference in nearness to God is abrogated only by the being-in-Christ. It is in Christ that the elect portion of mankind first attains to homogeneity. That is why Paul so constantly proclaims as something deeply significant that in Christ there is no longer Jew nor Greek, slave nor freeman, male nor female, but that in Him all possess the same essential being and personality.

The conception of a homogeneous humanity, which the Stoic mysticism takes for granted as self-evident, is therefore so remote from Paul's thought that in order to reach it he must call in the aid of the mysticism of being-in-Christ. How then could he possibly arrive at the Stoic mysticism of the physical being-in-God!

The other reason why the Stoic pantheistic mysticism is impossible for Paul is that the pantheistic conception of God is utterly foreign to his thought. It is not only that, as was customary in Jewish thinking, he holds the world and God firmly apart; on the ground of his own eschatological world-view he further assumes that, so long as the natural world endures, even down into the Messianic period, angelic powers stand between man and God and render direct relations between the two impossible. At the end of the eighth chapter of Romans there rises a hymn of joy over the relations to God which those who are elect in Christ assume on the ground of that election. And what is the gain which he celebrates? Precisely this, that henceforth no accusing angels have any right to appear before God against these elect; that no angel powers whatsoever shall henceforth succeed in interposing between them and the love of God.

Rom. viii. 38-39: "For I am certain that neither death nor life nor angels nor principalities nor powers, nor things present nor things to come, nor powers of the height, nor powers of the deep, nor any other being shall be able to separate me from the love of God which is in Christ Jesus our Lord."

The one thing that is attained by the being-in-Christ is just that this relation between the Elect and God is established. They have received a place in that world-process, which is now once more directed towards God.

Here we have the fundamental distinction between that world-view in which the 'natural' being-in-God is possible and that other in which it remains unthinkable. And in addition to the distinction between the immanence and transcendence of God there is the further contrast between the natural and the supernatural views of world history.

In the Stoic view the world is thought of as static and unaltering. The world is Nature, which remains constantly in the same relationship to the world-spirit pervading it and pervaded by it. For Paul, however, the world is not Nature but a supernatural historical process which has for its stages the forthgoing of the world from God, its alienation from Him, and its return to Him.

This dramatic view of world history is also in its own way a kind of mysticism, a mysticism which can assert that all things are *from* God and *through* God and *unto* God. But what it can never assert is that all things are *in* God. This is for it simply not the case so long as there is a sensible, material world, and a sensible world history. It is only when the End comes, when time gives place to eternity and all things return to God, that they can be said to be in God.

Since Paul lives in the conceptions of the dramatic world-view characteristic of the late Jewish Eschatology, he is by consequence bound to the logic of that view. He concludes the hymn to God at the end of the 11th chapter of Romans with the declaration "For *from* Him and *through* Him and *unto* Him are all things" (Rom. xi. 36); but he cannot take a step further and add that all things are *in* God.

Under the enchantment of the sound and splendour of the passage Eduard Norden, who in general takes up a sceptical attitude about Hellenism in Paul, feels that here he cannot do otherwise than assume the presence of Stoic mysticism.[1] He sets Paul's

---

[1] Eduard NORDEN, *Agnostos Theos*, Berlin, 1913: 410 pp.; pp. 240-250. *Eine Stoische Doxologie bei Paulus. Geschichte einer Allmachtsformel* ("A Stoic Doxology in Paul. History of an Omnipotence-formula").

saying beside the well-known address to Nature in the Reflections of Marcus Aurelius (iv. 23): "From thee is all, in thee is all, unto thee is all." But in so doing he overlooks what is precisely the decisive point, namely, that in Marcus Aurelius the second clause (of the saying) runs "in thee is all," whereas in Paul it is merely "through Him is all." In the difference between *in* and *through* lies the great gulf which divides the static mysticism of the Stoic from the dynamic mysticism of Paul.

R. Reitzenstein in his *Poimandres* (1909), p. 39, thinks that "in Paul (Rom. xi. 36) the supreme basic formula of the Egypto-Greek mysticism appears almost word for word." He quotes in illustration the inscription on a magic ring (Berthelot, *Alchimistes grecs*, introd. p. 133) ἐν τὸ πᾶν καὶ δἰ αὐτοῦ τὸ πᾶν καὶ εἰς αὐτὸ τὸ πᾶν, "all things are one and through it are all things and unto it are all things."

In other sayings also Paul avoids the conception of being-in-God. 1 Cor. i. 30: "From Him (God) are you, in Christ Jesus"; 1 Cor. viii. 6: "God the Father from whom is all and unto whom we are, and one Lord Jesus Christ through whom is all, and we through Him."

The being-in-Christ is not expanded into being-in-God until we reach the Johannine theology. John xvii. 21: "In order that all may be one as Thou, Father, art in me, and I in Thee, that they also may be in us"; 1 John iv. 15: "If any man confesses that Jesus is the Son of God, God abides in him and he in God."

According to the Eschatological view the elect man shares the fate of the world. Therefore, so long as the world has not returned to God, he also cannot be in God.

That Paul does not think of Sonship to God as a being-in-God depends ultimately on the fact that this sonship is for him, as it also was for Jesus, a thing of the future. Not until the coming of the Messianic Kingdom will men be Children of God. Before that, they are those who have the assurance of having been called to this sonship and are therefore, by anticipation, denominated Children of God.

Being-in-God is for Paul impossible so long as the angelic beings still possess some kind of power over man. Once Christ has, in the progress of the Messianic Kingdom, overcome them and has destroyed death as the last enemy, He will Himself give back His now unneeded power to God "in order that God may be all in all" (1 Cor. xv. 26-28). Then only will there be a being-in-God. Paul does thus recognise a God-mysticism; but it is not in being contemporaneously with the Christ-mysticism. The presuppositions of his world-view make it impossible that they should co-exist, or that one should necessitate the other. They are chronologically successive, Christ-mysticism holding the field until God-mysticism becomes possible.

The peculiarity that the mysticism of Paul is only a mysticism of being-in-Christ, and not also a mysticism of being-in-God, has thus its foundation in the fact that it originally had its place in an eschatological world-view.

One thing which surprises us in the Pauline Christ-mysticism is its extraordinarily realistic character. The being-in-Christ is not conceived as a static partaking in the spiritual being of Christ, but as a real co-experiencing of His dying and rising again.

The very fact that the new condition which is reached through this mysticism is concerned as an anticipated Resurrection is itself remarkable. The simple and natural expression 'rebirth' is entirely passed over by Paul, who goes on to deal with this other difficult and, indeed, rather violent conception of an already experienced resurrection.

This is the more surprising because in the mysticism of the Hellenistic mystery-religions, as well as in the Johannine literature, the new condition to which the mystic is introduced is regularly described as rebirth (regeneration). This conception, with the relevant metaphors about being begotten and born, dominates the Hermetic writings,[1] the picture of the Hellenistic-Oriental Mystery-religions and that of the Mithras cult. Since it is so natural in itself and so familiar to Greek thought, it maintains its hold even in cases where the character of the particular myths and mysteries would give appropriateness to the metaphors of dying and rising again.

For example, in the Phrygian Taurobolia the *mystes* is placed in a grave, which signifies that he, like Attis, is dead. The blood of an ox sacrificed over the grave trickles down upon him and, by the communication of the vital power contained therein, rouses him to life again. Although he ought, in view of the facts, to be thought of as

[1] The Hermetic writings are 18 tractates containing the revelations of the Egyptian god Hermes Trismegistos and of other Egyptian divinities. Their central doctrine is that of liberation from the tyranny of fate or natural necessity (*Heimarmenē*) through the mystic contemplation of God. These writings originated in the second and third centuries A.D., doubtless in Egypt.

having undergone a resurrection, he is nevertheless described as born again.[1]

Similarly the initiate in the Isis mysteries is spoken of as born again although he has undergone a voluntary death (Apuleius, *Metamorph.* xi. 21).[2]

That the conception of a resurrection, appropriate as it is to the symbolism, could in this way be thrust aside by the inappropriate one of a birth shows how entirely natural and obvious the conception of rebirth was to the Greek imagination. While in the Hellenistic mystery-religions the two mystical conceptions of resurrection and rebirth thus interpenetrate, Paul is a one-sided representative of resurrection-mysticism. With consistent logic he applies to the renewal of being which originates from fellowship with the risen Christ only the term resurrection, which is alone appropriate.

It is true he tells the Corinthians that he is their father because, in Christ Jesus, he has begotten them through the Gospel, whereas the others who have had to do with them could only claim to be teachers (παιδαγωγοί). So too he calls the Galatians his children, for whom he travails in birth till Christ be formed in them (Gal. iv. 19), and Onesimus the son whom he had begotten in his bonds (Philem. 10). But the birth metaphor refers always and only to the fact that he is the father of their faith and not to their being born again.

It is only in the "deutero-Pauline" literature that the concept of rebirth appears. Baptism, which according to Rom. vi. 4 signifies a being buried and rising again with Christ, is in the Epistle to Titus (Tit. iii. 5) the "Bath of Rebirth." And subsequently, in the Johannine theology and in Justin, the doctrine of Redemption is entirely dominated by the notion of rebirth.

1 Peter i. 23: "Born again not from corruptible but from incorruptible seed through the living and abiding word of God." See also 1 Peter i. 3 and ii. 2.

John iii. 5: "Whoever is not born of water and spirit cannot enter the Kingdom of God."

1 John iii. 9: "Everyone who is begotten of God, does not sin."

Justin, 1 *Apol.* 61: "Then they are brought by us to a place where

---

[1] A detailed description of the ceremony is found in the Christian writer Prudentius (b. 348) in *Peristephanon*, x. 1006-1050, reproduced in Hugo Hᴇᴘᴅɪɴɢ, *Attis, seine Mythen und sein Kult*, Giessen, 1903, p. 65 ff. The Taurobolium is also referred to in the inscription *Taurobolio criobolioque in aeternum renatus aram sacravit* ("This altar is dedicated by one who by the *Taurobolium* and *Criobolium* [similar ram sacrifices] was born again into eternity").

[2] Aᴘᴜʟᴇɪᴜs, *Metamorph.* xi. 21, *renatos ad novae . . . salutis curricula.*

there is water, and are born anew in a kind of rebirth, which we ourselves have experienced in ourselves."
Justin, *Dialogue with Trypho*, 138. 2: "Christ, although He is the first-born of all creation, has also become the beginning of a new race. This He has brought to birth through water, faith, and wood."
The Pauline assertion that he who is in Christ is a new creature (καινὴ κτίσις, Gal. vi. 15, 2 Cor. v. 17) has nothing to do with the notion of rebirth. He who has his being in Christ is a new creature because, inasmuch as he has died and risen again in Christ, he belongs already to the new world.

The fact that in Paul we find only Resurrection-mysticism and not also Rebirth-mysticism has hitherto not received from Pauline scholars the attention it deserved. As a rule it is simply overlooked. Even Richard Reitzenstein and Adolf Deissmann, who have gone so fully into the problem of Paul's relation to Hellenism, take no notice whatever of the absence in him of the expression rebirth. But how significant it must be for the solution of this problem that a so dominant conception of the Hellenistic mysticism finds no expression in him although his whole thinking is so deeply concerned with the new life!

That Paul, in view of his familiarity with the Greek language, must have known the term rebirth and its significance for Hellenistic personal religion, is doubtless to be assumed. But he is unable to make use of it because his thought follows logical and realistic lines. Dying and rising with Christ is for him not something merely metaphorical, which could at need be expressed also in a different metaphor, but a simple reality. It is because his thinking is wholly conditioned by the eschatological expectation that it is unable to find a place for the notion of rebirth.

.   .   .   .   .   .

One consequence of this realism and the un-Hellenistic character of Paul's mysticism is that the concept of deification is foreign to it. According to the conceptions prevailing in the Hermetic writings, the man who is born again has in a certain sense himself become God. In the Mithras mystery of the heavenly pilgrimage and in the mysteries of Isis the initiate undergoes a deification, and is even prayed to as a god. This conception is conditioned by the fact that Hellenistic mysticism is dominated by the idea of symbolic influence. By the symbolic imitation of the actions of the divinity the initiate becomes in a sense what the divinity is. But Paul thinks realistically. For him the believer experiences the dying and rising again of Christ in actual fact, not in an imitative representation. And he does not thereby become in a sense the same as Christ. Paul goes no further than the thought that he has fellowship with Christ and in this way shares the experience of Christ. Through this alone it is clear that Hellenistic and the Pauline mysticism belong to two different worlds. Since the Hellenistic mysticism is founded on the idea of deification and the Pauline on the idea of fellowship with the divine being, it is impossible to find in the Hellenistic literature parallels for the characteristic phrases "with Christ" and "in Christ" which dominate the Pauline mysticism.

Another profound difference is the fact that Hellenism, unlike Paul's teaching, does not postulate any connection between predestination and mysticism. In the Hellenistic mysticism with its basis of symbolism it is open to every man, by the appropriate imitative experience of the dying and rising again of the divinity, to become, as a deified being, freed from the natural world in which necessity rules (*Heimarmenē*).

In Paul, on the contrary, the idea is, that by a predestined necessity some share the fate of the world while others, through Christ, become participants of the future glory. This combination of mysticism with the idea of predestination—and a kind of predestination which is wholly foreign to Hellenism!—marks in its own way a no less profound distinction between Hellenistic and Pauline mysticism than that involved in the presence or absence of the notions of rebirth and deification.

The difference of kind between realistic and symbolic mysticism cannot therefore be too much emphasised. In the Hellenistic Mystery-religions the symbol is enhanced and solidified into reality. Through the believer's intensively imagining the symbolised experience and undergoing it in an imitative act, it becomes for him reality. In Paul, however, there is no staging of symbolism. He is content simply to assert the inconceivable view, that the historic fact of the dying and rising again realises itself in the believer.

One consequence of this realism is that, whereas in the Greek Mystery-religions the dying and rising again is a single experience undergone in the act of initiation, or at most revived from time to time in repetition of the initiatory act, for Paul it is an experience which, from the moment of his baptism, is constantly repeating itself on the believer. In the Hellenistic mysticism the believer lives on the store of experience which he acquired in the initiation. With Paul, his whole being, from his baptism onwards, is a constantly renewed experiencing of the dying and rising again which began in that act. As he says in 2nd Corinthians: "For we the living are constantly given up to death for Jesus' sake that the life of Jesus may also be manifested in our mortal flesh" (2 Cor. iv. 11). It is the realism of the Pauline mysticism which finds expression in this conception of the continuous dying and rising again with Christ. If sufficient attention had been paid to it, the question would long ago have arisen whether the mysticism of Paul and that of the Hellenistic mysteries were in any way comparable.

But both those who asserted Hellenistic influence in Paul and those who denied it closed their minds against any recognition of the realism of his mysticism. The former did so because they felt that by this realism he differentiated himself from the mysticism of mystery-religions; the latter were loth to admit any realism at all, because they feared that its presence would offend our religious sensibilities.

When Hermann Lüdemann[1] and Otto Pfleiderer[2] first described the train of thought connected with "being-in-Christ" in its full peculiarity and significance, their work met with scant approval. Up to that time this train of thought had been regarded, so far as it had been accorded a place alongside of the Pauline doctrine of justification, as the ethical complement of that doctrine. Now, however, it had to be admitted that the ethical was not present in a pure form, but was intermingled with physical conceptions. Lüdemann accordingly defined this doctrine of redemption as ethico-physical, Pfleiderer as mystico-ethical. It would have been better if it had from the first been designated mystico-natural. For the ethical element is not its motive force; it is the resultant of the process.

Under the influence of the distaste felt for the realism of Paul's mysticism, efforts have constantly been made to represent the being-in-Christ as an essentially ethical relation, only obscured a little at times by the shadow cast by a naturalistic conception. A typical example of these attempts to soften it down is the descrip-

---

[1] Hermann LÜDEMANN, Die Anthopologie des Apostels Paulus (1872).

[2] Otto PFLEIDERER, Der Paulinismus (1873: Eng. trans. by E. Peters, 1877); Das Urchristentum (1887), Eng. trans. from the second edition (1902), by W. Montgomery, "Primitive Christianity" (London, 4 vols. 1906-11). See on these A. SCHWEITZER, Geschichte der paulinischen Forschung (1911), Eng. trans. by W. Montgomery, "Paul and his Interpreters" (1912), pp. 28-34.

tion of Paul's mystical doctrine of redemption given in H. J. Holtzmann, *Neutestamentliche Theologie*, at the end of the nineteenth century.[1]

Later, Richard Kabisch[2] and William Wrede[3] carry on the work begun by Lüdemann and Pfleiderer. Indeed, right down to the present day Pauline study has endeavoured to evade the recognition of the result, because it could make nothing of it. But the plain fact is that we must resign ourselves to allow the Pauline sayings to retain their plain meaning. Treating it in a way incomprehensible to us as a self-evident thing he speaks of living men as having already died and risen again with Christ.

.   .   .   .   .

We have seen how Pauline mysticism contrasts with Hellenistic; on the other hand it offers a striking analogy to the mysticism of the Hellenistic mystery-religions, and to primitive mysticism in general, in the fact that it is sacramental mysticism.

The recognition of the sacramental in Paul has become, if possible, even more difficult for theological science than the physico-realistic character of the having died with Christ. That Paul should have regarded Baptism and the Lord's Supper as inherently efficacious acts, and redemption as being bound up with them, seems to us inconsistent with the deep spirituality which is elsewhere the shining characteristic of his religion. What tribulation the sacramental mysticism of Paul still has in store for theology becomes evident in Deissmann. He takes the desperate course of denying its recognition. "I hold it," he says, "to be untrue, that for Paul baptism is the way of attaining to Christ. There are passages which, taken in isolation, can be alleged in favour of this view, but there can be no doubt that it is more correct to say: Baptism does not operate but only seals the fellowship with Christ."[4]

---

[1] Heinrich Julius HOLTZMANN, *Lehrbuch des neutestamentliche Theologie* (Tübingen, 1897), vol. ii. 532 pp. On Paulinism see pp. 1-225. Cf. SCHWEITZER, *Gesch. d. paul. Forsch.* pp. 79-91 (Eng. trans. by W. Montgomery, "Paul and his Interpreters" (London, 1912), pp. 100-116).

[2] Richard KABISCH, *Die Eschatologie des Paulus in ihren Zusammenhängen mit dem Gesamtbegriff des Paulinismus*, 1893: 338 pp.

[3] William WREDE, *Paulus*, 1903: 113 pp. See SCHWEITZER, *ut sup.* pp. 45-50 and 130-140 (Eng. trans. 58 ff., 166 ff.)

Among later works, Ernst SOMMERLATH, *Der Ursprung des neuen Lebens nach Paulus* (Leipzig, 1923), seeks to do justice to the realism of the dying and rising again with Christ.

[4] Adolf DEISSMANN, *Paulus*, 2nd ed., 1925, p. 115.

Of such fine distinctions Paul knows nothing. He simply asserts that it is with Baptism that the being-in-Christ and the dying and rising again have their beginning. He who is baptized into Christ is united in one corporeity with Him and the other Elect who are "in Christ" (Gal. iii. 27-28), and undergoes with Him His dying and rising again (Rom. vi. 3-4).

The effect of Baptism is thought of so objectively that some in Corinth caused themselves to be baptized for the dead, in order that through this Baptism by proxy they might share in the benefits of the sacrament. Far from combating such a view as superstitious, Paul uses it as an argument against those who cast doubt upon the resurrection (1 Cor. xv. 29).

It is noteworthy that Deissmann in his denial of the fundamental significance of the sacraments in Paul does not deal with this recalcitrant passage.

The idea that it is only through a believing self-surrender to absorption in Christ that the Elect can bring about the mystical fellowship with Him is quite outside of Paul's horizon. He assumes as self-evident that a grafting into Christ takes place in Baptism and is bound up with this ceremonial act.

In primitive Christianity Baptism guaranteed the forgiveness of sins and allegiance to the coming Messiah, and the prospect of sharing the glory which is to dawn at His coming. In this significance Paul takes it over, but he explains its operation by his Christ-mysticism. On this basis he asserts that what takes place in Baptism is the beginning of the being-in-Christ and the process of dying and rising again which is associated therewith. He makes no use of the symbolism of the ceremony to explain what happens. He does not make it an object of reflection. In Rom. vi. 3-6 he nowhere suggests that he thinks of Baptism as a being buried and rising again with Christ just because the baptized plunges beneath the water and rises out of it again. These ingenious explanations have been read into his words by interpreters; Paul himself follows no such roundabout ways. Baptism is for him a being buried and rising again, because it takes place in the name of Jesus Christ, who was buried and rose again. It effects what the mysticism of being-in-Christ accepts as the effect of redemption.

How soberly realistic is this sacramental view compared with that of the Greek mystery-religions! In these everything is founded upon the symbolic ceremony. The rite effects that which it represents. He who receives the initiation outwardly performs that which he inwardly experiences. Every detail has its own significance.

For Paul the sonorous symbolism of the ceremony plays no particular part. The solemn preparation which is indispensable with Hellenistic mysteries is wholly lacking. He attaches to the sacred ceremony only that significance which his mysticism inevitably gives it. The impressive atmosphere which surrounds the mystagogue is wholly foreign to him. He, Paul, converts men, but he does not care whether he baptizes them or no. In 1 Corinthians i. 14-17 he puts on record that he himself at Corinth baptized but few. Christ had not sent him to baptize but to preach the Gospel. This sober matter-of-fact sacramentalism is absolutely un-Hellenistic.

The fact of holding a sacramental mysticism seems to place Paul in the same category as the Hellenistic mystagogues. But his position is really quite different from theirs, and he has another spirit than theirs. With them mysticism and sacraments grow up intertwined from a common root idea. But Paul deliberately brings the sacraments, which he found already present in the primitive Christian community, into relation with his mysticism of the dying and rising unto Christ, and explains them in the light of ideas originally foreign to the ceremony which he took over.

Like Baptism, the Lord's Supper is brought into relation with the mysticism of the being-in-Christ. It effects fellowship with Christ. Paul does not scruple to develop this significance by a reference to the pagan sacrificial feasts (1 Cor. x. 14-22). As the Lord's Supper effects fellowship with the Christ who died, so do sacrificial feasts effect fellowship with the demons.

The Old Testament analogies to Baptism and the Lord's Supper which Paul cites in 1 Corinthians x. 1-6 are interesting. The passing of the Children of Israel under the Cloud and their crossing of the Red Sea are described as a Baptism unto Moses. The eating of Manna and the drinking of the water from the Rock are the counterpart of the eating and drinking of the Lord's Supper. Paul here raises to the rank of Sacraments experiences undergone by a whole nation, which neither the participants, nor anyone else subsequently, had regarded as sacramental. That he can in this way make sacraments out of such events is characteristic of his view of sacraments, at once simple and realistic. Had he been in any way possessed with that sense of the symbolism of the sacraments which is characteristic of Hellenistic mysticism he could not have taken such liberties with them. For him all that is needed to make a sacrament is that the ceremonial act, carried out in a fashion willed by God, contributes to salvation. Baptism and the Lord's Supper effect an initiation of the believer of the "last times," which entitles him to participate in the glories of the Messianic Kingdom. For the Israelites on their march out of Egypt the salvation which lay before them was to attain to the Promised Land. Their experience with water in their wanderings with the Cloud and in the crossing of the Red Sea are thus a counterpart to Baptism—in the sense, namely, that in a mysterious fashion water was employed to help and deliver them. The feeding with Manna and the giving to drink out of the Rock continued this wondrous deliverance, as the Lord's Supper continues the work of Baptism. They were thus on their wanderings consecrated[1] to the attainment of the Promised Land by saving acts of God. These events are therefore prototypes of Baptism and the Lord's Supper, by which the Elect, "on whom the ends of the world are come" (1 Cor. x. 11), are consecrated to the attainment of the Messianic Kingdom.

The members of God's people, however, though they were consecrated thereto by such sacraments, nevertheless did not attain to the Promised Land, because in the meantime, through unchastity, idolatry, and other ungodly acts they fell from grace and must therefore die. So too the effect of Baptism and the Lord's Supper can be annulled by ungodly conduct. Thus, in spite of its apparent contrariness, the equating of these events which took place on the way to the Promised Land with the Sacraments which point to the Messianic Kingdom is, from Paul's point of view, perfectly logical.

That the realistic view of a sacrament is thus conditioned by the notion of an annulment of its effect by unworthy conduct is a still further proof that Paul's thought does not move in the same world as the Hellenistic mystery-religions. These avoid entering into the question which the Apostle here decides so confidently. They concern themselves with the initiation only, or if they do consider the subsequent life and activities of the initiate they incline to assume that the reborn is raised above all the conditioned-ness of the natural life. Attempts to preserve the rights of the Ethical within the Sacramental only occur in isolated instances and are not pressed

---

[1] The same word is used in German for the biblical 'consecrate' and the mystical 'initiate'.

home with any energy. The realistic simplicity of Paul's sacramentalism makes him unreceptive for the romanticism of the
Hellenistic Mysteries.

It is interesting to observe that Paul brings Baptism and the
Lord's Supper into connection with his Christ-mysticism, and finds
the explanation of them in it. This clearly shows that the Christ-
mysticism is the centre of his thought, and, further, that the sacraments are not for him something merely traditional, standing outside of his world of thought, but form a living part of his faith.

For us modern men it goes against the grain to have to recognise
this realistic sacramentalism in Paul. But reverence for truth must
be placed above this distaste. We must let his sayings mean what
they say, and not what we should like them to mean.

.   .   .   .   .   .

In dealing with the problem why for Paul God-mysticism does
not take its place alongside of Christ-mysticism, we have already
seen that his mysticism does not exist for itself alone but has its
part to play in a world drama. He has no God-mysticism, because
the existing condition of the world makes God-mysticism for the
present impossible.

The Sacraments are similarly conditioned. They do not directly
communicate eternal life, as is the case with the Greek mystery-
religions, but a participation in a world-condition which is still in
preparation. The Sacrament is related to the Cosmic event. This
view finds expression in the fact that for Paul the Sacraments are
ephemeral institutions. In the Hellenistic mystery-religions it is of
the essence of the sacrament that it reaches back into the mysterious
past of the world, and is efficacious for all times and all generations
of mankind. For Paul it is far otherwise. His Sacraments have their
beginning in the death of Jesus—that is, in the immediate present—
and continue until His return in glory—that is, into the immediate
future. It is only for this span of time that they exist. Before, they
were impossible; after, they will be unnecessary. They were created
ad hoc for a particular class of men of a particular generation, the
elect of that generation "upon whom the ends of the world are
come" (1 Cor. x. 11).

As temporary *ad hoc* institutions they have their counterpart in
the sacraments of the Israelites on their way from Egypt to Canaan;
these also were valid for one generation and with reference to a
benefit expected in the near future.

The character of Paul's sacramental views is clearly indicated by the fact that he can regard as sacraments events experienced once or a few times only, and by a great multitude of men, such as the passing through the Red Sea, or the wanderings beneath the Cloud, the feeding with Manna, and the drinking of the water from the Rock.

The fact, to which for him mysticism and sacraments alike go back, is the dying and rising again of Christ, which took place in the immediate past. This fact is a cosmic event. In the death of Jesus begins the cessation of the natural world, and in His resurrection the dawning of the supernatural world. This cosmic event translates itself in the created being, man, as a dying and rising again.

Paul's mysticism is then historico-cosmic where that of the Hellenistic religions is mythical. The difference is fundamental. Mythical mysticism is orientated towards the remote beginnings of the world, historico-cosmic mysticism towards the times of the end. In mythical mysticism an event lying in the past acquires universal significance and efficacy, by being repeated in symbol, and in a sense re-experienced, by a person who makes a conscious effort to that end. The myth is brought down into the present. In the mysticism of Paul, on the other hand, the whole happening is objective. World-transforming forces, which are manifested for the first time in the dying and rising again of Jesus, began thenceforward to show their efficacy in a certain definite category of mankind. The only necessary condition is to belong to the Elect and to be subjected through Baptism to the working of these forces.

The mysticism of the mystery-religions is individualistic; that of Paul collectivistic; the former has an active character, the latter has something peculiarly passive about it.

In the Hellenistic mysteries the initiate acquires immortality, entering into possession of it on his death. Pauline mysticism is concerned with the passing away and restoration of the world, and the fate of the Elect amid these events. It does not even assume that all will die, but expects that many of them will live to see the end of the world while still in their mortal bodies, and will enter, transformed, into the glory to which they have become entitled through the being-in-Christ.

The fact that it occurs in connection with the expectation of the end of the world, and is founded upon cosmic events, gives its distinctive character to the Pauline mysticism. It is in vain that literary

artifice has been applied to give to the expectation of death in the
Hellenistic mysticism some faint suggestion of the expectation of
the end of the world, in order to bring the Hellenistic sacramental
mysticism into closer touch with the Pauline.

In advocacy of its expectation of the end of the world Pauline
mysticism is something absolutely unique. There is no mysticism,
whether earlier, contemporary, or later, which comes into comparison with it.

.   .   .   .   .   .

A further peculiarity of the mysticism of Paul is that he is not
wholly and solely a mystic.

As a rule, the man who has once penetrated to the recognition
and experience of the eternal amid the transient thenceforward
scorns to have anything to do with the inadequate conception of
ordinary thought and everyday piety. He is a mystic and nothing
but a mystic. As possessed of a mode of apprehension coming from
within and directed towards that which is within, he is exalted
above all knowledge coming from without. If he tolerates naïve
statements about the temporal and eternal as traditional pictures,
he nevertheless constantly endeavours to illuminate this exoteric
material with the penetrating light of mysticism and to show it up
clearly in its inadequate relativity. But Paul's mysticism behaves
quite differently. It shows no hesitation in allowing non-mystical
views of redemption to take their place alongside of it as having
equal right to expression.

It is true no doubt that Paul is convinced that there is a conception of redemption 'having knowledge', which goes further than the
views of ordinary faith. Of such 'wisdom' he speaks in the first
three chapters of 1st Corinthians. He defines it as the wisdom which
comes from God, in which the things of God, as they really are,
manifest themselves in the Spirit of God, which dwells in the man
who has become spiritual. But he never exalts this mysticism of
being-in-Christ, which is the content of this full knowledge, above
other foundations of redemption. He lets it take its place alongside
of them. What he is concerned for is that men should perceive the
full extent and scope of the redemption wrought upon the Cross,
and to estimate the full splendour of the wealth "which God has
gifted to us" (1 Cor. ii. 12). The mystical knowledge does not de-
preciate faith, but completes it. For those who through the Spirit
have attained fullness of knowledge the whole panorama to its

furthest ranges lies in clear daylight; for those who are "babes in Christ" only the nearest hills are visible; for those who are wise "with the wisdom of this world" all is still veiled in cloud.

There are in fact three different doctrines of redemption which for Paul go side by side: an eschatological, a juridical, and a mystical.

According to the eschatological the Elect are saved because by the death and resurrection of Jesus Christ the end of the dominion of the angelic powers, and therewith the end of the natural world, is brought about. It is therefore certain that He will soon appear in His glory and open the way for His Elect, whether they be already dead or still living, to enter the Messianic glory.

The juridical doctrine of righteousness through faith rests in the idea of the atoning death of Jesus. It is carried through by the aid of scriptural arguments. That God, before there was a Law, declared Abraham righteous because he believed His word (Gen. xv. 6), signifies that the true seed of Abraham are those who, for the attaining of the Messianic blessedness, rely not on the works of the Law but solely on faith in the salvation given by God in Christ.

Thus Paul lives at the same time in the simple ideas of the eschatological doctrine of salvation, in the complicated Rabbinical and juridical conceptions, and in the profundities of the mysticism of the being-in-Christ, passing freely from the one circle of ideas to the other. If the co-existence of such disparate views is in itself difficult enough to conceive, it becomes a complete enigma when we find it in a mystic. For when all is said and done, Pauline personal religion is in its fundamental character mystical. It can no doubt find expression for its thought in the eschatological and juridical doctrines of salvation, but its own essential life lies in the mystical.

Paul is therefore a mystic. And yet he has not the usual mentality of a mystic. The exoteric and the esoteric go hand in hand. This too goes back ultimately to the fundamental fact that in him mysticism is combined with a non-mystical conception of the world.

CHAPTER II

HELLENISTIC OR JUDAIC?

OUR review of the characteristics of the Pauline mysticism has shown that it is closely connected with the eschatological world-view; that it finds no place for the conceptions of rebirth or deification; that it is dominated by the eschatological idea of predestination; that it has a kind of realism which is foreign to the Hellenistic mysticism; that its conception of the Sacraments is quite different from the Hellenistic; and that the symbolism which plays so essential a part in the sacramental side of Hellenistic mysticism here plays no part at all. Thus, when any attempt is made to explain the Pauline doctrine as Hellenistic, it finds itself confronted with the greatest difficulties.

Ferdinand Christian Baur and Heinrich Julius Holtzmann, and the other representatives of the historico-critical school of the nineteenth century, simply take for granted a Hellenistic element in Paul alongside of the Jewish without attempting to point out in detail what the Hellenistic element is, or whence it is derived.[1] It was not until the advent of Comparative Religion about the end of the nineteenth century that the need was felt to offer proof of this assumption. The first to undertake the task of explaining Paul by the aid of all the available material of religious history was Richard Reitzenstein.[2]

The book is an expansion of a lecture, which the author gave on the 11th November 1909 before the Clergy Theological Association of Alsace-Lorraine at St. Nicholas' Church in Strasburg, on the Influence of the Mystery-Religions upon Paul. In the 3rd edition the lecture occupies pp. 1-91, the appendices and excursuses pp. 92-438.

[1] See Albert SCHWEITZER, *Geschichte der paulinischen Forschung*, pp. 54-78, 86-88 (Eng. trans. pp. 81 f., 100-116).

[2] *Die hellenistischen Mysterienreligionen. Ihre Grundgedanken und Wirkungen.* Leipzig, 1910: 222 pp.; 3rd ed., 1927, 438 pp.

Without in any way disparaging the merits of H. Usener, A. Dieterich, E. Rohde, F. Cumont, G. Anrich and others, it may be fairly said that it was Reitzenstein who in his successive works introduced the world of Hellenistic personal religion to theological scholars. He has shown us how Oriental cults, carried beyond the limits of their original territories by the wide dissemination of the Greek language, entered into relations with one another and gradually, under the influence of the Hellenistic religious spirit, became fused in a universal religious attitude, the characteristics of which were a longing for salvation and immortality, and the belief that these could be attained through initiation. How great, for example, was the significance of the appearance of Reitzenstein's *Poimandres* (1904) for all those who were endeavouring to realise to themselves the spiritual background of the Christianity of the first generations!

The manner, however, in which Reitzenstein approaches the problem of the influencing of Christianity by Hellenism is not particularly happy. He does not enter into any general consideration of the questions how and when the primitive Christian belief in the Messiahship of Jesus and the Kingdom which was just about to dawn could come to take up into itself pietistic ideas drawn from the Hellenistic Mystery-religions, and what must have been the subsequent cause of development, but is content to assert that in Paul a synthesis of Jewish and Hellenistic Mystery-conceptions is already an accomplished fact. Further, in dealing with Paul himself he neglects to investigate the distinctive character of his ideas and the connections which obtain between them. All his efforts are directed exclusively towards explaining him without more ado by any Hellenistic views which have any kind of resemblance to his. Before the poor Apostle can get in a word he has overwhelmed him with a shower of parallel passages from the Hellenistic literature.

Reitzenstein the linguistic scholar is so completely under the influence of Reitzenstein the champion of Comparative Religion that he neglects the most primary linguistic foundations. He never so much as mentions the fact that Paul makes no use of the concept of rebirth. He never mentions the fact that Paul's mysticism is dominated by the idea of predestination and in many other ways is closely bound up with eschatology, or that from the side of Hellenism nothing can be adduced tending to explain Paul's 'in Christ' and the mystical body of Christ. He is so completely under the conviction that Paul, if he uses the same expressions which occur in

the Hellenistic mystery-faiths, must also have received his ideas
from this source, that his mind is inaccessible to the simplest
logical considerations. Thus, for example, he never gives due
weight to the fact that the whole of the literature which he uses in
explanation of Paul's thought belongs to a much later period.

A further point which Reitzenstein takes for granted is that Paul
was acquainted with the Hellenistic religious ideas, not only from
the everyday language of the Greeks but also through a thorough
study of Hellenistic religious literature. Through these works of
edification and revelation (with which he had been acquainted even
in his Jewish period) the Apostle is assumed to have been capable
of making out of the Damascus experience what it came to mean
for him, and so of breaking away from his ancestral religion. "A
renewed study became necessary from the moment when the
Apostle was preparing to give himself wholly to preaching among
Ἕλληνες. He had to acquaint himself with the language and the
world of ideas of the circles which he wished to win over, and to
find models for the communities which he wished to create and yet
could not conform to the model of the primitive community; and
similarly for the religious forms of worship which he desired to
establish among them." [1] The Paul who thus prepares himself by a
course of reading for his missionary calling is, in fact, so travestied
into the Professor that he retains scant resemblance to the Paul we
meet in the letters.

In a series of investigations into the Pauline conception of Baptism
as having died with Christ, into his conceptions of Gnosis and Pneuma,
his expectation of transfiguration, his self-consciousness, his Christ as
the new Adam, his formula Faith, Love, Hope, Reitzenstein exerts
himself to show that Paul can only be made intelligible in the light of
the ideas associated with the Hellenistic Mystery-religions. His acute-
ness in the discovery of interesting parallels is not more surprising than
his capacity for overlooking the obvious.

If he is to carry through his theory he cannot assume that Paul is a
thinker who works up his own ideas into a system. He is obliged to
make his activity consist solely in welding into a unity in his own mind

[1] R. REITZENSTEIN, *Die hellenistischen Mysterienreligionen*, pp. 209-10. In the
3rd edition this sentence takes the following form (p. 419): "Finally from the
moment when he consciously began to prepare himself for preaching among
the Ἕλληνες he must have entered upon a system of study of their religious
language and world of ideas, and this would be further deepened by his constant
intercourse with these communities."

material ready to his hand in his Hellenistic and Judaic environments, in the process of which "out of the Jewish Messianic hopes the belief in an emissary of God sent forth to deliver men, who has already appeared and now continues to work with His chosen ones," emerges and attains consistency.[1] In his preoccupation with the mixture of religious ideas in the Greek Orient Reitzenstein has lost all sense for the essential character of the actual thinker.

Reitzenstein indeed brings together rich stores of material relating to the problem of the Hellenization of Christianity, and in particular to the origin of the Christian Gnosis, and for this we are deeply indebted to his erudition. But he fails to recognise the exact character of the Pauline problem, and he never faces the difficulties of a Hellenization of Christianity taking place within the primitive Christian community.

.   .   .   .   .

Much more thorough is Bousset's grasp of the problem.[2] He starts from the conviction that the transformation of Christianity into conformity with the spirit of the Greek Mystery-religions cannot have been the act of one man. Had Paul been alone in undertaking such a task this would have been for the Christian communities a new thing. But from the Letters it is clear that there was no question of a difference of belief. The one point in which Paul departed from the accredited views was that he denied the validity of the Law for the converts from paganism. So the only solution to be considered is to make Paul and the primitive Christian communities both borrow from the Hellenistic Mystery-religions.

Bousset accordingly assumes that Hellenization began in the Church at Antioch in Syria, which was in existence before Paul appeared on the scene, and perhaps in other churches of contemporary foundation, before Paul's advent and independently of him.

Christians drawn from Hellenistic cults brought with them the cult of a Kyrios and transferred it to Jesus Christ. This is the explanation of the fact that the designation of Jesus as *Kyrios* (Lord) appears alongside of *Christos* (Messiah). Out of this worship of Jesus as Lord arose the Pauline Mysticism.

The Kyrios of the "Hellenistic primitive Church" is, according

[1] 3rd ed. pp. 90, 91.
[2] Wilhelm BOUSSET, *Kyrios Christos*. A History of Christology from the Beginnings of Christianity down to Irenaeus. Göttingen, 1913: 474 pp.; 2nd ed., 1921.

to Bousset, an element present in the cultus and the services of the Church, and it was in conformity with this that Paul's personal religion bases itself upon an intense consciousness of spiritual unity with the exalted Lord;[1] and it found further support in the primitive Christian conviction, associated with the fact of "speaking with tongues," that the Spirit had taken possession of the believers. Relying on this, Paul declares the Spirit to be the basis of the new life which is attained by fellowship with Christianity. He thus makes the Kyrios doctrine into a Pneuma-Kyrios doctrine.

The sacramental element is also, according to Bousset, found by Paul already present in the Kyrios cult of the Hellenistic churches. The idea that in the initiatory act of Baptism fellowship with the dead and risen Christ had its beginnings, was not invented by him, but only spiritually interpreted and raised to the ethical plane. "Behind the great and weighty ideas of dying and rising with Christ stand sacramental experiences and moods which the early Christian Church associates with Baptism."[2] The whole Christian life becomes for Paul a cultus feast. But "everywhere the Apostle passes beyond the world of cultus and sacrament which surrounded him on every side, and rises to the higher plane of purely ethical religion, to the intellectual and personal."[3] That is why he does not import into his mysticism the Hellenistic idea of deification. The believer does not become Christ, but is only taken up into His being.[4]

He also rejects the individualism of the Hellenistic mysticism. The correlative to Christ is for him not the believer but the Church. In the Hellenistic mystery-religions the man who has passed through all grades of initiation to perfection feels himself to stand alone, aristocratically exalted to a lofty elevation, to which he gradually admits only a chosen few, while the majority even of the initiates, who have attained only to the lower grades, stand far below him.[5] In the Christ-mysticism of Paul, on the other hand, there reigns a fellowship, in which all who are in Christ are felt to be equal with and bound up with one another. Paul is therefore not so much the Hellenizer of Christianity as the cleansing filter through which the waters of the Christian faith which have been muddied by Hellenism pass.

[1] Bousset, p. 126.   [2] Ut sup. p. 172.   [3] Ut sup. p. 148.
[4] Ut sup. p. 151.   [5] Ut sup. p. 154.

The rôle which he there assigns to Paul permits Bousset to maintain the Hellenistic origin of the Pauline mysticism while admitting that a large number of its utterances differ from those of the Hellenistic mystery-religions. The whole structure, however, falls to the ground owing to the fact that it is impossible to prove the existence of the Kyrios cult which the Hellenistic churches are assumed to have taken over. Bousset can no doubt produce passages to prove that Kyrios occurs as a designation of the divinity in the Isis and Osiris cult, and in some of those of Asia Minor and Syria, and then again later in the Emperor-Caesar cults. That, however, proves nothing more than that in Hellenistic Greek Kyrios was the most usual designation of a divine Being, and this indeed is already evidenced by the fact that the Septuagint renders the unspeakable name Jahwe by Kyrios.

The case is different when we consider the sacramental side of the Kyrios cult, which is one of the presuppositions of Bousset's theory. For this he can produce no evidence at all. The assertion that in the Hellenistic churches the Christian faith took on a sacramental character owing to Hellenistic influence remains unsupported.

But even supposing that there were some glimmer of possibility of proving the existence of a Hellenistic Kyrios cult, that would not prove that the Hellenistic churches had in fact really borrowed it. The importation of paganisms of this kind into the faith would certainly have brought them into conflict with the primitive Church in Jerusalem.[1] But we know nothing of any such controversy. The Hellenistic Christians were on the best of terms with Jerusalem. In fact they allowed themselves to be influenced by the original Apostles in opposition to Paul. In Antioch Peter counted for more than Paul. Even Barnabas took Peter's side on the question whether it was right to eat with Gentiles (Gal. ii. 11-14). In all the conflicts to which Paul's attitude to the Law gave rise in Asia Minor, the influence of Jerusalem showed itself stronger than his. The Christians from among the Gentiles and those from the Greek-speaking Jews ranged themselves under the authority of the

---

[1] How clearly the first Christian Church was bound up with Jerusalem is shown in Karl HOLL's study *Der Kirchenbegriff des Paulus in seinem Verhaltnis zu dem der Urgemeinde* (Gesammelte Aufsätze zur Kirchengeschichte, vol. ii., *Der Osten*; 464 pp. Tübingen, 1928, pp. 44-67).

See also Julius WAGENMANN, *Die Stellung des Apostels Paulus neben den Zwölf in den ersten zwei Jahrhunderten*, Giessen, 1926.

Christians drawn from Palestinian Judaism, even though they were numerically the stronger. How then can we reconcile with this the supposition that in the development of the belief and cultus they went their own way? And what a way! In order to leave something for Paul to do as the spiritualiser of this Hellenistic Christianity, Bousset is obliged to assume that the faith of the churches of the Diaspora had taken over the sacramental mysticism of the mystery-religions in all its primitiveness and crudity.

The question whether the adoption of sacramental mystic ideas from Hellenistic Mystery-religions would not have been felt in the first Christian generation to be an innovation, and been resisted as such, cannot be evaded, whether we put down this innovation to the account of the Christians of the Diaspora or of Paul himself. How sensitively, even a couple of generations later, a Christianity which in the meantime had been largely Hellenized by the adoption of the Logos theory reacted against the ideas of the Hellenistic mystery-religions when it encountered them in the guise of Gnosticism! Is it conceivable that the first generation should have tamely accepted such conceptions from the Christians of the Diaspora?

Another point which Bousset fails to explain is that Paul alone among these Hellenistic Christians denied the validity of the Law. This is for him Paul's only original act.[1]

Had the churches of the Diaspora really been under the influence of the Hellenistic mystery-religions, then for them too the Law must have been a thing of small account. Men who in the mystic fellowship of the cult had become beings raised along with the Kyrios-Christ above all earthly limitations, could surely not have conceived themselves as still standing under the Jewish law. That Paul should have been the only one to draw the natural conclusion from this mysticism would be difficult enough to understand. But that the churches of the Diaspora, if they had really lived in the conceptions of the Hellenistic mysticism, could have taken sides against the champion of the liberty which had its source in this mysticism (as they actually did)—that would be frankly unintelligible.

One great difficulty which Bousset creates for himself is that in

---

[1] *Ut sup.* p. 161: "Only in a single point is Paul certainly original, namely in bringing the death of Christ on the cross into relation with the abrogation of the Law." Bousset overlooks the fact that Paul derives the abrogation of the Law directly from the being-in-Christ.

order to be able to assert the Hellenistic origin of the Christ-mysticism he has to make it grow up out of the worship of a Kyrios-Christos thought of as present in the cultus. He thereby brings himself into conflict both with what we are told about the earliest church services and with the earliest conceptions of Christ. For a Christ worshipped as present in the cultus we have no evidence whatever, not even a passage which could be distorted to bear this construction. Paul and the Didache agree in bearing witness that the celebration of the Lord's Supper—and this was in fact the cultus—looked to the Christ whose Parousia was expected in the near future. The Aramaic exclamatory prayer *Maranatha!* (May our Lord come!) of the Didache is also familiar to Paul (1 Cor. xvi. 22). The Lord's Supper is for him a proclamation of the death of the Lord which looks forward to His return (1 Cor. xi. 26). Nowhere do we find a word which implies that he assumes Christ to be present in Baptism and the Supper. That these celebrations affect fellowship, not only with the Christ who is expected at the Parousia but also with the Christ who dies, does not signify that He is present in the cultus. For Paul, as for all the believers of his generation, Christ is in Heaven, with God, and nowhere else (Phil. iii. 20; 1 Thess. iv. 16).

Nor is there any support in the Letters for the suggestion that Paul was consciously drawing material from the Church's cultus and spiritualising the mysticism which he took thence. Everywhere he takes the position of one who contrasts the doctrine of the being-in-Christ as a higher stage of knowledge with the undeveloped belief in Christ, in order to draw from it inferences regarding the invalidating of the Law and the validating of the Law of the Spirit. Clearly as this appears in the text, Bousset cannot recognise it, because he believed himself bound to explain the sacramental mysticism of Paul by deriving it from cultus ideas.

.   .   .   .   .   .

Adolf Deissmann [1] is more cautious than Reitzenstein and Bousset, estimating the significance of the Hellenistic Mystery-Religions for Paul much lower than they do. He assumes that the Jewish-Hellenistic elements, which he brought with him from his pre-Christian period, played in conjunction with the purely

---

[1] The following account is based on the second completely revised edition of Adolf DEISSMANN'S *Paulus* (1st ed., 1911, 202 pp.), Tübingen, 1925: 292 pp. English translation, *St. Paul*, 1912.

Jewish a decisive part in the moulding of his doctrine. Alongside of it in his mysticism, it is assumed that there are ceremonial images and conceptions drawn from the Hellenistic mystery-religions which derived from the Greek language and from the world of religious ideas familiar to him in his youth in Asia Minor.

In thus representing the influence of the mystery-religions as of more or less subordinate importance Deissmann is prevented from recognising the full extent of the sacramental element in the Pauline mysticism. Now from the Jewish-Hellenistic element it is not possible to make a sacramental doctrine of redemption conceivable. He is therefore obliged to assume that Paul did not think of redemption as bound up with Baptism, although he sometimes expresses himself as if this were the case.

Deissmann, like Bousset, thinks of the Christ-mysticism as the centre of the Pauline thought. He does not grant any independent value alongside of it to the conceptions of atoning sacrifice and justification by faith, but regards them as merely another form of pictorial expression of the same facts. The realistic character of this mysticism he cannot recognise to the full extent that Paul's words require and as Reitzenstein and Bousset do. He has constantly to keep in view the necessity of so expounding the Pauline teaching as being explainable from Jewish-Hellenistic elements.

Like Reitzenstein and Bousset, Deissmann is concerned with denying that the Pauline mysticism forms a consistent system, and he is more emphatic than they in doing so. The tendency of his representation is to get rid of the idea that Paul was a thinker. "Reasoning in the strict sense of the word, an orderly progression of connected thought, is not Paul's strong point." [1] "In the handling of religious problems he is in general more successful in the intuitive and contemplative side than in the purely speculative." [2] Accordingly, Paul has not left us any consistent system. The Letters contain only "Confessions of faith in Christ in unsystematic order," in which the writer "delivers his message in constantly new variations of pictorial expressions of similar import, and often in a way that recalls prophetic extravagance." [3] It is precisely the mistake of thinking it possible to construct from these utterances a systematic Pauline teaching that has hitherto, according to Deiss-

[1] *Ut sup.* p. 84.   [2] P. 85.
[3] P. 130 ("des prophetischen Pathos").

mann, blocked for the students of Paul the way to a real understanding of him.

What, then, was the origin of this Christ-Mysticism which flashes up like a will-o'-the-wisp in disconnected sayings? in the main it goes back to the vision on the Damascus road. "Everything which can be called Christ-Mysticism in Paul comes from his reaction to this initiatory experience."[1] In the Damascus experience Paul attained to the conviction not only that Jesus was the expected Messiah but also to the "in Christ" and "Christ in me." His Christ-Mysticism is only the radiation of the energy which thenceforth was concentrated in his soul.[2] To the further development of this mysticism Jewish-Hellenistic and Hellenistic-Mystical ideas contributed their part, so far as he was acquainted with them.

In what way the belief in the Messiahship of Jesus attained on the Damascus road immediately grew into a mysticism of being-in-Christ Deissmann does not attempt to explain. He does not seem to have any consciousness of the difference between the two convictions.

Deissmann thus falls in the footsteps of Karl Holsten, for Holsten was in fact the first to explain the special character of the Pauline thought as a psychological result of the unique Damascus experience.[3] At bottom this method amounts to explaining the obscure by the more obscure. Of the spiritual significance of the Damascus experience, as apprehended by Paul, we know much less than we do of his teaching. He nowhere expresses his views upon the subject. He nowhere gives any hint that his doctrine of the being-in-Christ had so subjective an origin. On the contrary, he everywhere represents it as a logical inference from the Christian faith as such, and everywhere proclaims the being-in-Christ as something that is equally valid for all believers.

Thus Deissmann, not feeling able to represent Paul's teaching as a Hellenization of the original Christian faith, traces it back to a unique experience expressed in Jewish-Hellenistic thought-forms. In doing so he lays his attempted explanation open to the objection that, if Paul's teaching was really founded upon Jewish-Hellenistic ideas, it must have some kind of affinity with Philonian ideas. Now it is remarkable that Paul's teaching contains no trace of the Jewish

---

[1] P. 105.   [2] P. 125.

[3] Karl HOLSTEN, Das Evangelium des Paulus, vol. i., 1880, 498 pp.; vol. ii., 1898, 172 pp. See Albert SCHWEITZER, Geschichte der paulinischen Forschung, pp. 30-32 (English translation, pp. 38-40).

philosophical Hellenism as we find it in Philo. Deissmann is therefore obliged to assume that it is connected with some other kind of
Jewish Hellenism. But of this he fails to prove the existence.

In his statement of the problem Deissmann has shown clear insight. If Paul really did think Hellenistically, he must necessarily
have had his roots in a Hellenism which had already become Jewish.
The fact that his solution fails to be carried through proves that to
Paul Mysticism had nothing Hellenistic in it at all.

Deissmann makes the spirit of Paul's Gospel, which stands behind all the presentations of it, live as scarcely any writer before
him has done. Even if he is obliged to leave in its obscurity the
enigma of the thought-forms in which this spirit has expressed
itself, he yet succeeds in finding words to bring it vividly near to us.

.   .   .   .   .   .

Why has the task not yet been undertaken of explaining the
Pauline Mysticism from Eschatology, seeing that it is clearly apparent from the actual substance of his teaching that his mysticism
of the Dying and Rising again with Christ is centred in an ardent
eschatological expectation? Kabisch and Wrede [1] took the first
steps in this direction. How is it that they have had no successors?

It is obvious that, as a sacramental Mysticism, Paul's teaching
had a certain resemblance to that of the Hellenistic Mystery-
religions. It seemed therefore a more promising task to bring it into
relation with those than to make the attempt to derive it from the
eschatological world-view, which itself is innocent of mysticism,
and indeed shows no tendency in that direction. How, indeed, was
the fruit of mysticism to be sought on the tree of Judaism? The
transcendental character of the Jewish conception of the Deity and
the naïve antithesis of present and future, this world and the other
world, are opposed to mysticism. In the prophets, in the Scribes,
and in John the Baptist no hint of Mysticism is to be discovered.
How could it have been expected that the way to the rich fields of
Pauline Mysticism should lie through the rugged heights of the
Late-Jewish Eschatology?

Led by these obvious reflections Pauline scholars felt themselves

[1] Richard KABISCH, *Die Eschatologie des Paulus in ihrer Zusammenhangen mit dem Gesamtbegriff des Paulus*, 1893, p. 338.

William WREDE, *Paulus*, 1904, 113 pp. On these works see Albert SCHWEITZER, *Gesch. d. paul. Forschung*, pp. 45-50 and 130-140 (English translation, pp. 58 ff. and 166 ff.).

bound to bring Pauline Mysticism into relation with the Hellenistic Mystery-religions, or at least to regard it as the realisation of the possibilities of a Messiah-mysticism possibly present in Jewish Hellenism. But in fact the apparently so promising undertakings of Reitzenstein, Bousset, and Deissmann proved to be impossible of execution. So that, if scholarship is not to resign itself to be content with a mere description of the Pauline Mysticism, there remains nothing for it but to try the so unpromising road through the Late-Jewish Eschatology.

Closer reflection shows that it is by no means so unpromising as had hitherto been assumed.

What kind of mysticism is impossible to Judaism, and to the primitive Christianity which took its rise from Judaism? The answer is God-mysticism. But as a matter of fact what we find in Paul is not God-mysticism but Christ-mysticism. And this is in no way opposed to the transcendentalism of the Jewish and Early-Christian conception of God.

And why should there not be possibilities of mysticism in eschatology? For, after all, eschatology undertakes to get rid of transcendence. It lets the natural world dissolve into the supernatural, and sees this event as having its beginning in the dying and rising again of Jesus. Is it not possible that for a speculative mind, moving amid ardent eschatological hopes and fears in the moment when the expected transformation was being prepared, the two worlds might appear to coincide? That would provide the necessary conditions for the experiencing of the future in the present and the eternal in the temporal, which is the characteristic procedure of mysticism. The *differentia* of a mysticism which arose in this way would be precisely that the interpenetration of present and future did not in it come about by an act of thought, but was a simple reality, which thought only needed to apprehend. Now, in point of fact, the peculiar traits which distinguish the Pauline mysticism from that of the Hellenistic mystery-religions, and indeed that of every other form of mysticism, are directly derived from the fact that this mysticism stands in close relation with the cosmic Events which were to mark the times of the End.

There are other considerations, too, which make the prospects of such an undertaking appear brighter. One of the greatest problems of Paul's teaching is that it is something unique in Early Christianity, and yet is not felt to be essentially different from it.

The well-known epigram of the Basle theologian, Franz Overbeck, "No one has ever understood Paul, and the only one who did understand him, Marcion, misunderstood him," does not apply, at all events, to Primitive Christianity.[1]

Paul could assume that his mysticism, as well as the rest of his teaching, was understood by his fellow-believers, otherwise he could not have called it up as a reinforcement for his teaching of liberation from the Law. That can be understood only if the presuppositions of his mysticism were already present in Early-Christian eschatological belief. He is asking nothing more of his hearers and readers than to draw the natural inferences which they had not yet drawn for themselves. If to Paul mysticism had its roots in the eschatological expectation, then it became explicable how it could be a personal creation and yet at the same time could fairly claim to appeal to his fellow-Christians, not as something foreign to them but as something perfectly comprehensible.

There is no justification for citing 2 Peter iii. 15-16 as evidence that Paul was unintelligible to his fellow-believers.[2] The author, who here writes under the name of Peter, lived decades later, at a time when the Gnostic heresies which appealed to Paul's teaching had already appeared upon the scene. He is warning the Christians of the beginning of the second century not to allow themselves to be confused by the Gnostic interpretations of those passages of Paul which lent themselves to a Gnostic interpretation.

The problem why Paul's teaching did not appear strange to the Christians of the first generation has its counterpart in the similarly puzzling fact that it did become strange to the immediately follow-

[1] This well-known *mot* was made by Overbeck in the middle 'eighties in table-talk with Adolf Harnack. He coined it in imitation of the saying current among Hegel's disciples that the only one who had understood him had misunderstood him. Harnack quoted it in his Lectures on Dogma, and it became widely known through his students. That is how Overbeck tells the story in his posthumous book *Christentum und Kultur*, 1919, pp. 218 ff.

[2] This somewhat confused passage runs: "And consider the longsuffering of our Lord as salvation, as also our beloved brother Paul, according to the wisdom bestowed upon him, has written to you, as also in all his Letters when he speaks in them of these things, in which are some things hard to be understood, which the ignorant and unstable wrench to their own destruction, as they do also the other scriptures " (2 Peter iii. 15-16).

It is true that the author of the Epistle of James has misunderstood Paul in his polemic against faith without works (James ii. 14-20). But the doctrine of faith without works does lend itself to misunderstanding, as is shown by the controversy which had raged about it for centuries.

ing generations. In his Letters Ignatius, the representative of the theology of Asia Minor which set itself to Hellenise Christianity, appears on a superficial view to be completely under the influence of Paul. He moves in an atmosphere of Pauline reminiscences, and builds up his doctrine on the idea of the being-in-Christ which derives from the Pauline teaching. But the very fact of his familiarity with the Pauline teaching makes it the more apparent how foreign to him the Pauline teaching really is. He never explains the being-in-Christ by authentic Pauline conceptions! He never quotes any sayings about the dying and rising again with Christ; and he never develops the teaching about righteousness through faith. He takes over the idea of being-in-Christ, but without its Pauline content. For this he substitutes new and simpler ideas of Hellenistic origin. Ignatius, in fact, and the Johannine school which was nearly related to him, Hellenize Christianity as if Paul had not already done so. For them—and after all we must credit them with some sense for what was and what was not Hellenistic—the idea of having died and risen again with Christ is not Hellenistic, otherwise Christianity would have taken it over along with the idea of being-in-Christ, instead of substituting for it a view which is derived from the Logos idea.

Had Paulinism been a Hellenized Christianity it would have been influential as such in the immediately following period. The fact that even the second generation does not know what to make of his teaching, suggests the conjecture that he built his system upon a conviction which ruled only in the first generation. But what was it that disappeared out of the first Christian generation? What but the expectation of the immediate dawn of the Messianic Kingdom of Jesus?

If Paulinism is explained from Hellenistic mysticism, then the two facts which are in themselves difficult enough to explain—the fact that primitive Christianity did not reject his teaching as foreign to it, and that the immediately following generations could make nothing of it—become wholly inexplicable. If, on the other hand, we can succeed in deriving it from Eschatology, the two facts throw light upon each other. The prospect which it opens up of explaining the hitherto never fully explained relation of Paul, on the one hand to his contemporaries, and on the other to the immediately following generations, would alone suffice to justify the attempt to derive his mysticism from eschatology.

And there is yet another argument in its favour, namely, that such a representation has the great advantage over all previous ones, that it arises in a natural way. In the effort to understand Paul some started out from his anthropology, others from his psychology, others from his manner of thought in his pre-Christian period (as though we knew anything about that!), others from his personal idiosyncrasy, others from his attitude to the Law, and others from the experience on the way to Damascus. In thus taking hold of any thread which came to hand they tangled the skein to start with, and condemned themselves to accept an inexplicable chaos of thought as Pauline teaching. The only practical procedure is to begin with the simple material which Paul shares completely with the Early Church, and then to see how his doctrine develops out of these. Until it is explained in this way it is not explained at all. This simple material is the eschatological expectation. In that conviction Paul was at one with all those who at that time were preaching the Gospel—the conviction that through the death and resurrection of Jesus the proximate coming of the Messianic Kingdom with Jesus as its ruler was assured. It was this elementary teaching which formed the burden of the discourse when he journeyed as a missionary from place to place. To it he constantly recurs in his Letters. With this therefore the exposition of Paulinism must logically begin.

CHAPTER III

THE PAULINE EPISTLES

WHAT are the writings which can be accepted as authoritative sources for Paul's teaching?

As regards the speeches of Paul in the Acts of the Apostles, it is possible that they are based upon traditions of speeches which he actually delivered, but in the form in which we have them they doubtless belong to the author of Acts, and are adapted to his representation of the facts. As authentic testimony to the teaching of Paul they are consequently not to be trusted.

As certain sources we have, in the first place, the four main Epistles, that to the Galatians, the two to the Corinthians, and that to the Romans. The authenticity of these are accepted by F. C. Baur (1792–1860) and the Tübingen school which derived from him, though they declared the other writings attributed to St. Paul to be spurious and sought the author of these writings in the ranks of the Gentile Christian party which, after Paul's death, was involved in controversies, on the one hand with Jewish Christianity, and on the other with the beginnings of Gnosticism. The four great Epistles were called in question only by Bruno Bauer (1809–1882), and the Dutch radicals Allard Pierson and A. D. Loman, and those who as their successors in this line of criticism endeavoured to prove Paulinism to be a literary creation of the second century.[1]

Since Baur's day the objections brought by the Tübingen school against the genuineness of the First Epistle to the Thessalonians, the Epistle to the Philippians, and to Philemon have been shown to be untenable. These writings, in addition to the four main Epistles, may now be treated as unquestionably genuine.

[1] On the criticism represented by Ferdinand Christian Baur and his followers see Albert SCHWEITZER *Geschichte der paulinischen Forschung*, pp. 10-22 (Eng. trans. pp. 12 ff.); on the radical criticism of Bruno Bauer and the Dutch schools, *ibid.* pp. 92-111 (Eng. trans. pp. 117 ff.).

On the other hand, the Second Epistle to the Thessalonians, the two Epistles to Timothy, and the Epistle to Titus are not genuine. Against the genuineness of 2nd Thessalonians, in addition to the suspicions roused by the language, there is the difficulty that it explicitly opposes the idea that the Return of Jesus is immediately at hand, and enumerates all that must happen before that Day can dawn (2 Thess. ii. 1-12). It was only at a period subsequent to the death of Paul that Christian teachers found themselves obliged to find such means of reconciling believers to the delay of that event.

The Epistles, generally known as Pastoral, to Timothy and Titus, offer Pauline ideas only in quite general phraseology. The exhortations to fellow-workers of Paul's, now become leaders of the churches, which form their principal content, presuppose the struggle with Gnosticism; that is to say, we have here to do with writings dating from the end of the first or the beginning of the second century. It is in vain that repeated attempts have been made to prove their genuineness, or, at the least, to discover in them short notes written by Paul, which were later worked up in these forms in order to make them serviceable to the Church in its struggle with Gnosticism.

A special problem is presented by the Epistles to the Colossians and Ephesians. They differ in a peculiar way from those to the Romans, Corinthians, Galatians, and Philippians. At the same time they have so much in common with these that the assumption of spuriousness offers almost as many difficulties as that of genuineness. The style of these two writings is more elaborate and, at the same time, clumsier than that of the others. The length of the periods and the coinages of compound words arrest attention. The thoughts of Paul are present here, but they no longer present the same clear outlines as do the other Epistles, and in part have begun to undergo a process of transformation. The struggle against circumcision seems to have reached an issue, as well as that with the Jewish zealots and the Apostles at Jerusalem who stood behind them. The Paul of the Epistle to the Ephesians speaks of the "Holy Apostles" as though he did not belong to the same generation and did not hold himself to be an Apostle (Eph. iii. 5).

Whatever solution may be given, however, to the complicated literary problem of the Colossian and Ephesian Epistles it is not of primary importance for the exposition of Paul's teaching. There is so much that is peculiar in their ideas that these cannot in any case be simply dovetailed with those from the certainly genuine Epistles, but must in some way be allowed to take a place alongside of them.

Similarly 2nd Thessalonians and the Pastorals, if an attempt is made to use them as genuine, neither enrich nor make clearer the picture of Paul's doctrine arising from the other Epistles.

The course which commends itself therefore is to portray the Mysticism of Paul on the basis of the seven certainly genuine Epistles (Romans, 1st-2nd Corinthians, Galatians, Philippians, 1st Thessalonians, and Philemon), referring in detail to the ideas of the others where they appear of interest, but not including them in the picture.

.   .   .   .   .   .

Paul's Letters are 'occasional' writings. He did not compose them with a view to giving a connected account of his teaching, but expounded his views only as fully as the circumstances which gave rise to the Letters appeared to demand. We have to try to re-create a connected picture of his teaching from fragments which owe their existence to a particular polemical or apologetic interest. The fact that this is to some extent possible shows that we are dealing with ideas which are derived from a fundamental conception and are closely connected with one another.

The first Letter to the Thessalonians is doubtless to be regarded as the earliest of these Letters. Paul takes up his pen in order to give the newly founded church, from which he had been driven away by a persecution set on foot by the Jews, news of his welfare, to strengthen them in their faith and in steadfastness under persecution.

The Letter to the Galatians was written by the Apostle to the church which he had founded on his second missionary journey in north-eastern Phrygia, which he had visited again on his third journey, in order to defend his authority. Zealots from Jerusalem were on the point of convincing the Gentile converts that in order to be true Christians they must accept the Jewish Law and the rite of circumcision. They were endeavouring to persuade these people that Paul was keeping something back from them if he had not given them this teaching. And, moreover, they were denying that he was an Apostle at all in the same sense as those in Jerusalem.

The Letter in which Paul repels this attack upon his teaching and his authority dates probably from the time when, in his third missionary journey, he spent two and a quarter years in Ephesus

(Acts xix. 8-10). Whether he succeeded in preventing the apostasy of this church or not we are not informed.

It was also during the sojourn at Ephesus that the First Epistle to the Corinthians was written. The latter was occasioned by news of occurrences and circumstances in the Church at Corinth, in regard to which Paul had to state his attitude. At the same time he had to answer questions which had been submitted to him. And here too he was obliged to defend his apostolic authority, for his opponents were asserting that he was postponing his visit because he had not the courage to face and answer them. So far had things gone that Paul asks whether he is to come with a rod or in the spirit of meekness (1 Cor. iv. 21).

He holds out a prospect of an early visit. He intends after Pentecost to come by the land route through Macedonia and to remain with them for some time, perhaps throughout the winter (1 Cor. xvi. 5-9). He says he has already begun to collect funds, which he will later deliver, as a tribute from the Gentiles to the Church at Jerusalem. (1 Cor. xvi. 1-4). Meanwhile he sends Timothy in advance to deal with urgent matters.

A few months after this Letter a second became necessary. This is almost entirely devoted to the controversy with his opponents, who were becoming more and more arrogant. Against these agitators Paul was forced to take up the pen while still on his journey from Ephesus to Corinth. He won at least a partial victory. Titus, sent on by him to Corinth, was able on his return to Macedonia, to report to him that the opponent who had been bitterest against him had been condemned by the church by an impressive majority, though he had very soon after been received into favour again, a proceeding to which Paul had to give his retrospective approval (2 Cor. ii. 1-11, vii. 5-13). And Titus was able to tell them that zeal on his behalf and a longing for his presence were manifest in the Corinthian church (2 Cor. vii. 7). In the middle of the Letter he recurs again to the matter of the collection for the Jerusalem Christians.

Thus the first Letter to the Corinthians was written from Ephesus in the spring, the second Letter to the Corinthians from Macedonia in the autumn. In the following winter at Corinth the Epistle to the Romans was composed. These three main Epistles thus originated at short intervals in the course of a few months.

In the Epistle to the Romans Paul is preparing the way for a visit to the west. He finds that there is no longer any room for him in the region between Jerusalem and Illyria (Rom. xv. 23). He has a mind to go even as far as Spain (Rom. xv. 24). What urges him to this decision is the conviction that he is called to preach the Gospel throughout the whole world. Another thing that suggests to him working in the west is that the enmity of the Jews, as well as that of the Jewish Christians behind whom stood the Apostles at Jerusalem, made any hope of successful missionary work in the east for the present impossible. He does not indeed explicitly say this to the Romans, but what is in his heart they could gather from the fact that he entreats them to pray to God that he might be delivered from the unbelievers in Jerusalem, and that the offering which he was taking with him for the saints at Jerusalem might be well-pleasing to them (Rom. xv. 20-31).

As he has to reckon with the possibility that the Church at Rome might have been prejudiced against him, or, when his travel plans became known, might have adverse influences brought to bear on it, he seeks to put himself right in advance by setting forth in this Letter his attitude towards the Law. In this Apologia he does not deny the ground principles of his teaching, but he walks as warily as it is possible to do. All polemic against the Apostles in Jerusalem is avoided, and his attachment to his ancestral race is emphasised to the utmost.

What kind of reception this Apologia met with we do not know. It was not as he purposed in the following autumn that he found his way to Rome, but only two and a half years later (in the spring), and then not in the course of a journey to Spain but as a prisoner. Christians from Rome who had heard of his arrival from the brethren at Puteoli went to meet him on the Appian Way as far as Appii Forum, forty-three Roman miles from Rome (Acts xxviii. 14-15).

During his imprisonment in Rome Paul wrote the Epistle to the Philippians. They had sent him a gift, and had probably also intended that Epaphroditus the bearer of it should remain with him as his attendant. This intention, however, was not realised, for Epaphroditus fell dangerously ill, and after his recovery desired to return home (Phil. ii. 25-30). He took with him Paul's Letter with the expression of his gratitude and his exhortations to the Philippians. The Apostle takes an optimistic view of his own situation. Though he has to take into account the possibility of a fatal outcome of his imprisonment (Phil. ii. 17), he nevertheless has great hopes of being soon set at liberty and of coming again to Philippi (Phil. i. 25-26, ii. 24).

Another Letter written during his imprisonment was that to a Christian named Philemon, who probably lived at Colossae. Paul had become acquainted with a runaway slave of his named Onesimus and had converted him. He had charged him to return to his master, and now gives him a note of a few lines, in which he begs Philemon to pardon him, and henceforth to count him no longer as a slave but a brother in Christ. In this Letter also Paul expresses the hope of soon being set at liberty and revisiting the churches of Asia Minor.

Objection has been taken to the slave's having run away to Rome, and returning to his master from so far away, over land and sea, and it is suggested that the situation would be more intelligible if the Letter had been written during one of his Asian imprisonments—for we know Paul was frequently imprisoned (2 Cor. xi. 23) —or from his prison at Caesarea. And in the case of the Letter to the Philippians also it has been suggested that it dates from one of the earlier imprisonments rather than from the Roman. This is not impossible. But the fact that Paul sends greetings from "those of Caesar's house," that is to say, slaves from the Imperial household (Phil. iv. 22), makes it on the whole most probable that the writing originated in Rome. It is true that we know from inscriptions at Ephesus that there existed there, and no doubt elsewhere in the province, associations of freed slaves and Imperial slaves (*servi domini nostri Augusti*). But the most natural interpretation of the phrase "they of Caesar's house" is that it really does refer to a church formed among the slaves of the Emperor's household.

And in view of the constant coming and going which at that time took place over the Mediterranean area it is quite conceivable that the Church at Philippi should have sent a gift to Paul at Rome, and that he should have sent back to Asia Minor a runaway slave from those parts.

.   .   .   .   .   .

In what years were these Letters written? The fixed points for a chronology of Paul's activities are the date at which the Nabataean King Aretas IV. (9 B.C. to A.D. 39)—whose ethnarch (meaning some kind of representative) endeavoured at Damascus to get Paul into his power, and from whom, according to 2 Cor. xi. 32-33, he escaped over the wall in a basket—had some authority in this city, which since the days of Pompey had belonged to the Romans; the expulsion of the Jews from Rome under Claudius, in consequence of which Aquila and Prisca came to Corinth, where Paul worked with them (Acts xviii. 2, 3); the proconsulate of Gallio, brother of the philosopher Seneca, in Achaia, before whose judgment-seat Paul was dragged by the Jews (Acts xviii. 12); the entry into office of the Procurator Festus, who in the autumn after his arrival sent Paul from Caesarea to Rome (Acts xxv. 1-xxvii. 3). And we have, from Paul himself, an important statement in Galatians (i. 17-ii. 2) about the way in which he spent the time subsequent to his conversion. From this it appears that between the time of his conversion and his journey to Jerusalem to the so-called Apostolic Council (Acts xv.), after his first missionary journey, a period of at least seventeen years must have elapsed. From these chronological data it is evident that between the beginning of the second missionary journey to the end of the second year of the Roman imprisonment, from which time onward we have no further information about Paul's movements, we have to place a period of about twelve years, which are probably the years A.D. 52-64, but possibly from 50-62, if not still earlier.

The Letter to the Thessalonians is therefore to be placed at the beginning of the fifties; that to the Galatians and the two to the Corinthians and that to the Romans belong to the middle and the second half of that decade; the Letter to the Philippians and that to Philemon may be ascribed to the beginning of the sixties.

Do we possess these Letters in the actual form in which they were written? This question naturally suggests itself in view of the fact that they were copies, and collected not so much as letters, that is to say, historical documents, but as writings to be read at divine service. It is therefore conceivable that those who copied them may sometimes have been led by practical considerations to divide and arrange the material which lay before them in the manner most useful for this purpose. Another matter that must be taken into consideration is that the form of the writings might be influenced by the vicissitudes to which the papyrus on which they were recorded was exposed. They were written on papyrus strips which were attached to one another. If a strip at beginning or end became detached, the letter was without opening or close and might happen, when copied out again, to be attached to another Letter of Paul, and subsequently to become a permanent part of the MS. A similar fate might befall these detached beginnings and endings. And the possibility that several letters addressed to one church might subsequently be joined together into a single letter for public reading, is also to be taken into account.

1st Thessalonians and Galatians make the impression of lying before us in the original. In the case of 1st and 2nd Corinthians there are grounds for thinking that both really contain several letters. In 1 Cor. v. 9 Paul mentions a letter which he had sent them earlier, to exhort them to separate themselves from the unchaste. In 2 Cor. ii. 4, ii. 9, and vii. 8-16, he refers to a letter written with tears, in which he had sought to prove them, whether they were still loyal to him. This letter must have been severe in tone, for Paul had learnt from Titus that the believers had been deeply grieved by it. The letter thus referred to in 2nd Corinthians cannot be contained in 1st Corinthians, for this document does not make the impression of being written with tears or of summoning the church to return once more to its allegiance to the Apostle.

Paul must then, it would seem, have written no less than four letters to the Corinthians. If so, are we to believe that only two have been preserved? It is more natural to assume that two of them no longer exist separately, but in the course of being copied for use in public worship were interpolated into the two others. That would explain at once the bulk and the lack of unity of the two Letters which have come down to us. How their contents are to be distributed among the four letters can no longer be determined with certainty. The tearful letter, or at least a piece of it, is no doubt to be found in the so-called Four Chapters Letter (2 Cor. x. 1-xiii. 14). The moving arguments in which Paul shows why he, in spite of all the scorn of his opponents, has the right to hold himself to be a real Apostle and as such to demand their obedience, does really make the impression of being written with tears. And the searing irony with which they are written is sufficiently wounding to grieve the Corinthian readers. The hypothesis that these four chapters, although they now come after 2 Corinthians i.-ix., came in point of time before them was first put forward by Adolf Hausrath in the year 1870.

The identification of the earlier letter mentioned in 1 Corinthians v. 9 is rendered difficult by the fact that we know too little about its character and contents. The only thing we are told about it is that it commanded the readers to separate themselves from the unchaste. A fragment of this letter is doubtless to be found in 2 Corinthians vi. 14-vii. 1, where an exhortation of this kind appears in an argument by Paul about his attitude to the Corinthians. It is also possible that the warnings against partaking in idolatrous feasts, and the references to the Israelites who perished in the wilderness on account of unchastity and idolatry in 1 Corinthians x. 1-33, may have come from this letter, since in their present place they do not connect either with what precedes or what follows them.

Speaking generally, indeed, how many passages in the Corinthian Letters lie side by side without obvious connection! The arguments about the rights of an Apostle in 1 Corinthians ix. come in quite unexpectedly and break off equally abruptly. Chapters ix., x., and xi. of 1st Corinthians are three separate blocks, not even connected with one another, which break into a series of explanations of which each begins with "As concerning" ($\pi\epsilon\rho\grave{\iota}$ $\delta\acute{\epsilon}$, 1 Corinthians vii. 1, vii. 25, viii. 1, xii. 1), which according to 1 Corinthians vii. 1 are answers to questions which had been communicated to the Apostle in a letter from Corinth. In the second Letter the two tame chapters, in which directions are given for the collection from Jerusalem (2 Cor. viii.-ix.), stand in marked contrast with their surroundings.

This kind of disconnectedness and dislocation is most simply explained, if we assume that in 1st and 2nd Corinthians we have really the substance of four letters.

Philippians, again, may possibly consist of two distinct letters. It has always been noticed that, with the beginning of the third chapter, the tone suddenly changes. The excited lines against the 'dogs' (Phil. iii. 2) and the "enemies of the cross of Christ" (Phil. iii. 18), aimed at the Jewish Christian zealots, come as a bolt from the blue. It is therefore worthy of consideration whether the section Phil. iii. 2–iv. 9 may not be a fragment of a letter from the time when Paul in Macedonia had to defend himself against Jewish Christian opponents. For even in these churches conflicts must have taken place. When Paul at the end of his third missionary journey, instead of taking ship from Ephesus to Corinth, chose the land route via Macedonia, that was doubtless because his presence here was necessary. At that part of his journey he found, as he tells the Corinthians, no rest for his flesh; nothing but afflictions, fighting without and fears within (2 Cor. vii. 5).

In Romans the long list of greetings which are to be given to beloved friends (Rom. xvi. 1-23) certainly cannot belong to the original of this letter. How could Paul have so many personal relations with a church with which, on his own showing, he is not yet acquainted? It is therefore probable that Romans xvi. 1-23 originally formed part of a letter addressed to a church which he knew well in Asia Minor, and in a later copying became attached to the Epistle to the Romans. Since Aquila and Prisca are mentioned among those to whom greetings are to be given, Ephesus seems to be the most probable destination of the letter. This view regarding the list of greetings in the Epistle to the Romans was first expressed by David Schulz in the year 1829.

But if the Epistle to the Romans contained the list of greetings belonging to another letter, it is possible that it has also preserved some other portions of the latter's content. Is it not a little remarkable, that Paul writing to an unknown church should give directions as to what attitude should be taken up towards those who rejected the use of flesh and wine and other things, and approved nothing but vegetarian food for believers (Rom. xiv. 1-xv. 13)? These explanations about the strong and the weak would be much more intelligible if, having received news of a church well known to him, he is giving directions for the settlement of a controversy. If so, the case is that the Epistle to the Romans, at a time when it was being copied for reading in public worship, has taken up into itself a letter of which the Roman church at that time possessed a copy, but which had not been originally addressed to this church.

We have therefore to reckon with the possibility that the copy of a collection of the Pauline Epistles, on which our knowledge of the Apostle's letters rests, did not contain the Epistles to the Corinthians, Philippians and Romans in the original form, but in the version which they had assumed in the copies prepared for the purpose of reading at public worship.

But that means no more than that the order of the several sections is not always the original connection. It does not mean that there had been a real working over of the text. Here and there no doubt the marginal gloss of a copyist may have become interpolated into the text; but all efforts to prove any systematic interpolation have proved impossible to carry out. In the second half of the nineteenth century Christian Hermann Weisse and Daniel Völter and others thought it necessary to seek for an original text of the Pauline

Letters behind that which has come down to us.[1] The net results of their efforts was to show how arbitrary these proposed excisions were.

Have all the Epistles which Paul wrote come down to us? A possibility that some of them may have been lost must be admitted. We have constantly to remind ourselves that the reason why the Epistles were preserved was simply that they were treated as edifying writings for use in public worship, and as such were copied and circulated among the various churches. It is thus possible that many shorter letters of the Apostle's, or even those of some length, through the accident of not being transmitted from the churches to which they were addressed, and thus being included in the collection of Pauline letters which was continually recopied, fell into oblivion and so perished.

The wonder is, indeed, that so many were preserved. Writings like the Letter to the Galatians and the second to the Corinthians do not really seem destined to live. How came the churches to preserve documents which redounded so little to their credit? And it is still more astonishing that they allowed their shame to be continually recalled in public worship. How strong must have been the magic of the name of Paul, whose writings dealing with obsolete and therefore unintelligible questions and controversies, writings which contained such severe strictures on the contemporary churches, instead of being handed over to oblivion received the status and respect of edifying treatises! The fact that writings, the content of which was so unfavourable to their survival, have nevertheless come down to us makes it probable that circumstances were favourable to the preservation of the Pauline Epistles. What has been lost was lost through accident or carelessness, and doubtless at a very early date.

In any case, what has survived, be it much or little in proportion to the total amount of Paul's actual writings, is sufficient to give us some conception of his vigorous intelligence. We can never be thankful enough to those unknown church leaders and copyists through whose action these treasures have been preserved to us.

---

[1] On these investigations see Albert SCHWEITZER, *Geschichte*, pp. 111-116 (Eng. trans., pp. 141 ff.).

CHAPTER IV

THE ESCHATOLOGICAL DOCTRINE OF REDEMPTION

FROM his first letter to his last Paul's thought is always uniformly dominated by the expectation of the immediate return of Jesus, of the Judgment, and the Messianic glory.

In the first Thessalonian Epistle sayings constantly occur which give expression to this ardent expectation.

1 Thess. i. 10: "To await the Coming from heaven of His Son whom he raised from the dead, Jesus, who has delivered us from the Wrath which is on its way."

1 Thess. ii. 19: "For who is our hope, our joy, our crown if it be not you (to present you) before the face of our Lord Jesus Christ at His appearing" (Gr. παρουσία).

1 Thess. iii. 13: "To confirm your hearts that they may be blameless in holiness before God our Father at the appearing of the Lord Jesus Christ with His saints."

1 Thess. v. 23: "May He, the God of Peace, make you holy through and through, and keep you, spirit, soul and body complete, blameless at the appearing of our Lord Jesus Christ."

The Letters to the Galatians, Corinthians, and Romans are in the main so occupied with arguments about the Law, righteousness of faith, being-in-Christ, predestination, and the particular affairs of the churches, that it is possible to forget the expectation which dominates the soul of the writer. But suddenly, in some incidental saying, the eschatological belief stands there in all its strength as something which always underlies the whole.

Gal. i. 4: "Jesus who gave Himself for our sins that He might pluck us forth from this present evil world."

Gal. vi. 10: "Therefore, so long as we have time, let us do good. . . ."

In the 1st Epistle to the Corinthians the directions about marrying and remaining single are dominated by the conviction that the time is short (1 Cor. vii. 29) and that "the fashion of this world is passing away" (1 Cor. vii. 31). Believers are reminded that they are the generation "that will outlive the end of time" (1 Cor. x. 11), and that in the time to come they will pronounce judgment upon angels (1 Cor. vi. 3), that they themselves must be present at a judgment in which all things shall be tested by fire (1 Cor. iii. 13-15), and that the celebration of the Lord's Supper is a remembering of the death of Jesus which looks to His coming again (1 Cor. xi. 26). At the beginning of the Letter there is a reference to the revelation of the glory of Christ (1 Cor. i. 7-8) and it closes with the exclamatory prayer *Maranatha* ("Our Lord, Come!", 1 Cor. xvi. 22).

In 2nd Corinthians also there is frequent reference to the expectation of the day of the Lord.

2 Cor. i. 14: "That we are your boasting, as you also are ours in the day of our Lord Jesus."

2 Cor. v. 10: "For we all must be made manifest before the judgment-seat of Christ."

2 Cor. xi. 2: "For I have betrothed you to a husband, to present you as a pure virgin to Christ."

Imposing expressions of this eschatological expectation are found also in the Epistle to the Romans. The Apostle represents the whole creation as yearning for the day of the revelation of the sons of God (1 Rom. viii. 19). He holds that Redemption is nearer now than at the time when he and the Roman Christians first believed (Rom. xiii. 11), that the morning of the expected day is already beginning to dawn (Rom. xiii. 12), and that God will shortly tread Satan underfoot (Rom. xvi. 20).

In the Epistle to the Philippians eschatological expectation recurs again and again, as in 1st Thessalonians.

Phil. i. 6: "That He who has begun in you a good work will complete it against the day of Christ."

Phil. i. 10: "That you may be pure and without offence for the day of Christ."

Phil. ii. 10: "That you hold fast by the word of life, so that you may be my boast for the day of Christ."

Phil. iii. 20-22: "For our home is in heaven, from whence also we expect the Lord Jesus Christ as our Deliverer, who shall change the body of our humiliation that it may be conformed to the body of His glory."

Phil. iv. 1-5: "Rejoice in the Lord at all times! And once more I say, rejoice! . . . The Lord is at hand!"

If then Paul's thought underwent a development it certainly did not consist in the slacking of his eschatological expectation as time went on.

.   .   .   .   .   .

The conception of Redemption which stands behind this eschatological expectation is, to put it quite generally, that Jesus Christ has made an end of the natural world and is bringing in the Messianic Kingdom. It is thus cosmologically conceived. By it a man is transferred from the perishable world to the imperishable, because the whole world is transferred from the one state to the other, and he with it. The redemption which the believer experiences is therefore not a mere transaction arranged between himself, God, and Christ, but a world-event in which he has a share. It is impossible to form a right conception of the view of redemption held by the Early Christians without taking into count the fact that it was thus cosmically conditioned.

The writings which have to be considered as documents for the Jewish eschatological view are, in addition to the earlier and later Prophets, mainly the Book of Enoch, the Psalms of Solomon, and the Apocalypses of Baruch and of Ezra.

The Book of Enoch consists of a series of Apocalypses (revelations) which came into existence between 160 and 70 B.C.: written no doubt originally in Aramaic, it has come down to us in the Ethiopic language.[1] It was first brought to Europe from Abyssinia in 1773 by the English traveller James Bruce. In the main it continues the eschatology in the Book of Daniel. The most important part of the book consists of the so-called Similitudes (Enoch xxxvii-lxxi), in which are portrayed revelations regarding the times of the End which were vouchsafed to "Enoch the seventh from Adam" (*i.e.* before the Flood) by angels in the form of explanations of visions seen by Enoch.

The Psalms of Solomon were written shortly after the taking of Jerusalem by Pompey (63 B.C.). The existence of this work had long been known from its having been cited in canonical lists of early Christian date. The Greek translation of the book, which was originally

---

[1] In addition to this Ethiopic Book of Enoch there is also a Slavonic "Book of Enoch." This Slavonic book no doubt had its origin in the Jewish Diaspora, perhaps as early as A.D. 70 (Slavonic edition, 1880; English, 1896 and 1913 [on its possibly Byzantine date and origin see *Journal of Theol. Stud.* xxiii. 49-56]). There is, further, also a Hebrew "Book of Enoch" which doubtless originated in the second and third century A.D. (Hebrew-English edition by Hugo Odeberg, Cambridge, 1928).

written in Hebrew, was rediscovered at the beginning of the seventeenth century and published by the Jesuit de la Cerda.

The Apocalypses of Baruch and Ezra were written under the impression of the destruction of Jerusalem by Titus (A.D. 70). They profess to be revelations granted to Baruch the scribe of Jeremiah at the time of the destruction of Jerusalem in his day, and to Ezra at the time of the proclamation of the Law and the return to Jerusalem. In these two Apocalypses we no doubt have the expectations of the future held by the Scribes of Paul's day. The Apocalypse of Ezra, which is also known as the Fourth Book of Ezra, has always been known, as it was included in the Vulgate Apocrypha. The Apocalypse of Baruch is preserved in a Syriac translation, and was first published in 1871 by Ceriani. Both writings, which are closely connected in subject, were no doubt originally written in Hebrew.

Besides these four there should be mentioned the Book of Jubilees, dating from about 120 B.C., a paraphrase of Genesis and of Exodus as far as the Passover at Sinai; the Testament of the Twelve Patriarchs, which has come down to us in a form bearing some traces of a Christian working-over, while the underlying Jewish document, allied in spirit to the Book of Jubilees, doubtless also originated about 120 B.C.; and the Ascension of Moses, dating from the beginning of the first century A.D.

The natural world is, in the eschatological view, characterised not only by its transience, but by the fact that demons and angels exercise power in it: to what extent they do this is not completely clear from the various references. The Jewish eschatology does not recognise a real dualism, although it was strongly influenced by Zoroastrianism. The angels who in Gen. vi. 1-4 revolt against God are, according to the Book of Enoch, immediately overcome and kept in durance against their final punishment at the Judgment. But their progeny, begotten of the daughters of men, are the demons, who trouble the world until the end (Enoch xv. 8-xvi. 4). Their leader bears various names, and is often identified with Satan (the Accuser), who was originally not an enemy of God, but only the Accuser of men, whom God permits to act as such.

In general, the view of Jewish eschatology is that the evil of the world comes from the demons, and that angelic beings have, with God's permission, established themselves between Him and mankind. In its simplest form the conception of redemption is that the Messianic Kingdom puts an end to this condition.

. . . . . .

Jesus and Paul are at one in assuming that demons and angels exercise power in the world.

The mentally afflicted are held by Jesus to be possessed of demons. The fact that He heals them is explained by the Pharisees by His being in league with Beelzebub the Prince of the Demons, and having received power from him to do so. Jesus, however, gives the much more natural explanation that the Prince of the Demons has now lost power, and therefore is obliged to allow it. He compares him to a strong man who is overcome and bound by a stronger, and now can only look on while his house is plundered (Mt. xii. 22-29).

Not only possession, but also corporal suffering is for Jesus the work of the demons. In sending out the disciples He gives them power to cast out unclean spirits and heal all sickness and diseases (Mt. x. 1), which they are successful in doing (Mk. vi. 13, 30).

The head of the powers of evil is called by Jesus the 'Wicked One' (πονηρός). In the Lord's Prayer He makes believers pray to God that God will not lead them into 'temptation' (πειρασμός), that is to say into the afflictions brought about by the powers of evil which will precede the Messianic Kingdom, but will deliver them forthwith from the power of the 'Wicked One' (Mt. vi. 13). Peter, in the moment when he seeks to turn Him from the thought of suffering, becomes for Him a tool of Satan (Mt. xvi. 23).

The word Diabolos (διάβολος, slanderer), with which Matthew and Luke render an Aramaic designation of the Wicked One, is in sense identical with Satan. In the Septuagint Satan is translated by διάβολος. The word also occurs in the Wisdom of Solomon (ii. 24).

That this Wicked One is thought of not only as the lord of the demons but also an angelic power opposed to God, is clear from the saying about the eternal fire which is prepared for the devil and his angels (Mt. xxv. 41).

The view found in the Book of Enoch comes nearest to that of Jesus, and the representations found in this book of the Angels, who maintain the cause of the Elect in God's presence against the accusations of Satan, is familiar to Him.[1] This is evidenced by His

---

[1] Enoch xl. 1-10: The four Angels of the Presence are Michael, Raphael, Gabriel, and Phanuel. Of Phanuel it is said "the fourth voice I heard opposing the Satans and not permitting them to appear before the Lord of the spirits to accuse the inhabitants of the earth." See also Enoch civ. 1: "I swear to you, ye righteous, that the angels in heaven before the glory of the Great One remember you for good. Your names are inscribed before the glory of the Great One. Be of good hope."

saying that we must beware of causing offence to "these little ones" because their angels in heaven continually behold the face of God, that is to say, have constant access to His presence in order to intercede for them (Mt. xviii. 10).

It is interesting, and has not hitherto been sufficiently noticed, that, to judge from the Psalms of Solomon and the Apocalypses of Ezra and Baruch, the Scribes seem to have taken little account of the fantastic legends of angel domination. In the Psalms of Solomon the Angels have no rôle assigned to them at all. The Apocalypses of Ezra and Baruch mention angels only as obedient servants of God and never as adversaries and oppressors of men. Only the Angel of Death, whom (according to the Apocalypse of Baruch xxi. 23) Baruch prays God to reprove in order that mortality may cease and "that the store-chambers of souls may allow those who are shut up in them to return", has a sinister office. But he too is thought of as standing in the service of God.

It is significant that God in the Apocalypse of Ezra explicitly assures Ezra that He alone created the earth and alone will visit judgment upon the creation at the end of the Time (4 Ezra v. 56-vi. 6). This excludes also the Jewish-Hellenistic conception of the co-operation of personified powers—Spirit of God, Wisdom of God, Word of God—in the creation of the world.

Both Jesus and Paul stood closer to the world of thought represented by the Book of Enoch than the Scribes seem to have done, to judge from the Apocalypses of Baruch and Ezra.

. . . .

The elements of the eschatological doctrine of redemption are thus found in Jesus' teaching also.[1] He held the conviction that His presence in the world meant the beginning of the downfall of the demons' tyranny.

But the eschatological view is also a determining factor in Jesus' conception of the significance of His death. His death contributes to the destruction of the power of 'the Evil One', because it has for consequence His elevation to the Messiahship. As Messianic King He then has the heavenly angels at His command, in order to overthrow finally all that is opposed to God. But even the view that His death is "a Ransom ($\lambda\acute{v}\tau\rho o\nu$) for many" (Mk. x. 45), and His blood "the blood of the Covenant shed for many" (Mk. xiv. 24), is

---

[1] On Jesus' conception of His suffering and death see Albert SCHWEITZER, *Geschichte der Leben-Jesu-Forschung*, 2nd and later editions, pp. 408-411 and 432-437.

brought by Him under the eschatological conceptions of redemption. The historic Jesus does not die for humanity as a whole, and not for a universal forgiveness of sins, but for a definite number, namely, those who are elect to the Kingdom of God. The thought that He must suffer and die was present with Him from the first, but in the earlier period it took a different form from that which it assumed later. In the first period He associated it with the pre-Messianic tribulation. He expected that He, with his Elect gathered about Him, would be delivered over for a time by God into the power of 'the Evil One' and have to endure 'temptation', that is, suffering and death. With an eye toward this he exhorted the faithful fearlessly to surrender this life for the sake of that which is to come, and above all not to be offended in Him when they saw Him in His humiliation. With unmistakable clearness He announces in the discourse at the sending forth of the disciples that great troubles are about to begin, amid which his followers must preserve their loyalty to Him even unto death.

Mark viii. 34-38: "And He called the multitude to Him with His disciples and said to them, If any man will follow me he must deny himself and take up his cross and follow after me. For he who would save his life will lose it, but he who loses his life for my sake and the Gospel, will save it. What shall it profit a man to gain the whole world and lose his own life? For what can a man give in exchange for his life? For he who is ashamed of me and of my words in this adulterous and sinful generation, of him shall the Son of Man be ashamed when He comes in the glory of His Father with the holy angels."

Matt. x. 34-39: "Think not that I am come to bring peace on earth; I am not come to bring peace, but the sword. I have come to set a man at variance with his father, the daughter with her mother, the daughter-in-law against her mother-in-law, yea, a man's foes shall be they of his own house. He who loves father and mother more than me is not worthy of me; he who loves a son or daughter more than me is not worthy of me; and he who does not take up his cross and follow after me is not worthy of me. He who saves his life will lose it, and he who loses his life for my sake will save it."

Jesus thus believes that by sending forth the disciples He is unleashing the pre-Messianic tribulation, at the end of which the Kingdom of God shall come. But instead of the Son of Man's appearing before they had "gone over the cities of Israel" (Mt. x. 23), they simply returned to Him again. Therefore He withdraws with them into solitude to seek the meaning of this incomprehensible thing. He finds it in the prophet Isaiah (Isa. liii.), namely, that God has appointed Him to die alone, and that this death is to be a ransom, freeing the Elect from the pre-Messianic tribulation. From the first, Jesus had held it a possibility that God might dispense with the final tribulation: that is shown by the petition to be spared it in the prayer for the coming of the Kingdom. Now He is convinced that this prayer has been heard for others but not for Himself. He therefore goes up to Jerusalem intent on compelling the rulers of the people to put Him to death.

Jesus therefore applied to the Messiah the descriptions of the sufferings of the Servant of the Lord in Isaiah liii. It is interesting to note that in the Apocalypses of Enoch, Baruch, and Ezra we already find expressions used about the Messiah and the Son of Man which go back to the Deutero-Isaiah passages about the servant of the Lord. Thus in Enoch the Son of Man is called, in imitation of Isaiah liii. 11, "the Righteous" (Enoch xxxviii. 2, xlvi. 2, xlvii. 1, xlvii. 4), and in accordance with Isaiah xlii. 1 "the Chosen" (Enoch xxxix. 6, xlv. 3, xlviii. 6, xlix. 2). In the Apocalypse of Baruch (lxx. 9) and of Ezra (4 Ezra vii. 28) the Messiah is designated by God as His servant; in the Apocalypse of Ezra (4 Ezra xiii. 32) "the Son of Man" also.[1] The connection of the Messiah—Son of Man—with the suffering Servant of the Lord, which was completed by Jesus, was thus already more or less current in the language of Later Jewish Eschatology. (See Gerhard Kittel, "Der Menschensohn im Neuen Test.", in *Religion in Geschichte und Gegenwart*, 2nd ed. vol. iii., 1929, pp. 2118-2121.)

That Jesus in contemplating His mission dwelt in thought on Deutero- and Trito-Isaiah is evident from sayings of His which allude to passages in this part of the Book of Isaiah (Mt. viii. 11, cf. Isa. xlix. 12; Mt. xi. 5, cf. Isa. lxi. 1; Mt. xxi. 13, cf. Isa. lvi. 7). Even the "many" ($\pi o \lambda \lambda o i$), for whom, according to Mt. xx. 28 and xxvi. 28, His death is to be a ransom, are without doubt derived from Isaiah liii. 11-12.

It is probable too that the impression made by the death of John the Baptist played its part in determining the resolution of Jesus to suffer and die.

That Jesus, as a consequence of His death, expected His resurrection and, closely following thereon, His appearing in the clouds of heaven and the immediate coming of the Messianic Kingdom is clearly apparent from His saying to the disciples on the way to

---

[1] *Sic*, but the text in 4 Ezra has 'My Son', *not* 'Son of Man'.—F. C. B.

Gethsemane (Mk. xiv. 27-28) and His words to the High Priest at His trial (Mk. xiv. 62).

The Kingdom cannot come until the pre-Messianic tribulation has taken place. If Jesus suffers a death which God can accept as the equivalent of that tribulation, He can thereby bring in the Kingdom at once.

Since He thinks of the Kingdom as the New Covenant promised by God through Jeremiah (Jer. xxxi. 31-34), Jesus can say at the Last Supper that His blood is the blood of the New Covenant which is shed for many (Mk. xiv. 24). He feels Himself to be the sacrifice offered at the bringing into force of this new Covenant, parallel to the sacrifice at the conclusion of the Covenant at Sinai, whose blood Moses sprinkled partly on the altar and partly on the people (Ex. xxiv. 5-8).

According to Mark Jesus said only "This is my blood of the Covenant, that is shed for many"; Matthew adds "for the forgiveness of sins" (Mt. xxvi. 28). If the saying in this expanded form is not certainly authentic it is nevertheless true in substance. The blood shed for many has in Jesus' thought something to do with the forgiveness of sins. For with the conception of the pre-Messianic tribulation there is somehow bound up the idea that the Elect, in those sufferings, are not merely handed over to the power of the Evil One, but in their sufferings make atonement for their sins. The death of Jesus, which by God's merciful will is substituted for the Tribulation, therefore takes place for the forgiveness of their sins. Until the sins of the Elect are atoned for, God cannot bring in the Kingdom. Jesus thus suffers an atoning death, which has for its consequence God's forgiveness of sins to the Elect: thus the coming of the Kingdom, the forgiveness of sins, and the consequent rendering possible of the coming of the Kingdom are for Him the same thing.

As the sacrifice of the New Covenant Jesus' death has also in His eyes an atoning significance. It is expressly said in Jeremiah that the forgiveness of sins will accompany the making of the Covenant; Isaiah too had said that in the New Jerusalem there would be forgiveness of sins.

Jer. xxxi. 34: "For I will forgive their guilt, and their sins will I remember no more."

Isa. xxxiii. 24: "The people that dwelt there (in Zion) has forgiveness of sins."

Since God grants to the people of the New Covenant forgiveness of their sins, the inaugural sacrifice of the New Covenant, which Jesus offers by His dying, acquires the significance of an atoning sacrifice.

It is true that the sacrifice at the making of the Covenant at Sinai—not an atoning sacrifice, since in the rite performed by Moses the sprinkled blood is thought of as a binding together of the two parties—is a purely covenant-solemnising sacrifice. But the thoughts of Jesus are not so strictly determined by Comparative Religion that He must distinguish as scrupulously between the two kinds of sacrifice as a modern theological candidate under examination. For Him the sacrifice by which He offers Himself to God for the Elect is at once covenant sacrifice and atoning sacrifice. Similarly He ignores the distinction between Ransom and Atonement, which attempts have been made again and again to introduce in order to avoid the admission that He really looked on His death as an atoning death.

Only from the eschatological point of view does it become intelligible how Jesus could come to regard His death at one and the same time as an atoning death and a deed which ushers in the Kingdom. But for the light which the idea of pre-Messianic tribulation sheds on His saying about the significance of His suffering and death, they would remain entirely obscure. Because God recognises His suffering as an equivalent for that atonement for the sins of the Elect, which but for this they would have had to make by their own sufferings in the pre-Messianic tribulation, He can remit these, put an end at once to the power of the Evil One, and forthwith bring in the Kingdom.

The death of Jesus makes possible the fulfilment of the petitions of the Lord's Prayer for forgiveness of sins, for exemption from the 'temptation', and for deliverance from the Evil One.

Only from the point of view of the eschatological doctrine of redemption does it become intelligible why Jesus, when Peter seeks to dissuade Him from His purpose of dying, hears in his voice the voice of Satan. For Satan has an interest in His giving up that purpose. If Jesus does not die the dominion of the Evil One will continue.

Foreign to our ideas as is the thought of Jesus' atoning death as shaped by the eschatological idea of redemption, it is nevertheless both simple and profound. The atoning tribulation, which man was to suffer in order to obtain the forgiveness of sins, the future

Messiah takes, by the gracious permission of God, upon Himself. How much more living and fruitful is this historically true version of Jesus' thought, growing naturally as it does out of the universal attribution of atoning value to suffering, than the host of theological or untheological inventions which have been foisted upon Him!

. . . . . .

Jesus did not find it necessary to instruct His disciples and converts about His atoning death. It avails for them objectively, without their needing to know or believe in it. He therefore contents Himself with obscure hints. In the Kingdom of God they will come to understand how it all came about.

The Early Church explains Jesus' death on the basis of the tradition of Jesus' sayings and its own eschatological conception of redemption, namely, that through death and resurrection He had become the Messiah in Glory, who would shortly bring in the Kingdom, and that He had won for them an atonement for sin, which would assure to the Elect at the Judgment the forgiveness of their sins. The original idea of Jesus that His death is to take the place of the pre-Messianic Tribulation, and by thus making an end of this should bring in the Kingdom, was not known to them, and in the actual progress of events it lost its applicability. Whereas for Jesus the forgiveness of sins is identical with "deliverance from the Trial", the Early Christians believe in forgiveness of sins because of the death of Jesus, and still expect the pre-Messianic Tribulation, interpreting the suffering and persecution which they undergo as a chastisement which is to precede the appearing of the Messiah. That means that the thought of the atoning death and that of the bringing in of the Kingdom by the death of Jesus no longer form a unity, but become distinct conceptions. As the second can have no independent existence it becomes lost as a separate entity, and survives only in the form that the Jesus, who in His death and resurrection has become the Messiah, will bring in the Kingdom. This explains why the belief of the Early Christians, starting at the death of Jesus, expressed itself in the two parallel assertions that through it He won for Himself exaltation to the Messiahship and also has obtained for His people the forgiveness of their sins. The two apparently disconnected ideas remain, however, in accordance with their origin, attached together by the belief in the nearness of the Kingdom.

That is the Early Christian teaching about the death of Jesus, as proclaimed by Peter and Paul in the Acts, and as we find it given in the 1st Epistle of Peter.

.   .   .   .   .

The simple Early Christian teaching about the atoning death of Jesus is taken for granted by the Paul of the Epistles also. To the Corinthians he speaks of it as the basis of his teaching.

1 Cor. xv. 2: "For I delivered to you among the first things, as I have also received it (by tradition), that Christ died for our sins according to the scriptures."

It is interesting that Paul, who elsewhere claims to have had his teaching direct from Christ, here expressly appeals to tradition.

The Scriptural proof that Christ must die for the sins of the faithful is not given by him in the Epistles. Once (Rom. iv. 25) he has an allusion, in the words "who was delivered up for our offences," to passages which speak of the suffering servant of the Lord (Isa. liii. 5, 12), but without quoting directly. It is possible that his reason for not giving this scriptural evidence is that to him, and to primitive Christianity in general, it was self-evident that the "Servant" passages in Isaiah referred to Jesus.

In Gal. iii. 13 what he is proving by the quotation "Cursed is every one that hangeth on the cross" (Deut. xxi. 23) is not the atoning death of Jesus, but the annulling of the Law by his crucifixion.

This doctrine of the atoning death is then developed by Paul into the doctrine of righteousness by faith alone.

The other traditional assertion that Jesus, in virtue of His death and resurrection, is the Messiah, now exalted to glory and soon to appear as such, also plays its part in his teaching.

Rom. i. 4: "Who has been marked out the Son of God with power according to the Spirit of Holiness because of the resurrection from the dead."

Phil. ii. 8-11: "He humbled Himself, becoming obedient unto death, even the death of the Cross. Therefore God has highly exalted Him, and has given Him a name which is above every name, that at the name of Jesus every knee shall bow, both of those in heaven and those on earth, and those under the earth, and every tongue shall confess that Jesus Christ is Lord to the glory of God the Father."

By His death and resurrection, therefore, Jesus has been exalted above all angelic beings. But He is only to enter fully into this authority on the day of the beginning of the Messianic Kingdom.

Dowered with such might He will then deliver His followers from the coming wrath (1 Thess. i. 10).

But Paul does not limit himself to the doctrine that Jesus through the forgiveness of sins which He has won, and His Messianic power over the Angels, will shortly take up His followers into the Messianic Kingdom; he asserts that, because of the death of Jesus, they are no longer subject to the Angels in the same measure as before. Everywhere is apparent the tendency of the Pauline teaching to represent the Coming Redemption as having already begun to come into operation. One part in which, according to Paul, Redemption is already attained is that the accusing Angels, when they now appear before the throne of God against the Elect, no longer have to do with the Angels of the Presence as the representatives of the accused, but with God and Christ, and God and Christ declare the accused innocent.[1]

Rom. viii. 31-39: "If God be for us who can be against us? He who did not spare His own Son but gave Him up for us all, how shall He not with Him freely give us all things?

"Who shall bring anything to the charge of God's elect? It is God that justifieth.

"Who shall condemn? It is Christ Jesus who died, nay rather that is risen again, who is there at the right hand of God and appears on our behalf.

"Who then shall separate us from the love of Christ? Shall tribulation or distress or persecution or hunger or nakedness or peril or sword? As it is written, 'For Thy sake we are slain all the day long, we are accounted as sheep for the slaughter' (Psalm xliv. 23).

"But in all these things we are victorious through Him who loved us. For I am persuaded that neither death nor life, nor angels nor principalities, nor things present nor things to come, nor powers whether in the height or in the depth, nor any other created things, can separate us from the love of God which is in Christ Jesus our Lord."

Justin Martyr too, about the middle of the second century, maintains the doctrine that the work of Jesus Christ consisted in making an end of the angels and demons, who through their deceit kept men in subjection to them (1 *Apol.* 54, 58, 62, 64; 2 *Apol.* 4, 5, 7).

Dialogue with Trypho, 49: "You may acknowledge that the crucified Christ possesses the secret power of God; before Him the Demons shrink in terror, and indeed all the forces and powers of the earth."

---

[1] In regard to angels which accuse the just and angels which defend them see pp. 57-59. In the Book of Daniel it is a question of *nations* accused and defended by angels.

The result is that the Angels have now no power to effect anything against the Elect. And once these are sure of the love of God and justification through God, it matters little that, for the short time in which the power of the Angels, now doomed by the death of Christ, enters on its death struggle, they are variously tormented by it.

The persecutions which assail the infant Church of Thessalonia, and the circumstances which make it impossible for Paul to return to them to strengthen their faith, are represented as the work of Satan (1 Thess. iii. 3-5, ii. 18).

The view that married couples which had become Christians should live with one another as though they were not married is countered by Paul with the argument that Satan might take advantage of their continence to cause them to fall into sexual sin (1 Cor. vii. 1-6).

In the matter of the opponent who arose against him in Corinth, Paul yields to a degree bordering upon weakness, because he fears that the continuance of this quarrel might serve the cause of Satan, who seeks to disturb the church by such quarrels (2 Cor. ii. 5-11).

It is to Satan also that he attributes his own terrible bodily sufferings. Because he has been caught up into Heaven and Paradise and has heard things "which it is not lawful to utter," he has been delivered up in a special manner to "the Angel of Satan," who has authority to buffet him to the end that he may not be exalted overmuch (2 Cor. xii. 1-7).

. . . . ‘ .

The destruction of the dominion of the Angels will be completed by the Return of Jesus. His appearing will not be announced by preliminary signs (1 Thess. v. 1-4). Suddenly He is there. At His coming there will sound from heaven a voice of command; the voice of the Angel will be heard; the trumpet of God rings out. Those believers who have already 'fallen asleep' will awaken, and those who are still alive will pass through a transformation into the mode of being which belongs to the resurrection. All together will be caught up into the clouds of heaven to meet the Lord in the air, and will thenceforth abide with Him for ever (1 Thess. iv. 16-17).

The Archangel whose voice utters the command is probably Michael. The sound of the trumpet was originally intended (Isa. xxvii. 13) to call the dispersed of Israel together. For Paul it calls the dead to rise to take part in the Messianic Kingdom. 1 Cor. xv. 52: "For the trumpet shall sound, and the dead shall arise incorruptible, and we shall be changed."

Then follows the Messianic judgment held by the Messiah. As in the post-Exilic and Danielic eschatology God Himself was to be the Judge, and only from the Book of Enoch onwards is the Messiah once more, as in the old prophetic eschatology, the Judge. The language of Paul, like that of Jesus Himself, varies from time to time; sometimes the judgment is called the judgment of God, sometimes the judgment of the Messiah.

Christ as Judge: "For we must all be made manifest before the judgment-seat of Christ" (2 Cor. v. 10). See also 1 Thess. iv. 6; 1 Cor. iv. 4-5, v. 5; 2 Cor. i. 14; Phil. i. 10, ii. 16.—God as Judge: "For we must all stand before the judgment-seat of God" (Rom. xiv. 10). See also Rom. i. 18, ii. 2-10, iii. 6. God judges through Christ (Rom. ii. 16).

Jesus, or 'the Son of Man', as Judge: Mt. vii. 21-23, xiii. 41-43, xix. 28, xxv. 31-46.—God as Judge: Mt. vi. 4, 6, 14, 18, x. 33, xviii. 35.

We have from Paul no description of the Messianic Kingdom. That the conception of the heavenly Jerusalem means something for him we learn incidentally in Galatians (iv. 26). He therefore no doubt expects that this Jerusalem will in the Messianic time descend together with Paradise upon the earth, as is assumed in the Apocalypses of Ezra (4 Ezra vii. 26) and of John (Rev. iii. 12, xxi. 2).

That for Justin too the expectation of the Messianic Kingdom is associated with that of the New Jerusalem is evident from the *Dialogue with Trypho* (lxxx. 1-2).

As is implied in the eschatological doctrine of Redemption, Paul expects that in this Messianic time the whole of nature will pass through a transformation from mortality to immortality (Rom. viii. 19-22).

The Kingdom he conceives, strangely enough, not as peaceful blessedness but as a struggle with the angelic powers. One after another these powers will be overcome by Christ and His people, until at last Death also shall be robbed of his power (1 Cor. xv. 23-28).

That Death here is thought of as one of the Angel-powers is evident from the context. The Angel of Death is mentioned in the Apocalypse of Baruch also (xxi. 22-23).[1] Whether this Death actually causes mortality or is only the lord of the dead is not entirely clear from the present passage. But the former alternative seems the more likely. In

[1] See p. 57, *sup.*

any case he is an Angel-power who has his home in the underworld. In the Apocalypse of John, Death appears as a figure mounted on horseback, with Hades in his train, to whom in the pre-Messianic Tribulation power is given to bring all manner of death upon one-fourth part of the earth (Rev. vi. 8). In Rev. xx. 13-14 Death and Hades are compelled, after the end of the Messianic Kingdom, to give up their dead, and are themselves thrown into the Lake of Fire to undergo eternal torment.

In the Book of Jubilees, in which the Angels all appear upon the first day of Creation, the Angel of Death is not specifically named among these creations. It is no doubt included among the Angels of the abysses and of the darkness (Jubilees ii. 2). Paul also appears to assume that the Angel of Death not only has power over the dead but also causes death. In 1 Cor. xv. 55 he speaks of the sting of Death. Whether the "Destroyer" to whom, according to 1 Cor. x. 10, the Israelites who murmured in the wilderness fell a prey is to be identified with the Angel of Death cannot be determined.

The one thing certain is that it is after the overcoming of the Angel of Death that the general Resurrection becomes possible, as is also implied in the Apocalypse of John (Rev. xx. 13).

With the overcoming of Death the Messianic Kingdom comes to an end. Its duration is not mentioned by Paul any more than in the Apocalypse of Baruch. According to the Apocalypse of Ezra it lasts for 400 years (4 Ezra vii. 26-42); according to the Apocalypse of John (Rev. xx. 1-7), a thousand years. Whereas Paul expects Satan to be trodden under foot, doubtless at the very beginning of the Messianic Kingdom (Rom. xvi. 20), the Apocalypse of John (Rev. xx. 2-3, 7-10) represents him as thrown into chains during the period of the Messianic Kingdom, but as being let loose again to cause new commotions later, and finally delivered over to eternal torture in the Lake of Fire.

In the general resurrection at the end of the Messianic Kingdom all men arise who have ever lived upon the earth, unless they have already done so as partakers in the Messianic Kingdom. Then follows the Last Judgment, in which is decided which beings shall enter into eternal blessedness and which are given over to eternal death. This eternal death is called in the Apocalypse of John the Second Death (Rev. xx. 6, 14, 15), and it is there represented as consisting in eternal torment in the Lake of Fire.

The general Resurrection, and the immediately following judgment upon all men and upon the defeated Angels, are not mentioned in the series of events enumerated by Paul in 1 Cor. xv.

23-28. All this falls for him under the general concept of 'the End' (τέλος, 1 Cor. xv. 24), and is taken for granted as well known. It is not his purpose to give a description of the times of the End, he merely alludes in passing to its events in the course of confuting the view which had arisen at Corinth that there was no resurrection of the dead. But the 'judging' of the world and the Angels which, according to 1 Cor. vi. 3, is apportioned to the believers who have entered into the Messianic glory, no doubt takes place at that Last Judgment. The Angel-powers who are to be judged are overcome gradually in the course of the Messianic reign. Furthermore, according to the Book of·Enoch (xix. 1, xxi. 10), the Angels who fell in the first beginnings of the world (Gen vi. 1-4) are kept in prison, to be judged at the beginning of eternity. It is therefore to be assumed that at that day all the disobedient Angels will receive their sentence together.

According to Jesus also the Devil and his Angels will at the end of the age be thrown into the eternal fire along with the damned of mankind (Mt. xxv. 41).

What Paul is principally concerned about is to make clear that the Messiah, after subjugation of the angel-powers, will render up His authority to God, "that God may be all in all." In that moment world history will have reached its consummation. All beings who by coming forth from God and returning to Him have proved their allegiance to Him belong to Him thenceforward without distinction, and are in Him. All others are given over to eternal damnation.

Eternal Blessedness is thought of by Paul not as a purely spiritual existence, but as an existence in the condition incident on the bodily resurrection. The Elect who have been partakers of the Messianic Kingdom remain in eternal blessedness in the mode of existence which they already possess. When the condition which, at the Return of Jesus, they receive, either by resurrection or by 'being changed', is spoken of as a condition of incorruption, that means that it is thought of as eternal. What happens is just this, that after a Messianic reign all the dead who at the Judgment are found to be destined to blessedness enter likewise into this condition of imperishable bodily existence.

·   ·   ·   ·   ·

Into this eschatological conception of the dominion of the Angels and the termination of it by the Messiah, Paul strangely imports a view peculiar to himself, namely, that the Law was given by Angels who desired thereby to make men subservient to themselves, and that by the death of Jesus their power has already been so shaken that the Law has now no more force.

This assertion is inspired by his desire to conceive of the future redemption as already in large measure present. That the Law comes to an end when the Messianic reign begins is for Jewish thought self-evident. But Paul represents it as already invalidated by Jesus' death.

Paul is not alone in holding—though the Scripture says nothing of this—that at the law-giving in Sinai (Ex. xix. and xx), Moses did not receive the Law direct from God but from the Angels. In Later Judaism in general God is conceived as a being so transcendent that any direct contact with men becomes difficult to imagine. Moreover, the Scriptures also record that in the Patriarchal period He had intercourse with men through His messengers. In Alexandrian circles, which pushed the conception of transcendence to an extreme, the view developed that wherever in Scripture there is reference to God's intercourse with men this is to be understood as taking place through the mediation of Angels.

That Moses received the Law through Angels is asserted by Stephen in his speech before the Council (Acts vii. 38, 53). The same view is found in Heb. ii. 2 and in Josephus, who was a younger contemporary of Paul (*Ant.* xv. 5, 3). He represents Herod, in an address to his soldiers before a battle with the Arabs, as saying that the Jews had received their most important ordinances and a most sacred part of their Law through Angels sent from God. This assertion is made in the course of a pronouncement upon the inviolability of envoys. Jewish envoys had been killed by the Arabs, an inviolability established not only by Gentile but also—still more authoritatively—by Jewish Law.

In the Book of Jubilees also (Jub. i. 27-ii. 1, l. 1-2) the view that the Law was communicated by Angels is implied, since Moses is represented as being in company with an Angel upon Mount Sinai.

The Hebrew text of Deut. xxxiii. 2 reads "Jahwe came from Sinai . . . on His right was flaming fire." For this the Septuagint has "on His right His Angels with Him." Here, therefore, the Angels are the attendants of God at the Law-giving.

In the Rabbinic tradition, too, the Angels are present on Sinai at the Law-giving. In *Pesiqta Rabbati* reference is made to a tradition dating from the time of the Exile, that "two myriads of . . . angels descended with God upon Mount Sinai, to give Israel the Law."

That the Law was actually given by Angels is asserted by Paul in Galatians in the words "ordained by angels though by the hand of a mediator. Now a mediator does not represent one only; but God is one" (Gal. iii. 19-20). The logic which makes use of Rabbinic arguments and revolves about the conception of a mediator (μεσίτης) is as follows: If God, who is one, desired to give the Law to the People, which is a plurality, there would be no need of a mediator, for a single person can deal direct with a plurality. Two pluralities, however, cannot deal with one another, but need a single person to mediate between them. If then the Law was given through a mediator, that implies that on both sides pluralities were concerned. On the heavenly side this cannot have been God, who is one; the only plurality which can here come into question is that of the Angels. A point to be noted is that the word 'mediator' on which the argument depends is not in the text of Leviticus (xxvi. 46), to which Paul is here alluding, but is interpolated into it.

Lev. xxvi. 46: "These are the ordinances and laws and directions which Jahwe appointed for the Israelites on Mount Sinai, by the hand of Moses." That Paul, instead of this, can use the phrase demanded by his argument "by the hand of a mediator" is due to the fact that in the Rabbinic writings the view of Moses as כרסור (sarsōr, negotiator, μεσίτης) was widely current.

But from this theory, that the Law was given by Angels, Paul draws inferences which are quite foreign to the other representations of the view. Whereas these do not go beyond saying that the Law was made known on God's behalf by Angels, he advances to the statement, which occurs only in him, that the obedience rendered to the Law was rendered not to God but only to the Angels. By means of the Law men were placed in pupilage to the World-Elements (στοιχεῖα τοῦ κόσμου, Gal. iv. 3, 9), who kept them in dependence upon themselves, until God, through Christ, set them free from the curse of the Law (Gal. iv. 1-5). Accordingly when those who had been heathens submitted themselves as Christians to the Law this means, according to Paul, nothing else than that, instead of serving solely the one God, they once more (though in another form) submit themselves to the World-Elements, now rendered powerless by Christ, observing the "days, months, seasons, and years" which belong to their service (Gal. iv. 8-11).

Philo and, still earlier, about 100 B.C., the Wisdom of Solomon (Wisd. xiii. 2), assert that the heathen worship the Elements—Earth, Water, Air, Fire—as well as the stars. To this view Paul gives the special turn that these beings are in reality Angels and stand behind the Jewish Law.

.   .   .   .   .   .

With his assertion that the Law signified the dominion of Angels, and not the dominion of God, Paul took a step outside the Jewish world of thought and prepared the way to Gnosticism. A thinker comes upon the conception that the Law was valid only until the coming of the Messianic Kingdom, and then had to give place to something perfect. He can no longer understand this according to the usual view, which sees the Divine administration in the imperfect no less than in the perfect: he feels obliged to regard the imperfect as an activity, permitted by God, of Powers that do not comprehend what is perfect. In point of fact Paul, in his determination to find a logical conception of the history of redemption, started on the road which leads to the conception of the Demiurge.

He follows this road, however, only so far as the Law is concerned. The thought that it is God who maintains the world is not implicated. In dealing with those who abstained from the use of meat which had come from the altars of the heathen gods he uses the argument that all things are from God (1 Cor. viii. 6), quoting the Psalm passage (1 Cor. x. 26 = Ps. xxiv. 1) "The earth is the Lord's and the fullness thereof." In arguing with those who sought to distinguish between permitted and unpermitted foods he sets up, in Rom. xiv. 14, 20, the principle that all things are in themselves pure, that is to say, come from God. He even goes so far as to represent temporal authorities as standing in the service of God, not in that of the Evil One (Rom. xiii. 1-7).

The Gnostic hypothesis of an Angel domination exercised through the Law demands also a Gnostic solution of the problem which it involves. And Paul in fact gives such a solution. He affirms that the death of Jesus was a deed of ignorance on the part of the Angels, which led to the destruction of their power. According to him the Sanhedrin and the Scribes, who caused Jesus to be crucified, were only tools of the Angel-Powers. These, having no knowledge of the Divine plans, slew Jesus of Nazareth without recognising in Him the Lord of Glory over whom they had no power.

1 Cor. ii. 6-8: "We speak wisdom among them that are perfect, but not the wisdom of this world nor of the rulers of this age who are now

being overcome, but we speak the hidden wisdom of God, which God before the beginning of times has prepared for our glory, and which none of the rulers of the world have known. For had they known it they would not have crucified the Lord of Glory."

The end of the domination of the Angels was brought about by the death of Jesus, because in compassing it they brought about that which God had appointed to bring in the Time of the End. They have no power to hold this murdered person, as they had held other dead persons, prisoner in the grave. He rises again to newness of life, and He comes, precisely in virtue of His death and resurrection, as the Messiah in Glory, who with His hosts of faithful angels will straightway fall upon them.

But it was not only that they thus prepared the ending of their dominion; by the death of Jesus they also lost the power which they had exercised through the Law.

For in the Law it stands written that whoso hangeth on the Cross is accursed (Deut. xxi. 23). Jesus had hung upon the tree but could not be accursed. Therefore a case has occurred for which the Law is not valid. But as it must either be valid absolutely or absolutely invalid, it is by this one case rendered wholly invalid. The Angel-Powers thus help Jesus to redeem the Elect from the curse of the Law by fulfilling this curse in Himself (Gal. iii. 13-14). If they had known what was best for their power they would have done everything possible to prevent His death. For without His death there would have been no immediate appearing of the Messiah, and the validity of the Law could not have come to an end.

Gal. iii. 13-14: "Christ has redeemed us from the curse of the Law, being made a curse for us. For it is written 'Cursed is everyone who hangeth on a tree'."

Deut. xxi. 22-23: "If any have committed a crime which deserves death, and is condemned for it, and thou hang him on a tree, the body shall not continue overnight upon the tree; thou must bury him the same day; for he that is hanged is accursed, and thou shall not defile the land which Jahwe thy God hath given thee for a possession."

These provisions of the Law which are applied by Paul to the crucifixion have in reality nothing to do with it. They cannot refer to this mode of execution, which was not practised by the Jews, but to the ceremonial exposure of malefactors previously slain by stoning or otherwise. Such a corpse, as being accursed, would defile the land, and must therefore not be left hanging, but be buried on the same day.

Probably in this advance the Law is merely codifying an ancient usage which was no longer understood. The original conception is no doubt that the spirit of the dead man ranges about until the body is buried. It is therefore a duty, both in the interest of the land, which might be punished by this spirit, and in that of the dead man himself, whose spirit should be granted its rest, that the punishment of the malefactor should not be carried so far as to leave his corpse hanging for days.

In order, so far as possible, to rob their defeat of its effect these Angel-Powers produced the doctrine that the Law is necessary even alongside the belief in Christ, and that the Gentiles after their conversion must submit themselves to it and accept circumcision.

So definitely does Paul conceive the conflict with the Law as a strife with Angel-Powers that, in writing to the Galatians, he suggests as an absurdity the possibility that a heavenly Angel might be so foolish as to preach the Gospel of the Law to them. Such a one he declared in advance accursed, as also any being whatsoever who should seek to pervert the Gospel of Christ (Gal. i. 6-9).

Paul's doctrine of the annulment of the Law as having taken place upon the Cross is of special significance because it again revives the conception, which had already been given up in Primitive Christianity generally, that the death of Jesus had a direct effect in bringing in the Kingdom. Whereas, in the general belief, Jesus is the bringer of the Kingdom because through death and resurrection He becomes the Messiah, Paul takes this death as the deed by which the Stronger overcomes the Strong and takes his possessions from him (Mk. iii. 27). The miracles and healings with which Jesus in His lifetime combated the powers which opposed the Kingdom of God are for Paul, in comparison with the great final blow which He struck by His death, of so small account that he never refers to them at all.

But if the Law which stood between God and man is annulled, that means that the Kingdom has already begun. For it is the characteristic feature of the Messianic period that the Law in it is no longer valid. As serving God direct without the intervention of the Law, and warranted in regarding the Angel domination as for them no longer subsisting, believers are already redeemed in much fuller measure than they realise.

In order to be able to assert that redemption is there already present, Paul had further developed the eschatological conception of redemption upon Gnostic lines. All the elements of Gnosticism are already present in him. However much obscurity surrounds the rise of Gnosticism, the one thing which is certain is that Christian-Hellenistic Gnosis arose out of Christian Eschatological Gnosis. In both cases the general structure is the same, only that the material out of which it is built consists in the one case of purely eschatological, in the other of Oriental-Hellenistic ideas. If to Paul's eschatologic doctrine of redemption thought out on Gnostic lines we add the distinction between the God of the Jews who created the world and the purely spiritual supreme God, together with the spiritualistic conception of redemption as the recovery of the spiritual from the material which has overlaid it, we have the essential elements of the later Gnosis.

But not in every case where Paul seeks to prove the present existence of redemption and the freedom from the Law does he bring the eschatological Gnosis into play. It is only in the Epistle to the Galatians and the beginning of the Epistle to the Corinthians that he expounds it. The Epistle to the Romans, on the other hand, presents the appearance of an attempt to dispense with it. The fact is, that alongside of this eschatological Gnosis Paul has something else which gives the same results, only in a more complete form, namely, the Eschatological Mysticism. It also has the power of showing that redemption is already present, while it is superior to the eschatological Gnosis in that it replaces the external interpretation of the death and resurrection of Jesus by an internal interpretation. For that reason the eschatological doctrine of redemption remains something occasional, whereas the mystical is the centre of Paul's thought.

CHAPTER V

THE PROBLEMS OF THE PAULINE ESCHATOLOGY

PAULINE study has hitherto taken it as something requiring no explanation that in Paul there appears not only a Faith but a Mysticism. It finds no difficulty in the fact that he is not, like others, content with a confident expectation of a future redemption in consequence of the death and resurrection of Jesus, but seeks through the mystical conception of being-in-Christ to conceive it as something which is realising itself in the present. What was it that urged him to this undertaking, which forces him into such paradoxical assertions, and compels him to maintain the abolition of the Law for believers, a thing which brought him into irreconcilable conflict with the Early Church?

To find the clue to the explanation of the mystery of the Pauline Mysticism we must therefore investigate the circumstances which rendered it necessary. Since Paul's conception of redemption is eschatological, it is natural to assume that it is problems of eschatology which force him to the assertion of a redemption which is realising itself in the present.

It has been too easily assumed in the study of the subject that those who lived in an eschatological world of thought regarded it as a confused welter of expectations, without feeling any need of attaining a definite conception of these hopes. Hitherto studies of Jewish eschatology have been too little concerned to point out the problems which arose from the concourse of expectations of divers kinds, and of pursuing the question how far these were consciously felt, and so exerted an influence upon the shaping of the traditional material.

For in this eschatology not only inspiration but thought is at work. Jesus, Paul, and the authors of the Apocalypses of Baruch and Ezra do not simply take over traditional expectations of the future, but seek also to make out a logical satisfying whole.

The problems of Pauline eschatology all go back to the two circumstances that it is, in the first place, like the Apocalypses of
Baruch and Ezra, a synthesis of the eschatology of the Prophets and
of the 'Son-of-Man' eschatology of Daniel; and, in the second place,
that it has to reckon with the facts, wholly unforeseen to Jewish
eschatology, that the Messiah has already appeared as a man, has
died, and is risen again.

The pre-Exilic and Exilic prophets expect a Messiah of David's
line to come as the God-anointed Ruler, endowed with wisdom and
power, to rule the great Kingdom of Peace which was to form the
consummation of world history. This future—though still terres-
trial—they paint with supernatural colours. But it is only a glorified
transfiguration of reality. The Messiah is a real scion of the House
of David, who, however, receives from God supernatural powers.
The partakers of the Kingdom are men whom God enables to survive the tribulations with which He sifts the nations and on whom
He bestows existence long beyond all conception and full of joy, by
granting them to live amid a 'nature' which fulfils all their needs.

At the return from the Captivity the prophets Haggai and
Zechariah, about 550 B.C., see in Zerubbabel, the leader of the first
caravan of the returning exiles and the satrap of Judaea, who was a
Prince of David's line, the person who in the coming Day of God
shall be exalted to be ruler of the Holy City and the Lord of all
Nations. But the Day of the Lord does not come. Zerubbabel disappears from the picture. The rôle of the House of David is at an
end: in history, for ever; in eschatology also, for the time.

In the expectation of the future, which was developed on the
prophetic writings of the subsequent period, the Messiah no
longer plays a part. In the place of the Messianic Kingdom appears
the Kingdom of God, in which God rules directly. Typical of this
eschatology without a Messiah are the Book of Malachi, written
about 400 B.C., and a prophetic writing, preserved in Isaiah xxiv.-
xxvii., which dates doubtless from 300 B.C. or later.

This development reaches its conclusion in the Book of Daniel,
written in the years 168–164 B.C. under the influence of the desecra-
tion of the Temple by Antiochus Epiphanes. According to this conception God rules in the Kingdom of God by the Son of Man, that
is, by an Angelic Being who has the appearance of a son of man.

Very significant is the change which the idea of the tribulation

which is to precede the Kingdom undergoes. In the earlier prophets it was a means designed by God to sift out His people. In the
passages referring to the Suffering Servant in Deutero-Isaiah
(Isa. liii.) it is appointed by God for the spreading abroad of His
name and the revelation of His glory among the heathen. In Daniel
it consists in this: that the God-opposing world power, now engaged in its last struggle against God, wreaks its rage upon the
saints who are called to His Kingdom and gives them the opportunity to prove by their loyalty that they belong to God.

A special turn is given to the Danielic eschatology by the fact
that it takes up into itself the idea of Resurrection. In the earlier
expectation only those took part in the Kingdom who belonged to
the then living generation.[1] But now the conception, demanded by
ethics and suggested by the Zarathustrian religion, makes good its
place: namely, that in the times of the End the dead arise either to
receive sentence at the judgment-seat of God, or else to enter into
the Kingdom.

Dan. xii. 1-3: "And at that time shall arise Michael the great Prince
who protects the sons of the people. There shall be a time of tribulation
such as has not been, since the nations were, up to this time.

"But thy people shall be saved on that day, every one whose name is
found written in the book.

"And many of those who sleep in the dust of the earth shall arise.

"Some to eternal life and others to shame eternal.

"But the wise shall shine like the brightness of the firmament.

"And they that have turned many to righteousness shall shine as the
stars for ever and ever."

The hope of the future in Daniel has thus become something
transcendent. The Kingdom is no longer, as in the Prophets, the
outcome of an evolution brought to a happy conclusion by God's
omnipotence, but arises by a cosmic catastrophe. To this corresponds the fact that it has a super-earthly character. An Angel
Prince rules in it, over men who through the resurrection have
become supernatural beings.

The Book of Enoch takes over this Danielic eschatology and
develops it further. It knows nothing of a Messiah any more than

---

[1] It is possible that the prophetic writing, Isa. xxiv.-xxvii., already includes
this idea of resurrection. Isa. xxvi. 19: "Thy dead shall live, my dead bodies
shall arise, they shall awaken and rejoice who lie in the dust."

does the Book of Daniel.[1] In accordance with the supernatural character of the Kingdom of God which is ruled by the Son of Man the conception is developed that all the good things which are to be revealed in the Last Times have been there from the beginning of the world, and have always been intended for the righteous and the Saints. Belief in the Resurrection forms for the Book of Enoch an integral part of the eschatological world-view, as is evidenced by a long polemic against those who deny it.[2]

Thus it appears that the Messiah-eschatology of the Prophets was thrust aside by the Danielic Son-of-Man Eschatology. But in the Psalms of Solomon, which originated under the influence of the taking of Jerusalem by Pompey (63 B.C.), it appears as though it had always been there, and the Book of Daniel never been written.

How is this revival of the Messianic expectation of the Prophets to be explained? It arose from the study of Scripture. As a student of Scripture the author of the Psalms of Solomon lives in the world of thought of Isaiah and Deutero-Isaiah, and makes it his own.

And there was another influence at work. Through the Hasmoneans the Jewish people had again become a nation ruled by kings, whereas previously, since the Exile, it had been a mere appendage belonging to one foreign state after another. Since it had again become familiar with the idea of the Kingdom, these devout students of Scripture could once more think themselves into the Messianic expectation of the future. They interpret the fact that God by the hand of Pompey had made an end of the Hasmonean Kingdom, which was displeasing to Him, as an indication that He will before long clothe with power the Messianic Ruler of David's line promised by Isaiah, and will bring in the Times of the End. The Hasmonean Kingdom created the conditions necessary for the reintroduction of the Davidic Messiah into Eschatology.

In reality no doubt King Herod came in place of the Messiah, but the ideal of the Messianic Kingdom, once reawakened, maintained itself.

No doubt there is much in the revival of the old Prophetic eschatology by the Psalms of Solomon that remains inexplicable. How was it that the Danielic Son-of-Man Eschatology, which had been further developed by the Book of Enoch, simply became as

---

[1] The occurrence of the expression 'His Anointed' constitutes a separate problem.

[2] Enoch cii.-civ., esp. civ. 6-12.

though it had never been? Had it been only the view of a limited circle? Or did the Scriptural scholarship of the Scribes make a point of ignoring it and recognising only the old Prophetic view? The judgment described by the Psalms of Solomon deals not with Angels but with nations. It is held by the Scion of the House of David as the commissioned representative of God. God girds him with might that he may purge Jerusalem of the heathen and destroy the godless by the breath of his mouth. The nations are held captive beneath his yoke that they may serve him. No foreigners are allowed to dwell in Jerusalem in the Messianic times.

A resurrection of the dead precedent to the judgment and the Kingdom is not implied by the Psalms of Solomon any more than by Isaiah. Entrance into the Kingdom is the privilege of the Elect of the generation in whose time it came. The righteous of earlier times remain dead.

Ps. Sol. xvii. 44-45: "Blessed is he who shall live on that day, and is suffered to behold the salvation of Israel in the union of the tribes which God shall bring about.

"May God soon let His mercy come upon Israel."

Wherever in the Psalms of Solomon eternal life is mentioned, what is meant is the blessed existence which the righteous, who are alive in the Time of the End, enter upon at the judgment while sinners shall be destroyed (Ps. Sol. iii. 12, xiii. 11, xiv. 3-5). So far as the wording of the Greek goes, iii. 12 might be understood as referring to a Resurrection, but the other passages cancel this impression. The absence of the Hebrew original permits of no clear decision. But since the author never speaks of a judgment held upon those who have risen, he did not make the conception of a resurrection of the dead an essential part of the Messianic expectation.

.   .   .   .

Thus in the time previous to the appearance of John the Baptist and Jesus two quite distinct expectations of the future existed side by side.[1] Which of the two was held by the Baptist cannot be determined, since we know too little of his teachings.

But in the case of Jesus it is clear that He lives entirely in the Son-of-Man eschatology of the Book of Daniel and Enoch. He

[1] On this fact, which has so far received too little attention from scholars, see Joachim JEREMIAS, *Erlöser und Erlösung im Spätjudentum und Urchristentum* (Deutsche Theol. ii., Göttingen, 1929, pp. 106 ff.). Some remarks on this same subject by August VON GALL, Βασιλεία τοῦ θεοῦ, Heidelberg, 1926, pp. 491 f.

announces the coming of the Son of Man, surrounded by His Angels, upon the clouds of heaven. Instead of speaking of the Messianic Kingdom He speaks of the Kingdom of God. He thinks of this as entirely supernatural. From the saying in which He promises the Disciples that they shall sit upon twelve thrones, judging the twelve Tribes of Israel, we learn that the judgment of the Son of Man coincides with the 'Palingenesia' (παλινγενεσία), that is to say, the creation anew of the heaven and the earth (Mt. xix. 28).

The creation of the eternal heaven and the eternal earth is the last of all the eschatological events: Enoch xci. 16-17; Apoc. Bar. xxxii. 6, xliv. 11-12, lvii. 2; 4 Ezra vii. 75; Rev. xxi. 1.

In agreement with this Jesus declares that the Law shall abide "until Heaven and Earth pass away" (Mt. v. 18), and represents the Judgment as taking place in the Times of the End (Mt. xiii. 40). That this Judgment will include the Angels, as in the Book of Enoch, may be inferred from the fact that the Son of Man condemns the reprobate to the Furnace of Fire prepared for the Devil and his Angels (Mt. xiii. 42, xxv. 41). The Angel hosts which surround Him carry out the sentence (Mt. xiii. 41).

A point which is decisive as regards the character of Jesus' conception of the Kingdom is that He represents men belonging to earlier generations as arisen again and taking part in it. Thus He thinks of Abraham, Isaac, and Jacob as being fellow-guests at the Messianic feast (Mt. viii. 11). All in fact who have a part in the Kingdom will be in the resurrection form of existence, and be like the Angels of Heaven, as is clear from the replies of Jesus to the Sadducees' question about the Resurrection (Mk. xii. 24-25). When, with allusion to passages of Daniel and Enoch, He promises the righteous that they shall shine as the sun in the Kingdom of their Father (Mt. xiii. 43), He means that they will then be supernatural beings.

Dan. xii. 3: "And they that be wise shall shine like the brightness of the firmament, and they that have turned many to righteousness shall shine as the stars for ever and ever."

Enoch civ. 2: "Now ye shall be bright and shining as the lights of heaven."

Matt. xiii. 43: "Then shall the righteous shine as the sun in their Father's Kingdom."

It is for Jesus so self-evident that the partakers in the Kingdom will possess the resurrection form of existence that He exhorts the faithful not to care whether they lose their lives in the present persecution, but to be concerned only to obtain the life to come.

Mark viii. 35: "For whoso will save his life, the same shall lose it; but whoso loseth his life for my sake and the Gospel's, he shall save it." See also Mt. x. 39.

Matt. x. 28: "Fear not them who kill the body, but cannot kill the soul. Rather, fear Him who can destroy body and soul in hell."

That Jesus reckons with the dying of the Elect in the pre-Messianic Tribulation is—though this has never been noticed before—something new. He thus brings to an end a line of development which had begun with Daniel. Whereas in the Prophets the final tribulation proceeds from God and follows such a course that the wicked perish while the righteous are saved to be included in the Kingdom, with Daniel the tribulation is the work of the God-opposing powers. This conception has its origin in the fact that he regards the campaign of Antiochus Epiphanes against God and His saints as the commotion in the course of which the final tribulation and the Kingdom of God will come. Although Daniel has already taken up into his eschatology the thought of the resurrection, he nevertheless retains, as regards the final tribulation, the old conception that the Elect are made manifest as those upon whom this persecution has no power. He represents them as under the special protection of the Archangel Michael.

Dan. xii. 1: "And at that time shall Michael arise, a great Prince which standeth for the children of thy people, and there shall be a time of trouble such as never was since there was a nation even to that time, but at that time thy people shall be delivered, every one that shall be found written in the book."

But Daniel has also to reckon with the facts and recognise that some of the righteous became victims of the persecution.

Dan. vii. 25: "And he shall speak words against the Most High, and shall ill-treat the saints of the Most High, and think to change times and laws, and they shall be delivered unto his power until a time and times and half a time."

Dan. xi. 33: "The wise among the people bring many to understanding; for a time they shall fall by sword and flame, by captivity and spoiling."

Dan. xi. 35: "And some among the wise shall fall, to refine them and to purify them and to make them white against the Times of the End, for it continues yet until the time appointed."

The conception in Daniel is, therefore, that so long as the persecution has still a natural character the righteous perish, but that from an appointed moment onwards, when the persecution takes on an unprecedented intensity, the Elect stand under the protection of Michael. As he is unable to keep these persecutions clearly separate, he is unable to carry through the conception consistently. He has retained from the prophetic representation of the Divine testing the idea of miraculous preservation, although it no longer corresponds with his new conception of the final Tribulation and is now superfluous. It was created for an eschatology which did not as yet reckon on a resurrection, and only in this has it relevance.

In the Book of Enoch also the empirical idea of martyrdom and the dogmatic idea of the preservation go side by side. The latter, however, is the dominant conception, as also the idea that the final Tribulation is appointed by God for the destruction of sinners.[1] In some passages the expression is so vague that it is not clear whether it is the Tribulation or the judgment itself which is meant.

Jesus thus carries the Danielic view of the final tribulation to its logical conclusion. He abandons the idea of the prophetic eschatology that God will destroy the wicked and save the Elect alive, and substitutes for it the view, which from the point of view of the Son-of-Man eschatology is the only logical one, namely, that in the final Tribulation the Elect are in God's hand and are assured of partaking in the Kingdom, whether they live or die. In this way the conception of Martyrdom came into being and was taken up into Eschatology.

·   ·   ·   ·   ·   ·

A synthesis of the Danielic and Prophetic eschatologies is only effected by Jesus in so far as He identifies the Son of Man with the Messiah of David's line. He, who is Himself the descendant of David, expects, at the coming of the Kingdom, to be transformed into the Son-of-Man Messiah. In this way He solves the problem created by the transcendentalising of Eschatology—how the Ruler of the Times of the End can have a human origin, and at the same time be a supernatural being. In the Temple at Jerusalem He puts

[1] Enoch xlv. 5, xlviii. 7, lvi. 1-8, xci. 5-10, xcvi. 1-3, xcix. 3-10, c. 1-5.

this to the Scribes as an enigma, asking them how it is possible for David to call his descendant 'Lord'.

Mark xii. 35-37: "How can the Scribes say that the Messiah is David's son? Has not David himself in the Holy Spirit said, 'The Lord said unto my Lord, "Sit thou on my right hand until I put Thine enemies beneath Thy feet".'[1] If David himself calls Him Lord, how is He then his son?"

The solution of the riddle is that the Messiah, all unsuspected by the Scribes, lives at first in the person of Jesus humbly among men as a human descendant of David's line, but afterwards will be transformed into the super-earthly Messiah, in which capacity, although David's son He is David's Lord, since He now wields authority over all beings, men as well as angels. That New Testament scholarship down to the present day usually interprets this question to the Scribes, which goes to the heart of the Messiah problem, as though it was intended either to dispute the descent of the Messiah from David, or to leave it on one side as meaningless, only shows how little it realises that the problems which inevitably arise in connection with eschatology were apprehended as problems by the representatives themselves of the eschatological world-view.

Although He thus brings together Messiah and Son of Man, Jesus does not undertake any more comprehensive synthesis between the Prophetic and the Danielic eschatologies, but draws His picture of the events of the End exclusively from the scheme known to us from the Books of Daniel and Enoch; and it is left an open question how far He was directly influenced by these books, and how far He simply adopts their views as current in His time in certain circles.

His Eschatology is thus simple and self-consistent. He expects a Judgment, which at the appearing of the Son-of-Man Messiah will include the Angels as well as all generations of men. He assumes, as did also the Book of Daniel, that prior to this Judgment and in preparation for it the general resurrection of the dead takes place. The survivors of the final generation, along with all those of previous generations who have risen again, receive their sentence, some to damnation, others to life. In the Kingdom of God there thus live,

---

[1] Ps. cx. 1. On the interpretation of this question see SCHWEITZER, *Geschichte der Leben-Jesu-Forschung*, 2nd and following editions, p. 393.

under the rule of the Son of Man, the Elect of all generations, living now in the resurrection mode of life, whether they as survivors received it by a transformation, or whether they had arisen to it from the dead. This Kingdom is something final; it is not to be replaced by something else; it is the consummation of the process of history, and endures for ever.

.　　　　.　　　　.　　　　　.　　　.　　　.

Completely different from the eschatology of Jesus is that of the Apocalypses of Baruch and Ezra. These attempt to bring the Prophetic and Danielic Eschatologies into harmony. They do so by the simple method of regarding the Messianic Kingdom of the Prophets as something temporary, which is to give place to the eternal Kingdom of God, which latter is to be the consummation of history. They are thus enabled to picture the Messianic Kingdom in exactly the same manner as the ancient Prophets have described it.

The partakers in this Kingdom are, for the Apocalypses of Baruch and Ezra, only the Elect of the final generation of mankind who are alive in the Times of the End. The Prophetic view of the pre-Messianic tribulation as a time of sifting ordained by God continues to hold the field. Those who are destined for the Kingdom are preserved amid this tribulation by God, so that at the coming of the Messiah they are still alive.

Apoc. Bar. lxx. 2-lxxi. 1: "Behold, the days are coming when it shall come to pass that when the time of the world is ripe, and the harvest of the sowing of evil and good is come, the Almighty shall send upon the earth and its inhabitants and upon their rulers confusion of mind and paralysing dread. And they shall hate one another and rouse themselves to war against each other. . . . And he who shall save himself from war shall die by earthquake, and he who shall save himself from earthquake shall be burned by fire, and he who shall save himself from the fire shall perish of hunger, and all who shall save themselves and shall escape the perils aforesaid—whether they have conquered or been conquered—shall be given into the hands of My servant the Messiah. For the whole earth shall devour its inhabitants. But the Holy Land shall have mercy upon that which belongs to it and will in that time shelter its inhabitants."

The Judgment which the Messiah holds at the end of the Tribulation is held upon the living only, not upon the dead. Those belonging to foreign nations who have never sinned against Israel he leaves alive, merely subjugating them. But all who have fought against Israel he delivers to the sword (Apoc. Bar. lxxii).

In the Kingdom of peace which now begins there is neither pain nor grief, joy walks freely over the whole earth. No one will die prematurely. The wild beasts will come forth out of the wood and make themselves the servants of men. Women will bear children without pains of child-bearing (Apoc. Bar. lxxiii). Behemoth and Leviathan will serve as food for the Elect. The earth will yield its fruit ten thousand-fold, one vine will bear a thousand grapes.[1] Supplies of manna will again fall from the skies. The companions of the Lord shall eat of it in those years, since they have survived to Times of the End (Apoc. Bar. xxix).

The Messianic Kingdom thus pictured in the colours of the Third Isaiah (Isa. lxv. 17-25) has a temporally limited duration. When it is ended there will take place the resurrection of the dead (Apoc. Bar. xxx. 1-4).

In their manner of depicting the End of the Messianic Kingdom the Apocalypses of Baruch and Ezra diverge from one another. The Apocalypse of Baruch makes no statement about the duration of this period, simply asserting that the Messiah, when the time of his rule is over, will return to heaven, whereupon the resurrection of the dead will take place.

Apoc. Bar. xxx. 1-4: "And thereafter when the time of the Coming of the Messiah is ended, he shall return into glory (to Heaven). Then all they that have fallen asleep in hope of Him shall arise. And it shall come to pass in that time that the storehouses in which the number of the souls of the righteous have been preserved shall be opened, and they shall go forth; and the numbers of souls shall appear all together like a troop having one mind. And the first shall rejoice and the last shall not grieve. For everyone shall know that the time has come which is called the Time of the End. But the souls of the godless when they see all this shall utterly perish (for dread). For they know that their pains are come upon them and their destruction is at hand."

---

[1] Irenaeus (v. 33, 3) quotes from the 4th Book of the *Exposition of the Lord's Sayings* (λογίων κυριακῶν ἐξήγησις) by Papias a supposed saying of Jesus about the fruitfulness of the Messianic Kingdom, according to which every vine shall have 10,000 branches, every branch 10,000 clusters, every cluster 10,000 grapes, and every grape shall yield 25 measures of wine, other fruits will bear in the same proportion, and animals shall live at peace with one another and with men.

According to the Apocalypse of Ezra the Messianic Kingdom lasts 400 years and comes to its end by the Messiah, and with him all that has the breath of man, undergoing death; and on that follows the resurrection of all who have ever lived.

4 Ezra vii. 26-33: "For behold the days come when the signs which I have spoken of before shall come to pass, and then shall the invisible city appear and the hidden land shall show itself; and everyone who is saved from the plagues of which I have told you, shall behold My wondrous deeds, for My servant [1] the Messiah then shall reveal himself with all them that are with him, and will give to those who remain alive joy for 400 years. After these years shall My Son the Messiah die, and all that have the breath of man. Then shall the earth be turned to the silence of the primeval time, seven days long, as at the beginning, so that none shall be left alive. But after seven days the Age (aeon) which now sleeps shall awaken, and corruptibility itself shall be done away. The earth shall give up those who rest therein, and the dust shall deliver up those who sleep therein, and the storehouses shall give back the souls which have been committed to them. The Highest shall appear upon the Throne of Judgment."

As the Apocalypse of Baruch represents those who partake in the Messianic Kingdom as not dying, it has to assume that at the ensuing Judgment they attain, by a transformation, the resurrection mode of life. But it does not enter further into this question. The solution of the Apocalypse of Ezra, according to which the Messiah and his associates in the Messianic Kingdom die, and are afterwards raised again along with the dead in general, is simpler.

Both writings represent the Messianic Kingdom as something in which the natural and supernatural worlds meet. In accordance with this the Apocalypse of Baruch characterises the Messianic time as "the end of that which is perishable and the beginning of that which is imperishable" (Apoc. Bar. lxxiv. 2). Fundamentally, however, it is the character of the natural world which is dominant, since the partakers in the Messianic Kingdom are still natural men, even though they have abnormally long lives, and according to the Apocalypse of Baruch even beget children.

---

[1] In KAUTZSCH, Apokryphen und Pseudepigraphen des Alten Testaments, this phrase is translated, following the Latin [and Syriac] text, as "For my Son the Christ." As is evident from the Ethiopic text in this passage and the two Arabic versions at xiii. 32, the original was παῖς, which in the Septuagint is used to translate the Deutero-Isaiah עֶבֶד. (See Bruno VIOLET, Die Ezra-Apokalypse, pt. i., Leipzig, 1910, pp. 140 ff. and 384 ff.)

The most obvious thing would appear to have been for both Apocalypses to distinguish between this temporary Kingdom of the Messiah of David's line and the eternal Kingdom of the Son of Man. In this way the Messiah might, as in the earlier Prophets, have been born of David's line and endowed with power by God, giving place in the fullness of time to the Son of Man who appears upon the clouds of heaven. But for both Apocalypses this solution is impossible, because their Messiah is already too much a supernatural being. He is no longer thought of as born; he appears. In the Apocalypse of Baruch he comes from Heaven and returns thither. That the Messiah is a scion of David's line is not said in the Apocalypse of Baruch; but neither is he designated in it 'Son of Man'.

In the Apocalypse of Ezra the Messiah is a scion of the House of David (4 Ezra xii. 32) and at the same time the Son of Man, who is caught away out of the depths of the sea to heaven, and from there appears to bring in the Messianic Kingdom (4 Ezra xiii. 1-52).

The Davidic sonship of the 'Son-of-Man Messiah' is therefore asserted, but not made intelligible. It was left for Jesus to give the solution of the problem how the Son-of-Man Messiah could be born of David's race, and at the same time be a supernatural figure.

In the Judgment which is held upon those who have risen again after the Messianic Kingdom, it is decided which of them shall enter into eternal blessedness and which shall be given over to eternal torment. They all alike arise in their previous shapes. But the faithful are then changed into beings whose glory is greater than that of the Angels. The suffering which they have borne in the world for righteousness' sake has earned them this blessedness. The wicked are changed into revolting forms, and go away into torture (Apoc. Bar. l.-lii).

In the Kingdom which follows after the resurrection of the dead neither the Messiah nor the Son of Man have any part to play; it is thought of as a pure theocracy.

Participation in the Messianic Kingdom is therefore, according to the Apocalypses of Baruch and Ezra, the privilege of the Elect of the last generation of mankind who are kept safe through the tribulation and are alive at the appearing of the Messiah. After the Messianic Kingdom they pass into resurrection-life and as such participate also in eternal blessedness. Two blessednesses are thus conferred upon them—the Messianic and the Eternal. Those of the Elect who lived and died in earlier generations can attain only to the eternal blessedness, which begins after the resurrection of the dead.

As the righteous of the last generation of mankind, before they enter into the Messianic Kingdom, must all pass through the dreadful pre-Messianic tribulation, the Apocalypse of Ezra raises the question whether it is better to be among those who died earlier, and experience neither the pre-Messianic tribulation nor the Messianic Kingdom, or whether the Messianic glory outweighs the pains of the Tribulation. The answer is that God, who in that day brings in the Tribulation, will also preserve those who are subjected to it, if they have works and faith in Him. "Know, therefore, that those who live to see that time are by far more blessed than they who have died" (4 Ezra xiii. 14-24). For these experience not only the eternal but also, before that, the Messianic blessedness.

According to both the Apocalypses of Baruch and Ezra the course of events is as follows: pre-Messianic Tribulation, in which those who are elect to the Messianic Kingdom remain alive; appearing of the Messiah; Judgment of the Messiah upon all survivors, at which those who are not worthy of the Messianic Kingdom are condemned to death; Messianic Kingdom; End of the Messianic Kingdom and return of the Messiah to Heaven; Resurrection of the dead of all generations and Last Judgment upon them by God; eternal blessedness in the Kingdom of God or eternal torment.

This eschatology recognises therefore two blessednesses (the Messianic and the eternal); and two Judgments (the judgment of the Messiah at the beginning of the Messianic Kingdom upon the survivors of the last generation of mankind, and the final judgment of God upon the whole of risen humanity after the Messianic Kingdom); and two Kingdoms (the temporary Messianic and the eternal theocracy). Jesus expects one blessedness only (the Messianic, which is also eternal); one Judgment (the Judgment of the Son-of-Man Messiah and the beginning of the Kingdom of God, which includes both the survivors of the last generation and also the whole of risen mankind); and one Kingdom (the Kingdom of the Son-of-Man Messiah, which is also the eternal Kingdom of God).

The whole difference between the two views goes back to the fact that Jesus, like the Book of Daniel, represents the Resurrection as taking place at the beginning of the Messianic Kingdom, whereas the Apocalypses of Baruch and Ezra put it at the end. The

Apocalypses of Baruch and Ezra represent the eschatology of the Scribes, which accepts all the expectations expressed in the Books of the Prophets, including Daniel, and seeks to bring them into harmony. One cannot refuse a certain admiration for the way in which they bring order out of chaos. It is the work of theologians who were capable thinkers.

A first attempt at an outline of the events of the End is found in the so-called "Ten Weeks' Apocalypse," one of the oldest portions of the Book of Enoch (Enoch xciii. 1-9, xci. 12-17). Here the events from the beginning to the end of the world are arranged in 'world-weeks.' The Messianic Kingdom begins in the 8th world-week, in which the sinners are given over into the hands of the righteous and the House of the Great King arises in glory to endure for ever. In the 9th week takes place the Judgment of Righteousness, in consequence of which the works of the godless disappear from the earth and the world is appointed to destruction. In the 10th week, in its 7th part, the great Eternal Judgment takes place in which the punishment of the Angels is carried out. Thereafter the first Heaven passes away to give place to a new one, whose coming marks the end of all history (Enoch xci. 12-17). Here then there are two judgments in the cause of an eternally enduring Messianic Kingdom. When the resurrection of the dead takes place is not stated. The conception seems to be that at the last judgment the risen dead of the earlier generations are added to the survivors of the last generation, who must logically be thought to be in the resurrection mode of existence. Similar is the view in the "Similitudes of Enoch" (Enoch xxxvii.-lxxi), in which first the appearing and the Judgment of the Messiah are described (Enoch xlv.-l). Then follows a mention of the resurrection of the dead (Enoch li). But in the Similitudes each episode is joined to the last by "In those days," so that we are not told clearly whether the events are contemporaneous or successive. One decisive point is that according to the Book of Enoch the Kingdom of the Son of Man is eternal, from which it necessarily follows that those which participate in it must possess the resurrection mode of existence. The Scribes, however, as the Apocalypses of Baruch and Ezra show, did not accept this view, but held with the earlier Prophets that participation in the Messianic Kingdom was the privilege of the survivors of the last generation of mankind.

As the Apocalypses of Baruch and Ezra were not written until after the destruction of Jerusalem by Titus, it might be questioned whether the Eschatology which they offer was really that held by the Scribes of an earlier period. Paul, however, is the proof that this was actually the case. The eschatology which he presupposes is, as regards its scheme and the events of the end, the same as that of the Apocalypses of Baruch and Ezra. This therefore must have been the accepted view of the Scribes among whom he was brought up.

. . . . . .

That Paul conceives the sequence of events of the time of the End in accordance with the two-fold eschatology of the Scribes, is shown by the fact that he represents death as being destroyed only at the end of the Messianic Kingdom. This means that, according to his assumption, the resurrection of the dead and the Judgment of the risen of all generations takes place only after the conclusion of the Messianic Kingdom.[1] Like the Scribes, he regards the Kingdom as the privilege of the Elect of the last generation, and thinks of it as transient.

Paul accordingly distinguishes between two blessednesses—the Messianic and the eternal. The Elect of the last generation are the participants in both; those which died earlier can obtain only the eternal, which begins after the conclusion of the Messianic Kingdom. During the Messianic Kingdom they are still dead. The eschatology of Paul is therefore quite different from that of Jesus, a fact which has been hitherto never duly appreciated. Instead of thinking as Jesus did along the lines of the simple eschatology of the Books of Daniel and Enoch, he represents the two-fold eschatology of the Scribes.

It is probably connected with the eschatological view of the circles from which he came that Paul never uses the expression "Son of Man." This is absent from the Apocalypse of Baruch also. Nevertheless he thinks of the Messiah as the Son-of-Man Messiah, because he represents him as appearing upon the clouds of heaven.

The most curious thing, however, is that Paul does not simply take over the eschatology of the Scribes in its actual form, but imports into it a conception which is at variance with its whole logic. For he asserts that the first participators in the transient Messianic Kingdom already have the resurrection mode of existence, and that the Elect of the last generation, even if they have died before the beginning of the Kingdom, will be able, through the resurrection, to become participants in it. This self-contradictory eschatology takes a middle place between that of the Scribes and that of Jesus. Paul

---

[1] For Paul's scheme of the Events of the Resurrection see pp. 65-68, *sup.*

shares with the Scribes their conception of the course of events; and with Jesus that of the mode of being which those who participate in the Messianic Kingdom possess.

In assuming that the Elect in the Messianic Kingdom possess the resurrection mode of existence, Paul is not asserting something more or less self-evident, but something *extraordinary*, something at variance with the character of his eschatology. This has not heretofore been sufficiently realised. Jesus assumes a resurrection to participation in the Messianic Kingdom, and this assumption is also held in the Johannine Apocalypse (Rev. xx. 4-6): [1] it therefore would have seemed quite natural that Paul should hold the same view. But the eschatology with which he started out does not assume any resurrection or resurrection mode of life for the Messianic Kingdom. If this Kingdom is itself transient, obviously the participants in it cannot be in a condition of immortality. Now if Paul finds himself obliged to assert this illogical thing, he cannot feel it to be self-evident. And in point of fact the way in which he informs the Thessalonians that believers who have died will rise again for the Messianic Kingdom, makes it clear that this is not immediately obvious either to them or to him. He appeals in confirmation of it to a "saying of the Lord," that is to say, to a revelation which he has received from Christ.

i Thess. iv. 13-18: "We desire, therefore, that you should not be in ignorance regarding those that sleep, in order that ye may not sorrow as those which are without hope. If we believe that Jesus died and rose again, God will also bring through Jesus those which have fallen asleep together with Him. For thus we say unto you in a saying of the Lord— We who live and are still living at the coming of the Lord shall have no advantage over those who sleep. He, the Lord, will descend from Heaven when the shout is heard and the voice of the angel and the trumpet of God, and first shall arise the dead which are in Christ and then we which survive shall be caught up with them in the clouds, to meet the Lord in the air, and henceforth we shall be always with the Lord. Encourage one another with these words."

---

[1] Rev. xx. 4-6: "And the souls of those who have been executed for the testimony of Jesus and for the word of God, and who had not worshipped the devil or his image and had not received the mark of the beast on their forehead or on their hands, came to life and reigned with Christ 1000 years. The rest of the dead did not come to life until the end of the 1000 years. That is the first resurrection. Blessed and holy is he that hath part in the first resurrection. Over these the second death has no power."

To understand how the problem of the fate of these believers who died before the return of Jesus presents itself to Paul, we must realise that he, like the Apocalypses of Baruch and Ezra, expects the Resurrection only after the Messianic Kingdom. He must therefore assume that all the dead, including those which have fallen asleep only a little while before the Return of Jesus, have no part in the Messianic Kingdom but must wait until the Resurrection of the dead. But the case of those who had died believing in Jesus was a case not foreseen in the traditional eschatology, because it did not look for a coming of the future Messiah before the appearing of the Kingdom.

But by their belief in Jesus those who had thus fallen asleep had put beyond doubt their loyalty to the Messiah and their right to be participants in His Kingdom. Thus there occurs the question whether by dying they had come into the condition of all the earlier dead, and must await along with them the resurrection at the end of the Kingdom, or whether they have not the standing with God of those who through their belief in Jesus have secured to themselves the prerogative of the last surviving generation and as such shall have part in the Messianic glory. The problem of the fate of those who had died in faith in the Messiahship was thus the first of the problems raised by the delay in the Return of Christ. Paul's decision was to the effect that these dead have not to wait for the resurrection which takes place at the end of the Messianic Kingdom, but that by an earlier special resurrection they became participants in the glory of the Messianic Kingdom just as much as the other Elect of the last generation.

The idea that the Messianic Kingdom is the prerogative of the last generation is thus maintained, though by connecting with it the conception of the resurrection of the dead. Only those who have fallen asleep believing in Jesus, not the remainder of the dead, share, according to Paul, in the Messianic Kingdom.

That the death of believers before the Return of Christ constituted a grievous difficulty for the Early Church is evident from the fact that Paul explains cases of death in the Church of Corinth as a punishment of God for the unworthy celebration of the Lord's Supper (1 Cor. xi. 29-32). It is conceivable that such deaths before the Return had been interpreted in the earliest times as meaning that those who died were not granted the Messianic blessedness, in spite of their belief in Jesus.

As a matter of fact, the view that only survivors at the time of Jesus' Return had a share in the Messianic Kingdom had its representatives in early Christianity: this is evident from the existence at Corinth of persons who denied the resurrection (1 Cor. xv. 12-18, 29-33), who were evidently very troublesome to Paul, and have been even more so to his interpreters: to these persons we owe the fifteenth chapter of 1st Corinthians. For who were these deniers of the Resurrection? Were they sceptics? If so, it is difficult to explain how they had wandered into the Christian Church. And Paul does not dismiss them as such, but seeks to show from the fact of the Resurrection of Jesus, which was admitted by them also, that they are mistaken. The most interesting point, which is generally overlooked, is that these deniers of the Resurrection had no doubt at all about the Resurrection of Jesus, but only of that which believers expected for themselves. Paul therefore refutes them by the argument that, if there is no resurrection of the dead, Christ Himself cannot have risen.

1 Cor. xv. 13: "For if there is no resurrection of the dead, then Christ is not risen."—1 Cor. xv. 16: "For if the dead are not raised, then has Christ not been raised from the dead."

These deniers of the Resurrection were therefore no sceptics, but representatives of the ultra-conservative eschatological view that there was no resurrection. According to them, only those have anything to hope for who are alive at the Return of Jesus. They thus deny not only the resurrection to the Messianic Kingdom, but that to eternal blessedness. Their position is the same as that of the Psalms of Solomon and the eschatology of the Prophets.

What solutions the problem of the dying of believers received among the Early Christians in general we do not know. When death was seen to be the rule, the Christian faith could not simply leave it unsettled, but, if the Christian Hope was not to fail, was forced with Paul to the solution, that the dead in Christ arise at His Return. Thus arises the necessity of assuming two resurrections: a first in which believers in Christ attain to a share in the Messianic Kingdom, and a second in which all men who have ever lived upon earth, at the end of the Messianic Kingdom, appear for final judgment before the throne of God, to receive eternal life or eternal torment.[1]

[1] Rev. xx. 4-6; cf. pp. 91-92, *sup*.

In any case the creator of this doctrine of the two Resurrections was Paul.

.   .   .   .   .   .

The doctrine of two Resurrections was not found by Paul already in existence. All eschatology previous to him knows only one resurrection, which either, as in the Books of Daniel and Enoch and in the sayings of Jesus, is placed before the Messianic Kingdom, or as in the Apocalypses of Baruch and Ezra is placed after it.

That those who have fallen asleep in Jesus enter the Messianic Kingdom as men who have arisen can be maintained by Paul only if he assumes at the same time that those who are alive at its coming enter it not with a natural being, however ideally enhanced, but as those who by a transformation have taken on the resurrection mode of existence, which is thought of as eternal. This he actually does. In doing so he is quite conscious that he is asserting something which is not self-evident, but in fact departs from the ordinary view. The logical thing would be that, if the Messianic Kingdom is a transient entity, those who participate in it shall possess a temporary, not an eternal mode of existence. Therefore he communicates it to the Corinthians as a mystery that they are not to enter the Kingdom as flesh and blood, but, whether they are at the coming of the Kingdom alive or dead, they shall equally exchange the mortal mode of existence for an immortal one.

1 Cor. xv. 50-53: "But this I say unto you, brethren, that flesh and blood cannot inherit the kingdom of heaven nor corruptibility inherit incorruptibility. Behold, I show you a mystery. We shall not all sleep but we shall all be transformed, in a moment, in the twinkling of an eye, at this last trumpet. For the trumpet shall sound, and the dead shall be raised up incorruptible, and we shall be transformed. For this corruptible must put on incorruptibility and this mortal must put on immortality."

So far as the wording goes, Paul might have been speaking of the resurrection of the dead in general. But he means, as in 1 Thess. iv. 16 and 1 Cor. xv. 23, only those who have fallen asleep in Jesus. Only these are to be raised to life again at the time of the coming of Jesus and the transformation of the survivors.

According to the eschatology of the Scribes, as set forth in the Apocalypses of Baruch and Ezra, the righteous inherit the Kingdom in their actual flesh and blood.

What is it that causes Paul to take such liberties with the eschatology of the Scribes, which he elsewhere treats as authoritative?

Is it the influence of the eschatology of Jesus? But had he been in any way influenced by this he would have taken over from it the much simpler solution of placing the general Resurrection before the Messianic Kingdom. This he cannot do, for it would have meant abandoning the belief that the Messianic Kingdom is the prerogative of the Elect of the last generation. When he decides to put upon the old garment of the two-fold eschatology of the Scribes the new patch of the resurrection-and-transformation concept, he does this under the influence not of the teaching of Jesus but of the fact of His death and resurrection. This is evident from the way that in 1st Thessalonians he deduces the resurrection of those who have died in Christ from the resurrection of Jesus.

1 Thess. iv. 14: "If we believe that Jesus has died and has risen again, God will also bring with Him those who have fallen asleep through Jesus."

Whether we are to interpret that those shall be brought again who have fallen asleep through Jesus (*i.e.* in Him), or that those who have fallen asleep shall be brought again through Jesus, cannot be decided. But in any case the reference is only to those who have died in Christ.

The argument against the deniers of the Resurrection at Corinth (1 Cor. xv.) is a further proof that it is the resurrection of Jesus which led Paul to the adoption of the view that believers possess in the Messianic Kingdom the resurrection mode of existence. Since the future Messiah Himself lived, died, rose again before the coming of the Kingdom, Paul can no longer hold to the traditional eschatology of the Scribes. As a thinker he is bound to bring it into harmony with that fact, and he can do this only by the assumption of two resurrections.

Since he assumes that the participants in the Kingdom possess, like the Messiah, the resurrection mode of existence, he is able to solve the otherwise insoluble problem of the fate of believers who have died before the Return of Jesus, by assuming that the resurrection takes place before the coming of the Kingdom. Otherwise he would have to suppose natural men and resurrection-men living side by side with one another in the Kingdom, which is unthinkable.

.   .   .   .   .   .

But what difficulties are raised by the assumption of the pre-Kingdom resurrection of believers! Death, thought of as an angelic being, is after all in power up to the end of the Kingdom. How is it then thinkable that some of the dead can escape his clutches before he is compelled to release them all at the Resurrection?

Almost greater difficulties confront the assumption that survivors enter by a transformation into the resurrection mode of existence. How can men come into this condition without being obliged to pass beforehand the gates of death and resurrection? This problem was already there for the Eschatology represented by the teaching of Jesus, but without being recognised. The Scribes, however, were conscious of it. In the Apocalypse of Ezra it is got rid of by assuming that the partakers of the Kingdom at last die all together, in order along with the rest of the dead to become through the resurrection possessed of the eternal life.

For Paul the problem is inescapable. Since Jesus had passed through death in order to attain the mode of existence appropriate to the Messianic Kingdom, these two events could not be simply ignored in the case of those who, being alive at His Return, then exchange the natural mode of existence for the supernatural. They also must in some way have passed through death and resurrection.

It is not as though Paul could simply assert the pre-Kingdom resurrection of believers and transformation of the survivors without more ado. For those who later take over the doctrine of the twofold resurrection, it was something self-evident. For him, asserting it for the first time, it needed to be supported by argument and based on a theory. And he can find a basis for it only in the mystical being-in-Christ.

Only as those who are 'in Christ' can these believers, who at the Return of Jesus are still alive, pass by transformation out of the natural mode of living into the eternal; only because the believers who have fallen asleep are 'in Christ' (1 Thess. iv. 16; 1 Cor. xv. 18, 23) are they not dead as others are, but are capable of the preliminary resurrection at the Return of Jesus.

Paul's conception is, that believers in mysterious fashion share the dying and rising again of Christ, and in this way are swept away out of their ordinary mode of existence, and form a special category of humanity. When the Messianic Kingdom dawns, those of them who are still in life are not natural men like others, but men who have in some way passed through death and resurrection along with

Christ, and are thus capable of becoming partakers of the resurrection mode of existence, while other men pass under the dominion of death. And similarly, those who have died in Christ are not dead as others are, but have become capable through their dying and rising again with Christ of rising before other men.

It is just because this assumption, that believers who have died rise up at once at the beginning of the Messianic Kingdom and that the survivors are at the same moment changed into immortal beings, constitutes for Paul a difficult problem, that he is obliged, with a view to its solution, to assert the mystical doctrine of the dying and rising again with Christ. And his mysticism must remain unintelligible, because purposeless, until we recognise the peculiarity of his eschatology and the difficulty it involves of asserting that the participators in the Kingdom possess the resurrection mode of existence. The great mistake which has hitherto been made in dealing with the subject was to assume that what was self-evident from the eschatology of Jesus was also self-evident for the eschatology of Paul.

.   .   .   .   .   .

But it is not only the problem of the mode of existence of the Elect in the Messianic Kingdom which leads Paul as a thinker to his Mysticism, but also direct reflection upon the import of the death and resurrection of Jesus.

The general belief merely regarded the death and resurrection of Jesus as the events which made possible His coming as Messiah in glory and heralded the dawn of the Messianic Kingdom. It adopted a purely expectant attitude, and held simply that the natural world would go on until the coming of the Messianic Kingdom. The view of a more thoughtful belief might be different. For the thinker the fact of the Resurrection of Jesus must raise the remarkable question whether men were still living in the natural world-period (aeon), or had already entered upon the supernatural. The simple antithesis between Then and Now is no longer sufficient, because the resurrection of Jesus, if strictly considered, was not a pre-Messianic but a Messianic event. In the natural world-period it is possible for the faithful to be rapt away into heaven to be kept safe until the Times of the End, as happened to Enoch, Elijah, and, according to the Apocalypses of Baruch and Ezra (Apoc. Bar. lxxvi. 1-4; 4 Ezra xiv. 49), to Baruch the scribe of Jeremiah and to Ezra himself; and also for these to return from heaven, as Elijah was expected to do,

according to the well-known passage in the Book of Malachi (Mal. iv.
5-6, E.V.). But a resurrection of those who had died was only to take
place when the supernatural age had dawned. If Jesus has risen,
that means, for those who dare to think consistently, that it is now
already the supernatural age. And this is Paul's point of view. He
cannot regard the resurrection of Jesus as an isolated event, but
must regard it as the initial event of the rising of the dead in general.
According to his view Jesus rose as "The First-fruits of those that
had fallen asleep" (ἀπαρχὴ τῶν κεκοιμημένων, 1 Cor. xv. 20). We
are therefore in the Resurrection period, even though the resurrection of others is still to come. Paul draws the logical inference
from the fact that Jesus, after His earthly existence, was not simply
rapt away to heaven in order to return thence in glory as the
Messiah, but Himself passed through death and resurrection.

In the Apocalypse of Ezra also (4 Ezra vii. 29-32) the Son of Man
dies, and thereby brings it about that all who have breath die with
him and afterwards rise again with him. But this happens at the end
of the Messianic Kingdom. Although this Messiah is not born but
simply 'appears', he has this in common with men, that in order to
attain to immortality he must pass through death and resurrection. In
this we see the influence of the prophetic view that he is a natural
descendant of David endowed by God with supernatural power. This
conception also throws light upon the conscious intention of Jesus. For
what He does is, under the influence of the eschatology of Daniel and
Enoch, and under the compulsion of His own self-consciousness, to
transfer the dying and rising again of the Messiah to a point previous
to the Messianic Age, and in this way to explain how the bodily descendant of David can become the Son-of-Man Messiah, and how the
resurrection of the dead takes place in preparation for the coming of
the Son of Man.

The appearing of the future Messiah before the Messianic Age,
His dying and rising again, nothing of which was foreseen in the
traditional eschatology, gave a problematical character to the period
between the Resurrection of Jesus and His Return. Evidently Christ
had not yet appeared, and the world had still its natural aspect. If
we judged by external appearance it was still the natural world-age.
But what is decisive for the character of the period between the Resurrection of Jesus and His Return was not outward appearance but
the nature of the powers which were at work in it. Through the
Resurrection of Jesus it had become manifest that resurrection

powers, that is to say, powers of the supernatural world, were already at work within the created world. Those who had insight, therefore, did not reckon the duration of the natural world as up to the coming of Jesus in glory, but conceived of the intervening time between His Resurrection and the beginning of the Messianic Kingdom as a time when the natural and the supernatural world are intermingled. With the Resurrection of Jesus the supernatural world had already begun, though it had not as yet become manifest.

While other believers held that the finger of the world-clock was touching on the beginning of the coming hour and were waiting for the stroke which should announce this, Paul told them that it had already passed beyond the point, and that they had failed to hear the striking of the hour, which in fact struck at the Resurrection of Jesus.

Behind the apparently immobile outward show of the natural world, its transformation into the supernatural was in progress, as the transformation of a stage goes on behind the curtain.

.   .   .   .   .   .

For the man of insight who dares to see things as they really are, faith ceases to be simply a faith of expectation. It takes up present certainties into itself. This invasion of a belief in the future by a belief in the present has nothing to do with the spiritualising of the eschatological expectation; it arises in fact from the intensification of it. During that world-period between the Resurrection of Jesus and His Coming again the transient and the eternal worlds are intermingled. Thereby the conditions for a peculiar Mysticism are created.[1] In consequence of the actual condition of the world, not merely by a pure act of thought as in other mystical systems, he who has the true knowledge can be conscious of himself as at one and the same time in the transient world and the eternal world. He need only to realise in thought what is happening to him and to the world; namely, that powers of supernatural existence are engaged in so transforming him—and all about him, so far as that is its destiny—in such a way that their outward appearance is still that of the transient world while the reality is already that of the eternal world. In the Elect who are destined at the coming of Christ to be made manifest immediately in the resurrection mode of existence the work of those supernatural powers must have proceeded furthest.

[1] See p. 37, *sup*.

This objective mysticism of facts necessarily arose as soon as the thought which was latent in the eschatological expectation realised the significance of the death and resurrection of Jesus as cosmic events, and saw that the resurrection of Jesus was the beginning of the resurrection of the dead in general. Paul, alone among the believers of his time, gave due weight to the consideration that the traditional eschatology could not maintain itself unchanged: the Messiah having already appeared in the flesh, having died, having risen again, the eschatological expectation had to recast itself to those facts. Thus he comes, contrary to the concepts in which he is accustomed to move, to postulate for the Elect in the Messianic Kingdom the resurrection mode of existence, and to maintain, contrary to the existing naïve belief, that with the resurrection of Jesus the Messianic period had actually already begun and that the resurrection of the dead in general was in progress. Thus the direction of his thought was forced from all sides by the problems of eschatology itself to the paradoxical assertion that the powers manifested in the dying and rising of Jesus were already at work in those who are elect to the Messianic Kingdom.

CHAPTER VI

THE MYSTICAL DOCTRINE OF THE DYING AND RISING
AGAIN WITH CHRIST

IN consequence of his eschatological view of redemption Paul is obliged to maintain that the powers of death and resurrection which were made manifest in Jesus, now, from the moment of His dying and rising again onwards, are at work upon the corporeity of those who are elect to the Messianic Kingdom and render them capable of assuming the resurrection mode of existence before the general resurrection of the dead takes place.

On what lines, then, does he work out this assumption? In some way or other he must call to his aid the conception that those who are elect to the Kingdom stand in a relation of fellowship with Christ, which makes this overflow to them of the powers which are at work in Him intelligible. In point of fact, eschatology offers such a conception. It is that of the preordained union of those who are elect to the Messianic Kingdom with one another and with the Messiah which is called "the community of the Saints."

This conception arises as a natural consequence from the idea of predestination to the Messianic Kingdom. In principle this glory was destined for the nation as such. The fact that transgressors were found in it rendered necessary the assumption that only a part of Israel would attain to it. Consequently in the earlier as well as in the later Prophets the idea of sifting became bound up with that of election. Only those who amid the disasters which were coming upon Israel were kept alive by God, were destined to the Messianic Kingdom.

Isa. iv. 3: "And those survivors in Zion and those who are left in Jerusalem shall be called holy, every one that is inscribed to life in Jerusalem."

They are called holy because they are to live close to God, who will be over Jerusalem as a cloud and as a flaming fire.

Mal. iii. 16-17: "Then they that feared Jahwe talked with one another, and Jahwe hearkened and heard, and a book of remembrance was written before Him for those who feared Jahwe and gave heed to His Name. They shall be mine own, saith Jahwe of Hosts, in the day when I intervene, and I will have pity upon them as a man has pity upon his son who serves him."

The idea that the saints who are destined to the Kingdom are all inscribed in the Book of Life appears thenceforward again and again in eschatology (Ps. lxix. 29; Dan. xii. 1; Enoch ciii. 2, civ. 1, cviii. 3). According to the Psalms of Solomon they bear God's mark upon them, which safeguards them when the wrath of God goes forth to destroy the ungodly (Ps. Sol. xv. 4-6).

A "people of the Saints of the Most High" is spoken of in the Book of Daniel (Dan. vii. 27). And the concept of the "community of the Saints" which is also called "the community of the righteous" is further developed in the Book of Enoch. It is here thought of as a pre-existent entity, which at the beginning of the Messianic period is made manifest along with the Messiah (Enoch xxxviii. 1-5).

Enoch lxii. 7-8: "For the Son of Man was formerly hidden, and the Highest kept him in the presence of His power and has revealed him to the Elect. The community of the Saints and Elect shall be sown (*sic*), and all the Elect shall stand before him in that day."

Enoch lxii. 14-15: "The Lord of Spirits shall dwell over them, and they shall eat with that Son of Man, shall lie down and rise up to all eternity. The Righteous and Elect shall raise themselves from the earth and shall cease to cast down their eyes, and shall be clothed with the garment of glory."

Both Jesus and Paul include this concept of the predestined community of saints in their eschatology. Jesus speaks in parables about the Kingdom of God in order that only those "who have ears to hear," that is to say, those who are appointed to accept His message, may understand it, and that those who are not called to the Kingdom may not repent at His preaching and thus establish a claim to the forgiveness of sins at the Judgment and participation in the Kingdom (Mk. iv. 9-12).[1] "Many are called (that is, hear the call to the Kingdom) but few are chosen" (Mt. xxii. 14). The man in the parable of the Royal Marriage who sits down among the guests but has no wedding-garment is one who has followed the call, without being predestined. He is therefore thrown out into

[1] On predestination in the teaching of Jesus see Albert SCHWEITZER, *Geschichte der Leben-Jesu-Forschung*, 2nd and following editions, pp. 400-402.

the darkness (Mt. xxii. 9-13). The Kingdom has been prepared for
the Elect "from the beginning of the world" (Mt. xxv. 34).

In the saying to Peter "Thou art Peter, and upon this rock will I
build my community (ἐκκλησία), and the gates of hell shall not
prevail against it" (Mt. xvi. 18), Jesus is clearly referring to the
"community of the Saints" of the Book of Enoch, which is bound
up from eternity with the Son of Man and is to be made manifest
at His coming.

In the same way Paul's thought follows predestinarian lines.
Believers are for him "called" (κλητοί), and in Paul's writing
"called" has the significance of elect—to be saints (1 Cor. i. 2;
Rom. i. 7).   The beautiful saying that all things work together for
good "to those that love God" applied only to "those who are
called according to His purpose" (Rom. viii. 28).

The pre-existing community of the saints is identified by Paul,
as also by the Apocalypse of Ezra (4 Ezra ix. 38-x. 57), with those
who belong to the pre-existent heavenly Jerusalem. To them he
applies the saying of Isaiah (liv. 1): "Rejoice thou barren, that hast
not borne, break forth into singing thou that travailest not, for more
are the children of the desolate than of her that hath a husband"
(Gal. iv. 26-27).

Although Paul here shows acquaintance with the concept of
the ideal "community of God," Protestant scholarship was long
unable to rid itself of the prepossession that by the term "community" (ἐκκλησία) he always meant only a particular individual
church and never the ideal general community (the Church). It was
here influenced by the desire to show that the Catholic concept of
the Church had arisen empirically, and believed itself able to show
that in Paul the particular community was the original entity, and
that from the totality of these particular communities there gradually grew up the concept of the community as a single whole.

The word ἐκκλησία is used of any religious fellowship. It can there-
fore mean both the ideal eschatological entity of the community of the
Elect to the Messianic Kingdom (the "Community of the Saints," the
"Community of God") or each particular religious community.

It is, no doubt, a fact that Paul in most passages means by the
term an actual particular community in a definite place. That is
sufficiently evident from the fact that he uses it in the plural in
about twenty passages. But he also uses it in connections in which

it is only intelligible as a designation of the community as a whole. He accuses himself of having persecuted "the community of God" (Gal. i. 13; 1 Cor. xv. 9). He blames the Corinthians for treating contemptuously "the community of God" (1 Cor. xi. 22), and exhorts them to be blameless towards "the community of God" (1 Cor. x. 32).

The ideal concept of the "Community of God" does therefore occur in the certainly authentic Epistles of Paul, and was not first created by the second generation. It is derived from eschatology and belongs to Messianic doctrine.

For Paul the Community in a particular place is the general community of the Saints as there locally manifested.

The Catholic conception of the Church as found in the earliest Christian theology goes back to the eschatological entity, the Community of the Saints. It is not explainable in any other way. As early as Ignatius it is clear that the realistic concept of the Church is founded upon an ideal mystical concept.

The denial of this general conception of the Community to be the teaching of Jesus and of Paul was due to the difficulty of explaining how it should come to be there. So long as the attempt was made to explain the beginnings of Christianity apart from eschatology, it was impossible that conceptions which could only be understood from eschatology should find recognition. Therefore in the passages where they occurred the meaning was disputed, or else it was maintained that they were due to later interpolation.

Since both Jesus and Paul move in an eschatological world of thought, the concept of this "Community of the Saints," in which by the predestination of God the Saints are united with one another and with the Messiah as the Lord of the Elect, is to them perfectly familiar.

In the Jewish eschatology, where the manifestation of the Messiah and his Elect is purely a matter of the future, this concept is not of special importance. In essence it asserts no .more than the obvious fact that the Elect and the Messiah would be united together in the Messianic Kingdom. But the case is altered when that which had not been foreseen in the Jewish eschatology occurred, namely, that the Messiah appears before the beginning of the Kingdom as a man among men. Once it was attempted to work out an eschatology with such a prelude the concept of the predestined union of the Elect with one another and with the Messiah acquires a remarkable vitality. For in it the natural and the Messianic world are now brought into connection. The union of the Elect with one another and with the Messiah receives an anticipatory realisation. Relationships between them, which were first to be made manifest in the Messianic world, now, since they have already come into contact in the natural world, come into force forthwith: on the other hand, the relationships which arise between them in the natural world are to be continued in the Messianic. Thus it comes about that, in an eschatology which has to reckon with the coming of Jesus into the world, the concept of the predestined union of the Elect with one another and with the Messiah necessarily gave rise to a Christ-Mysticism, that is to say, to the concept of a fellowship with the Messiah, which realises itself already in this natural world. And it does not first begin to do so in the writings of Paul, but already in the preaching of Jesus.

.   .   .   .   .   .

For the preaching of Jesus itself contains Christ-Mysticism. It is simply not the fact that Jesus' preaching dealt with nothing but the nearness of the Kingdom of God and the ethic to be practised during the period of waiting; He also declared that in the fellowship with Him on which they had entered His followers had already the guarantee of future fellowship with the Son of Man. This Christ-mysticism He offers as a mystery. For the hearers do not know that it is He Himself who shall one day appear as Son of Man, and therefore cannot understand why fellowship with Him signifies also fellowship with the Son of Man. Had it ever been foreseen in eschatological thought, that the Son-of-Man Messiah before His appearing would first enter unrecognised upon a human existence, His hearers could not but have gathered from His words that the solidarity which He asserted between Himself and the future Son of Man was nothing less than identity. But the connection between a human existence and the appearing of the Son of Man depends upon an act of the self-consciousness of Jesus, and as such is known to Him only. He can therefore go so far in His assertions that the identity between Him and the Son of Man sounds forth in every tone of them, and yet the hearers can only understand from these assertions that the Son of Man will display in all things His solidarity with Him who now proclaims His coming. And it is all they need to know. For their salvation what matters is only that through fellowship with Jesus they should attain the fellowship with the

Son of Man, not that they should understand how this comes about.

In point of fact this teaching, that the attainment and maintenance of fellowship with Him signifies fellowship with the Son of Man, dominates the preaching of Jesus in a way which, in the accounts hitherto given of that preaching, has never received its full significance.

Looking forward to the sufferings which He expects for Himself and His followers in the pre-Messianic tribulation, Jesus exhorts them to be faithful to Him in His humiliation, if need be even unto death, since suffering along with Him means glory along with the Son of Man in the Messianic Kingdom.

Matt. v. 11-12: "Blessed are ye when men shall despise you and persecute you and say all manner of evil against you falsely for my sake. Rejoice and be exceeding glad, for your reward is great in the Heavens."

Mark viii. 35: "He who shall lose his life for my sake and the Gospel's, the same shall save it."

Mark viii. 38: "For he who is ashamed of me and of my words in this adulterous and sinful generation, of him shall the Son of Man be ashamed when He comes in the glory of His Father, with His holy angels."

Even to the Baptist, when he sent to ask Him who he was, Jesus cannot give up His secret. He evades the question, pointing to the signs by which the nearness of the Kingdom is made manifest, and closing with the words "Blessed is he, whosoever shall not be offended in me" (Mt. xi. 6). He thereby makes known to him, as to the disciples and the people, the one thing needful.

Later, when He has come to know that others shall be spared the tribulation, and He alone shall suffer and die, He reveals this to His disciples, opening to them at the same time the secret of His Messiahship. He does this in order that, when the time comes, they shall not be offended in Him. He who shall desert Him in His humiliation will thereby forfeit his claim to be with Him in His Messianic glory.

For election is not, for Jesus, an unalterable thing. Although His thought, like Paul's, follows more frankly predestinarian lines than those of earlier Jewish eschatology, His conception of election nevertheless retains the vacillation which clung to it from the Jewish eschatology. This vacillation comes from the meeting of predestinarianism and ethics. Because he is elect, the elected person is righteous; and because he is righteous he is elect. For Jesus, too, predestinarianism and ethics still hold the field alternately. If election is not confirmed by entering into fellowship with Him and cleaving faithfully to Him, it becomes invalid. On the other hand, one who is not actually elect, but through his conduct enters into fellowship with Jesus, can thus acquire the right of an elect person to be with the Son of Man in the Messianic Kingdom. Thus in the ultimate result everything depends upon the realisation of fellowship with Jesus.

That men can also acquire election by their own act is implied by Jesus when, at the beginning of His mission, He speaks of the Kingdom of God in parables, that the non-elect may not understand and may not through repentance acquire a claim to the forgiveness of sins and participation in the Messianic blessedness (Mk. iv. 10-12).[1]

At the Lake of Gennesareth Jesus confirms the election of believers by an act proceeding from Himself. In the meal which has come down to us as a miraculous feeding, He distributes to each participant food from His own hand. It is in fact a cultus-feast which looks forward to the Messianic feast. The intention is not the satisfaction of hunger. Jesus is concerned only that each one shall receive from His hand consecrated food, and so enter into table-fellowship with Him. They thereby receive that fellowship with the Son of Man, with whom the Elect shall in the future sit at the Messianic feast, and they thus acquire a claim to participate in the Messianic feast. The recipient does not understand the significance of Jesus' action, nor does he need to do so. Without knowing it he has entered upon this table-fellowship with the Son of Man.

Since the significance of this mysterious distribution of small portions of food to a great multitude still remained obscure, it was made by tradition into a story of the miraculous increase of bread and fish in the hands of Jesus (Mk. vi. 34-44).[2]

It is not only through the establishment of a direct relation of fellowship with Jesus that a place among those who belong to the Son of Man is secured; it may also be acquired indirectly, through fellowship with anyone who belongs to Jesus or even merely to the circle of His followers. To the disciples He explains, in sending

[1] See p. 102, *sup.*

[2] On this explanation of the miraculous feeding of the multitude at the Lake see Albert SCHWEITZER, *Geschichte der Leben-Jesu-Forschung*, 2nd and subsequent editions, p. 421.

them out, that whoever receives them receives Himself (Mt. x. 40). The places which refuse to have anything to do with them prepare for themselves a fate which is worse than that of Sodom and Gomorrah (Mt. x. 14-15). Without knowing it, they have rejected the Son of Man. He who receives a child in His name receives Him; he who offends against one of the least of those who believe in Him prepares for himself a fate so terrible that it would have been better for him if he had never been born (Mt. xviii. 5-6).

In consequence of the belonging-to-the-Son-of-Man, which has been unconsciously acquired or missed, there will be great surprises in the Day of Judgment. Men will be declared by the Son of Man to be righteous and partakers in the Kingdom, with the explanation that they have fed Him when He was hungry, given Him to drink when He was thirsty, given Him hospitality when He was a stranger, clothed Him when He was naked, visited Him when He was sick, come to Him when He was in prison. To their astonished question when they had done such things to Him, the reply is given that they did it to one of the least of those who were His brethren, and so have done it unto Him. And likewise others shall learn with astonishment that they are rejected because they neglected to show compassion to one of the least of the followers of the Son of Man at his need, and have thus failed to be numbered with those who belong to the Son of Man (Mt. xxv. 31-46). The least of the brethren of the Son of Man to whom the so wonderfully rewarded deed was done is not any chance person who happens to be in need, but one who belongs to the community of the Elect who are in fellowship with the Son of Man. The ethical obtains a special significance through the mystical.

To belong to the community of those who are called to the fellowship of the Son of Man annuls all other relationships. To those who tell Him that His mother and brethren are asking for Him, Jesus declares, with a glance at the believers who surround Him, that these are His mother and His brethren, because they are resolved to do the will of God (Mk. iii. 31-35). In the discourse at the sending out of the disciples He declares uncompromisingly that love of father, mother, brothers, and sisters must take second place to love to Himself (Mt. x. 37), the thought being that by love to Him a man enters the fellowship of the Son of Man and His followers. Even the title Master (Rabbi) is no longer to be used, since we should know only one Master (meaning the Messiah), and no one any more called Father, since (in the moment when the Community of the Saints, that is, God's Children, is just about to be made manifest) only the Father in Heaven can properly be called by this name (Mt. xxiii. 8-9).

The concept of the Community of the Elect, and of an adhesion to it and to the Coming Son of Man, which is to be realised even in this world, thus plays a large part in the teaching of Jesus. Without revealing to His hearers the content of His own self-consciousness, He brings them again and again face to face with the thought that by fellowship with Him they have fellowship with the Son of Man.

He thus teaches Christ-Mysticism in ways appropriate for the time in which the coming Messiah was walking unknown, in earthly form, upon the earth.

.   .   .   .   .   .

Paul, on the other hand, teaches Christ-mysticism in the way appropriate to the time immediately following on the death and resurrection of Jesus.

But is such a mysticism possible? How is it conceivable that the Elect, walking upon earth as natural men, should have fellowship with the Christ who is already in a supernatural state of existence? In face of such a difference of condition, how is an anticipatory realisation of their close connection with the Messiah possible? What meaning can be assigned to it?

In the intervening period between the Resurrection and the Return of Jesus it might well seem that the relation of the Elect to Him must be confined to their belief in His Messiahship and to their looking forward in hope to that future realisation of their solidarity with Him which was to take place in the Messianic glory. And this appeared self-evident to all believers of the earliest Christian community—with the exception of Paul. In face of all the facts which seemed to make against it, he asserted that the solidarity of the Elect with Christ was already working itself out in the period between His Resurrection and Return, and that only thereby would their union with Him in the Messianic Kingdom be rendered possible.

Of all that must be common to Jesus and the Elect, in order that they might be united together in the glory of the Messianic Kingdom, this stands for Paul in the foreground, namely, that they share together the resurrection mode of existence before the resurrection has begun for the remainder of the dead. The essential point in their predestined relation of solidarity is that they share a corporeity, which is in a peculiar measure open to, and receptive of, the influence of the powers of the resurrection. Their common predestination to the Messianic Kingdom is a predestination to the anticipatory obtaining of the resurrection state of existence. In accordance with this the eschatological concept of the Community of the Elect (that is to say, the predestined solidarity of the Elect with one another and with the Messiah) takes on for Paul a quasi-physical character. As such, it contains the solution of the eschatological problems with which he is concerned.

The fundamental significance of the dying and rising again of Jesus consists therefore, according to Paul, in the fact that thereby death and resurrection have been set afoot throughout the whole corporeity of the Elect to the Messianic Kingdom. This is, so to speak, a mass of piled-up fuel, to which the fire there kindled immediately spreads. But whereas this dying and rising again has been openly manifested in Jesus, in the Elect it goes forward secretly but none the less really. Since in the nature of their corporeity they are now assimilated to Jesus Christ, they become, through His death and resurrection, beings in whom dying and rising again have already begun, although the outward seeming of their natural existence remains unchanged.

In consequence of undergoing this mysterious process they are capable, on the Return of Christ, of immediately receiving, whether they are then surviving or already dead, the resurrection state of existence. Thus in 1st Thessalonians (v. 9-10) he can with a fine simplicity explain the deliverance effected by Jesus Christ as meaning that "He has died for us, in order that we, whether we wake or sleep, may be alive with Him."

Throughout the corporeity of the Elect who are thus united with Christ the springtime of super-earthly life has already begun, even though elsewhere in the world the winter of natural existence still holds sway.

The problem how natural men can be in union with the already glorified person of Jesus thus receives the solution, that these Elect are in reality no longer natural men, but, like Christ Himself, are already supernatural beings, only that in them this is not yet manifest.

.   .   .   .

By understanding and interpreting in this quasi-physical way the eschatological concept of the predestined solidarity of the Elect with one another and with the Messiah, the three problems of the Pauline eschatology are all solved together. For it thus becomes explicable—(1) that those who have died in Christ have not by dying missed the Messianic Kingdom, but, as being already risen with Christ, participate in it by means of a special pre-dated resurrection; (2) that at the Return of Christ those who are alive do not need first to die in order to enter on the resurrection state of existence, but, as having already died and risen again with Christ, can enter on it by a simple transformation, that is by sloughing off the natural existence which clings to them as a sort of outer covering; (3) that with the Resurrection of Jesus the resurrection of the dead in general—and therewith the supernatural world—has already begun, though the substitution of mortality by immortality is, to begin with, only operative in the corporeity of those who are elect to the Messianic Kingdom, and even in their case, without becoming outwardly manifest.

In the ruthless logic of its thinking the Christ-Mysticism of Paul does not hesitate to fly in the face of the course of events. It is concerned to dispose of the first and most immediate problem of the Christian faith, the temporal separation of the Resurrection and Return of Jesus Christ. For, properly, the Resurrection of Jesus, His manifestation as Messiah, and the beginning of the Messianic Kingdom in which is included the resurrection and transformation of the Elect, belong temporally and causally together.

Jesus' conception of the course of events was that after His resurrection He should go with His disciples to Galilee, and there experience the beginning of His exaltation as Son of Man. This is what He must mean when on the way to Gethsemane He says to the disciples "After my Resurrection I will go before you into Galilee" (Mk. xiv. 28). The appearing as Son of Man upon the clouds of Heaven which He foretells to His judges (Mk. xiv. 62) will therefore take place from Galilee.

Paul does not reckon on Jesus' coming first as a risen man to the disciples, but expects, since He is already in Heaven, that He will come, without further preliminaries, upon the clouds of Heaven.

But now there happens something unexpected and hard to understand, namely, that since a time-interval has been interposed between the Resurrection and Return, the Resurrection of Jesus has become an independent event. But Paul refuses to budge from the position that what belongs in fact together, even though temporally separated, must still, as at first, be regarded as a unity. That which was to happen along with the Resurrection of Jesus is for him actually involved in it even though it is not visibly manifest. The Elect are the risen-along-with-Christ, even though they still have the external seeming of natural men.

In a tremendous paradox Paul puts in the place of reality, as presented to the apprehension of the senses, the reality which is valid for a thinker who understands clearly what moment in world-time this is. He knows that the immortal world is about to rise by successive volcanic upheavals out of the ocean of the temporal. In the resurrection of Jesus, "the first-fruits of them that have fallen asleep" (1 Cor. xv. 20), one island-peak has already become visible. But this is only a part of a larger island which, still beneath the waves, is actually in process of rising, and is only so far covered as to be just invisible. This larger island is the corporeity of the Elect who are united with Christ. In their transformation and anticipatory resurrection the further portion of the immortal world will forthwith appear. Thereafter, in temporally separated upheavals, one portion of land after another will rise round about this island. In the Messianic period all nature will take on immortal being. And then, as the final event of the renewing of the world at the end of the Messianic Kingdom, will come the general resurrection of the dead. With that the whole continent of the immortal world will have become visible. Then comes the End, when all things are eternal in God, and God is all in all.

.   .   .   .   .   .

This whole mystical doctrine of the world as in process of transformation along with mankind is nothing other than the eschatological conception of redemption looked at from within. That with Jesus' death and resurrection the natural world is beginning to be transformed into the supernatural is only another way of expressing the idea that, from that moment onwards, the rule of the Angel-powers is passing away and the Messianic period is beginning.

That the Elect belong already to the super-sensuous world is a consequence of the fact that for them the rule of the Angels, which though broken still survives into the Messianic period, no longer applies to them.

That the Elect came to assume the resurrection state of existence even before the general Resurrection of the dead, corresponds to the fact that the Angel of Death has no more power over them.

That the general resurrection of the dead comes to pass as the last event of the transformation of the natural into the supernatural world is implied by the belief that the Angel of Death was to be the last power overcome by Christ in the course of His Messianic rule.

Since this mystical doctrine is only another expression of the eschatological concept of redemption, Paul is justified in regarding it as something which should be immediately obvious to those who held the Early Christian beliefs, and in arguing from it against those who wished to give to the Law and Circumcision a meaning for the Elect, as though these still belonged to the earthly corporeity of death.

.　　　　.　　　　.　　　　.　　　　.　　　　.

Thus Paul preaches Christ-mysticism on the ground of the eschatological concept of the predestined solidarity of the Elect with one another and with the Messiah, as Jesus had done before him, but with this difference, that Paul presents it in the form which it assumes as a consequence of the death and resurrection of Jesus.

What endless trouble theology has given itself about the problem of Paul and Jesus, and what shifts it has been put to to explain why Paul does not derive his teaching from the preaching of Jesus, but stands in this respect so independently alongside of Him! In doing so it is talking all round a problem, which it has first made insoluble by failing to grasp it in its completeness. The discovery that Paul takes up an independent attitude towards Jesus is misleading, unless one at the same time recognises all that he has in common with Him. For Paul shares with Jesus the eschatological world-view and the eschatological expectation, with all that these imply. The only difference is the hour in the world-clock in the two cases.

To use another figure, both are looking towards the same mountain range, but whereas Jesus sees it as lying before Him, Paul already stands upon it and its first slopes are already behind him. The features of the eschatological certitude take on a different aspect. Not all which then looked solid looks so now, and not all that is now valid seemed so formerly. Because the period of world-time is different, the "teaching of Jesus" cannot always lay down the lines for Paul. The authority of the facts must outweigh for him on a question of fact the authority claimed by the teachings of Jesus.　Truth is for him the knowledge of redemption as it results, on the basis of the eschatological expectation, from the fact of the death and resurrection of Jesus.

Those who continue to appeal, without further thought, to the teaching of Jesus, only show, according to Paul, that they have failed to understand how world-time has been advanced by the death and resurrection of Jesus. Against an error of this kind he dares the assertion that those who have known Christ in the flesh should henceforth know Him so no more.

2 Cor. v. 16: "If we have known Christ after the flesh, yet now henceforth we know Him no more."

In drawing the logical inferences from the altered world-circumstances Paul is forced by the position to take, in his teaching, an original attitude alongside of Jesus. But in this he is merely recasting in accordance with the conditions of the time the fundamental conceptions, derived from eschatology, which are common to them both. He does not abandon Jesus, but continues His teaching. Precisely because he does share with Jesus the conception that the redemption of men is the result of a change in the condition of the world, he is compelled, in his doctrine of redemption, to take account of the cosmic events which have happened in the death and resurrection of Jesus and, as a consequence, to maintain that the rule of the Angels is in process of being destroyed, and that the transformation from the earthly state of existence to the super-earthly is already going on. It is thus that he comes to regard what Jesus had said about the Law, or what, in ordinary circumstances, men would have been justified in inferring from His silence, as no longer authoritative. Although Jesus had recognised the Law, and had never said anything against Circumcision, both must now be regarded as no longer valid, since they presuppose that rulership of Angels which is now being destroyed and the continuance of the natural condition of the world which in regard to the corporeity of the Elect no longer obtains, and Law and Circumcision are only applicable to this natural condition.

Jesus Himself assumes that the Law will come to an end at the beginning of the Messianic Kingdom. He is also conscious that when He, the future Son of Man, appears, the Law and the Ordinances of the Scribes which were based upon it, no longer apply. To those who reproach Him because His disciples do not fast, as did those of the Baptist, He replies in the mysterious saying that they have no need to do this so long as the bridegroom is with them, but when he is taken away from them they shall do it (Mk. ii. 18-20). In this He is alluding to the time of the Messianic tribulation in which He expects for Himself persecution and death.

Jesus' attitude to the Law is not consistent. He recognises its continuance in solemn words (Mt. v. 17-19). But at the same time He teaches and demands a righteousness which is better than that of the Scribes, and explains in an interesting saying how foolish it is to put a new patch on an old garment or new wine into old wine-skins (Mk. ii. 21-22).

But that prior to the coming of the Messianic Kingdom the Law could be abrogated, He neither said nor thought. In view of His eschatological expectations such a declaration would have had no meaning. But Paul is confronted with the question whether the Law can still retain its validity, now that on the resurrection of Jesus the Messianic period has already begun.

From the eschatological acceptation, which he shared with Jesus, of the death and resurrection of Jesus as cosmic events, Paul, because these events have in the meantime happened, arrives at conclusions which lay far from the mind of Jesus. Similarly his mysticism, although it appears alongside the teaching of Jesus as something so wholly different from it, is not something absolutely new, but merely the recasting of a Christ-mysticism which Jesus had already derived from the predestined solidarity of the Elect with one another and with the Messiah.

Since Jesus expects the beginning of the Messianic Kingdom to take place immediately after His death, He does not presuppose any doctrine of redemption applicable to that period. When, in consequence of the delay of the Messianic Kingdom, such a doctrine had necessarily to be set up, others contented themselves with makeshifts. They still expected the redemption effected by Jesus to follow the lines of the traditional eschatology, which has no relevance to the fact that the future Messiah has previously died and risen again. Paul alone recast the doctrine of redemption in accordance with the facts, namely, that the Messiah is not only to appear in the future, but has already been present on earth in the conditions of human existence, and by His dying and rising again has made a first beginning of the resurrection of the dead.

.   .   .   .   .   .

The original and central idea of the Pauline Mysticism is there-

fore that the Elect share with one another and with Christ a corporeity which is in a special way susceptible to the action of the
powers of death and resurrection, and in consequence capable of
acquiring the resurrection state of existence before the general
resurrection of the dead takes place.

That this mystical doctrine is actually derived from the eschatological concept of the Community of God in which the Elect are
closely bound up with one another and with the Messiah is quite
clearly evident from the fact that inclusion in this favoured corporeity is not effected in the moment of believing, and not by
faith as such. It is first by Baptism, that is, by the ceremonial act by
which the believer enters the "Community of God" and comes into
fellowship, not only with Christ but also with the rest of the Elect,
that this inclusion takes place. The Pauline Mysticism is therefore
nothing else than the doctrine of the making manifest, in consequence of the death and resurrection of Jesus, of the pre-existent
Church (the Community of God). The enigmatic concept, which
dominates that mysticism, of the " body of Christ " to which all
believers belong, and in which they are already dead and risen
again, is thus derived from the pre-existent Church (the "Community of God").

In the whole literature of mysticism there is no problem comparable to this of the mystical body of Christ. How could a thinker
come to produce this conception of the extension of the body of a
personal being? How can Paul regard it as so self-evident that he
can make use of it without ever explaining it?

The expression "*mystical* body of Christ" is, however, not actually
found in Paul. He himself speaks only of the body of Christ, even when
he means the extended conception of the body which includes the
believers within its sphere.

Without admitting it, the explanation of Paul's mysticism has
always come to an end at the point where the mystical body of
Christ came in. The way in which it was attempted to explain it
could not lead to the goal. The idea was to drive it from the belief
in Christ and the being-in-Christ. The belief in Christ was supposed to become a being-in-Christ, and from the being-in-Christ
of the many believers Paul was supposed to have arrived at the
conceptions of the mystical body of Christ.

All attempts hitherto undertaken to pass from the concept of belief in Christ to that of being-in-Christ have proved a failure; and all that may be made in the future are equally without prospect of success. They all come to the same point, that the belief in Christ, growing in depth, is by verbal ingenuity made to figure as a being-in-Christ. That the being-in-Christ arises out of such an enhancement of belief in Christ is nowhere indicated by Paul and is nowhere presupposed by him. The relationship of faith in Christ to union with Christ is for him thus: that belief in Christ being present, union with Christ automatically takes place—under certain circumstances, that is to say, when the believer causes himself to be baptized. Without baptism there is no being-in-Christ! The peculiarity of the Pauline mysticism is precisely that being-in-Christ is not a subjective experience brought about by a special effort of faith on the part of the believer, but something which happens, in him as in others, at baptism.

And if belief in Christ cannot be simply made over into being-in-Christ, no more is the concept of the mystical body of Christ to be explained as a summation of the being-in-Christ of the multitude of believers. There is not to be found in Paul a single word which gives the slightest foundation for such an assumption.

Since in Paul we have to do, not with deductive but with speculative thinking, we must not follow the pathway of induction but of deduction; the general cannot here be explained from the particular. The mystical body of Christ remains an enigma so long as it is not understood in the light of the fundamental concept of the Community of God, in which by preordination the Elect are closely united with one another and with Christ. The "being-in-Christ" is in fact inexplicable until it is made intelligible by the concept of the mystical body of Christ.

Once it is perceived that we have to start from the conception of the predestined solidarity of the Elect with one another and with the Messiah, the mystical body of Christ is at once explained. Out of the conception of the preordained solidarity of the Elect with one another and with Christ there grew up in Paul's resurrection mysticism the conception of the common possession of a corporeity which, in respect of the resurrection, enjoys a favoured position. And from this again arises, by a justifiable simplification of expression, that of the mystical body of Christ. The participation of the Elect with Christ in the same corporeity becomes a being part of the body of Christ.

The corporeity, which is common to Christ and the Elect, is called the Body of Christ by reference to the most exalted personality which shares in it, and because its special character was first consummated and made manifest in Christ; the general is expressed through the individual. Because in Christ the process is already completed, the original conception that the Elect and Christ undergo, in the same corporeity, the same experiences is transformed into the conception that they experience that which He has experienced. The first act of the process is now conceived as continuously operative. In this way there arises out of the original conception the derivative and simplified conception that the Elect are taken up into the body of Christ. This, taken in isolation, is unintelligible. It becomes explicable only in the light of the original conception.

All attempts to distinguish in the relevant passages between the personal (historical) and the mystical body of Christ are inevitably doomed to failure. The obscurity was intended by Paul. The body of Christ is no longer thought of by him as an isolated entity, but as the point from which the dying and rising again, which began with Christ, passes over to the Elect who are united with Him; just as, on the other hand, the Elect no longer carry on an independent existence, but are now only the Body of Christ.

Since the concept of the mystical body of Christ and the concomitant concept of the being-in-Christ have their roots in eschatology it is impossible to find sources for them in Hellenistic literature.

.   .   .   .   .   .

The fact that believers are taken up by baptism into the "Community of God" gives rise in the logic and speech of mysticism to the affirmation that they are not only one body with Christ, but themselves are a body. The phrase "We are all baptized into one body" (1 Cor. xii. 13) is to be understood literally. Since the Elect form, with one another and with Christ, one body, Paul can equally well say that "the many are one body in Christ" (Rom. xii. 5) and that they with one another are "one body" (1 Cor. x. 17). He even ventures on the expression that they are "One (person—*masc.*) in Christ Jesus" (Gal. iii. 28), that is to say, that they, with one another and with Christ, form a joint personality, in which the peculiarities of the individuals, such as are constituted by race and sex and social position, have no longer any validity.

Gal. iii. 27-28: "So many of you as are baptized into Christ have put on Christ. There is neither Jew nor Greek, neither bondman nor freeman, male nor female; for you are all one in Christ Jesus."

Since in the mystical body of Christ dying and rising again with Christ have taken place, the Elect from Judaism have been "through the body of Christ made dead to the Law," and in relation to the Law are counted as dead men over whom the Law has no more authority (Rom. vii. 4-6). They have ceased to be fleshly existences, and as such "to be in the flesh" (Rom. vii. 5, viii. 9) or "to walk after the flesh" (Rom. viii. 4-5, 12). Their flesh, with its passions and lusts, has been destroyed, as though they had been crucified with Christ (Gal. v. 24).

As those who are properly to be considered dead they are removed not only from the flesh but from sin (Rom. vi. 2, 6-7). In everything they are like men who have been buried with Christ and now live in a new state of existence (Rom. vi. 4-5). The essential character of this new state of existence is that they are men who have been dead and have been made alive (Rom. vi. 13). If in their outward seeming they are still natural men, yet the life-power which is in them is no longer of a natural but of a supernatural character. Their whole experience is summed up in the statement "though our outward man perishes, yet our inward man is renewed from day to day" (2 Cor. iv. 16).

As their life-power they have the Spirit of God, which is also the power which lives in Jesus and goes forth from Him (Rom. viii. 9). Christ Himself is in them (Rom. viii. 10; Gal. ii. 20). Since the life-power of His resurrection state of existence is also theirs, they are a new creation (καινὴ κτίσις, 2 Cor. v. 17; Gal. vi. 15), that is to say, they are already creatures of the new world. The Spirit of Him that raised Jesus from the dead, which dwells in them, will also give life to their mortal bodies (Rom. viii. 11). Being grafted into Christ's death, they are also grafted into His resurrection (Rom. vi. 5) and have the certainty that they will live with Him (Rom. vi. 8).

The mysticism of Paul marks the last stage in the struggle that the resurrection idea waged to make good its place in eschatology.

The realism and the logic of this mysticism carry the consequence that the conception of the new condition as a Rebirth, near at hand as it seemed to be, and familiar as it was to the Hellenism with which Paul as a thinker must have had some kind of acquaint-

ance, can never find a place in it.[1] He who has a part in the body of
Christ becomes a new creature by an anticipatory experience of His
resurrection. That the idea of Rebirth is so often taken for granted
in Paul only shows how remote from the reality the explanations
which introduce it are.

In Paul's mystical doctrine of being part of the body of Christ
his hope of the Kingdom of God and his assurance of sonship to
God are both included; that is why he has so little to say directly
dealing with these two points.

I Thess. ii. 12: "God, who called you to His Kingdom."

Gal. v. 21: "Those who do such things shall not inherit the Kingdom
of God."

I Cor. iv. 20: "The Kingdom of God is not in word but in power."

I Cor. vi. 9: "The unrighteous shall not inherit the Kingdom of God."

I Cor. vi. 10: "Neither the unchaste, nor idolaters . . . nor revilers
nor robbers shall inherit the Kingdom of God."

I Cor. xv. 50: "Flesh and blood cannot inherit the Kingdom of God."

Rom. xiv. 17: "For the Kingdom of God is not eating and drinking,
but righteousness and peace and joy in the Holy Ghost."

Inasmuch as believers have died and risen again with Christ, and
possess the Spirit, they are already partakers of the Kingdom of
God, although they will not be made manifest as such until the
Kingdom begins.

Sonship to God is seen by Paul as guaranteed by the dying and rising
again with Christ and by the possession of the Spirit which results there-
from (Gal. iii. 26-27, iv. 6; Rom. viii. 14-16).

Since the doctrine of the mystical body of Christ contains within
it Paul's view of the pre-existent Church and its realisation in time,
he dces not otherwise enter upon the conception of the Church.
The occurrence in the Epistle to the Ephesians of speculation
about the Christian community as a whole (the Church) is an argument against the Pauline authorship.

Eph. i. 22-23: "And gave Him to be head over all the Church which
is His body."

Eph. iii. 21: "To him be honour in the Church and in Christ Jesus."

Eph. v. 23: "The Man is the head of the woman, as Christ is the
head of the Church."

[1] On the absence of the idea of Rebirth in Paul see pp. 13-15, *sup.*

Eph. v. 24-25: "As the Church is subject to Christ, so let the women be subject to their husbands in all things. Husbands, love your wives, as Christ also loved the Church, and gave Himself for it that He might make it holy."

Eph. v. 31-32: "And the two shall become one flesh. This is a great mystery: I refer it to Christ and the Church." [1]

In Paul's thought the union of Christ with the ideal entity of the Christian Community as a whole is associated exclusively with the concept of the Mystical Body of Christ in which the two are united together. The author of the Epistle to the Ephesians, by setting alongside of one another the concept of the Body of Christ and speculations regarding Christ and the Church, shows that the original nature of the conception of the Mystical Body of Christ is no longer present to his mind. He has no consciousness of the fact that in that conception everything that can be said about the Church, and about Christ and the Church, is exhaustively expressed.

.   .   .   .   .   .

Since the fundamental conception of the Pauline mysticism is that the Elect and Christ partake in the same corporeity, it is most accurately represented by those terms of expression in which it is still recognisable that they refer to an experience which is common to Christ and the Elect. These expressions, accordingly, in which "with Christ" becomes "in Christ" diverge from the original idea.

With Christ. "I am crucified with Christ" (Gal. ii. 20). "We have been buried with Him by baptism" (Rom. vi. 4). "If we have died with Christ, we believe that we shall also live with Him" (Rom. vi. 8).

Fellowship with Christ. "God is faithful, who has called us into the fellowship (κοινωνία) of His Son Jesus Christ, our Lord" (1 Cor. i. 9). "To know Him, and the power of His resurrection and the fellowship (κοινωνία) of His sufferings, being conformed unto His death, if by any means I may attain to the resurrection from the dead" (Phil. iii. 10-11).

Belonging to Christ. "If you are Christ's, then you are Abraham's seed" (Gal. iii. 29). "Those who are Christ's have crucified the flesh with its passions and lusts" (Gal. v. 24). "You are Christ's and Christ is God's" (1 Cor. iii. 23). "If any man is confident that he is Christ's, he should also think this, that just as he himself is Christ's so also are

---

[1] The German throughout these quotations is *Gemeinde* (community), the "non-technical" word for church, but as the author is here arguing that the whole Church, as a concept, is in view, it would be misleading to depart from the familiar English translation of ἐκκλησία.

we" (2 Cor. x 7.). "He who has not the Spirit of Christ, is not Christ's" (Rom. viii. 9).

To be laid hold of by Christ. "I pursue after Him, if anywise I may lay hold upon Him by whom I am laid hold of" (Phil. iii. 12).

To put on Christ. "As many of you as were baptized into Christ, have put on Christ" (Gal. iii. 27).[1]

.   .   .   .   .   .

Since "in Christ" is the more frequent expression, it has been held to be the most original, and the attempt has been made to take it as the starting-point in investigating Paul's mysticism. But that path led into a *cul-de-sac*. The phrase which is regarded as the most original is really a derivative one, from which the real nature of the conception cannot be apprehended. The very fact that alongside of the "in Christ" there occurs these other phrases, such as "with Christ," ought to have suggested the idea that possibly there should be sought behind the "in Christ" a more general conception, the common denominator for these various forms of expression. One thing which ought certainly to have led to this perception, was that alongside of the "we in Christ" there occurs the converse "Christ in us." How was it possible to overlook this problem of linguistic logic and treat the two opposite expressions as simply identical, without feeling the need of giving any explanation of their identity in terms of fact?

Christ in us. "My children for whom I am again in travail, till Christ be found in you" (Gal. iv. 19). "Do you not recognise that Christ is in you" (2 Cor. xiii. 5). "If Christ be in you, the body is dead because of sin, but the spirit is alive because of righteousness" (Rom. viii. 10). "Christ is magnified in my body, whether by life or by death" (Phil. i. 20). "You demand proof that Christ speaks in me, and He is not weak towards you, but mighty in you" (2 Cor. xiii. 3).

The original conception in which the various expressions find their common denominator is that of partaking with Christ in a special way in the corporeity which is capable of resurrection. As referring to this kind of union "Christ in us" and "we in Christ" are both equally intelligible.

.   .   .   .   .

The expression "being-in-Christ" is merely a brachyology for

---

[1] For proof that "to put on Christ" is not a Hellenistic expression see pp. 134-5, *inf.*

being partakers in the Mystical Body of Christ. Since it did not contain in itself the implication that the individual has his part in the Body of Christ along with the multitude of the Elect, it led investigators astray. It misled them into trying to explain as an individual and subjective experience that which according to Paul happens to believers as a collective and objective event.

"Being-in-Christ" is therefore the commonest, but not the most appropriate, expression for union with Christ. It becomes the most usual, not only because of its shortness but because of the facility which it offers for forming antitheses with the analogous expressions "in the body," "in the flesh," "in sin," and "in the spirit," and thus providing the mystical theory with a series of neat equations.

Thus "in Christ" forms the antithesis to "in the Law." No doubt the "in the Law" stands in most cases originally for "by the Law," corresponding to the linguistic usage of the Septuagint, which renders the Hebrew בְּ by ἐν. But when Paul speaks of sinning in the Law (Rom. ii. 12) and being justified in the Law (Gal. iii. 11, v. 4), there is suggested in it too the conception of a sinning and being justified in the condition of "being in the Law." The "being in the Law" is implied by the "being in the flesh." As a rule Paul uses, instead of it, the more natural expression "to be under the Law" (Rom. vi. 14; 1 Cor. ix. 20; Gal. iii. 23, iv. 4, 5, 21, v. 18); but for the sake of having a parallel expression to "being in the flesh" and "being in Christ" he can also speak of "being in the Law." Thus he says in Romans (iii. 19) that what the Law says applies to "those who are in the Law." The local significance of the Hebrew בְּ is combined by him with the instrumental.

Being in Christ. "The dead in Christ will arise first" (1 Thess. iv. 16). "Seeking to be justified in Christ" (Gal. ii. 17). "In Christ Jesus there is neither circumcision nor uncircumcision, but faith which expresses itself by love" (Gal. v. 6). "Sanctified in Christ Jesus" (1 Cor. i. 2). "Babes in Christ" (1 Cor. iii. 1). "Timothy, who is my beloved and faithful son in the Lord" (1 Cor. iv. 17). "He that is called in the Lord, being a slave, is the Lord's freedman" (1 Cor. vii. 22). "If Christ has not been raised up . . . then those also who have fallen asleep in Christ have perished" (1 Cor. xv. 17-18). "As in Adam all die, so in Christ shall all be made alive" (1 Cor. xv. 22). "If any man is in Christ, he is a new creation" (2 Cor. v. 17). "That we in Him" (Christ) "may become the righteousness of God" (2 Cor. v. 21). "I know a man in Christ" (2 Cor. xii. 2). "Through the redemption in Christ Jesus" (Rom. iii. 24).

"Dead for sin, but living for God in Christ Jesus" (Rom. vi. 11). "The grace of God is eternal life in Christ Jesus" (Rom. vi. 23). "There is thus no condemnation for those who are in Christ Jesus" (Rom. viii. 1). "The Law of the Spirit of Life in Christ Jesus" (Rom. viii. 2). "Therefore we, many as we are, are one body in Christ" (Rom. xii. 5). "Andronicus and Junias . . . who were in Christ before me" (Rom. xvi. 7). "Salute the family of Narcissus, who are in the Lord" (Rom. xvi. 11). "Salute Rufus, the elect of the Lord" (Rom. xvi. 13). "All the saints in Christ Jesus who are in Philippi" (Phil. i. 1). "That I may be found in Him" (Christ) (Phil. iii. 9). "The peace of God, which is higher than all intellect, shall keep your hearts and thoughts in Christ Jesus" (Phil. iv. 7). "As a beloved brother . . . both in the flesh and in the Lord" (Philemon 16). " Epaphras, my fellow-prisoner in Christ Jesus, greets you" (Philemon 23).

From the "being in Christ" is to be understood the "through Christ," in the sense in which Paul frequently uses it.

"I thank my God through Jesus Christ" (Rom. i. 8). "Thanks be to God through Christ Jesus" (Rom. vii. 25). "Peace with God through our Lord Jesus Christ" (Rom. v. 1). "To eternal life through Jesus Christ" (Rom. v. 21). "Who gives us victory through our Lord Jesus Christ" (1 Cor. xv. 57). "To obtain salvation through our Lord Jesus Christ" (1 Thess. v. 9).

The concept of being-in-Christ dominates Paul's thought in a way that he not only sees in it the source of everything connected with redemption, but describes all the experience, feeling, thought and will of the baptized as taking place in Christ. Thus the phrase "in Christ Jesus" comes to be added to the most varied statements, almost as a kind of formula.

The believer speaks the truth in Christ (Rom. ix. 1), knows and is convinced in Christ (Rom. xiv. 14), has a temper of mind in Christ (Phil. ii. 5), exhorts in Christ (Phil. ii. 1), speaks in Christ (2 Cor. ii. 17, xii. 19), gives out his Yes or his No in Christ (2 Cor. i. 19), salutes in the Lord (1 Cor. xvi. 19; Rom. xvi. 22), labours in the Lord (Rom. xvi. 3, 9, 12), labours abundantly in the Lord (1 Cor. xv. 58), presides in the Lord (1 Thess. v. 12), has freedom in Christ Jesus (Gal. ii. 4), rejoices in the Lord (Phil. iii. 1, iv. 4, 10), has hope in the Lord Jesus (Phil. ii. 19), has confidence in the Lord (Phil. ii. 24), is weak in Christ (2 Cor. xiii. 1), has power in the Lord (Phil. iv. 13), stands fast in the Lord (Phil. iv. 1), becomes rich in Christ Jesus (1 Cor. i. 5), glories in Christ Jesus (1 Cor. xv. 31; Rom. xv. 17; Phil. i. 26, iii. 3), is wise in Christ (1 Cor. iv. 10), is kept safe in Christ (Rom. xvi. 10), has love in Christ (1 Cor. xvi. 24; Rom. xvi. 8), receives a person in Christ Jesus (Rom. xvi. 2; Phil. ii. 29), is of one mind in Christ (Phil. iv. 2), has confidence in a person in the Lord (Gal. v. 10; Phil. i. 14), marries in the Lord (1 Cor. vii. 39), Paul's bonds become manifest in the Lord (Phil. i. 13).

Though the expression has thus almost the character of a formula, it is no mere formula for Paul. For him every manifestation of the life of the baptized man is conditioned by his being in Christ. Grafted into the corporeity of Christ, he loses his creatively individual existence and his natural personality. Henceforth he is only a form of manifestation of the personality of Jesus Christ, which dominates that corporeity. Paul says this with trenchant clearness when he writes, in the Epistle to the Galatians, "I am crucified with Christ, so I live no longer as I myself; rather, it is Christ who lives in me" (Gal. ii. 19-20).

The fact that the believer's whole being, down to his most ordinary everyday thoughts and actions, is thus brought within the sphere of the mystical experience has its effect of giving to this mysticism a breadth, a permanence, a practicability, and a strength almost unexampled elsewhere in mysticism. Certainly in this it is entirely different in character from the Hellenistic mysticism, which allowed daily life to go its own way apart from·the mystical experience and without relation to it.

.   .   .   .   .   .

Although in the expression of the Pauline mysticism the phrase "in Christ" is linguistically dominant, nevertheless the original conception is constantly breaking through, namely, the sharing by the Elect in the same corporeity with Christ. This makes itself felt especially in the fact that the relations prevailing in this mysticism can be stated in converse formulae. Not only can "Christ in us" be substituted for "we in Christ"; in place of "Christ for us" there similarly appears the converse "we for Christ." Paul boldly uses the phrase "Henceforth we, the living, are given up to death for the sake of Jesus, that the life of Jesus may also be made manifest in our mortal flesh" (2 Cor. iv. 11).[1] The union between the Elect and Christ has thus a meaning not only in relation to the Elect, but also in relation to Christ Himself. In the above passage the Elect are

---

[1] With the first part of the statement may be compared the quotation in Rom. viii. 36: "For Thy sake we are killed all the day long; we are accounted as sheep for the slaughter" (Ps. xliv. 23).

treated as fuel, the consumption of which extends the sphere of the dying and rising again of Jesus.

Paul even goes so far as to assume, for the existences which are united in the Body of Christ, the communicability of the mystical experience of the one to the other. Thus he affirms, in writing to the Corinthians, that they and he together are experiencing the dying and rising again in the body of Christ, in such a way that the powers of death are working themselves out in him, while the corresponding powers of life are made manifest in them. Therefore he is, for Christ's sake, foolish, weak, and despised, whereas they are in Christ, strong, wise, and honoured. Amid his sufferings he gains a consolation which is effectual in enabling them to bear suffering. The mystical character and the wide scope of this communicability of experience has not hitherto received the attention it deserves.

2 Cor. iv. 10-12: "We constantly carry about in our bodies the dying (literally—in both Greek and German—'the having-died') of Jesus, that the life of Jesus may also be made manifest in our bodies. For we, the living, are constantly beling delivered to death for Jesus' sake, in order that the life of Jesus may also be made manifest in our mortal flesh. Thus the death works in us, but the life in you."

2 Cor. xiii. 9: "For we rejoice when we are weak and you are strong."

1 Cor. iv. 10: "We are fools for Christ's sake; you are wise in Christ. We are weak, you are strong; you are in honour, we in contempt."

2 Cor. i. 5-7: "For as the sufferings of Christ abound in us, so abounds in us, through Jesus Christ, our consolation. If we are afflicted, it is for your consolation and salvation; if we receive consolation, it is for your consolation which is effectual in the bearing of the same sufferings which we suffer. And our hope for you is steadfast, since we know that you have part, as in the sufferings, so also in the consolation."

This passage, which might otherwise seem in its complicated involutions merely an elaborate complimentary opening to the Epistle, becomes simple and arresting once it is given its true meaning as a reference to the communicability of experience which obtains within the Mystical Body of Christ.

Whether the statement which puts this in its extreme form in the Epistle to the Colossians, "Now I rejoice in my sufferings on your behalf, and fill up in my flesh that which is still outstanding of the sufferings of Christ on behalf of His body, which is the Church" (Col. i. 24), is from Paul's pen or not cannot be determined with certainty. In any case, it is in the line of development of thought of

2 Cor. iv. 10-12 and of the thoughts relating to representation in the Epistle to the Philippians.

Phil. i. 20: "That Christ may be glorified in my body, whether by life or by death."

Phil. i. 29: "It has been granted to you for Christ's sake not only to believe on Him, but also to suffer for His sake."

Phil. ii. 17: "And even if I be poured out as a libation at the sacrifice and dedication of your faith, I joy and rejoice with you all."

The Mystical Body of Christ is thus for Paul not a pictorial expression, nor a conception which has arisen out of symbolical and ethical reflections, but an actual entity. Only so can it be explained that not only can Christ suffer for the Elect, but also the Elect for Christ and for one another. This reciprocity of relations is founded on the fact that the existences in question are physically interdependent in the same corporeity, and the one can pass over into the other. From the one-sided formula "being-in-Christ" such expressions would not be explicable.

.   .   .   .   .   .

That what is in view in the Pauline mysticism is an actual physical union between Christ and the Elect is proved by the fact that "being in Christ" corresponds to and, as a state of existence, takes the place of the physical "being in the flesh."

To what an extent the union with Christ is conceived of as physical is evident from the fact that it is thought to be of the same character as the bodily union between man and wife. Paul does not hesitate to use the same word—κολλᾶσθαι, 'cleave', derived from Gen. ii. 24—of bodily union between man and woman and union with Christ (1 Cor. vi. 16-17). He represents the two connections as of so much the same character that the one may be either included in the other, or may exclude it. In the case of morally blameless physical union between man and wife the connection with Christ continues through it; in the case of immoral intercourse the connection with Christ is broken by it.

It is on the basis of his mystical doctrine of physical union with Christ that Paul decides the question whether the believing husband or wife should continue in the married state with an unbelieving partner. He is in favour of the marriage continuing, because the unbelieving partner will be 'sanctified' by the believer. 'Sanctified' (made holy) is not here to be understood in some general sense, but signifies that the unbelieving partner, through bodily connection with the believing, has a share in the latter's being-in-Christ and thereby becomes with him a member of the Community of the Sanctified. Because the married pair belong corporeally to one another, the unbelieving partner becomes, without his or her co-operation, attached to Christ and susceptible of receiving the powers of death and resurrection which go forth from Christ and prepare the recipient for the "being-with-Christ" in the Messianic Kingdom. And similarly, children sprung from such a marriage belong to the community of the Sanctified.

1 Cor. vii. 12-14: "If a brother have an unbelieving wife and she be willing to live with him, he shall not put her away. And if a woman have an unbelieving husband and he be willing to live with her, she shall not put him away. For the unbelieving husband is sanctified by the wife, and the unbelieving wife by the husband; else were your children unclean, but now they are holy."

The significance of this passage for the interpretation of the Pauline mysticism has not hitherto been sufficiently emphasised. For it shows that Paul is prepared to accept in the fullest measure the implications of his doctrine of the union of believers with Christ as a physical bodily union.

.   .   .   .   .   .

Since the connection is of this physical character, it can be annulled by other physical connections which are not compatible with it.

Intercourse with a harlot is ruinous, because thereby a union is established which necessarily annuls the existence of union with Christ. For it is unthinkable that anyone can have bodily union with two such opposite beings at the same time. Every other sin is external to the body, and does not so directly affect the fact that our body belongs to the Lord and the Lord to our body.

1 Cor. vi. 13-19: "The body is not for unchastity but for the Lord, and the Lord for the body. . . . Know ye not that your bodies are members of Christ? Shall I then take the members of Christ and make them members of a harlot? Or know ye not that he who is joined to a harlot is one body with her. 'For the two,' as it is written, 'become one flesh.' But he who is joined to the Lord is with Him one Spirit. Flee unchastity, for every sin which a man commits is outside his body, but the unchaste sins against his own body. Or know ye not that our body

is a temple of the holy Spirit which is in us, which ye have from God, and that ye no longer belong to yourselves?"

Another way in which union with Christ can be lost is by trying to maintain in being alongside of it, or contemporaneously with it, the natural life; for that is nothing else than to suppose a man can be at the same time "in Christ" and "in the flesh." This is the case which arises when circumcision is demanded of believers. Those who put their trust in becoming members of the chosen People by means of this ceremonial act, which is concerned with the flesh, and so of attaining the possibility of entering into fellowship with the Messiah who is after the flesh of the Jewish race, fall into a fatal error. In making alteration of the natural corporeity by circumcision a necessity, they are asserting that, in spite of the being-in-Christ, natural corporeity still has its significance. But a man can only be either in Christ or in the flesh, not both at once. By circumcision a man decides for the being-in-the-flesh, for which the Law is valid, and thereby renounces the being-in-Christ. If the believer by dying with Christ is discharged from the Law, he is, if he places himself once more under the Law, in turn "discharged" from Christ.

Rom. vii. 4-6: "Even so, my brethren, you have been made dead for the Law by the body of Christ, in order to belong to another, even to Him that was raised from the dead. . . . Now we are loosed (κατ-ηργήθημεν) from the Law because we have died to that by which we were held fast."

Gal. v. 4: "You have been loosed (κατηργήθητε) from Christ, as many of you as are being justified by the Law; you are fallen from grace."

Yet another way of cancelling the union with Christ is by entering into union with the demons. Paul draws an analogy between the cultus-feasts in the temples, to which those who were offering sacrifice invited their acquaintances, and the Lord's Supper. The Lord's Supper signifies union with Christ. The sacrifices, since the heathen gods are no gods, are offered to demons. Therefore these feasts effect a union with the demons. Since union with Christ and union with demons are mutually exclusive, anyone who takes part in the heathen sacrificial feasts loses his union with Christ (1 Cor. x. 14-21).

1 Cor. x. 20-21: "I would not that you should have fellowship with demons. You cannot drink the cup of the Lord and the cup of demons;

you cannot be partakers of the table of the Lord and the table of demons."

On the basis of his mysticism Paul thus recognises three deadly sins—unchastity, acceptance of circumcision after baptism, and partaking in heathen sacrificial feasts. While all other sins are only prejudicial to the union with Christ these three destroy it at once. And since the obtaining of the resurrection state of existence at the Return of Jesus only takes place as a result of being-in-Christ, these sins cause death.

.   .   .   .   .   .

In what manner are the elect prepared through the dying and rising again with Christ for the preliminary resurrection?

If we are to understand Paul rightly, we must not attribute to him that conception of the resurrection of the flesh which we find in Ignatius, Justin, and the Johannine theology. According to this conception the fleshly body of the man acquires from the union of the Spirit with it the capacity to participate in immortality. Paul's manner of thought is quite different. He distinguishes between corporeity as such and the natural and glorified body. In accordance with this he assumes that the soul, that is to say, the indestructible personality of the individual, is something corporeal which is first united with a fleshly body and afterwards with a glorified body. The capacity which the elect person acquires through the dying and rising again with Christ is, that the soul-body which constitutes his essence is prepared to give up immediately its union with the fleshly body and enter upon that with the glorified body.

This conception of Paul's corresponds to the conception of dying and rising which was held by Late-Judaism. This also assumed that the soul after death carries on an individual corporeal existence, whether it sleeps in the earth (Dan. xii. 2), or lives in the dwellings which are prepared in the lower world for the sojourning of the souls of the dead. The latter view is the usual one. According to the Apocalypse of Ezra the fate of souls differs even in this intermediate state. The souls of the ungodly do not go into the chambers of rest, but wander about miserably, suffering seven-fold torment; the righteous dwell in peace and experience seven-fold joy.

The seven-fold torment of the souls of the wicked consists in this: That (1) they have despised the Law of the Highest; (2) can no longer find repentance; (3) see the reward of the righteous; (4) are aware of the torment which awaits them at the end of the world; (5) behold the dwellings where the souls of the righteous, watched over by angels, rest in peace; (6) bear the pains to which they are subjected even in this intermediate state; and (7) must endure the prospect of their final condemnation at the Judgment-seat of God (4 Ezra vii. 81-87). The seven-fold joys of the souls of the righteous are: (1) The consciousness of having fought a good fight; (2) witnessing the torment of the souls of the ungodly that wander to and fro; (3) being praised by God for their faithfulness to the Law; (4) having the guarantee that they shall rest in their chambers under the protection of angels until the Judgment; (5) looking back upon their afflictions, and forward to the glory of immortality; (6) awaiting the splendour in which they shall shine like the stars; and (7) have confidence that at the Judgment they shall stand fearless before God (4 Ezra vii. 88-99).

The condition of souls in this intervening period is described by Paul, quite in accordance with the Late-Jewish view as a being naked. The soul has put off its fleshly body, and has still to await the heavenly body. As he thinks of this nakedness, even for the souls of the righteous, as a rather miserable existence, he holds that those who remain alive up to the Return of Jesus, and then immediately undergo the transformation from the natural state of existence to the supernatural, are better off than those who, having "fallen asleep" in the meantime, have to pass through a period of this nakedness, and the kind of shadowy existence associated with it. He himself eagerly desires to be found alive at the Return of Jesus Christ, in order to be reclothed without being first unclothed.

2 Cor. v. 1-9: "For we know that, even if our earthly tent be broken up, we have a building of God, a house not made with hands, eternal in the heavens. For while we are in this tent we sigh with longing to put on over it our house from heaven, that when we have put this on we may not be found naked. For we who are in this tent-dwelling sigh and are heavy-hearted, not that we desire to put it off, but to put the other over it, in order that that which is mortal might be swallowed up by life. And He who has prepared us for this is God, who has given us the earnest of the Spirit. Therefore we are full of confidence, knowing that if we are at home in the body we are distant from the Lord, for we are walking by faith and not by sight. We are therefore full of confidence, and would rather remove out of the body and have our home with the Lord. Therefore we endeavour, whether at home or abroad, to be always well-pleasing to Him."

According to the Apocalypse of Baruch (xlix.-li), all the dead rise first in their original form, that they may recognise one another. Then follows the Judgment. Immediately after that some are changed into angelic beings, others into repulsive forms. This applies to the general resurrection, for the Apocalypse of Baruch, and indeed the Late-Jewish Eschatology in general, only recognise this one resurrection.

Paul's view of the rising again of those who sleep in Christ at the Return of Jesus is quite different. He represents them as clothed with the glorified body immediately upon the resurrection. This is what he means when, in 1 Corinthians xv. 52, he writes that the dead in Christ arise "incorruptible" ($\check{\alpha}\phi\theta\alpha\rho\tau o\iota$), while at the same moment the surviving are transformed.[1] The dead "in Christ" are in fact no ordinary dead. In their case it is not first decided, after the resurrection, whether they are to go into glory or into damnation. Their fate is already fixed. Moreover, by their membership in the glorified Body of Christ, they are already prepared to receive the glorified body which is destined for them. Consequently they can there and then arise in the glorified body.

Paul's description of the fleshly body which has been buried as the seed from which the incorruptible body is to spring (1 Cor. xv. 42-44), is a further proof that he expects for the dead in Christ, of whom he is there speaking, a resurrection taking place in the glorified body.

For the General Resurrection Paul cannot, of course, hold that the dead arise at once in the glorified body. At the Judgment, through which they have to pass after their resurrection, it is first decided whether they are to receive the body of glory, or in repulsive forms are to languish in eternal torment.

Paul of course holds that all human beings who have ever lived on earth are raised at the resurrection, with the exception of those who at the Return of Jesus are alive in Christ, and therefore enter into the resurrection state of existence by a transformation. The dead in Christ will rise at the Return of Jesus, all the remainder of the dead at the general resurrection after the Messianic Kingdom.

In order that they may rise again they must necessarily have first died. Paul therefore has to assume, that at the Judgment which

---

[1] Although, so far as the wording goes, Paul might be speaking in 1 Cor. xv. 52 of the dead in general, he actually means, as in 1 Thess. iv. 16 and 1 Cor. xv. 23, only the dead in Christ. See p. 94, *sup.*

takes place at the beginning of the Messianic Kingdom, all the survivors of mankind, with the exception of those who are in Christ, are delivered over to death. Whether it is thereby determined that at the Final Judgment to which they will later be raised up, they will be condemned to eternal damnation, cannot be clearly made out. It is conceivable that some of them may attain to eternal blessedness, although they have forfeited the Messianic Kingdom. Theoretically such, for example, might be the case of the Elect of the last generation of mankind whom no knowledge of Christ has reached, and who therefore have had no opportunity to confirm their election by the being-in-Christ. In consequence of that they would have lost the special prerogative of the last generation but not eternal blessedness.

On the other hand, it is quite clear that those who share in the Messianic blessedness thereby possess an unquestioned right to the eternal.

It is interesting to note that in the earliest attempt to combine the resurrection-idea with eschatology, which is undertaken in the Apocalypse contained in Isa. xxiv. 27, the resurrection is assumed to be, not of all but only of those who are well-pleasing to God.

Isa. xxvi. 14: "(Their) dead shall not live, the shades do not arise; thou hast punished them, rooted them out, and made the thought of them to perish."

Isa. xxvi. 19: "Thy dead shall live, my dead bod(ies) shall arise; awake and rejoice shall they that lie in the dust."

Here the idea of the resurrection is combined in a simple way with that of the preservation of the Elect in the final tribulation. With the righteous who are preserved alive at the sifting of the nations there is associated a company of those who have been raised from the dead in order to share in the Messianic Kingdom (Isa. xxvi. 7-21).

Even in the Book of Daniel it is stated only that many of those who sleep in the dust shall arise. But here already the idea of a judgment of those who have arisen is presupposed, since the resurrection brings blessedness to some and suffering to others.

Dan. xii. 2: "And many of those who sleep in the dust of the earth shall awake, some to eternal life, some to shame and everlasting contempt."

Once the idea of a resurrection is associated with eschatology in such a way that a judgment is assumed to be held upon those who have arisen, there is necessarily a further development in the direction that all the dead arise in order all to receive sentence. This inference is drawn in the eschatology of the Apocalypses of Enoch, Baruch, and Ezra, as well as by Jesus and by Paul.

.   .   .   .   .   .

Paul's statements about a being clothed upon with the heavenly tabernacle (2 Cor. v. 2-3), and a putting on of imperishability and immortality (1 Cor. xv. 53-54), are fully explained by the Late-Jewish view which was thoroughly familiar to him, that the soul, thought of as corporeal, at death puts off the fleshly corporeity and thenceforth in a state of nakedness awaits the heavenly corporeity. It is therefore not necessary to cite for their explanation Hellenistic views : they do not thereby become clearer than they were, but decidedly more obscure. The only reliable commentaries upon Paul's conception of death and resurrection are found in the Late-Jewish Apocalypses of Enoch, Baruch, and Ezra.

That these Late-Jewish views are not themselves genuinely Jewish but are taken over, along with the idea of resurrection, from Parsism and Oriental religion in general, is a separate question. Whatever their origin, Paul comes into possession of them by way of the Jewish tradition, and feels no need to deepen or extend them by such ideas about mortality and immortality as he might have learned from the Hellenistic world about him.

Since the being-in-Christ in itself signifies a partaking, even though still hidden, in the heavenly corporeity of Christ, Paul can describe it as a putting on of Christ.

Gal. iii. 27: "For as many of you as have been baptized into Christ have put on Christ."

Rom. xiii. 14: "Put on the Lord Jesus Christ."

It is not therefore necessary, for the explaining of this putting on of Christ, to cite evidence that the initiate into the Isis mysticism, after the wanderings through the underworld and the heavenly region, which he undergoes in the Mysteries, is sanctified by the putting on of twelve garments, and finally, clothed with the heavenly garment, is presented to the Isis Community and by it worshipped as a god (Apuleius, *Metam.* xi. 23 ff.). Paul's thought differs fundamentally from all the Hellenistic views which seek to realise themselves in this kind of theatrical ceremony, in that he thinks of a collective and permanent experience, which, moreover, is only intelligible in the light of his conception of the Mystical Body of Christ. For the Elect, in common and constantly, are in a mystical fashion clothed with the glorified corporeity of Christ. And the act by which it was bestowed upon them—baptism—was not associated with any ceremonial with which this assumption of a garment is connected.

.   .   .   .   .   .

In 2nd Corinthians (v. 1-9) Paul, in harmony with the Late-Jewish view, represents dying as a becoming unclothed, and expresses the desire not to have to go through this condition, but to be alive to experience the transformation from the natural to the supernatural state of existence. But in the Epistle to the Philippians he holds another language. Here death is not for him the beginning of a pitiable state of intermediate existence. On the contrary, he expects to enter immediately at death into the being-with-Christ. Were not his remaining in the flesh necessary for the Church's sake he would rather depart at once.

Phil. i. 21-24: "For to me life is Christ and death is gain. But if life in the flesh means seeing the fruit of my labour, I know not which I shall choose. I am urged this way and that; I have a desire to depart and be with Christ, which is far the better; but to remain in the flesh is more necessary for your sake."

How is this revolution in his view of death to be explained? It has been suggested that when he wrote the Epistle to the Philippians Paul no longer expected the Return of Jesus so soon as he had done earlier, and had therefore begun to reckon with the death of believers as the normal case. In order to rob of its bitterness this death which was now expected for all, he had, with the aid of the Hellenistic individualistic view of immortality, arrived at the conviction that everyone who died in Christ would immediately after death enter upon the resurrection state of existence and, by being rapt away to Christ, would attain to heaven. This took the place of his earlier view that all those who had fallen asleep in Christ would arise at His Return, and would be caught up to meet Him in the clouds.

In regard to this explanation, it is, in the first place, not the fact that Paul in the Epistle to the Philippians is less confident about the speedy Return of Jesus than he was earlier. Against this we have to begin with the statement "The Lord is at hand" (Phil. iv. 5), and the exhortation to "Rejoice," which is founded on this confi-

dence (Phil. iv. 4).[1] Further, it is not obvious why this hope of
an immediate and individual resurrection should be something
Hellenistic, which here comes into play alongside of eschatology.
What is there Hellenistic in the idea of being rapt away to
Christ?

It is much more natural to explain this hope of immediate rising
and being rapt away as due to the extreme intensity of the hope of
resurrection, which resulted from this mystical doctrine of the
being-in-Christ.

We have to begin by recognising that Paul in Phil. i. 21-26 is
speaking only of what he expects for himself. He is not setting up a
new teaching about dying and rising again, which is to take the
place of the old; he is only giving expression to an individual hope,
which he cherishes on the ground of his own self-consciousness.
And his thoughts are turned to it in view of a particular death,
which he may be destined to undergo. For he has to reckon with
the possibility that his imprisonment may end with a martyr's death.
For this particular case he has the expectation of being rapt away to
Christ in an immediate resurrection.

Thus it is not Paul's general doctrine of death and resurrection
which changes. It is only that he expects, on the ground of his own
self-consciousness, that in case of his dying a martyr-death a special
kind of resurrection will be vouchsafed to him.

How strongly his self-consciousness is involved in the thoughts
which he thinks about his possible condemnation to death is evident from the fact that he gives it the significance of a sacrifice
offered for his churches.

Phil. ii. 17: "But even though I be poured out as a libation upon the
sacrifice and the priestly offering" (*priesterliche Darbringung*—the Greek
is λειτουργία) "of your faith, I joy and rejoice with you all."

In this consciousness, the strength of which we can hardly over-
rate, Paul expects that the same fate will be allotted to him as to
Enoch, Elijah, Ezra, and Baruch. It is possible also that the ecstatic
experience, in which "whether in the body or out of the body" he
was "caught up into the third heaven and into Paradise" (2 Cor.
xii. 2-4), contributed to the creation of his hope of being rapt away
to Jesus.

[1] On the undiminished liveliness of the eschatological expectation in Philippians see p. 53, *sup.*

This experience, which is referred to in 2nd Corinthians as having happened fourteen years before, was no doubt at the time of the Philippian Epistle some twenty years behind him. But the high importance which Paul always attached to it is to be judged from the fact that in his struggle to vindicate his Apostolic authority he makes reference to it, holding it to be a unique distinction, from which must at once be evident his equality with the other Apostles, if not indeed his superiority to them. It was to Paradise that Enoch was translated when he was rapt away (Enoch lx. 8, lxx. 3). Paul had thus had an experience comparable to that of these pious men of early times, and remained for a time in the place which he visited! Which of the original Apostles had been granted such a favour!

The challenge to his Apostleship had had the effect of inflaming and intensifying his self-consciousness. And this self-consciousness gives him the hope of a resurrection taking place immediately after his death, and connected with his being rapt away to Christ, Eschatological mysticism permits him to extend it. He had already come to the conclusion, as regards the dead in Christ, that they, as having already undergone with Christ a dying and rising again, do not arise in the same condition as the rest of the dead, but on their awaking from the sleep at death immediately possess an imperishable corporeity, and in this will be rapt away to meet Jesus in the air (1 Thess. iv. 17). The thought of being rapt away to Jesus is thus really contained already in the concept of the resurrection of the dead in Christ. Paul, who is conscious of having undergone in a unique fashion the dying with Christ and of having already experienced being rapt away to heaven, may well therefore, in face of his probable martyr-death, have attained to the expectation of experiencing a still more privileged resurrection than that of the others who have died in Christ. Thus there arises in him the hope that in case of his martyr-death he will be rapt away, by an immediate individual resurrection, to where Christ is. In his imprisonment his mind plays with this possibility; but his sense of reality still keeps the upper hand. When he asks himself whether God has appointed for him death or liberation, his dominating conviction is always that the latter is the case, because his remaining in the flesh is necessary for his churches. So, with the desire to live which this conviction makes a command of God, Paul looks for a liberation from prison and a return to his churches and continues to expect his transformation to take place at the Return of Jesus.

Phil. i. 24-26: "To remain in the flesh is more necessary for your sakes. And in this conviction I know that I shall remain, and shall sojourn with you all again to aid your progress and to have joy in your faith, that your glorying may abound in Jesus Christ in me, because of my being present with you again."

.   .   .   .   .   .

The problems which made his mysticism necessary, and the general conception on which it is based, are never expounded by Paul. Indeed even the doctrine of being-in-Christ is never systematically developed; its implications are simply stated as though they were self-evident. But behind the phrases in which he expresses his mysticism lie the problems by which it was called into being, and the fundamental conceptions out of which it arose stand forth with such clearness that they would always have been visible if only theologians had had the courage to endeavour to understand this mysticism in the light of the eschatological expectation. It was, however, held to be self-evident that it must be, to a greater or less degree, Hellenistic.

The possibility that Paul through the Greek language absorbed some Hellenistic ideas, and that these were not without influence upon his mysticism, is by no means to be disputed, even though most of what has hitherto been adduced from Hellenistic literature for the explanation of the Pauline world of thought has not thrown as much light upon it as was expected. It is, in any case, certain that this mysticism as a whole cannot be reconstructed out of a patchwork of Hellenistic ideas, but only becomes intelligible in the light of eschatology. The explanation from the eschatological point of view has the advantage at every point over that from Hellenism. It is able to show that the Pauline Mysticism is demanded by eschatological problems, and is therefore necessary; it shows how the most various tenets are derived from a single fundamental conception; it makes clear the origin of the idea of the Mystical Body of Christ, before which the Hellenistic explanation found itself helpless; from this it is able to derive the view of the "being-in-Christ," for which no satisfactory parallels have been found in Hellenism; it is able to explain the quasi-physical character of the union with Christ, and the realism of the dying and rising again with Him; it makes intelligible why the concept of rebirth is absent in Paul and the new condition of the believer is thought of always and only as an anticipatory resurrection.

Further points which it makes intelligible are: the connection between this mysticism and predestination; the peculiarity that the being-in-Christ is not a subjective but a collective experience; the absence of symbolism; the fact that the whole life of the believer, even in its most everyday manifestations, is thought of as taking place "in Christ"; the possibility of the results of the death of Christ, which works itself out in the Elect, being communicated to others and becoming manifest in them as the life of Christ. Thus both as a whole and in its details the mysticism of Paul is immeasurably better explained by deriving it from eschatology rather than from Hellenism.

The superiority of the eschatological interpretation is further apparent in the fact that it sets the problem of Jesus and Paul in a new light, and gives it a much more satisfactory solution than has hitherto been the case. At the same time it makes it clear why Paul was obliged to create a new teaching for himself. The theory of Paul's defection from Jesus, without which the Hellenistic and semi-Hellenistic explanations of the Pauline Mysticism cannot make out their cases, becomes purposeless for the eschatological explanation.

And the latter has this further advantage, that it brings Paul into a natural relation to Early Christianity. It makes that which is common to both, and that in which he goes beyond it, alike intelligible, by showing that his thought has as its sole presupposition the eschatological beliefs of the primitive Church, while he draws from them inferences which ordinary reflection had not arrived at.

The decisive point is, however, that the eschatological explanation is able to show that the Pauline Mysticism is something which necessarily arose out of the problems raised by the conception of redemption. Here, as elsewhere, the principle is exemplified that that which is shown to be necessary is really explained.

And how totally wrong those are who refuse to admit that Paul was a logical thinker, and proclaim as the highest outcome of their wisdom the discovery that he has no system! For he is a logical thinker and his mysticism is a complete system. In the interpretation and application of Scriptural passages he may proceed by the leaps and bounds of the Rabbinic logic, but in his mysticism he proceeds with a logical consistency, which in its simplicity and clearness compels assent as a piece of thinking. His paradoxical assertion that those who are in Christ are only in outward appearance natural men, and are to be considered as having in reality already died and risen again, is irrefutable, once the two-fold fact of the dying and rising again of Jesus has been given the place of importance in the eschatological expectation which it actually possesses for eschatological thought.

Understood on the basis of eschatology, Paul becomes a thinker of elemental power who was alone in recognising the special character of the period which interposed itself between the Resurrection and Return of Jesus, and the first to seek a solution of the problem raised by the delay of this Return. Since all his conceptions and thoughts are rooted in eschatology, those who labour to explain him on the basis of Hellenism, are like a man who should bring water from a long distance in leaky watering-cans in order to water a garden lying beside a stream.

As the spider's net is an admirably simple construction so long as it remains stretched between the threads which hold it in position, but becomes a hopeless tangle as soon as it is loosed from them; so the Pauline Mysticism is an admirably simple thing, so long as it is set in the framework of eschatology, but becomes a hopeless tangle as soon as it is cut loose from this.

CHAPTER VII

SUFFERING AS A MODE OF MANIFESTATION OF
THE DYING WITH CHRIST

As a consequence of his mystical teaching Paul is in the position of having to assert the existence of death and resurrection even where nothing of the kind is visible. He can, however, produce indications of them. The dying which the believer experiences with Christ is made manifest in suffering which destroys, or tends to destroy, his life. The resurrection state which is in process of formation is manifested by the presence of the Spirit as a supernatural life-principle. The diminution of the natural life and the expression of supernatural life in the natural are, for the knowledge which can look into the depths of things, indications of the displacement of the natural state by the supernatural which is in progress in the believer.

Consistently with this view Paul treats all suffering as dying, and characterises it by that term. This explains why the thought of suffering either passes into that of dying with Him, or, as is more usual, is simply replaced by it. This makes an obvious point of distinction between Pauline and non-Pauline theology. In the First Epistle of Peter—from whatever pen and from whatever time it may have originated—there is found more about suffering, and suffering with Christ, than in all the Pauline Epistles put together. On the other hand, the idea of dying with Christ does not occur in it.

1 Peter i. 6-7: ". . . though you now suffer affliction by various temptations, that your faith may be found more precious than gold, which is perishable."—1 Peter i. 11: "The sufferings with a view to Christ ($\epsilon\dot{\iota}s$ $X\rho\iota\sigma\tau\acute{o}\nu$) and the glory that follows after them."—1 Peter ii. 20-21: "If you are steadfast under suffering, that is the grace of God. For thereto are you called, because Christ also suffered for us, leaving us an example, that you might follow His footsteps."—1 Peter iii. 14:

"But if you suffer for righteousness' sake you are blessed."—1 Peter iv. 1: "Since, then, Christ has suffered in the flesh, arm yourselves with the same mind, for he who has suffered in the flesh is loosed from sin."—1 Peter iv. 13: "In so far as you have a share in the sufferings of Christ, rejoice, that at the revelation of His glory you may have bliss and joy."—1 Peter iv. 16: "But if he suffer as a Christian let him not be ashamed; let him glorify God in this name."—1 Peter iv. 19: "Those who suffer according to the will of God."—1 Peter v. 9: "Knowing that the like sufferings are fulfilled in your brotherhood throughout the world."—1 Peter v. 10: "The God of all peace . . . will after short sufferings make you perfect."

There are only a few passages in which Paul speaks of suffering with Christ.

2 Cor. i. 5: "For as the sufferings of Christ abound in us, so also through Christ shall our consolations abound."

Rom. viii. 17: "Fellow-heirs with Christ, if we suffer with Him, that we may be also glorified with Him."

Rom. viii. 18: "I reckon that the sufferings of the present time signify nothing in comparison with the glory that will be revealed to us."

Paul usually, as though he were following some inner necessity, lets the thought of suffering merge into that of dying. In Philippians iii. 10-11 he speaks of fellowship with the sufferings of Christ, but immediately adds that he is therein conformed to Christ's death. In Romans viii. 35-36 he concludes the list of sufferings with the quotation, "For Thy sake we are slain all the day long" (Ps. xliv. 23). In 2 Corinthians i. 8-10 Paul describes a deliverance from severe affliction in Asia as a deliverance from death by God "who raises the dead." In 2 Corinthians iv. 8-12 he interprets his troubles as a bearing about in his body of the dying of Jesus. Especially instructive is 2 Corinthians xi. 23. Here he is about to close the list of distresses and dangers in which he has been preserved with the mention of deadly perils, but uses instead the word death, the illogical plural of which ($\dot{\epsilon}\nu$ $\theta\alpha\nu\dot{\alpha}\tau o\iota s$) he has to form for this purpose!

As a rule, however, he spares himself the detour by way of the idea of suffering, and speaks simply of dying where he might more logically speak only of suffering. In order to make the paradox complete he can express the dying as a being crucified and buried with Christ.

"I die daily"[1] (1 Cor. xv. 31).—"We have been buried with Christ by being baptized into death" (Rom. vi. 4).—"If we have died with Christ" (Rom. vi. 8).—"Reckon yourselves therefore to be dead" (Rom. vi. 11).—"We who have died to sin" (Rom. vi. 2).—"Even so, brethren, you have been made dead to the Law by the body of Christ" (Rom. vii. 4).—"If Christ is in you, then is the body dead" (Rom. viii. 10).— "Always bearing about in our body the having-died of Jesus" (2 Cor. iv. 10).—"From henceforth we who live are constantly delivered up to death for the sake of Christ" (2 Cor. iv. 11).—"Far be it from me to boast except in the Cross of our Lord Jesus Christ, by which the world is crucified to me, and I to the world" (Gal. vi. 14).—"With Christ I have been crucified" (Gal. ii. 20).—"Henceforward let no man trouble me; I carry about in my body the marks (*stigmata*, στίγματα) of Jesus" (Gal. vi. 17).

The marks (*stigmata*) mean primarily the brandings by which a slave or an animal was made recognisable as his master's property. The sign of belonging to Christ is suffering. Gal. vi. 17 therefore means, like 2 Cor. iv. 10, that Paul carries about with him the having-died of Christ. It is possible that by the stigmata he means also the scars which must have remained from his various scourgings. It is possible that he means to claim that he is one who is in such fashion crucified with Jesus, that he is to be regarded as one who shows the marks of the crucifixion. As one who has been crucified unto Christ, he demands that no one shall henceforth make trouble for him, as though he were still going about as a mere natural man.

This claim of Paul's, as is well known, is the starting-point of a phenomenon, which has occurred in a series of abnormally suggestible persons, of the visible appearance of bleeding wounds upon hands and feet. What happens is that, through intense imagining of the wound marks as known from pictures, and through the conscious or unconscious desire to share the experience of stigmatisation which is attributed to Paul, such wound marks actually occur in consequence of the accompanying vasomotor excitation. What Paul meant metaphorically, here becomes literal.

.   .   .   .   .   .

In enunciating the dynamic conception of union with Christ in His death, Paul is simply giving to an idea derived from eschatology, preached by Jesus, and held in primitive Christianity, the form of expression which it must logically assume in consequence of the death and resurrection of Jesus.

[1] Karl von Weizsäcker, in his well-known translation of the New Testament, does not venture to give the full force of the thought: he has "Death is daily before me."

Up to the sending forth of the Twelve Jesus taught that His followers must suffer with Him and endure, even unto death, in order to be acknowledged by the Son of Man as belonging to the Messianic Kingdom.[1] The kind of persecution which He expects for Himself and for believers in the Kingdom, is that implied in the general conception of the pre-Messianic tribulation. Later, in consequence of the delay of this tribulation He arrived at the conviction that a dying which He should voluntarily bring upon Himself would be accepted by God as an atonement for the Elect, and that these would consequently be spared the tribulation.[2] Since He kept this thought secret to Himself, only making veiled allusions to it, primitive Christianity grasped only, in regard to His death, that He had thereby made an atonement, in consequence of which the Coming of the Kingdom becomes possible and the Elect receive in Baptism forgiveness of sins, as will be made manifest at the Coming Judgment. Moreover, persecution and tribulation continue, indeed it is now that they really first begin. Consequently the original idea with which Jesus had gone to His death, if it had ever been understood, was now set aside by the reality. The idea of the pre-Messianic tribulation still persisted. Believers understood the persecution which they encounter as being a part of it. They thus naturally brought these sufferings into relation with that of Jesus, since that was also an event of the pre-Messianic tribulation. Their suffering is connected with His and continues it. However purely believing and expectant the attitude of the first Christians was, there was, nevertheless, already present, in their conception of suffering, one element in the mystical doctrine of union with Christ, in so far as they, in virtue of the concept of the pre-Messianic tribulation, are fellow-sufferers with Him.

In primitive Christianity the thought of following Christ in the path of suffering hardly occurs apart from that of fellowship with Christ in suffering. The believer thinks of his suffering as included in the Great Tribulation which, according to the Divine Decree, is brought by the God-opposing powers upon those who belong to the future Messianic Kingdom, Messiah and Elect alike, in order that they may be purified and may prove their loyalty to God and make good a claim to the future glory.[3] That these

---

[1] *Vide sup*. pp. 57-61.

[2] On Jesus' view of His own suffering and death see pp. 57-61, *sup*.

[3] On the Final Tribulation see pp. 79-82, *sup*.

sufferings really belong to the same whole as those of Jesus Christ is not invalidated by their separation in point of time. Nay more, humiliations suffered before the Coming of Christ belong together with His. In the Epistle to the Hebrews, Moses' refusal to be called the son of Pharaoh's daughter is praised on the ground that he, with forward-looking faith, "held this humiliation of Christ to be wealth greater than the treasures of Egypt" (Heb. xi. 24-26).

Only in a few passages of the New Testament is the thought expressed of following Christ's example in His sufferings.

1 Peter ii. 21: "Thereto (viz. the suffering) are you called, because Christ has suffered for you, leaving you an example that you might follow in His footsteps."

1 Peter iv. 1: "Since Christ has suffered in the flesh, arm yourselves with the same mind."

Heb. xiii. 12-13: "Therefore Jesus also, in order that He might sanctify the people by His own blood, suffered outside the gate. So let us go out to Him, outside the camp, bearing His humiliation."

In the First Epistle of Peter the idea of imitating Christ in His sufferings takes its place alongside of that of fellowship in His sufferings. In Paul's writings it does not occur at all.

The First Epistle of Peter is indeed built up upon the idea of the connection of the suffering of the believer with that of Christ; the same idea lies at the base of numberless passages in the Catholic Epistles, in the Apocalypse, and in the Apostolic fathers. It is the original correlative to the concept of the atoning death of Jesus. Later dogmatic theory as a whole is unable to give any logical and satisfactory answer to the question how that which Jesus gained in His suffering can be communicated to others. It is not in a position to explain satisfactorily the solidarity necessary for such a communication, since it has at its disposal only the concept of faith and a concept of the Church which has lost its original vitality. Primitive Christianity, however, was acquainted with a living relation of the suffering of Christ to that of the believer, which came into visible manifestation. What Christ has won in His sufferings is passed on to those who are partakers with Him in suffering. In this concept of fellowship with Christ in suffering, founded in the idea of the pre-Messianic tribulation and the pre-existent Church, and kept alive by the fact of constant persecution, lies the immediacy of the primitive Christian belief in the forgiveness of sin. It is in this spirit that the author of

1st Peter teaches that he who has suffered in the flesh is freed from sin (1 Peter iv. 1). It corresponds to the elemental thought of Paul which stands behind the statements about justification by faith, that he who has died with Christ is free from sin.

1 Peter iv. 1-2: "He who has suffered in the flesh is loosed from sin, that for the rest of his time in the flesh he should live, not according to the lusts of men, but for the will of God."

The meaning of the passage is not that by suffering his flesh has been made dead, so that he no longer has any impulse to sin; by loosing from sin is meant forgiveness on the ground of the atoning power of suffering.

According to the Psalms of Solomon also suffering has this sin-annulling power.

Ps. Sol. xiii. 10: "For the Lord spares His righteous ones and their transgression he annuls by chastising."

Ps. Sol. xviii. 4-5: "Thy chastening is exercised upon us as upon a first-born only son, that thou mayest turn away obedient souls from their unconscious errors. May God purify Israel against the day of His healing mercy, against the day of choosing, when His anointed shall come to rule."

That suffering annuls sin is also expressed in the conception of the suffering servant (Isa. liii.). He suffers that others may not have to bear the penalty of their misdeeds.

Since Paul puts dying in the place of suffering, we get the statement (Rom. vi. 7): "For he that has died is justified ($\delta\epsilon\delta\iota\kappa\alpha\iota\omega\tau\alpha\iota$) from sin." He means, as the context shows (Rom. vi. 4-11), the dying with Christ.

There is a passage in Ignatius, which seems not to recognise the atoning significance of suffering. In his Epistle to the Romans (*Ad Rom.* v. 1) he says, with reference to the sufferings which he has to endure from his guards, "Under their ill-treatment I am better schooled, but I am not thereby justified." But this is the martyr-modesty. He means to say that in comparison with the wild beasts at Rome he does not consider his present hardships as belonging to the sufferings which possess atoning power: in the same way he says that he is only now beginning to be a disciple (*Ad Rom.* v. 3).

Moreover, his phrase "but I am not thereby justified" is suggested by a reminiscence of 1 Cor. iv. 4: "For though I am not conscious of anything in me, yet I am not thereby justified."

Fellowship with Christ in suffering and death is the solution of the problem of post-baptismal sin. According to the view of Paul, as of primitive Christianity in general, the atoning death of Christ does not procure continuous forgiveness of sins, but only the release obtained in baptism from previously committed sins. For subsequent transgressions atonement is secured by suffering with Christ. But this view is only tenable as long as the eschatological expectation, and the accompanying view of the pre-Messianic tribulation, are in being. From the moment when the conviction is no longer present to believers that they are actually in the pre-Messianic tribulation, and are therefore suffering along with Christ, the problem of the forgiveness of post-baptismal sin immediately presents itself in the form of the question of a second repentance—and has never found a satisfactory solution.

The thought of having a share in the atonement procured by Christ is therefore only intelligible in connection with the concept, originally closely attached to it, of fellowship in the sufferings of Christ. With the disappearance of the latter the doctrine of the forgiveness of sins passes through a stage of obscurity, to become finally, in Catholicism as in Protestantism, something quite different from what it was in primitive Christianity.

The concept of the fellowship of suffering with Christ did not, therefore, as is often assumed, originate with Paul, it follows immediately from the concept of the pre-Messianic Tribulation. Paul shares it with Jesus and with primitive Christianity, but, in accordance with his mystical doctrine, must necessarily intensify it into that of the dying with Christ. After the death and resurrection of Jesus there cannot, according to his view, be any further pre-Messianic tribulation; for the Messianic time is already present. The only course open is to treat suffering as a dying with Christ.

Bold as it is to regard suffering as the equivalent of dying, Paul is nevertheless entitled to expect that those who are already familiar with the thought of suffering with Christ will recognise and understand it in the intensified form, which it has become necessary to give it, of fellowship in the death of Christ.

.   .   .   .   .   .

The logic of his mystical doctrine compels Paul, as we have seen, to treat suffering as a form of manifestation of the dying with Christ. The excessive sufferings, which were his lot from the moment of his beginning to preach Christ, helped him to arrive at this conception.

It has often been suggested that the Pauline teaching is to be explained by the unique character of his experience at his conversion. His Mysticism, so the theory goes, is just that experience expressed in terms of universal application. But if there is really anything of his peculiar personal experience recognisable in his doctrine, it is not so much the vision of Christ on the Damascus road, as the fact that his Christ-dedicated life could really appear to him as a being delivered over to death. To the peculiar character of his conversion he hardly makes any allusion in his letters. Again and again, however, he speaks of his so numerous and so heavy sufferings. It is here, then, if we are to accept his own evidence, that the experience lies which he has generalised in his teaching.

The Acts of the Apostles tell us of a part only of the heavy trials which befell him. And even so, how much there is! In Damascus, immediately after his conversion, the only way in which he can escape from the Jews and the ethnarch of King Aretas, who were seeking to do away with him, was by being lowered over the city wall by night in a basket (Acts ix. 23-25; 2 Cor. xi. 32-33). In Jerusalem the Hellenistic Jews seek his life, for which reason he is brought by the brethren to Caesarea, and from there goes away to Tarsus (Acts ix. 29-30).

On the First Missionary Journey he was driven out of Antioch in Pisidia in consequence of a disturbance stirred up by the Jews (Acts xiii. 50-51). In Iconium he had to escape by flight from an attempt to stone him (Acts xiv. 5-6). In Lystra he is stoned, dragged out of the city, and left for dead by the populace (Acts xiv. 19-20).

On the Second Missionary Journey he was first scourged and then thrown into prison by the Roman authorities (Acts xvi. 22-24). From Thessalonica he had to flee from the populace, which had been roused against him by the Jews (Acts xvii. 5-9). He meets with the same fate later on at Beroea (Acts xvii. 13-14). In Corinth he is dragged before the Proconsul Gallio, brother of the philosopher Seneca, who, however, refuses to have anything to do with religious controversies of the Jews among themselves (Acts xviii. 12-17).

On the Third Missionary Journey an uproar is raised against him at Ephesus (Acts xix. 23-xx. 1). In Corinth he is unable to carry out his plan of travelling to Syria by sea, because the Jews were planning an attack upon him (which they apparently intended to carry out either as he was going aboard or at sea), and was obliged to take instead the land route through Macedonia, guided and guarded by brethren who travelled with him (Acts xx. 3). Then in

Jerusalem the multitude, excited against him by Jews from Asia, sought to kill him outside the Temple. He was saved from this fate by the captain of the Roman guard. But this rescue was the beginning of the imprisonment which was to lead up to his death (Acts xxi. 27-35).

.   .   .   .   .   .

It is only from the Epistles, however, that we hear the full tale of all the miseries of his existence. In Ephesus he had fought with men as with wild beasts.

1 Cor. xv. 32: "If after the manner of men I underwent a beast-fight (κατὰ ἄνθρωπον ἐθηριομάχησα) at Ephesus, what does that profit me?"

An actual fight with wild beasts cannot be meant. If Paul had been condemned as a disturber of the peace to fight with beasts, he would thereby also have lost his Roman citizenship. But at his arrest at Jerusalem he still possesses it. He probably means to say, therefore, that in Ephesus men had raged against him like wild beasts. Does that mean that there was another uproar besides that set afoot by Demetrius? (Acts xix. 23-xx. 1)—for in the latter, according to Acts, he was not actually exposed to the violence of the populace?

It is no doubt with allusion to Paul's words that Ignatius speaks of the fighting with beasts, which he had to undergo upon his journey as a prisoner. *Ad Rom.* v. 1: "From Syria to Rome I fight with beasts by land and sea, by day and night, chained to ten leopards, that is to say, to a detachment of soldiers. These become the worse, the better they are treated."

It is to be noticed also that Paul's words can be taken as referring to an imaginary case. "If I, after the fashion of men, had had to fight with beasts in Ephesus, what would it have profited me?" In this case he would be alluding to the fact, known to his readers, that at Ephesus he had almost been condemned to fight with beasts in the arena. But in this case would the words κατὰ ἄνθρωπον (after the manner of men) have any proper sense? Ignatius, in any case, thinks of this fighting with beasts as metaphorical.

Five times was Paul scourged by the Jews; three times he was beaten with rods; repeatedly he was put in prison; three times he suffered shipwreck, being a night and a day adrift on the sea; he suffered hunger, thirst, and nakedness, and was in danger in deserts and from robbers.

1 Cor. iv. 9-13: "For I think that God has set forth us the Apostles last, as men condemned to die. For we are become a spectacle to the

world, both to angels and to men.[1] We are foolish for Christ's sake, you are wise in Christ; we are weak, you are strong; you are in honour, we in dishonour. For up to this present hour we are hungry and thirsty and are naked and mishandled and have no fixed abode and make shift to support ourselves by the work of our hands. Being reviled, we bless; being persecuted, we endure; being treated with contumely, we answer kindly. We have become as the filth of the world, the offscouring of all things to this day."

2 Cor. vi. 4-5: "In all things showing ourselves servants of God; in much enduring of affliction, in trouble, in necessity, in distresses, in blows, in imprisonment, in tumults, in labours, in night-long vigils."

2 Cor. xi. 25-30: "Are they servants of Christ? (I speak as a fool)—I am more. In labours more abundant, in prisons more, in stripes beyond measure, in deaths often. Of the Jews received I five times forty strokes save one; three times was I beaten with rods; once was I stoned; three times I have suffered shipwreck, a night and a day have I (as a ship-wrecked man drifting about the sea) been carried over the abyss; in journeys often (thus more a servant of Christ than the others); in perils of rivers, in perils by my own people; in perils from the heathen; in perils in the city; in perils in the desert; in perils on the sea; in perils among false brethren; in toil and travail; in wakefulness by night; in hunger and thirst; in fastings often, in cold and nakedness, not to speak of the other things which press upon me daily, anxiety for all the churches! Who is weak, and I am not weak? Who is offended, and I burn not. If I must needs boast, I will boast of the things in which I am weak."

.   .   .   .   .   .

The Jewish authorities punished by beating with a whip, the Romans with rods, that is to say, with blows with a stick. In the punishment by the Synagogue authorities it was not a case of scourging strictly so-called, but of beating with a four-thonged plait of calf-leather, very much what we might call a horse-whip. The terrible process is described, with reference to Deut. xxv. 2-3, where the beating is ordered, in the Mishna tractate "Makkot" ("Blows"). This was originally the second part of the famous

[1] This figure, drawn from the arena, is found already in Enoch (lxii. 9-12). Here the kings and mighty ones of the earth at the Judgment beseech the Son of Man to beg for God's mercy upon them. He, however, delivers them to the Angels of Punishment, who take them and wreak vengeance upon them for having ill-treated His children and elect. They shall be a spectacle for the righteous and His elect; these shall rejoice over them, because the wrath of the Lord of Spirit is laid upon them. In the Stoic rhetoric also the wise men struggling with fate is said to be a spectacle for gods and men.

Mishna tractate "Sanhedrin" (*Synedrium*), which dealt with Jewish criminal law. The oldest parts of both tractates are probably derived from a record, made in the second century A.D., of the old traditional Jewish criminal law. The directions given in them therefore no doubt correspond to the legal practice of the time of Jesus and the Apostles.[1]

Deut. xxv. 2-3: "When the guilty man deserves beating as a punishment, the judge shall cause him to lie down, and shall cause to be given to him a number of strokes proportionate to his offence. Forty (strokes) he may give him but no more, that thy brother may not be dishonoured in thine eyes if more strokes were given him."

Tractate *Makkot* iii. 10: "How many strokes shall be given him? Forty, less one; for it is written (Deut. xxv. 2-3) 'up to forty strokes,' (therefore) a number close on forty."[2] The usage of giving just less than forty strokes is also evidenced in Josephus (*Antiq.* iv. 8, 21): "He who transgresses these commandments shall receive publicly thirty-nine strokes." Similarly in iv. 8, 23.

Tract. *Makkot* iii. 12-14: "(One) binds his hands to the pillar on this side and on that, and the attendant seizes (him) by his clothes—if they tear, they tear, and if they come to pieces, they come to pieces—until he has laid bare his heart. And the stone is placed behind him, and the servant of the community takes his stand upon it and (holds) a thong of calf's leather in his hand, plaited one to two and two to four, two thongs going over and two under it. (This no doubt means the two thongs which plait the others together.) The grip of it (measures in length) a handbreadth, and its width (is likewise) a hand-breadth (and it must be of such a length that) it reaches to his navel. And (the attendant) gives him a third (of the strokes) in front and two-thirds behind. And while he is beating him, the criminal neither stands (upright) nor sits, but takes up a bowed position . . . and he who strikes, strikes with his full strength with one hand.

"The Reader reads out: 'If thou dost not observe to do all the words of the law which are written in this book, to fear this glorious and fearful name,'" etc. (Deut. xxviii. 58-59). ". . . and he begins again.

"And if the (the criminal) dies under his hand (that of the attendant), then he (the latter) is free of punishment; (but) if he gives him one

---

[1] Gustav HÖLSCHER, *Die Mischnatraktate Sanhedrin und Makkot ins Deutsche übersetzt* (Tübingen, 1910: 143 pp.).

[2] Lest, owing to a mistake in counting, more than forty strokes should be given, it is laid down that the criminal should receive fewer than forty. "Rabbi Juda (on the other hand) says: 'He receives forty strokes. Where does he receive the extra one (fortieth)? Between the shoulders.' " Tract. *Makkot* iii. 10.

(stroke with the) thong too many and he. dies, then shall he be banished for this.

"If he (the criminal during the infliction of the strokes) defiles himself either by evacuation or by urine, he is free (of punishment)."

Tract. *Makkot* iii. 11: "If he has been sentenced to receive forty strokes, (and) he has received a part of the strokes, (and) it is said that he cannot endure the forty, then he is free."

This cruel torture, carried out amid the reading of Scripture, was endured by Paul five times. Each time he received, as he expressly records, the full permitted number of strokes, even though as we know from his letters he was delicate and sickly. Although he was a Roman citizen he submitted himself as a Jew to the jurisdiction of the Synagogue authorities of the town in which he happened to be.

The beating with rods he suffered at the hands of the Roman authorities. Properly speaking, his Roman citizenship should have protected him from this. No doubt in these three cases he was given no time to appeal effectively to it. How ready the Roman authorities were to inflict corporal punishment is shown on the occasion of Paul's arrest in Jerusalem. Scarcely has the officer of the guard who has rescued him from the Jews brought him into the castle when he proposes to "examine him by scourging" in order to extract the truth regarding the Jewish charges against him (Acts xxii. 24).

Thus Paul, Jew by race and Roman citizen, experienced at the hands of both Jewish and Roman authorities ill-treatment, of the extent of which we should have had no idea if he had not been forced in dealing with the Corinthians to make a catalogue of his sufferings in order to prove his claim to Apostleship by showing what he had endured for Christ's sake.

.   .   .   .   .   .

And the man who in this way, in addition to the hardships and dangers of constant journeyings, underwent imprisonment, stonings, scourgings, and beatings was a sick man. What form his bodily sufferings took cannot be precisely determined from the statements which he made about it. That he suffered from attacks of some kind which were calculated to humiliate him in the eyes of men, we learn from the Epistle to the Galatians. He thanks the Galatians for not spurning or contemning him because of his sufferings.

Gal. iv. 13-14: "You know how amid sickness of the flesh I preached the Gospel to you the former time, and your temptation which was in my flesh you did not despise or spit out, but received me as if I were an angel from heaven, as if Jesus Christ Himself."

It was usual to spit out in the presence of men who had mysterious illnesses, in order to protect oneself against the demon, to whom the sickness in question was attributed. This means of arresting evil was practised especially in the case of epileptics and the mentally afflicted.

The most natural hypothesis is therefore that Paul suffered from some kind of epileptiform attacks, which does not by any means necessarily mean that he was a real epileptic. It would agree with this, that on the Damascus road he hears voices during an attack, and suffers afterwards a temporary affection of the eyesight, if his experience at his conversion really happened during such an attack (Acts ix. 3-9). A rapture into the third heaven and into Paradise, during which he heard unspeakable words, is thought of by Paul as a special mercy which has been granted to him (2 Cor. xii. 1-4).

2 Cor. xii. 1-4: "If I am to boast, though boasting is not an expedient thing, I will come to visions and revelations of the Lord. I knew a man in Christ Jesus, who fourteen years ago—whether in the body, I know not, or out of the body, I know not—was caught up into the third heaven. And I know that this man—whether in the body or out of the body, I know not, God knows—was caught away into Paradise and heard unspeakable words, which it is not lawful for a man to utter."

It is possible that the rapture into the third heaven and that into Paradise are one and the same experience, which Paul, in the style of the Jewish parallelism, describes twice over.

According to the Slavonic Enoch and the "Life of Adam and Eve," Paradise is situated in the third heaven. *Slav. Enoch*, rec. A, chap. viii. (ed. Bonwetsch, p. 7): "And they brought me to the third heaven and set me in the midst of Paradise." According to the "Life of Adam and Eve" (chap. xxxvii.), Adam after his death is brought by the Archangel Michael to Paradise and into the third heaven. The number of seven heavens which is accepted in the Slavonic Enoch, the Greek Apocalypse of Baruch,[1] the Testament of Levi (chap. iii.), and other writings which originated later than the first century A.D., is no doubt not yet taken for granted in Paul's writings. Before the second century A.D. it was usual in Judaism to enumerate three heavens. This number was arrived at by the Scribes on the basis of a passage in the Book of Kings. In 1 Kings viii. 27 Solomon says of God: "Behold the heaven and the

---

[1] This work, in seventeen chapters, has been edited by M. R. JAMES, *Apocrypha Anecdota*, ii. pp. 84-94.

heaven of heavens cannot contain Him." This makes, according to the Rabbinic exegesis, three heavens. Midrash on Ps. cxiv. § 2: "The Rabbis have said: There are two firmaments (heavens), for it is written 'He that rideth into the heaven of heavens' (Ps. lxviii. 34). Our Teachers have said (There are) three (heavens), for it is written 'The heaven and the heaven of heavens'" (1 Kings viii. 27). See L. STRACK and P. BILLERBECK, *Die Briefe des Neuen Testaments und die Offenbarung Johannis erläutert aus Talmud und Midrasch* (The Epistles of the New Testament and the Revelation of St. John illustrated from Talmud and Midrash), Munich, 1926, p. 531.

According to the Apocalypse of Enoch, which knows only one heaven, Paradise, which it describes as the Garden of the Elect and the Righteous (Enoch lx. 23, lxi. 12), lies at the furthest end of heaven. It serves as dwelling for those who are of the fellowship of the Son of Man. To this Paradise Enoch is translated at the end of his life (*Hen.* lx. 8, lxx. 3). Whether Paul, who only counted three heavens, thinks of Paradise as lying in the third heaven (as the later writers do, who hold that there are seven heavens) we do not know. If Paradise is not a part of the third heaven, then there is reference in 2 Cor. xii. 1-4 not to one only, but to two ecstatic experiences.

By the pains which he has to bear Paul comes to be aware that he is a sick man. He explains this as due to an angel of Satan's being permitted to buffet him, in order that he may not be exalted above measure by the privilege of having been rapt into the third heaven and into Paradise.

2 Cor. xii. 6-9: "But I restrain myself, that no man may think of me more highly than he ought to think, even in respect of the abundant revelations. In order that I might not be exalted above measure, there was given me a thorn in the flesh, an angel of Satan to buffet me, that I might not be exalted above measure. About this I have three times besought the Lord that he might depart from me. And He said to me: My grace must be sufficient for thee, for strength is made perfect in weakness."

What was the character of his pains, and how they were connected with the attacks, is not clear. But how greatly Paul must have suffered when he can speak thus of them!

.   .   .   .   .   .

And not for a moment of his life was this so often maltreated sick man safe. How much must be behind those words "perils from my own people!" (2 Cor. xi. 26). The Hellenistic Jews, of whom, as one of themselves, he had been a leader at the stoning

of Stephen, had sworn his death.[1] From the moment when he returned to Jerusalem as a converted man (Acts ix. 29) they constantly plotted against him, not only because he had become a
believer in Christ, but also, and more especially, because he declared circumcision and the Law to be no longer valid. What a
light is thrown upon his precarious life by the brief statement that,
when returning home from Corinth to Jerusalem, instead of
crossing by ship to Asia Minor as he had planned, he was obliged
to travel by the land route through Macedonia in order to evade
an attack which had been planned by the Jews (Acts xx. 3)! After
his arrest at Jerusalem forty Jews took an oath neither to eat nor
drink until they had killed him; so that the captain of the guard,
informed of the plot by Paul's nephew, decided to send him away
by night hastily and secretly with a strong military escort—400
footmen and 70 horsemen—to conduct him in safety to Caesarea
(Acts xxiii. 12-24).

Not less persistent was the persecution of the zealots for Jewish
Christianity, though their enmity was directed not against his
life, but against his teaching and his work. Behind them stood the
Apostles at Jerusalem. His teaching, that converts from heathenism
did not need to take upon them the burden of circumcision and the
Law, was to the believers at Jerusalem unintelligible and intolerable.

The attempt to make an agreement on the basis that Paul
should devote himself to the Gentiles, while the Apostles at
Jerusalem should reserve to themselves the Mission to all the
Jews, proved to be impossible in practice, if it was ever seriously
meant.[2] A local division was also impossible in view of the position of matters. In the struggle which followed it was Paul who
was defeated. The leaders at Jerusalem did not find it difficult,
by means of their emissaries, to estrange his churches from him.

---

[1] Jews of Cilician and Asian origin at Jerusalem, together with other Hellenistic Jews, had disputed with Stephen and accused him before the Council
(Act. vi. 8-14). At the stoning, at which the witnesses must cast the first stones
(Deut. xvii. 7), these, to free their hands, laid down their garments at the feet
of Saul of Tarsus in Cilicia, who is thus shown to have been the leader in the
action (Act. vii. 58). The mention of the witnesses and of the part which they
played in the stoning shows clearly that the stoning of Stephen was not the act
of an excited mob, but a regular execution, such as is described in the Mishna
tractate "Sanhedrin" (German translation by Gustav HÖLSCHER, Tübingen,
1910: 143 pp.; pp. 75-78).

[2] How wide is the diversity between Acts xv. and Gal. ii. even in the interpretation of the attempted agreement !

On his side he had only truth; they had on their side tradition and commonsense, which clearly asserted that whoever wished to share in the hopes of the people of Israel must attach themselves to it by circumcision and the observance of the Law. Paul had nothing to fall back upon but the authority of his own personality, while they had behind them that of the Church. That there was even then something in the nature of a church, and that the Jerusalem community incorporated this church, is usually denied. It was however the fact. For the Christians of the churches in Asia Minor and Greece the Church at Jerusalem was an authority, in the same sense and to the same extent as the Sanhedrin was for the Synagogues of the Diaspora. The collection which they made for it was not so much a gift sent to the poor as a levy comparable with the Temple tax of the Jewish proselytes, which they paid to it.[1] And what pains Paul takes, as we see from the Epistle to the Corinthians, to ensure that through his efforts the tribute shall be a large one! On his arrival, however, it is laid upon him by the Apostles that he should take upon him a vow along with four designated men, in order to make plain to the world that he walks according to the Law. He humbly accepts, but the vow they forced upon him becomes fatal to him. As in the fulfilment of it he stands with shaven head in the Temple, Jews from Asia Minor recognise him and raise a tumult against him, which leads to his arrest (Acts xxi. 20-36).

The personal authority which the Apostle to the Gentiles could oppose to that of the Jerusalem church was not great. At moments violent, and then again extremely submissive, he can have organised no considered resistance. He is only a thinker, not a tactician. His violence no less than his submissiveness puts him in disadvantageous positions. The reflections, open or indirect, which he makes upon the original Apostles go so far that they put him in the wrong and give them a weapon which can be turned against him. He indulges in irony about the respect which is paid to them; charges one of them, Peter, with hypocrisy before all the believers of Antioch;[2] claims a higher place than they, because he has done

---

[1] Karl HOLL shows a clear grasp of the question in his full and reliable study *Der Kirchenbegriff des Paulus in seinem Verhältnis zu dem Urgemeinde*. See also p. 31, *sup.*

[2] Gal. ii. 11-14. Peter had then at first sat down to table with the Gentile Christians, but ceased to do so when some persons from the circle of James the Just arrived.

and suffered more; hints that they are in favour of circumcision in order to avoid the persecutions which the true teaching of the Cross of Christ brought upon those who preached it; and finally asserts, in the terrible excitement in which he threw off the second Epistle to the Corinthians, nothing more or less than that they in their blindness, and deceived by Satan, are actually serving Satan's cause against the Church.

Gal. ii. 6: "But if those who seemed to be somewhat—whatsoever they were makes no matter to me; God accepts no man's person."— 2 Cor. xi. 5: "For I hold that I am in no way inferior to those who are Super-Apostles" (τῶν ὑπερλίαν ἀποστόλων). Similarly in 2 Cor. xii. 11.— 1 Cor. xv. 10: "I have laboured more than they all."—Gal. v. 10: "He who troubles you shall bear his punishment, whosoever it may be."— Gal. v. 12: "I would that they were unmanned that trouble you."— Gal. vi. 12: "They force you to be circumcised only in order that they may have no persecution through the Cross of Christ."—2 Cor. xi. 13-15: "Such men are false apostles, deceitful workers giving themselves the appearance of Apostles of Christ. And this is no wonder, for Satan himself disguises himself as an angel of light, so that it is in no way strange if his servants disguise themselves as servants of righteousness, and their end will be according to their deeds."

In this last passage Paul does not directly name the Apostles at Jerusalem. But he can hardly have meant any others by "those who are 'Super-Apostles' " (2 Cor. xi. 5). It is these that he has in view in these last chapters of 2nd Corinthians.

That Paul was sometimes again inconceivably compliant is evident from the fact that his opponents could assert (Gal. v. 11) that he still preached circumcision. According to Acts. xvi. 2 he circumcised Timothy, and from the involved and uncompleted argument of Gal. ii. 3-5 it is not quite certain that he did not consent to the circumcision of Titus also.

Paul himself at the beginning of the Epistle to the Galatians alludes to the prevalent opinion about him, that he used conciliatory language and sought to please men.

Gal. i. 10: "Do I now seek to conciliate men, or God? Or do I seek to please men?"

.   .   .   .   .   .

But even if his tactics had been better, his cause would have been hopeless. His claim to be an Apostle of Christ, in the same sense as the original Apostles and James, could not be substantiated. The others had their authority in virtue of having been called by Christ when He walked on earth, or of near relationship to Him. And Paul claims the same authority, only in order to oppose their views regarding the Law and circumcision. His deeper knowledge of the scope and significance of the death and resurrection of Jesus compels him to do so. The Apostle of the Gentiles is the first to oppose the authority of the Church; the first also to feel its weight.

At the end of his three years' sojourn at Ephesus, which lasted from about 54–57, his defeat must have been evident to him. The churches of Galatia had fallen away from him. In Corinth his authority had been undermined. His opponents here pour scorn upon him, alleging that he does not venture to claim to be supported by the churches, because he knows himself not to be an Apostle (2 Cor. xi. 7-9). They say that in his Letters he talks big against them, but when it comes to word of mouth he is weak, and imputes his repeated delays in coming to his fear of them (2 Cor. x. 1-2, x. 10, i. 23). Further, no reliance can be placed upon his word (2 Cor. i. 17). He writes something different from what he means (2 Cor. i. 13); he uses guile (2 Cor. xii. 16-17); he is fond of boasting (2 Cor. iii. 1); he has become a fool in his self-exaltation (2 Cor. xi. 1, xi. 16, xii. 11).

Even though by the greatness of his personality he may again and again defeat such adversaries, and though churches like that of the Philippians show their love of him, he cannot in the long run make headway against the authority of Jerusalem. He cannot hope even to get clear of the enmity against him which takes its rise there.

By the time when he wrote, at Corinth, his Epistle to the Romans, in order to keep a clear road open to him in the West, it must have become evident to him that further work in the regions of his earlier activity was for the present barred to him by the enmity of the Jews, and the opposition which emanated from the Apostles at Jerusalem. But this only strengthened him in his conviction that it was appointed to him to carry the knowledge of the Gospel to regions where it had not been preached.

This man, maltreated, sick, going in constant danger of his life, had thus in addition an excessive burden of mental and spiritual troubles to endure. But he understood the meaning of that suffering. It is because he alone dares to speak out the full truth about the significance of the Cross that he has to suffer the greatest persecution. In this it is made manifest that he alone is the true Apostle of Jesus Christ, even though his right to bear this name is denied. Behind all the troubles he encounters stand those Angel-powers, who have directed their enmity against him because he is endeavouring to prevent men from falling again under their dominion owing to false ideas about the Law and circumcision. Even though, like a man condemned to death in the arena, he has become "a spectacle to angels and to men" (1 Cor. iv. 9), he knows that that only shows how far he has already advanced in the dying with Christ, and accordingly, how vigorously the life of Christ is unfolding itself in him. Thus in the end his sufferings come to mean more to him than even being caught up into the third heaven and into Paradise. He closes the record of his ecstasy and of his bodily sufferings with the enthusiastic, "Now I will most gladly boast of my weakness, that the power of Christ may dwell in me. Therefore I rejoice in weakness, ill-treatment, hardship, persecution and affliction for Christ's sake. For when I am weak, then am I strong" (2 Cor. xii. 9-10).

CHAPTER VIII

IN regarding the possession of the Spirit as a sign of the resurrection which is already in process of being realised in the believer, Paul is asserting something which, from the point of view of an eschatology which has Christ's death and resurrection behind it, is self-evident, but which was not foreseen in the thought of the traditional eschatology, the teaching of Jesus, or the belief of the primitive Christian community.

According to the prophetic eschatology the Messiah of David's line is endowed with the Spirit of God, and thereby becomes capable of bringing in the Kingdom of Peace. In Ezekiel this conception widens into the view that the whole Messianic people becomes the bearer of the Spirit. That is also what Jeremiah means when he makes the New Covenant consist in God's writing it, His Law, into all hearts and upon all minds. Deutero-Isaiah also expects that the Spirit shall come upon all. For this prophetic conception, therefore, the Messianic Kingdom consists in the Messiah and all his subjects being guided in all their thinking and doing by the Spirit of God.

Isa. xi. 1-2: "There shall grow up a shoot out of the stem of Jesse and a branch shall grow out of his roots. And the spirit of Jahwe shall descend upon him, the Spirit of wisdom and understanding, the spirit of counsel and of power, the spirit of knowledge and of the fear of Jahwe."

Ezek. xxxvi. 26-27: "And I will give you a new heart and put a new spirit in your inward parts. . . . And I will put my spirit within you and will cause you to walk in my statutes and keep my ordinances and to do according to them."

Jer. xxxi. 33: "Therein shall the covenant consist, which I will make with the House of Israel after this time, saith the oracle of Jahwe. I will put my law into their inward parts and write it in their hearts, and so will I be their God and they shall be my people."

Isa. xliv. 2: "My Spirit will I pour out upon thy (Jacob's) seed."

Isa. lix. 21: "As for me, this is my covenant with them, saith Jahwe. My Spirit that is upon thee, and my words which I have put into thy mouth, shall not depart out of thy mouth, or out of the mouth of thy seed's seed, saith Jahwe, from henceforth and for ever."

The Servant of the Lord is also described as a bearer of the Spirit (Isa. xlii. 1).

In the later eschatology the view that the Spirit was the life-principle of the participants in the Messianic Kingdom was given up. The coming of the Spirit becomes one of the miraculous events which, with others of like kind, proclaims the nearness of the Judgment of God. This transformation appears in the famous passage of the Book of Joel, which no doubt originated in the second or third century B.C.

Joel iii. 1-4 (A.V. ii. 28-31): "And afterwards I will pour out my Spirit upon all flesh; and your sons and your daughters shall prophesy, your old men shall dream dreams and your young men shall see visions. Also upon the bondmen and bondwomen will I pour out my Spirit in those days. And I will cause signs to appear in heaven and upon earth; blood, and fire, and columns of smoke. The sun shall be turned into darkness and the moon into blood before the coming of the great and terrible day of Jahwe."

This new conception of the coming of the Spirit is explained by the fact that the place of the Messianic Kingdom has been taken by the Kingdom of God. If the Kingdom is no longer under the headship of the anointed ruler of the race of David, then the view associated with this, that the participants in the Kingdom will be bearers of the Spirit, also naturally disappears. It was therefore the transcendental character of the expectation of the future, which superseded the prophetic view of the Coming of the Spirit.

In the eschatology of the Book of Daniel and the Apocalypse of Enoch the outpouring of the Spirit no longer plays the part even of a Sign of the End.

The Psalms of Solomon revert to the prophetic expectation, expecting as the ruler of the Last times a Son of David "whom God has made strong in the holy Spirit" (Ps. Sol. xvii. 37 (42)). It is not said, however, that the participants in the Kingdom will also be bearers of the Spirit.

.   .   .   .   .

John the Baptist combines the general outpouring of the Spirit, prophesied by Joel, with the coming of Elijah, which in Malachi is looked to similarly as belonging to the Last Days.

Mal. iii. 23-24 (A.V. iv. 5-6): "Verily I will send you the prophet Elias before the coming of the Day of Jahwe, that great and terrible day; he shall reconcile the fathers with (their) sons and the sons with their fathers, that I come not and smite the land with a curse." [1]

In the Apocalypse of Ezra (4 Ezra vi. 23-26) there appears the men "who in past times have been rapt away to heaven and have not tasted death from their birth" (*i.e.* Enoch, Elijah, and Ezra) at the end of the Final Tribulation, whereupon the "hearts of the inhabitants of the earth are altered and changed to a new spirit." Here the appearing of Elijah and the outpouring of the spirit are associated together, as they are by the Baptist.

The Baptist expects, therefore, that "He that shall come" shall "baptize men with the holy Spirit." He sees it as his own mission to be the forerunner of this one "who is to come," and to call men to repentance, that they may be capable of receiving the Spirit which is to be poured forth at his coming. He who is now baptized with water to repentance receives an initiation, by which he will then become a bearer of the Spirit, and at the same time a sign by which he will be known as one to be delivered from the Judgment.

That the view that the Baptist meant the Messiah by the designation "He who is to come" should have held its ground in the critical interpretation of the New Testament down to the most recent times, shows how difficult it is even for scientific study to displace the traditional view in favour of the right one.

He-who-is-to-come is Elias, who is to come down from heaven. No natural man could come forward with the claim to be this Elias, forerunner of the Messiah. And, on the other hand, expectation is not directed to the coming of the Messiah but, in the first place, to the appearing of "Him-who-is-to-come," that is, Elias. Until he is first come, the Messiah cannot appear.

How was it possible so long to misconstrue the clear language of the passage in which the Baptist's question to Jesus is narrated? The disciples of the Baptist put to Jesus, on his behalf, the question whether

---

[1] According to the Rabbis, Elias will decide all controversies which have not been decided from the times before the coming of the Messiah. See K. Heinrich RENGSTORF, *Jebamot* (Concerning Brother-in-Law Marriage), Giessen, 1929, p. 150.

He (Jesus) was "He who-is-to-come" (ὁ ἐρχόμενος, Mt. xi. 3). After they have been sent away with an obscure message—for He cannot yet make known the secret of His future Messiahship—Jesus reveals to the multitude which surrounds Him that the Baptist himself is the Elias who was to come ('Ηλείας ὁ μέλλων ἔρχεσθαι, Mt. xi. 14). And from that saying it is clearly evident that the Baptist in his question—and of course also in his preaching—by his "Him who is to come" meant Elias.

The revelation that the Baptist is himself the Elias who was to come is communicated by Jesus to His hearers as something difficult to understand. Mt. xi. 14-15: "*And if ye will receive it*, he is Elias who was to come. He that hath ears to hear, let him hear."

As a matter of fact, Jesus does violence to reality by this identification. Neither the picture of Elias given in the Scriptures, nor that drawn by John, is applicable to the Baptist, who is, and desires to be, nothing more than the preacher of Elias' coming. It is Jesus' own consciousness of His own person and mission which compels Him to make the Baptist into Elias. If He Himself is the future Messiah, then Elias must have already come. Therefore the Baptist is Elias." [1]

The Baptist goes beyond Joel in holding that the outpouring of the Spirit is not merely a miracle announcing the coming of the Times of the End, which might manifest itself in any chance person, but that it happens only to those who are destined to have a part in the Coming Kingdom, and who repent in preparation for it.

Jesus sees in Himself a bearer of the Spirit, and explains the miracles which He performs as being done by the Spirit. The assertion that they are not done in the power of the holy Spirit but in that of the chief of the demons He characterises as the sin against the holy Spirit, which can never be forgiven, even though all other sins, even blasphemy against the Son of Man, may find forgiveness (Mt. xii. 22-32).

In sending out the disciples on their mission, He holds out to them the prospect that in the Tribulation which is about to break out, when they will be brought before rulers for His sake, they shall find that the Spirit of God is speaking out of their mouths. He therefore shares with the Baptist the view of the Book of Joel,

---

[1] On this problem see Albert SCHWEITZER, *Das Messianitats- und Leidensgeheimnis*, Tübingen, 1901, pp. 44-48 (2nd, unaltered, edition, 1929), and *Geschichte der Leben-Jesu-Forschung*, Tübingen, 1906, 2nd edition (1913) and following editions, pp. 418-420.

that the outpouring of the Spirit is an event which indicates the immediate imminence of the End. The End means for Him the Coming of the Son of Man.

Matt. x. 17-23: "They will deliver you up to Councils and will scourge you in their Synagogues; and will bring you before Governors and Kings for my sake, for a witness to them and to the peoples. And when they bring you up for judgment, take no thought how or what you shall speak. For it is not you that speak, but the Spirit of your Father which speaks in you. . . . But he who endures to the end shall be saved. When they persecute you in one town, flee to another. Verily, I say unto you, you will not have gone over the towns in Israel before the Son of Man comes."

It is to be noticed that Jesus never represents the being-in-the-Kingdom-of-God as the being in possession of the Spirit. He assumes that the partakers in the Kingdom of God are already in possession of the resurrection state of existence. As those who have passed through the resurrection, they have no need of the Spirit. Only when the partakers in the Kingdom are thought of as natural men is there any purpose in representing them as endowed with the Spirit. Paul was the first to arrive at the conception of risen men who are also vehicles of the Spirit. Jesus combines in a simple fashion the view of the older Prophets with that of Joel by holding with the Prophets that He Himself, as called to be the Messiah, is the vehicle of the Spirit, and expecting with Joel the outpouring of the Spirit as a sign of the beginning of the End.

The occurrence of ecstatic phenomena in the Apostles at Pentecost, and later on among believers in general, was held by the primitive Christian Community to be the fulfilment of the prophecy of Joel. Peter's speech makes express reference to the Joel passage (Acts ii. 16-21). In the phenomena of ecstatic speech and in the gift of prophecy which appeared in various places the believers' hope, based on the death and resurrection of Christ, of the immediate nearness of the Messianic Kingdom, was apprehensible by the senses in a fact which constantly recurred. In his estimation of these facts in which faith seemed most clearly to apprehend its object, Paul was at one with primitive Christianity in general. But he cannot, like others, rest content with regarding the working of the Spirit as a miracle by itself; as a thinker he finds himself obliged to bring it into connection with the fact of the death and resurrection of Christ, and with his conception of the mode of being in the Messianic Kingdom. In accordance with this he explains it as a manifestation of the having-died and having-risen-again with Christ.

.   .   .   .

For naïve thinking the Spirit of God is manifested in natural man in the natural world by a miracle promised beforehand by God. For a deeper knowledge the matter takes a different aspect. If God's Spirit is poured out after the resurrection of Christ, that means that it is poured out in consequence of that resurrection. The Spirit of God is in men only since men have been "in Christ Jesus," and in union with His corporeity have also part in the Spirit of God by which this is animated. The holy Spirit, therefore, comes to the believer from Christ and as the Spirit of Christ. It is through the being-in-Christ that they have part in it. Not as natural men, but as those who are actually dying and rising again with Christ, are they vehicles of the Spirit. The conception of the early prophets, that the Messiah and the partakers in the Messianic Kingdom all possess the Spirit, is changed by Paul into the form that the Spirit of the Messiah passes over to the partakers in the Kingdom.

For the customary ways of thought the Spirit which manifests itself in believers is the Spirit of revelation, which was present in the prophets and in Christ. It is in this way that the First Epistle of Peter attributes the Spirit of Christ to the prophets.

1 Peter i. 10-11: "The salvation about which the prophets enquired and sought diligently, who prophesied of the grace which should come into you, seeking what or what manner of time the Spirit of Christ which was in them was pointing to, when it testified to the sufferings which were coming to Christ and the glory which should follow."

But for Paul the Spirit of Christ in which the believers have part is much more all-embracing than the former prophetic spirit. It is the life-principle of His Messianic personality and of the state of existence characteristic of the Messianic Kingdom. As such it is something unique, not previously known. As the predestined sharers in the glory of the Messiah, believers have a part in His Spirit.

Paul thus draws the full inference from the fact that the Spirit which has been granted to believers is the Spirit of Christ, and that the outpouring of the Spirit follows in point of time upon the resurrection of Christ. What ordinary beliefs regarded as a miracle of the pre-Messianic times becomes for him an essential event of the Messianic time. His conviction, that with the resurrection of Jesus the supernatural world-period has begun, makes itself felt in his thinking in all directions, and determines also his conception of the Spirit. Paul thus inevitably comes to see in the manifestation of the Spirit an efflorescence of the Messianic glory within the natural world.

By bringing the miracle of the presence of the Spirit into connection with the Person of Christ as the Coming Messiah, and with the expected supernatural state of being of the believers in the Messianic Kingdom, Paul, passing over Joel, arrives back at the original prophetic view of the Spirit as the life-principle common to the Messiah and the members of his Kingdom. He fits this in with the expectation of the future, now become transcendental, by conceiving of the Spirit not only as a spiritual and ethical principle, like the representatives of the prophetic Messianic expectation, nor as a phenomenon of revelation, like Joel, but, in addition, as the power which communicates the resurrection mode of existence.

From the point of view of a deeper understanding, therefore, the dominant force of the situation is that the Spirit is the form of manifestation of the powers of the resurrection. Through their possession of the Spirit believers have the assurance of sharing in the same resurrection with Christ. The Spirit is the earnest, given to be a possession of their hearts, of the coming glory. As the vehicle of the resurrection-Spirit which is bestowed upon the Elect, Christ becomes the ancestor of an immortal race of men. He is the heavenly Adam, who takes the place of the earthly.

Rom. viii. 11: "If the Spirit of Him who raised up Jesus from the dead is in you, then shall He who raised up Jesus Christ from the dead also make alive your mortal bodies through the Spirit which dwells in you."

2 Cor. i. 22: "God, who has sealed us and has given us the earnest of the Spirit which is in our hearts."

1 Cor. xv. 45-49: "The first man, Adam, became a living soul; the last Adam has become a life-giving Spirit. . . . the first man is of the earth earthy, the second man is from heaven. . . . As we have borne the image of the earthy, so shall we also bear the image of the heavenly."

The Pauline doctrine of Christ as the Second Adam is so naturally explained from the mystical doctrine of the dying and rising again with Christ, and of the partaking of believers in the Spirit of Christ, that there are no grounds for connecting it with the Persian myth of the primal man Gayomart, with the Indian primal man Purusha, or the doctrine of the primal man in the Hellenistic tractate *Poimandres*. Nor has the incorporeal primal man, who (according to Philo) was before Adam and Eve, anything to do with those speculations. Philo deduces his existence from exegetical considerations regarding the presence of two accounts of the creation of man (Gen. i. 26-27, ii. 15-25).

As a pre-existent Being, Christ should really be designated in Paul's argument as the First Adam. But it is by His coming in the flesh and His dying and rising again that He first becomes man, from whom a new humanity can go forth. Since the humanity destined to Messianic glory, which takes its rise from Him, follows as the second humanity after the humanity which proceeds from Adam, Paul speaks of Him as the Second Adam. This designation should in itself be sufficient to make it clear that he has nothing to do with the primal man of the Indian, Persian, or Hellenistic myths. For He is thus not a Primal Man, but a Second Adam, and this in consequence of His resurrection, by which He becomes the Ancestor of those who are appointed to the resurrection. The Second Adam is, in Paul, an eschatological not a mythical conception.

.   .   .   .   .   .

The possession of the Spirit proves to believers that they are already removed out of the natural state of existence and transferred into the supernatural. They are "in the Spirit," which means that they are no longer in the flesh. For being in the Spirit is only a form of manifestation of the being-in-Christ. Both are descriptions of one and the same state.

As a consequence of being in the Spirit, believers are raised above all the limitations of the being-in-the-flesh. Through the Spirit the true Circumcision, that of the heart, is accomplished in them. In the Spirit the New Covenant comes into being. The Spirit is the New Law which gives life, whereas the Old Law, that of the letter, only made sin manifest and thereby delivered the man over to death. The Spirit gives believers the assurance that they are Children of God, and are justified in His sight. Through the Spirit they feel in their hearts the love with which they are loved by God.

Rom. viii. 1-2: "There is therefore now no condemnation for those who are in Christ Jesus. For the Law of the Spirit of Life in Christ Jesus has made them free from the Law of sin and death."

Rom. ii. 28-29: "He is not a Jew who is one externally, and circumcision is not that which is external in the flesh, but he is a Jew who is so in the secret life, and circumcision is a circumcision of the heart, in the Spirit, not a literal thing."—Phil. iii. 3: "For we are the Circumcision, we who pray to God in the Spirit, and have our boasting in Christ and do not trust in the flesh."

2 Cor. iii. 6: "God who has made us capable of becoming servants of the New Covenant, the covenant not of the letter but of the Spirit. For the letter kills, but the Spirit makes alive."

Gal. v. 18: "If your motive power is the Spirit, you are not under the Law."—Rom. vii. 6: "But now we are set free from the Law, having died to that in which we were held fast, that we might serve in the new existence of the Spirit and not in the old one of the letter."

Gal. iv. 6: "Since you are sons, God has sent forth the Spirit of His Son into our hearts, who there cries 'Abba, Father'."—Rom. viii. 14-16: "For so many as are moved by the Spirit of God, they are the Sons of God. You have not received a spirit of servility nor of fear, but a Spirit of Sonship in which we cry, 'Abba, Father'. The Spirit Himself witnesses to our spirit that we are God's children."

Gal. v. 5: "We await in the Spirit, through faith (the fulfilment of) the hope of (being pronounced) righteous."—Rom. viii. 4: "That the ordinances of the Law might be fulfilled in us, who walk not after the Law but after grace."—Rom. viii. 10: "But if Christ is in you, the body is dead because of sin, but the Spirit is Life because of righteousness."—1 Cor. vi. 11: "You have been justified through the name of the Lord Jesus Christ and the Spirit of our God."

Rom. v. 5: "The love of God is poured out in our hearts through the holy Spirit that is given to us."

Being in the Spirit, it rests with the believer to decide whether he will be in earnest about it, and consistently live in the Spirit. He must resolve to let the Spirit rule completely in all his thought, speech, and action. He must not suppose that he can be in the Spirit and at the same time live in the flesh. For those who are in Christ and in the Spirit, their being in the flesh is only a matter of outward appearance, not a real state of existence. This relation the elect man has to preserve by freeing himself from the thoughts and desires of his natural Ego, and submitting in all things to the ethical direction of the Spirit. If by his conduct he allows the being-in-the-flesh again to become a reality, he gives up the being-in-the-Spirit and the resurrection state of existence, of which this is the pledge.

Gal. v. 16-17: "Walk in the Spirit, and you shall not fulfil the desires of the flesh. For the flesh has desires contrary to the Spirit, and the Spirit contrary to the flesh; these are opposed to one another, in order that you may not do the things which you desire."—Gal. v. 25: "If we live in the Spirit, let us also walk in the Spirit."—Gal. vi. 7-8: "What a man soweth, that shall he also reap. He who sows to the flesh, will of the flesh reap corruption; but he who sows to the Spirit, will of the Spirit reap eternal life."—1 Cor. iii. 16-17: "Do you not know that you are the temple of God, and the Spirit of God dwells in you? If any man destroys the temple of God, him shall God destroy. For the temple of God is holy, and that temple you are."—Rom. viii. 5-6: "Those who are after the flesh think the thoughts which are after the flesh, but those who are after the Spirit think the thoughts that are after the Spirit; for the thoughts of the flesh are death, but the thoughts of the Spirit are life and peace."—Rom. viii. 13: "If you live after the flesh you will die, but if through the Spirit you make dead the deeds of the body, you will live."

.   .   .   .   .   .

In regard to himself, Paul knows that the Spirit acts through him. If his preaching is effectual, that is because it is done in the power of the Spirit; if signs and wonders proceed from him, they are wrought by the Spirit. In the same way all the gifts which manifest themselves in believers, however various they may be, are due to the Spirit. All that is truly spiritual and all exercises of power manifested in miracles proceed from the supernatural principle which is already at work in the world.

1 Thess. i. 5: "For our bringing of the Gospel message to you was not only in word, but in power and in the holy Spirit."—1 Cor. ii. 3-4: "I came to you in much weakness and fear and trembling, and my speech and my preaching were not in persuasive words of wisdom but demonstrations of the Spirit and of power."—Rom. xv. 19: "In power of signs and wonders, in power of the Spirit; so that from Jerusalem and its neighbourhood, even to Illyria, I have fulfilled the preaching of the Gospel of Christ."

Gal. iii. 5: "God who gave you the Spirit and wrought wonders among you."

1 Cor. xii. 4-11: "The gifts of grace are divided, but there is one Spirit; ways of service are divided, but there is the one Master; manifestations of power are divided, but there is one God who worketh all and in all. To each is given the revelation of the Spirit in the way most profitable. To one is given, through the Spirit, to speak with wisdom;

to another to speak with knowledge, by the same Spirit; to another, faith, in the same Spirit; to another, gifts of healing, in the same Spirit; to another, the working of miracles; to another, to prophesy; to another, distinguishing between Spirits; to another, various kinds of tongues; to another, interpretation of the speaking-with-tongues; but all this is wrought by one and the same Spirit, distributing to each as he will."

How fully Paul's actions were determined by the Spirit is evident from his telling us in the Epistle to the Galatians that it was in consequence of a revelation that, at the end of the First Missionary Journey, he went up to the Apostles at Jerusalem (Gal. ii. 2). In the Acts of the Apostles the Spirit prescribes to Paul and his companions the route to be followed at the beginning of the First Missionary Journey. The Spirit does not allow them to preach in the Province of Asia, and also not to go into Bithynia (Acts xvi. 6-7).

.   .   .   .   .   .

Of the manifestations of the Spirit the common judgment rated highest the ecstatic "speaking-with-tongues" (*glossolalia*), which occurred during divine service, since it was the most patent to the senses. Paul, however, values most highly the work of the Spirit in edification, and in the advancement of spiritual life which comes about through it. He therefore opposes the excessive estimate of the *glossolalia*, although, he thanks God, it is granted to him in fuller measure than to others (1 Cor. xiv. 18). He desires that it should not occupy too large a space in public worship, as was happening in Corinth. Speaking with tongues is, he pronounces, a speaking with God, of which others understand nothing. Therefore he would rather speak five words with the understanding, and to the edification of others, than ten thousand in ecstatic speech (1 Cor. xiv. 19). Ecstatic speech is for him a praying to God, in which the Spirit of God, dwelling in the man, brings before God in sighings which cannot be uttered those longings for deliverance from mortality, which are intense beyond all thought and word (Rom. viii. 26). Alongside of this prayer of the Spirit of God, "praying with the understanding" must also have its rights (1 Cor. xiv. 14-17). Accordingly, in the fourteenth chapter of the First Epistle to the Corinthians, where he is dealing with the matters connected with divine service, he ordains that on any particular occasion only two or three ecstatic speakers shall come forward, and that only when there is one present who possesses the gift of being able to interpret this ecstatic speech. If there are no interpreters present the ecstatic speaker shall not take part in divine service at all, but let him rather converse with God at home (1 Cor. xiv. 28).

Prophets—although their prophesyings were intelligible to all and served to edification—were only to speak two or three, one after another. If any one should make known, whilst a prophet is speaking, that he has received a revelation, the prophet is to be silent and give place to this man (1 Cor. xiv. 24-33).

An opportunity for their activities was afforded to the ecstatic speakers and the prophets by the thanksgiving of the Lord's Supper. This was the main feature of the service. At the celebration, according to the account which has come down to us in the Didache (the "Teaching of the Twelve Apostles," chaps. ix.-x.), there were three thanksgivings—one at the cup, one at the breaking of bread, and the other at the end of the feast.[1] How far this corresponds to the primitive Christian celebration we do not know. The important point is that we learn from the Didache the character of the Thanksgiving. It refers not only to the feast but also to the expected Kingdom and glory. And it is not confined to thanksgiving, but includes an ardent supplication for future blessings. It is thus easy to understand why the thanksgiving was committed to those who possessed the gift of ecstatic speech and to the prophets.

In the Didache, in which a form of thanksgiving prayer is already laid down, it is expressly remarked that in addition to this the prophets are to be allowed to give thanks as much as they will.

That Paul, in spite of sharing with his contemporaries the high estimation of the sensible manifestations of the spiritual, maintains with such decision the higher right of the rational manifestations of the spiritual, is a fact of tremendous importance.

Here too he shows himself as a thinker who goes to the heart of things. How sure an instinct guided him could first be appreciated by men of the present day, who have learned to recognise ecstatic speech as a merely psycho-physical phenomenon.

And what courage it must have demanded at that time, and especially in face of the Corinthians, who were so proud of the ebullient utterances of the Spirit in that assembly, to maintain

---

[1] The *Didache* was supposed to be lost until the Nicomedian Metropolitan, Philotheos Bryennios, in 1874 discovered a MS. (dated A.D. 1056) which contained it complete. The MS. was then at Constantinople, but is now No. 54 in the Patriarchal Library at Jerusalem. The text was first published by Bryennios in 1883.

the higher right of those spiritual manifestations which were in accordance with reason. Hardly anywhere else does Paul appear so markedly as possessing the greatness which not only belongs to its own time, but also stands above it, as in this fourteenth chapter of First Corinthians.

.   .   .   .   .   .

To have understanding in the Spirit, which Paul places above speaking in the Spirit, consists in being able to search the deep things of God, and understand "the Word of the Cross" (1 Cor. i. 18), which to earthly wisdom is folly, in its full content. What the natural man cannot understand (1 Cor. ii. 14), and what indeed had remained hidden even from the Angels (1 Cor. ii. 8), is made known by God to the Elect through His Spirit. The content of this inner revelation is the knowledge of the whole mystery of the dying and rising again with Christ.

1 Cor. ii. 10-13: "But to us God has unveiled it by the Spirit; for the Spirit searches all things, even the abysses of God. For who of men knows the thoughts of a man, except the spirit of the man which is in him? Even so, none knows the thoughts of God, except the Spirit of God. For we have not received the spirit of the world, but the Spirit of God, to the end that we might know what has been bestowed upon us by God. Of which we speak, not in words taught us by human wisdom but in words taught by the Spirit, interpreting spiritual things to spiritual men."

It is on the basis of revelations which came to him from the Spirit that Paul gives his decisions upon questions of belief and conduct. It is as a 'mystery', that is, as knowledge given by the Spirit, that he communicates to the Corinthians that at the coming of Christ both those who are still alive and the dead (meaning the dead in Christ) shall alike at once receive immortality ('incorruptibility', 1 Cor. xv. 51-52). And he makes the same communication to the Thessalonians (iv. 15-18) as "a Word of the Lord." He treats as a word received from Christ that which is revealed to him by the Spirit of Christ.

It is just because he receives communications direct from Christ through the Spirit that he can leave aside the teaching of Jesus of Nazareth as recorded by tradition. The alteration in world-conditions through the precedent death and resurrection of Jesus is so great that the teaching of Jesus, prior to it, can no longer be applied to it without more ado, and compels Paul to take up a creative attitude alongside of Jesus, and give the Gospel the form necessary to adapt it to the changed conditions. The certitude which he acquires from the revelation given him by the Spirit of Christ makes it possible for him to carry out this necessary task.

So far as possible he avoids quoting anything from the preaching of Jesus, or, indeed, mentioning it at all. If we had been dependent on him for our knowledge, we should not have known that Jesus spoke in parables, preached the Sermon on the Mount, or taught His disciples the Lord's Prayer. Paul even fails to mention sayings of Jesus in connections where they lay directly to his hand. For example, he quotes the command "Thou shalt love thy neighbour as thyself" as the summing-up of the whole Law, without making any references to the fact that Jesus Himself had spoken to this effect (Gal. v. 14; Rom. xiii. 8-10). To the Corinthians, when justifying himself for not carrying out his announced purpose of coming to them, he makes a detailed statement about making one's yea, yea, and one's nay, nay (2 Cor. i. 17-19). Now, there must lie behind this, in some form or other—perhaps it had been quoted by the Corinthians in writing to him—the saying of Jesus, "Let your speech be yea, yea, and nay, nay: whatsoever is more than these cometh of evil" (Mt. v. 37). But Paul makes no mention of it. Similarly, he is not concerned to establish the point that his exhortation, "Bless those who persecute you" (Rom. xii. 14), reproduces a saying of Jesus.

Indeed, in the Epistle to the Galatians he asserts in the most direct fashion that the Gospel which he preaches is in no way dependent on tradition relating to Christ and His teaching received through men.

Gal. i. 11-12: "For I give you to know, brethren, respecting the Gospel which I preach, that it is not dependent on men. For I have not received or learned it from a man, but through a revelation of Jesus Christ."

Naturally Paul is not able to carry through the theory of his independence of tradition with complete consistency. In his account of the Lord's Supper he is obliged to appeal, when writing to the Corinthians, to the tradition of Jesus' words at the Last Supper with the disciples (1 Cor. xi. 23-25). In support of his view that "they that preach the Gospel should live of the Gospel" he appeals to an ordinance of the Lord which is assumed to be well known (1 Cor. ix. 14). He had, according to 1 Cor. xv. 2, himself received from the tradition the teaching that Jesus according to the Scriptures died for the sins of His people. Probably, also, he is referring to the historic saying of Jesus about divorce (Mt. v. 31-32), when in 1 Cor. vii. 10, as a command from Christ, he forbids married believers to separate from one another ($\pi\alpha\rho\alpha\gamma\gamma\epsilon\lambda\lambda\omega$ $o\dot{v}\kappa$ $\dot{\epsilon}\gamma\dot{\omega}$ $\dot{\alpha}\lambda\lambda\dot{\alpha}$ $\dot{o}$ $\kappa\dot{v}\rho\iota\sigma$).

Apart from these unavoidable concessions to the tradition, Paul abides by the principle that the truth about Christ and redemption is not received from traditional narratives and doctrines, but from revelations given by the Spirit of Jesus Christ. This principle he cannot surrender, because his own interpretation of the death and resurrection of Jesus goes beyond the doctrine applied to Him by the tradition, while his view of liberation from the Law is in contradiction to it.

In 1 Thess. iv. 15 Paul cannot mean by the phrase "by a word of the Lord" ($\dot{\epsilon}\nu$ $\lambda\dot{o}\gamma\dot{\omega}$ $\kappa\nu\rho\dot{\iota}ov$) an utterance of the historic Jesus, but only a revelation of Christ made to him through the Spirit. How could he possibly have possessed a saying of Jesus to the effect that believers who had died since the death of Jesus nevertheless receive, along with those who remain alive at His Return, the resurrection state of existence? Moreover, he informs the Corinthians (1 Cor. xv. 51) that the simultaneous entry of the dead and the survivors upon the resurrection life was "a mystery" ($\mu\nu\sigma\tau\dot{\eta}\rho\iota\sigma\nu$), which can only mean a revelation made to him, not something known from a traditional saying of the Lord.

. . . . . .

Paul does not deal with the problem whether all that professes to be spoken by the Spirit of God really proceeds from the Spirit. He no doubt reckons with the possibility that Satan might disguise himself as an angel of light (2 Cor. xi. 14). But that a demonic spirit might speak with the voice of the Spirit of God he, curiously enough, does not seem to take into account. When anyone, speaking in the Spirit, acknowledges Christ as Lord, he takes it as a proof that the Spirit of God is speaking from him. A Spirit can, in Paul's view, only utter that which is in accordance with its nature.

1 Cor. xii. 3: "Therefore I give you to know that no one speaking in the Spirit of God says 'Jesus is accursed!' And no one can say 'Jesus is Lord!' except by the holy Spirit."

In 1 Cor. xii. 10 there is mentioned as a gift of the spirit the "distinguishing of Spirits" (διάκρισις πνευμάτων). What Paul means by this, we do not know. In any case, it cannot refer to a gift of distinguishing whether divine or demonic spirits are speaking. For, as we have seen, in 1 Cor. xii. 3 every spirit which confesses Christ is to be acknowledged as of a divine character.

This large simplicity in the treatment of utterances of the Spirit was only possible in primitive Christianity. If those who seek to show that the Pauline Epistles originated in the second century and were dated back into primitive Christianity were able to dispose of all the other passages which make against them, they could never deal satisfactorily with these. How could a later writer, who set out to produce primitive Christian Epistles under Paul's name, possibly have ascribed to him such a confiding readiness to acknowledge every spirit which confessed the name of Christ as genuine?

With the rise of Gnosticism, which also made appeal to the Spirit, such a simple-minded attitude as Paul's became untenable. A testing of the spirits became necessary. Such testing is actually prescribed in the First Epistle of John (1 John iv. 1-3). If a spirit confesses that Jesus Christ has come in the flesh ('Ιησοῦν Χριστὸν ἐν σαρκὶ ἐληλυθότα)—i.e. that the Logos was united with Jesus of Nazareth from His birth, and not only from His baptism onwards —it is of God. If its words are contrary to this, it is not of God.

Here it is no longer enough that the spirit should make a general acknowledgment of Christ; it must also hold the correct view in regard to His person. If it represents a Gnostic or a Judaising Christianity, it is not to be accepted as of God.

At the end of the first century the Didache attempted to give directions by which false prophets could be distinguished from true. It will not permit a testing of the content of their prophesying. This it regards as forbidden by Jesus' saying about the sin against the holy Spirit. But those who speak in the Spirit are to be judged upon the ground of their conduct. The somewhat halting explanation shows that by this time the testing of the Spirits was already in measure felt to be desirable, but was not yet boldly ventured on. The necessity, created by Gnosticism, of taking into account the dogmatic position of the Spirit in question had not yet made itself felt at the time of the Didache.

Did. xi. 7-12: "And every prophet who speaks in the spirit, you shall not test nor judge him; for every sin shall be forgiven, but this sin shall not be forgiven. But not everyone who speaks in the spirit is a prophet, but only when he has the way of life of the Lord; by their way of life you can recognise the false and the (true) prophet. And no prophet who with the spirit commands a feast to be prepared eats thereof, unless he be a false prophet. And every prophet, though he may teach what is right, is a false prophet if he does not do what he teaches. . . . If any says in the Spirit 'Give me money,' or the like, do not give heed to him, but if he asks for gifts for the needy, none shall judge him."

About A.D. 150 the author of the "Shepherd of Hermas," who was himself a prophet, also dealt with this thorny problem, still without applying a dogmatic criticism. He grapples with it more practically than the Didache.

Hermas, *Mand.* xi. 8: "In the first place, the man who possesses the spirit from above is gentle, quiet, humble, free from all wickedness and every evil desire for this world. He makes himself of less account than all other men. Never does the divine Spirit give anyone information in answer to questions, nor does he speak in secret for himself, or when someone wants him to speak. On the contrary, the divine Spirit speaks only when God wills that he should speak."—*Mand.* xi. 12-14: "Can a divine Spirit take payment and prophesy for pay? That beseems not a prophet of God; on the contrary, the spirit of such a prophet is of the earth. Further, he does not come at all into the assembly of righteous men, but avoids them. Instead, he associates with doubters and empty men, prophesies to them in corners and cheats them, by talking idle nonsense according to their desires. . . . But if he comes into an assembly of wholly righteous men, who have the divine Spirit, and when they pray, such a man stands there empty. The earthly spirit flees from him for fear, and so he becomes dumb and quite dismayed, so that he can say nothing at all."

One criterion here suggested is, therefore, that he who is truly gifted with the Spirit speaks only at divine Service, while the false claimant speaks elsewhere.

Amid such scruples about the genuineness of the Spirit the voice of Paul, still wholly filled with spiritual ardour, sounds as from another world when he exhorts the Thessalonians (1 Thess. v. 19-20) "Quench not the Spirit! Despise not prophesying!"

CHAPTER IX

MYSTICISM AND THE LAW

It was not necessary for Paul to contend for the idea that Gentiles also are called to the Messianic glory and that the Gospel of Christ was to be preached to them. He found it already in existence; his opponents were as much convinced of it as he was. But when the matter is looked into more closely, it becomes evident that his conviction is of a different kind from theirs, and that from this difference in universalism, and in the motive at the back of the preaching to the Gentiles, results the fact that others think it necessary to impose circumcision and the Law upon converts from heathenism, while he feels bound to oppose them in this.

In order to understand Paul's peculiar position, it is first necessary to make clear to ourselves how universalism arose in Jewish and Christian eschatology, and in what way it implies a preaching to the Gentiles.

Universalism was first introduced into eschatology by the Exilic and post-Exilic prophets. They expect that in the New Zion the Gentile nations will serve God along with Israel.

Zech. ii. 14-15 (A.V. ii. 10-11): "Rejoice and be glad, O daughter of Zion, for I will at once appear and dwell in the midst of thee; such is the oracle of Jahwe! Then in that day, many nations shall join themselves to Jahwe and shall belong to His people."

Zech. viii. 22-23: "Then shall many people and strong nations come to seek Jahwe of Hosts in Jerusalem and to seek the favour of Jahwe. . . . In that day it shall come to pass that ten men out of all languages of the world shall take hold of the skirt of him that is a Jew and say, we will go with you, for we have heard that God is with you."

Isa. lx. 2-3: "Jahwe's glory appeareth over thee (Zion). And the nations shall come to thy light, and Kings to thy resplendence."

Isa. xxv. 6-7: "And Jahwe of Hosts shall prepare for all nations upon this mountain a feast of fat things, of fat things full of marrow, of fermented wine well refined. And He will destroy in this mountain the veil which is upon the face of all nations, and the covering which is spread over all nations."

The eschatology of the Book of Daniel shows a retrogression in this respect. Judaism, contending with the heathen for the maintenance of the faith, loses all sympathy with the idea that these also are to have a share in the Coming Glory. From that point onward universalism hardly maintains a footing in eschatology. Only in the Book of Enoch does it emerge with some clearness.

Enoch xlviii. 4-5: "The Son of Man shall be the light of the nations and the hope of those who are sad at heart. All that dwell upon the earth shall fall down before him, and pray and praise."

The Psalms of Solomon reject universalism. They expect that in the Kingdom of the Messiah no strangers will be allowed to dwell among Israel (Ps. Sol. xvii. 25-28), in this contradicting the view of the Exilic and post-Exilic prophets.

Neither have the Apocalypses of Ezra or Baruch anything to say about the Gentiles sharing in the Messianic Kingdom.[1] The Scribes therefore no longer cherished any universalistic Messianic expectation. But in its place appears a universalism adapted to the circumstances of the time in the form of missionary activity. In this existing natural world-period they desire to convert Gentiles to Judaism; and these, having thus become Jews, will as such enter the Kingdom.

Of the vigorous missionary activity which the Pharisees developed in the light of this new universalism we are told by Jesus Himself.

Matt. xxiii. 15: "Woe unto you, Scribes and Pharisees, hypocrites, for ye compass sea and land to make one proselyte, and when he is made ye make him two-fold more a child of hell than yourselves."

.   .   .   .   .   .

Jesus does not share the missionary zeal of the Scribes and Pharisees, because His thought moves along the lines of the universalism of the old eschatological expectation, according to which those Gentiles who are called to the Kingdom will be made manifest when the Messianic Kingdom begins. To convert the heathen

---

[1] Traces of universalistic thought are found in Apoc. Bar. xlii. 5, and in 4 Ezra iii. 32-36.

beforehand is to take into one's own hands what God has reserved for Himself. The missionary universalism, which for the Scribes had taken the place of the 'eschatological' universalism, was the logical negative of the latter.

In consequence of the changed conception of the Kingdom, and of the significance which predestination has for Him, Jesus' 'eschatological' universalism is different from that of the Exilic and post-Exilic prophets. The latter expect the Kingdom for collective entities, the people of Israel and whole heathen nations. For Jesus, it is destined for individual elect men. And these, moreover, do not belong exclusively to the last generation of Israel and the Gentiles, but are drawn from all races who have ever at any time been upon earth.

There are many utterances of Jesus which seem to suggest that the Elect from among the heathen are destined to take the place of those among the Elect of Israel who have not obeyed the call.

Matt. viii. 11-12: "I say unto you, many shall come from the east and from the west, and shall sit down to meat with Abraham, Isaac and Jacob in the heavenly Kingdom. But the sons of the Kingdom shall be cast out into outer darkness, where shall be wailing and gnashing of teeth."

Matt. xii. 41-42: "The men of Nineveh shall stand up in the judgment alongside of this generation and shall condemn it; for they repented at the preaching of Jonah, and behold a greater than Jonah is here. The queen of the south shall stand up at the Judgment alongside of this generation and shall condemn it, for she came from the ends of the earth to hear the wisdom of Solomon, and behold a greater than Solomon is here."

Matt. xxi. 43: "Therefore I say unto you that the Kingdom of God shall be taken from you, and shall be given to a people which brings forth the fruits thereof."

Although he has such expectations for the Gentiles, and even from time to time finds among the Gentiles—as in the case of the Centurion of Capernaum (Mt. viii. 10) and the Canaanitish woman (Mt. xv. 28)—a faith which astonishes Him, Jesus directs His activities only to Israel, and prescribes a similar limitation to His disciples when He sends them forth.

Matt. xv. 24: "I am not sent but to the lost sheep of the House of Israel."

Matt. x. 5-6: "Go not along Gentile roads, and into any town of the Samaritans enter not; go rather to the lost sheep of the House of Israel."

This conduct is due to no narrowness of sympathy, and is not even to be explained exclusively by the shortness of the time available before the beginning of the Kingdom. It is connected with the character of Jesus' universalism. His 'eschatological-expectation' universalism forbids a mission among the Gentiles.

To the Jews He is sent both for mercy and for judgment. For the Elect among them His preaching is a touchstone. If they believe in it, then election becomes a reality; if they will not hear it, they forfeit their election. Those, however, who do not yet belong to the Elect, and in view of their outward conduct must obviously be considered as reprobate, can by accepting his preaching, confirmed as it is by miracle, enter into the rights of elect persons. Possibly Jesus cherished the notion that for all those of the Children of Israel who have been privileged to experience His unrecognised appearance among them, the possibility existed of obtaining election by means of fellowship with Him. According to this the prerogative of Israel and that of the last generation would both be preserved and brought into harmony with the conception of election in general. As regards the Gentiles, it is simply that God has chosen a number of them to be received into the Messianic Kingdom at its appearing. They cannot, however, acquire election, as the Children of Israel can, because there is no preaching of the Gospel of the Kingdom to them.

According to this the original idea of Jesus was that to all the living members of the people of Israel was given the possibility of acquiring as a reality that entrance to the Kingdom, which in principle stood open to them, by confessing allegiance to Himself, who was in appearance only the preacher of the Kingdom, but in reality the Son of Man. But in proportion as He found by experience that numbers of Israelites were not concerned about making their potential election into an actual one, He came to the conviction that the Elect from among the Gentiles would step into their places, in order that the number of the members of the Kingdom should be complete. These supplementary Elect are simply appointed by God to have a part in the Kingdom. They are not preached to. The privilege of entering upon the rights of the Elect by a free choice is reserved to the Children of Israel. This explains how it is that Jesus is universalistic in His thinking and Jewish-particularistic in His action.

.   .   .   .   .   .

After the death of Jesus the Gospel was preached to the Gentiles. How came this departure from His attitude?

It arose naturally from the fact that through Hellenistic Jews who accepted Christianity the Jewish mission in the Diaspora naturally passed into a Christian mission. According to the earliest stratum of narrative in the Acts of the Apostles, this happened first at Antioch in Syria. There, believing Hellenistic Jews, Cypriots and Cyreneans, who had belonged to the Jerusalem community, but after the stoning of Stephen were driven out, after at first preaching to the Jews only, began to preach the Gospel to the Greeks also (Acts xi. 19-21). On receiving accounts of their success, the Apostles at Jerusalem—who had remained there undisturbed (Acts viii. 1), because the persecution, and indeed the stoning of Stephen itself, really arose out of quarrels between different parties of Hellenists—sent Barnabas to Antioch. He brought Paul from Tarsus, and later on began, along with him, at the behest of the Spirit and under commission of the church, to engage in missionary work (Acts xi. 22-26, xiii. 1-3).

According to a passage from a later stratum of Acts, the Christians who were driven out of Jerusalem began preaching the Gospel at once in Samaria, which was thought of as Gentile (Acts viii. 11-13). And Peter himself is moved by a vision to go to the house of the Gentile Centurion Cornelius at Caesarea, and to baptize him and all his family (Acts x. 1-48, xi. 1-18).

How came Paul to devote himself so especially to the preaching among the Gentiles and to feel himself to be, in fact, the Apostle of the Gentiles? That his call, as is often assumed, took place in the moment of his conversion at Damascus is not really a necessary inference from the passage in the Epistle to the Galatians (i. 15-16) which is usually cited in support of it. What he says there is that God had appointed him, from his mother's womb, to preach to the Gentiles His Son who was now revealed to him.

Was it his failure among the Jews and success among the Gentiles which made him the Gentiles' Apostle? This would agree with the account in the Acts of the Apostles, according to which he always preached first in the Synagogues, and only after this was made impossible to him, turned to the Gentiles. Against that, however, is the fashion in which Paul in his Epistles makes the preaching to the Gentiles a matter of prime importance, with which, as such, he is charged.

Since Paul was regularly led to his characteristic convictions by inferences drawn from his doctrine, it is natural to ask whether that is not also the case here. And as a matter of fact his eschatology did contain a special motive for preaching among the Gentiles on account of the character of the universalist eschatological expectation which is peculiar to it.

This is of a totally different kind from that of Jesus. For Paul, this Messianic Kingdom is the prerogative of the Elect of the last generation of mankind, in so far as they are in the condition of being-in-Christ. Apart from the being-in-Christ they cannot obtain the capacity of sharing in advance in the resurrection state of existence, and so, in fellowship with the Risen Christ, entering with Him into the Messianic glory. For the Elect among the Gentiles this implies that their election cannot become actual unless they receive the knowledge of Christ, and in consequence enter upon the being-in-Christ.

As practised by others, the Christian preaching to the Gentiles aimed, in the analogy of Jewish missionary activity among Gentiles, at making the Gentiles into Christian Jews, in order that these Gentile converts, whatever their number might be, might be assimilated to the believers from Judaism, and with them might become partakers in the Messianic Kingdom which was about to begin with Christ. This relative necessity became for Paul an absolute one. He has the compelling motive of a number which must be filled up.

Very high importance is attached in the Apocalypse of Ezra to the completion of the number of the Elect. In answer to his question whether the coming of the glory of the Times of the End is being delayed by the sins of men, Ezra is told that this is not the case. So soon as the number of righteous dead is complete, those events of the End which have to do with the resurrection of the dead must begin. Then shall the Messianic Kingdom appear, which is only the prelude[1] to the rising of the dead. 4 Ezra. iv. 40-43: "Go, ask the woman with child whether, when she is nine months gone, her womb can still retain the child." I replied: "Assuredly not, O Lord." He replied: "The dwelling

---

[1] The German is *Auftakt*—anacrusis, the uncounted syllable at the beginning of a metrical line, the point emphasised being the preliminary character of the Kingdom.—TRANSLATOR.

of the souls in Hades are like the mother's womb; for, as the woman in travail strives to be eased of her pains so soon as may be, so the dwellings of the dead strive as soon as may be to give back what was committed to them at the first. Then shalt thou be shown that which thou desirest."

For Paul then the conception is that the End will come when the number has been completed of those who, by believing in Jesus, make actual their election to the Messianic Kingdom. If he feels himself under compulsion to carry the knowledge of Christ into the whole world, his purpose is to give to all the Elect from among the Gentiles the possibility of attaining to the condition of the being-in-Christ, and thus making their election a reality. It is from these theological motives that he desires to penetrate even to Spain.

His project of preaching the Gospel where it is not yet known is not first announced in the Epistle to the Romans (xv. 20-24), but is referred to earlier in an obscure passage of the Second Epistle to the Corinthians (x. 15-16): "Not boasting excessively in other men's labours, but having the hope that when your faith increases we shall be magnified among you, having our limit set more widely, by preaching the Gospel to the regions beyond you, not boasting of ready-made work within another's limits."

Since Paul is alone in apprehending a necessity of this kind for the preaching to the Gentiles, and in desiring to take the necessary action, he recognises in himself the God-appointed Apostle to the Gentiles, who must take his place as such alongside the Apostles of the Circumcision.

How deep a significance this gives to the passage in the Epistle to the Romans about the preaching of the Gospel which must be spread abroad everywhere!

Rom. x. 13-15: "For everyone who shall call upon the name of the Lord (Christ) shall be saved. But how can they call unless they have believed? And how can they believe on Him of whom they have not heard? And how can they hear without a preacher? And how can they preach if they have not been sent forth? As it is written, 'How beautiful are the feet of those that bring good tidings'."

It is only for Paul that the Gentiles really have a right to the preaching of Christ. Since they in consequence of their election have equal rights with the Jews, they also are to be given the same possibilities of learning to know Christ which the Jews already possess. Before the Return of Christ the Gospel must be preached throughout the whole world!

.   .   .   .   .   .

It is not only for the sake of the Elect among the Gentiles, but for the sake of Israel also, that the Gospel must be preached as speedily as possible throughout the whole world. Paul cannot reconcile himself to the thought that "they of the circumcision," who are the first to be called to true sonship to Abraham, will not make their election a reality. Wrestling with this most difficult problem of predestination, he finds the solution in the view that this hardening of heart can only be a temporary thing which has been foreseen in the Divine plan. Accordingly he makes known in the Epistle to the Romans, as a mystery, that so soon as the Elect from non-circumcision have all been made manifest through belief in Christ, then they of Israel, roused to jealousy by this, will put off the hardness of heart which has temporarily fallen upon them, and will themselves also enter into God's grace. This miracle he expects to take place before the Return of Christ! To aid in bringing it about he desires to carry the knowledge of Christ to the ends of the earth. The Return will indeed not take place until all the Elect from among the Gentiles have heard the call of the Gospel. It is therefore to save Israel that Paul exercises his calling as the Apostle of the Gentiles! He makes every effort to arouse the jealousy which shall turn his people decisively to salvation (Rom. xi. 13-14). When the wild olive branches which have been grafted into the olive tree of Israel have struck, its own branches which had been cut off shall again be grafted on (Rom. xi. 17-24).

Rom. xi. 13-14: "But to you the Gentiles I say, inasmuch as I am the Apostle of the Gentiles I am proud of my office, for it is my hope to stir up my brethren according to the flesh to jealousy, that I might save some of them."

Rom. xi. 23-24: "They, if they do not persist in their unbelief, shall be again grafted in. For if you were, out of the naturally wild olive tree and against nature, grafted into the good olive tree, how much more shall these, for whom it is according to nature, be grafted (again) into their own olive tree."

Rom. xi. 25-26: "For I would not have you ignorant of this mystery, that you may not value yourselves on your own wisdom, that a partial hardening of heart has come upon Israel, until the full number of the Gentiles has entered in (to the faith), and so shall all Israel be saved."

In the First Epistle to the Thessalonians Paul pronounces so hard a judgment upon the Jews that it is very difficult to understand how he can combine with it his hope of their becoming believers and being saved.

1 Thess. ii. 14-16: "For you have become imitators, brethren, of the churches of God which in Judaea are in Christ Jesus, for you have received the same from your own fellow-countrymen as they from the Jews, who killed the Lord Jesus and the prophets, and have persecuted us, and are unpleasing to God and at enmity with all men, hindering us from preaching to the Gentiles their redemption, that they might fill up the measure of their sins. But wrath is come upon them up to the end."

It is possible that Paul at the time of writing this Epistle had not yet fought his way to the belief in this ultimate redemption of all Israel. Many expositors see in the words "but wrath is come upon them to the end" the marginal gloss of a copyist which has found its way into the text, in which case it would be an allusion to the destruction of Jerusalem, which happened in A.D. 70. And indeed it is not easy to see what Paul could have meant by a Divine judgment which had already overtaken the Jews.

Formerly it was the Gentiles who were disobedient to God, now it is the Jews. For Paul this is not, as it appears on the surface, an annulling of election, but the course which the redemption of all the Elect takes by the Divine appointment.

Rom. xi. 29: "For the gifts of grace and the calling of God are irrevocable."

Rom. xi. 32: "God has shut up all under disobedience that He might have mercy upon all."

Hitherto exegesis has been at a loss as to how to deal with this redemption of all; and that for two reasons. First, it has overlooked the fact that by "all" is meant nothing more nor less than all the Elect; secondly, it does not distinguish between the Messianic and the eternal blessedness in the way which Paul takes for granted. That the passage in Rom. xi. 32 refers to eternal blessedness is, in view of the whole handling of the problem in Rom. ix. 11, impossible. Paul is not speaking here of a restoration of all the men who have ever lived upon earth (ἀποκατάστασις πάντων) as a conferring of universal blessedness, which is to happen in the moment when God becomes all in all. He is dealing only with the generation of mankind which is still alive in the Times of the End, and with their participation in the Messianic Kingdom. He is thinking only of the turning to belief of the whole of the Elect, both from the Gentiles and the Jews, in preparation for the Return of Christ—in short, of the miracle which his faith demands, in his concern for Israel, and which he hopes himself to experience in his earthly life.

In consequence of this expectation that all those who were called thereto would attain the righteousness which is by faith, the meaning of the delay of Christ's return becomes intelligible to him. Probably he assumes that the whole of Israel is destined to become believing (Rom. xi. 26). He, therefore, continues to hold the conception which Jesus had at one time held, but had given up in the course of His ministry.

.   .   .   .   .   .

From the fact that Paul's preaching to the Gentiles is based on his universalistic eschatological expectation, results its peculiar character. It is directed to Gentiles who are called as Gentiles, not to Gentiles who, as Jews believing in Christ, are to fill up the number of those who shall enter into the Kingdom. This theoretic difference seems at first glance of small account. It goes, however, very deep.   On it ultimately depends the fact that Paul cannot concede the submission to Law and circumcision, which was demanded of his Gentile Christian converts. It is not open to him to depart from the position that they have been called to the being-in-Christ as Gentiles, not as Gentiles who have been made into Jews. And the freedom from the Law, which follows from his universalistic eschatological expectation, is equally demanded for them by the being-in-Christ. Had there not been this question of the Law, Paul could have kept his mystical doctrine of the being-in-Christ to himself. For the believer does not necessarily need to know the whole mystery which proceeds within him from baptism onwards. If with the simple belief that he is still living in the natural world-era, he looks forward to the coming of Jesus as Messiah, and makes ready for His coming by repentance and sanctification, he will go to Him in His Messianic Kingdom with no less certainty than if he were already conscious that, through the resurrection of Jesus, the supernatural world-era had already begun, that the powers of death and resurrection were already, since his baptism, at work upon the believer, and that, in consequence, it was only in outward appearance that he was still a natural man.

But once the question of the Law has come up it is impossible to go further without the knowledge of the mystical doctrine of the being-in-Christ. If uninformed belief here attempts to make the decision for itself it will be exposed to the completely fatal error of treating the Law as still valid even after the death and resurrection of Jesus, and will consequently, in all simplicity, demand of the Gentile convert that he shall submit himself to it, in order (as one who has joined himself to the Chosen People) to establish his claim upon the promises which refer to them. But in reality the Gentile convert, if he does this, irrevocably falls away from Christ, even though he continues to acknowledge Him as Messiah, and to make ready by repentance and sanctification for His coming. For by his acceptance of the being-in-the-Law he gives up the being-in-Christ and therewith his redemption.

.   .   .   .   .

What actually is Paul's attitude towards the Law?

If the statements in the Epistles are looked at one by one an extraordinary complexity and inconsistency appears. He asserts roundly that the Law is no longer in force. But at the same time he admits its authority by his view that those who acknowledge the Law are subject to the Law, and so perish by the Law. And there is yet another unintelligible distinction. That believers from Judaism should continue to live according to the Law seems to him quite proper and in no way detrimental to their redemption. But if believers from among the Gentiles do the same thing, this is for him a denial of the Cross of Christ.

Paul's view of the Law cannot therefore be summed up in the simple statement that it is no longer to be regarded as valid. In order to understand his real meaning we must have present to our minds the questions with which he is concerned. There are two of these—one theoretical and one practical.

1. In what sense and to what extent is the Law no longer valid?

2. What is the right attitude of believers towards the Law, in so far as it is no longer valid?

If these two questions are rightly posed and rightly kept apart, the problem itself and Paul's decision both become clear. His apparently so complicated attitude towards the Law resolves itself into something simple and logical.

In what sense, then, and to what extent is the Law no longer valid?

The answer is easy. The Law belongs to that natural world which lies under the dominion of the Angels. In so far as this world, since the death and resurrection of Jesus, exists or does not exist, in so far is the Law in force or not in force. The dominion of the Angels has received a blow from the death and resurrection of Jesus, but for the present still maintains itself. It is in the same way—for Angel dominion and natural world-era are correlative—that the end of the natural world may be considered to have come or not come. At the present time the natural world is in process of being changed into the supernatural. Where the supernatural world is already a reality, Angel dominion and the Law have no more validity. Where the natural world still retains validity, Angel dominion and the Law are still valid.

The supernatural world already exists within the sphere of the corporeity of those who are in Christ, filled as it is with the death and resurrection-producing forces. Outside of that sphere all else, for the present, that is to say, until the coming of the Messianic Kingdom, is still natural world. The Law is no longer valid for those who are in-Christ-Jesus. As those who have died—died with Christ!—they are liberated from the Law in the same way as the dead and risen Christ. Upon the dead-and-risen-again it has no power.

Rom. vii. 1: "Know ye not, brethren—for I speak to men who know the Law—that the Law has dominion over a man just so long as he is living?"—Rom. vii. 4: "Accordingly, brethren, you have been made dead to the Law by the body of Christ, in order that you might become the property of another, namely, of Him who is risen from the dead, that you might bring forth fruit unto God." [1]

Gal. ii. 19-20: "I through the Law have died to the Law, that I might live unto God; I have been crucified with Christ." [2]—Gal. v. 18: "If the Spirit is your motive power you are no longer under the Law."

Thus, though Paul can say in quite general terms that Christ is the end of the Law (Rom. x. 4), what he means by this is only that with Christ the end of the Law has begun. But this has as

[1] As members of the Body of Christ they have died with Christ.

[2] He has died to the Law through the Law, because Christ, with whom he has died, was brought to the Cross by the Law, and there annulled the curse of the Law (Gal. iii. 13); and because the Law, when brought into contact with flesh and sin, causes the death of the man.

yet become a reality only for those who are in Christ. Those who have not yet passed from the being-in-the-Law to the being-in-Christ, and those who allow themselves to be misled into exchanging the being-in-Christ for the being-under-the-Law, are under the Law and are made to feel its power.

Gal. iii. 10: "As many of you as are of the works of the Law are under the curse. For it is written, 'Cursed is everyone who continues not in all that is written in the Book of the Law to do it'."

Gal. v. 2-5: "Behold, I Paul say unto you, If you allow yourselves to be circumcised, Christ can profit you nothing. And, again, I testify to every man who allows himself to be circumcised that he is strictly bound to keep the whole Law. If you seek to be justified by the Law, you are abolished out of Christ, you are fallen away from grace."

Paul thus affirms the co-existence of a validity and a non-validity of the Law corresponding to the difference of world-era within the sphere of the being-in-Christ and outside of it. And in so doing he is not indulging in some fancy opinion of his own, but simply drawing the logical conclusion from the fact that the Law ceases where the Messianic Kingdom begins.

.   .   .   .   .   .

The incompatibility of Law and eschatology becomes evident in the fact that the Law is constantly threatened by eschatology, and that in a two-fold fashion: by the intrinsic impulse of eschatology towards an immediate and absolute ethic; and by the supra-mundane character of the Messianic mode of being, to which the Law, established for the natural world, is not appropriate.

Post-Exilic Judaism and Rabbinism, however, make an attempt to unite these incompatibles. They combine Law and eschatology on the lines that the Law leads up to the Messianic Kingdom, and the observance of the Law guarantees the attainment of the Messianic state of existence. They thus build a bridge which looks quite well, but has no adequate carrying capacity. They can make no headway against the historical and logical fact that the eschatology of the pre-Exilic Prophets, who were its creators, was not orientated to the Law, which at that time did not exist, but to an immediate and absolute ethic. This connection of ethic and eschatology uncompromisingly asserts its rights, whenever eschatology is treated seriously; that is to say, whenever expectation-eschatology becomes in living personalities eschatology in action.

The immediate ethic then begins to shine through like an earlier colour which has been overlaid by a later one. It does not supplant the Law, but it relegates it to a lower place. Accordingly both the Baptist and Jesus demand repentance and an absolute and inward ethic, instead of enjoining a meticulous observance of the last detail of the Law, as the most obvious line of conduct in view of the nearness of the coming of the Kingdom. They have no reason to attack the validity of the Law; it does not stand in their path. And with the coming of the Kingdom it will, in any case, pass away. Thus Jesus solemnly affirms (Matt. v. 17-19) that the Law continues to be binding in all its ordinances. At the same time He robs it of all significance by the ethic of unworldliness, and His demand of a righteousness which is better than that of the Scribes (Mt. v. 20).[1]

Matt. v. 17-18: "Think not that I am come to destroy the Law and the Prophets. I am not come to destroy but to fulfil. For, verily I say unto you, until heaven and earth pass away, not one jot or one tittle of the Law shall pass away till all come to pass."

This saying does not mean, as is usually assumed, that Jesus here ascribes eternal validity to the Law. He represents it as continuing in force "until heaven and earth pass away"; that is to say, until the present heaven and the present earth give place, at the coming of the Kingdom of God, to a new heaven and a new earth. It is only on this interpretation that the apodosis "until all things have come to pass acquires a natural meaning." [2]

Jesus thus clearly affirms that the Law is only valid until the beginning of the Kingdom of God. How, indeed, could He have held that it would retain its validity for the men of the resurrection, the partakers in the Kingdom?

Judaism refused to acknowledge the incompatibility between Law and eschatology. The Exilic and post-Exilic Prophets make the attempt to conceive of the Messianic Kingdom as the Kingdom of the perfect observance of the Law. According to Ezekiel (xxxvi. 26-27) and Jeremiah (xxxi. 33), in the Messianic time God, by giving to men a new spirit, will give them the Law in their hearts, so that they cannot do otherwise than live in accordance with it.[3] In them the spirit is in the service of the Law. About

---

[1] On Jesus' attitude to the Law see also pp. 79-80, 114-115, *sup.*

[2] ἕως ἂν πάντα γένηται—A.V. misleadingly, "till all be fulfilled," as though the verb were the same as in v. 17.—TRANSLATOR.

[3] See pp. 160-161.

520 B.C., at the time of the restoration of the Temple, Haggai and
Zechariah proclaim as the Messianic Kingdom a Kingdom of
Peace which shall extend itself from Jerusalem over all nations,
and in which the Law rules. The same view is represented by the
fragment found in Isaiah ii. 2-4 and Micah iv. 1-4, which doubtless originated in the fifth century B.C., and in the prophecies, also
post-Exilic, of Isa. lx. and lxvi.

But the ideal of the Messianic Kingdom as the perfect Kingdom
of the Law becomes untenable in proportion as the Coming Kingdom is thought of as transcendental. The fact that the Law, designed for natural men, becomes purposeless when no longer
natural but supernatural beings are in view, made its influence
felt even when an effort was made to ignore it. It is true that the
Late-Jewish Apocalypses never go so far as to affirm in principle
that the Law will cease to have significance in the future Kingdom. But practically they are influenced by it, and take up a corresponding attitude. Surprising as it may appear, they never assert
that the Law will be in force in the Messianic Kingdom, and they
never picture the life of the Coming Kingdom as a life of perfect
Law-keeping, but always as a life in a new and blissful condition
which is enfranchised from all earthly limitations. How would it
be possible for the Book of Enoch, according to which the Saints
"become angels in heaven" (Enoch li. 4, lxi. 12), to carry through
the idea that they live according to the Law? But even the Psalms
of Solomon, and the Apocalypses of Baruch and of Ezra,
which picture the partakers in the Messianic Kingdom not as
risen men, but only as beings existing in ideal conditions of life,
make no attempt to represent the Messianic Kingdom as the
Kingdom of the perfected rule of the Law. Their point of view is
rather that by keeping the Law a man acquires a claim to the
Messianic Kingdom, but in the Messianic Kingdom such a man
walks according to God's will by natural impulse, in virtue of the
new condition.

When it is asserted in the Apocalypse of Baruch (xlviii. 47) that God
at the Day of Judgment punishes for transgression of the Law, that
does not imply that the Law will also be in force in the Messianic
Kingdom.

In support of the eternal validity of the Law 4 Ezra ix. 36-37 has
been quoted: "We who received the Law, must be lost on account of
our sins along with our hearts in which that was done. But the Law

is not lost, but abides in its glory." That the Law is eternal does not necessarily mean that it is of eternal application. It is eternal, because it is pre-existent. But just as it was in abeyance, although it existed, until it was given to the People of Israel at Sinai, so it can again rest in abeyance from the beginning of the Messianic period onwards. Paul also, when he speaks of the Law as holy (Rom. vii. 12), spiritual (πνευματικός, Rom. vii. 14), and "of God" (Rom. vii. 22), must think of it as eternal. This does not prevent him from affirming that it only has validity in the natural world, and that only during a relatively short period.

In any case the Apocalypse of Ezra pictures the new condition in the Messianic period without making any mention of the Law. 4 Ezra vi. 26-28: "Then shall the heart of the inhabitants of earth be altered and shall be changed to a new spirit. Then shall evil be rooted out and deceit destroyed, faith shall flourish, destruction shall be overcome, and truth shall be made manifest which so long has continued without fruit."

Where evil no longer exists the Law has logically no further office.

The supernatural character of the Kingdom therefore makes it in practice impossible for Late-Judaism to conceive of the Kingdom as the Kingdom of the Law. And similarly the conception that in the Kingdom of God the hearts of men are ruled by the Spirit swallows up the other that they are obedient to the Law, even though Ezekiel and Jeremiah may originally have meant that through the spirit of God the Law was given into their hearts. Men in whom God Himself works irresistibly do not need a Law in order to fulfil His Will.

In Paul's conception of an ethic inspired by the spirit of the resurrection the immediacy of this ethic combines with the supernatural character of the Messianic mode of existence in opposition to the Law. Paul is convinced in the same way as Jesus that the Law can only remain in force up to the beginning of the Messianic Kingdom. And since he holds that the Elect, so soon as they are 'in-Christ', no longer belong to the natural, but henceforth to the Messianic world, he is necessarily led to the conclusion that they are now no longer under the Law.

The historical and logical incompatibility continues its course inexorably. In Paul and in the Judaism of the immediately following generation appeared the inevitable outcome. Paul sacrificed the Law to eschatology; Judaism abandoned eschatology and retained the Law.

For the Rabbis, who had no longer a living conception of eschatology but only lived in it with the literary imagination, it became possible to do what the Late-Jewish Apocalypses had not found possible; to conceive of the Messianic Kingdom as the Kingdom of the Law. They often describe how the righteous in the Garden of Eden study the Torah. Sixty associations were supposed to occupy themselves with it under the Tree of Life (Midrash to the Song of Solomon vi. 9). Moses, who taught the Torah in this life, would do the same in the life to come (Exodus Rabba 2). According to other statements, it is God Himself (Tanchuma, ed. Buber, 106 *a*) or the Messiah (Targum to Song of Solomon viii. 1-2) who is thus occupied.

Of course we are not justified in concluding from this view of the later Rabbis that the Late-Judaism of the time of Jesus and Paul held similar views. It only shows that things were otherwise for the Rabbinic reminiscence-eschatology than they were for the living eschatology of the time previous to the destruction of Jerusalem.

What attitude then, in Paul's view, ought believers to take up towards this Law, which is for them no longer valid?

The simplest solution would have been if Paul had been able to declare it an *adiaphoron*, a thing indifferent, neither harmful nor useful. In that case he would have been able to live at peace with the original Apostles and to look on the activities of Judaising emissaries with a gentle smile, knowing and preaching that believers from among the Gentiles, who allowed themselves to be persuaded to take upon themselves circumcision and the Law, were merely burdening themselves unnecessarily. But the tragic thing was that he could not take up the ironic attitude towards this zealotry, but must needs treat it with all seriousness. For so was it required by the inexorable logic of the mystical doctrine of being-in-Christ.

But how are we to explain the apparently inconsistent decision that Jewish Christians might observe the Law as customary usage, while Gentile converts were forbidden to do so on pain of jeopardising their salvation? This too is a consequence of the same mystical doctrine.

The attitude towards the Law which Paul prescribes to his converts is in fact an application of a more comprehensive theory which he applies to other cases also. It runs: Whatever was the external condition in which a man has made his election a reality, that is to say, has become a believer, in that condition he is, as a believer, to remain. This theory of the *status quo* is twice enunciated by Paul in the same context.

1 Cor. vii. 17: "So, as God has allotted to each man, as God has called him, so let him walk. Thus I ordain in all the churches."

1 Cor. vii. 20: "In the state in which each was called, therein shall he continue."

If, therefore, a slave became a believer he should not, on this theory, if he were afterwards offered freedom, accept it (1 Cor. vii. 21-22);[1] if a man was married when he became a believer, he is to remain married and not persuade himself that he and his wife, as a means of sanctification in view of the coming Kingdom, should henceforth live as though they were not married (1 Cor. vii. 3-5, 10-11); if a man were unmarried or a widower, he is to remain so, and the further reason is given, that he is better in this condition because he can direct his thoughts wholly to Christ, whereas married people are preoccupied with family cares (1 Cor. vii. 8, 32-35).

Similarly he who is called as an uncircumcised man shall remain uncircumcised, and he who was circumcised at the time when he became a believer shall make no effort to be considered uncircumcised (1 Cor. vii. 18).

This theory of the *status quo* is again a necessary inference for the doctrine of the mystical being-in-Christ. From the moment that a man is in-Christ his whole being is completely conditioned by that fact. His natural existence and all the circumstances connected with it have become of no importance. He is like a house sold for breaking up, all repairs to which become irrational. If in spite of this he begins to make alterations in his natural condition of existence, he is ignoring the fact that his being is henceforth conditioned by the being-in-Christ, and not by anything else connected with

---

[1] This demand appears so unbelievable that many translators and exegetes take the text (1 Cor. vii. 21) differently. Instead of translating "Wert thou called as a slave; *care* not for that. *Even* if thou canst become free, rather remain as you are," they render the text (which runs ἀλλ' εἰ καὶ δύνασαι ἐλεύθερος γενέσθαι, μᾶλλον χρῆσαι) as if it meant "If thou art able to be freed, then by all means take advantage of this," which is both grammatically and logically impossible. Paul's decision figures in this erroneous form in the ordinary Biblical translations.

his natural existence. His natural condition of existence has therefore become of no importance, not in the general sense that it does
not matter what is done to it, but in the special sense that henceforth nothing must be done to it. The contract relating to the house
which has been sold specifies that it has been sold only with a view
to breaking up, and that consequently nothing must be done to
keep it in habitable repair, not to speak of alterations designed to
make it more commodious!

If Paul is exposed to the reproach that he did not in the Spirit
of Christ oppose slavery, and consequently for centuries lent the
weight of his authority to those who regard it as compatible with
Christianity, the blame rests on the theory of the *status quo*. His
mysticism did not permit him to hold a different view. For what
need has one who is already a free man in Christ Jesus, and mo-
mentarily expects to enter as such into the Messianic glory, to be
concerned about release from slavery for the few moments that he
has still to spend in the natural world? Accordingly Paul enjoins
upon Onesimus, the escaped slave whom he had come to know during his imprisonment, that he should return to his master Philemon, and although as a believer he is now a freeman like his master,
nevertheless to continue to serve him.

Paul's point of view is also adopted by Ignatius in his Epistle to
Polycarp. Ignat. *ad Polyc.* iv. 3: "Despise not bondmen and bondwomen; but they on their part must not be presumptuous, but for the
glory of God serve the more diligently, that they may obtain a better
freedom from God. They must not seek to be freed at the cost of the
Church, lest they be found to be slaves of their desires."

From this decision, that the believing slave must not seek freedom, we see how strongly the theory of the *status quo* is held. The
only concession that Paul makes is, that if continuance in the unmarried state involves a danger of unchastity, those to whom this
applies may marry even though they were unmarried when they
became believers. He thinks it necessary, however, to assure them
expressly that they are thereby committing no sin, since this is a
change of small importance and justified by the avoidance of the
greater evil (1 Cor. vii. 9, 28, 36-40).

Applied to the question of the Law and circumcision the theory
of the *status quo* requires that he who believed as a Jew must continue to live as a Jew, and the non-Jew as a non-Jew. Paul would

have been no more justified in permitting the Jew to abandon the ordinances of the Law, and the prescriptions of the Scribes which had come to be identified with it, than in requiring the non-Jew who had been baptized to place himself thereafter under the Law. He himself—we must not allow his protestations that he had become a Greek to the Greeks to introduce any confusion on this point—continued to live as a Jew. He even allowed himself to be persuaded by the original Apostles to take upon him a vow involving Temple sacrifices, in order that everyone might see that the rumour that he was teaching the Jews of the Diaspora to abandon Moses was without foundation (Acts xxi. 20-26). In so doing he was in no way acting contrary to his convictions.

Paul's preaching of freedom from the Law is thus by no means conceived in a spirit of freethinking. He compels Jews and non-Jews alike to remain in the state in which they first became believers. The champion of the freedom of Gentile Christianity is at the same time its tyrant. If it desired to become partaker in the blessing of the Law and circumcision, he would not suffer it to do so.

.　　　.　　　.　　　.　　　.　　　.

The putting into practice of this decision, however, encountered difficulties. If believing Jews celebrated the Lord's Supper along with Gentile brethren, they sinned against the prohibition of table-fellowship with Gentiles. On this question there arose at Antioch a breach between Paul and Peter (Gal. ii. 11-16). Peter, having at first been willing to celebrate the Lord's Supper along with Gentile Christians, ceased to do so after the arrival of certain brethren from the circle of James the Just, whether because these had made representations to Peter about it, or because Peter wished to avoid a controversy about it with the strongly Pharisaic James.

That the question at Antioch concerned eating together at the Lord's Supper is so obvious that Paul does not think it necessary to say so expressly. It can hardly be supposed that he would have been so deeply moved about Peter's refusal of private invitations to eat with Gentile Christians. In any case, the problem of table-fellowship with the Gentiles must have first become pressing where, as in the case of the Lord's Supper, it was a question of an unavoidable eating together.

In the Old Testament Law we do not find any statute forbidding Jews to eat at the same table with Gentiles. All that is prescribed is abstinence from certain foods and from the flesh of animals which had not been slaughtered in accordance with the provisions of the Law. It is the ordinances of the Scribes which first forbid such table-fellowshi Whether in the period prior to the destruction of Jerusalem their prescriptions were so fully developed and so universally acknowledged that every Jew who ate with Gentiles was conscious of eating contrary to the Law we do not in fact know with certainty. It is assumed in the Acts of the Apostles (x. 28 and xi. 3). And Paul seems to presuppose it when he makes the point against Peter, that by his partaking in a common celebration of the Supper he, a Jew, had lived Gentile fashion (Gal. ii. 14).

Following the example of Peter, the other Jewish believers, even including Barnabas, absented themselves from the common celebration of the Supper. Thereupon Paul rebuked Peter for acting contrary to his conviction, in deference to the strict view taken in Jerusalem. Since he had at first broken the Law by eating with Gentile Christians, he had now no right whatever to compel others to live as Jews (Gal. ii. 11-14).

It was no doubt precisely this question of table-fellowship at the Lord's Supper which led the authorities at Jerusalem to insist that the Gentile Christians, by accepting circumcision and the Law, should put themselves on the same footing as Jewish Christians. The great internal struggle in Early Christianity thus began as a Eucharistic controversy.

There were other points, too, in which Paul's decision, clear and logical as it appeared from the point of view of the mystical doctrine of the being-in-Christ, proved in practice difficult of application. The fact that it enjoins on some what it forbids to others, gives rise to misinterpretation from both sides. Thus, while some asserted that Paul was misleading the Jews of the Diaspora to abandon the Law (Acts xxi. 21), others, as we learn from the Epistle to the Galatians, were spreading the report that he himself was still preaching the circumcision which he had forbidden to the Gentile Christians (Gal. v. 11). It is possible that those who brought against him the charge that he could on occasion act contrary to his fundamental principle, had some grounds of fact to go upon. If the report in the Acts of the Apostles is correct, at the outset of his Second Missionary Journey he circumcised Timothy at Lystra, "because of the Jews who were in those parts," before taking him with him as his companion (Acts xvi. 1-3). And it is possible that he had done the like on an earlier occasion, at the time of the Apostolic Council at Jerusalem, in the case of Titus.

Gal. ii. 3-5: "But not even Titus my companion, although a Greek, was compelled to be circumcised. But on account of the surreptitiously introduced false brethren, who came in surreptitiously to spy out our liberty, which we have in Christ Jesus, to enslave us; to whom we did not give way for an hour by submission in order that the truth of the Gospel may remain with you. . . ." Here the sentence breaks off. The most natural explanation is that Titus was not circumcised; but another is possible, according to which the accent lies on "not compelled." In this case the meaning is that the circumcision took place, but not out of compulsion, being an act of conciliation for the sake of peace.[1]

In the case of Timothy the circumstances are rather different, inasmuch as he was "the son of a believing Jewess, but of a Greek father" (Acts xvi. 1-3). Since, in the Rabbinic view, in the case of children of a mixed marriage it is the national and social status of the mother which determines the legal status of the marriage, Timothy was a Jew. Nevertheless Paul, if he was to be true to his principles, ought not to have circumcised him after baptism.

Are we to suppose that Paul was not as certain as he later became that the man who was in-Christ might not afterwards take upon him circumcision and the Law? Or is it really the case that he was a man who could write in his letters impressive pronouncements, but who in face-to-face controversy was incompetent (2 Cor. x. 10), and consequently, in certain circumstances, in order to conciliate men (Gal. i. 10), could be got to consent to things which were really against his own convictions?

.   .   .   .   .   .

In any case, Paul holds firmly to the principle that the Gentile convert who allows himself to be persuaded into accepting the Law and circumcision becomes a castaway. For he who holds such alterations of the being-in-the-flesh, the external existence, to be imperative thereby shows that he regards himself as still in-the-flesh. He thereby annuls the being-in-Christ, and delivers himself into the hands of the Angel-powers who stand behind the Law.[2]

Law and circumcision, if adopted after a man has become a believer, are something quite different from what they are in the

---

[1] There is also an ancient various reading, actually omitting the 'not'!

[2] On the connection of the Law and the rule of the Angels see pp. 69-71, *sup.*

case of one who has lived in them previously. Paul exerts himself to procure the acceptance of this remarkable truth, in order to put an end to the delusion which is leading those whom he has won for Christ to their destruction. The Epistle to the Galatians is a veritable cry of the heart's anguish, making itself heard in words.

Gal. iii. 2-3: "One thing I would know of you. Did you receive the Spirit by the works of the Law, or by the hearing of the message of Faith? Are you so void of understanding that having begun in the Spirit you seek to reach your goal by the flesh?"

Gal. iv. 3-5: "When we were in our non-age we were in servitude to the spirits of the elements of this world. But when the fullness of time was come, God sent forth His Son, born of a woman and made subject to the Law, that He might redeem those who were under the Law, and that we might be put in the position of sons."—Gal. iv. 8-11: "At that time, when you knew not God, you served false gods which in reality are no gods, but now that you have known God, or rather have been known by Him, how can you turn back again to the powerless and miserable Element-Spirits to be in servitude to them once more? . . . I fear to have had my labour for you in vain."

Gal. iv. 16: "Have I then become your enemy because I have told you the truth?"—Gal. iv. 19-20: "My children, I travail for you in the pains of birth, till Christ be found in you; I would I were now among you and could change my voice, for I am in distress because of you!"

Gal. v. 1: "For freedom has Christ set us free; stand firm therefore, and suffer not yourselves to be harnessed again to the yoke of bondage."

Ultimately the whole deception proceeds from the Angel-powers. They want to keep for themselves what can possibly be kept. Since they cannot undo the death of Jesus, they do their utmost to make it have taken place in vain.[1] For if they can succeed in getting the error accepted that the Law and circumcision are necessary in addition to belief in Christ, then, in spite of the belief in the death and resurrection of Christ, there is no being-in-Christ. And thus they have succeeded in bringing it about that men who imagine themselves to belong to Christ have fallen back under their power again, Gentile and Jewish Christians alike. For not only have Gentile converts, who seek to bring in the being-under-the-Law as a supplement to being-in-Christ, "fallen from grace"

---

[1] On the part played by the Angel-powers in the strife about the Law see also p. 159, *sup.*

(Gal. v. 4); the same fate overtakes Jewish converts, if the Law and circumcision are anything more to them than a condition which has become indifferent to them but which they retain because they were already in it at the moment of their becoming believers. Whoever, as a baptized person, accepts anything connected with the being-in-the-flesh as of importance to redemption, thereby surrenders the being-in-Christ. The dread sentence that a man cannot be both in Christ and in the flesh is fulfilled in them even more relentlessly than in those who through sin, in consequence of weakness, remain entangled in the flesh. He is guilty in the same way as those who, by immoral bodily intercourse, or by taking part in idol feasts, annul their being-in-Christ.[1] Thus to attach value to the Law and circumcision, which in itself has nothing to do with sin, becomes the gravest transgression against Christ.

Anyone, therefore, who demands that believers should accept the Law and circumcision is supporting the cause of the Angel-powers. For Paul, the Apostles at Jerusalem and their emissaries are "blinded by Satan." Under the mask of Apostles of Christ they are acting as false Apostles. The evil that they thereby do they will one day have to answer for (Gal. v. 10; 2 Cor. xi. 13-15).[2]

Paul refuses to admit that the Jewish zealots are acting only because they are deceived. He holds that they are also moved by fear. They see in his own case what those who, by preaching the pure doctrine of the Cross, interfere with the plans of the Angels, have to endure in the way of persecutions and sufferings. This they desire to escape. That is why they set up the Law alongside of the Cross.

Gal. vi. 12: "Those who desire to make a fair show in the flesh seek to force you to be circumcised, only in order that they may not suffer persecution for the Cross of Christ."

For in Paul, as the only one who sees the real meaning of the insistence on the Law and circumcision, the Angel-powers wreak their vengeance. While the Apostles at Jerusalem live in peace and are held in high respect, he is in every way humiliated and tormented. If he bears about with him, more visibly than any other,

---

[1] On Paul's view of the three mortal sins see pp. 128-130, *sup.*

[2] That Paul means by the "false Apostles whom Satan has blinded" (2 Cor. xi. 13-15) the Twelve at Jerusalem, even though he does not expressly name them, see pp. 155-157, *sup.*

the dying of Christ, that is because the Angel-powers desire to destroy him, like Jesus before him. They reckon that they will have won their game if they can only get him out of the way.

For this reason he does not, he says, need to contradict the rumour that he still preaches circumcision. The persecutions which he endures suffice to prove the contrary.

Gal. v. 11: "But, I, brethren, if I shall really preach circumcision, why am I still persecuted? For in that case the offence of the Cross has ceased to be."

It is often assumed that, as time went on, Paul came to take a milder view about the question of the Law. It is said to be observable in the Epistles to the Corinthians and Romans that the struggle has slackened. That is a mistake. If the question of circumcision is not treated in the Epistles to the Corinthians, that does not mean that it no longer existed. The struggle had taken a different form. From the offensive Paul had been forced into a defensive position. Instead of debating with him about the Law and circumcision, the original Apostles and their emissaries were contesting his right to be called an Apostle at all. By these tactics he was forced into the position of having to wage the struggle about circumcision and the Law as a struggle for his own authority in his churches.

There are good grounds, too, for there being nothing about the struggle over the Law in the Epistle to the Romans. Paul wrote it in order to prepare the Church for his coming, and to predispose it favourably towards him. He is justifying himself to it in advance. Accordingly he expounds his attitude towards the Law in as conciliatory a manner as he possibly can.

In writing to the Philippians he does not need to proceed so cautiously. From the vehement words which he launches at them from his captivity it is obvious that the struggle was still raging, and that the Apostle's interest in it was as keen as ever.

Phil. iii. 2-3: "Beware of the dogs! Beware of evil workers! Beware of the 'Excision'; for *we* are the Circumcision, we who pray in the Spirit of God, and boast in Christ, and put no trust in the flesh."

It is the zealots for circumcision that Paul has in view in Phil. iii. 18-19: "For many walk—of whom I have told you often, and now tell you again with tears—that they are enemies of the Cross of Christ. Their end is destruction; their god is their belly; their glory is in their shame; their mind is set upon earthly things."

If the conclusion is rejected that these polemics are due to the struggle having continued during his imprisonment, this section of the Epistle would need to be ascribed to an earlier Epistle to the Philippians, which was worked up afterwards to form a whole, for purposes of public reading, with the imprisonment Epistle. And this is not inconceivable.[1] But even if that hypothesis were accepted, it certainly does not prove that Paul during his imprisonment held any different view on the question of the Law from that which he had held earlier.

That Paul's opponents continued to carry on the struggle during his imprisonment is evident from the passage in the Epistle to the Philippians, in which he speaks of brethren of Rome who preach Christ there in a way which is intended to cause him pain. He consoles himself with the thought that, whatever the motive, Christ is preached.

Phil. i. 15-18: "Many indeed (he means brethren at Rome) preach Christ out of envy and contentiousness, but others of good will. The one set do it of love, knowing that it is for the defence of the Gospel that I suffer imprisonment; the others preach Christ out of contentiousness, not single-mindedly, but in order to make trouble for me in my bonds. What then? In whatever way, whether in pretence or in truth, Christ is preached; and therein I rejoice."

Paul cannot indeed relax his view about the Law and circumcision without being untrue to himself. That he was forced to engage in this struggle is the tragedy of his life. All the difficulties which he experienced in the preaching of the Gospel flowed from the fact that the theory of the *status quo*, which resulted from his mystical doctrine of the being-in-Christ, demanded to be applied to the Law and circumcision. The struggle in which he thus involved himself was hopeless from the first. How could he hope to convince believing Jews that the Law and circumcision, in which according to the Scriptures they were to find righteousness, lost all importance from the moment when they became believers, though still obligatory? And how was he to make it clear to the Gentile Christians that observance of the Law and faith in Christ are indeed compatible in the case where the believer before his conversion stood under the Law and circumcision, but not if he places himself under them subsequently? And, when all was said and

---

[1] On the possibility that the Epistle to the Philippians had been worked up out of two documents see above, p. 49, *sup*.

done, he had to be inconsistent by demanding from Jewish believers that they should violate their legalism by table-fellowship
with Gentile believers.

At the time of writing the Epistle to the Galatians he believed
that he had agreed with Peter upon a solution, which would really,
if it had been maintained, have resulted in the formation of two
independent churches—the agreement, namely, that the Twelve
should be the Apostles of the Circumcision, he and Barnabas of
the Gentiles (Gal. ii. 7-9). This separation proved impossible of
execution because both churches were generally represented in
each church, and at the common celebration of the Lord's Supper
one section must surrender its point of view in deference to the
other, either by the Jews overriding the ordinances of the Law, or
by the Gentile Christians accepting circumcision and thus getting
rid of the question altogether.

Another reason why it was impossible was that the original
Apostles were bound to maintain that their authority extended over
the whole Church. Thus the struggle about the Law became a
struggle between the authority of the man who had been called to
be an Apostle by the glorified Christ upon the Damascus road, and
that of the men who had been appointed by Jesus of Nazareth in
Galilee to be His disciples and who had, ready to their hand, sayings of Jesus with which they could oppose any attack upon the Law.[1]

Thus the issue of the struggle was certain from the first. The
weight of common-sense opinion, of the Scriptures, of the authority
of Jesus and the authority of the Twelve, were all combined against
Paul. And the fact that his attitude towards the Law brought on
him the hatred of the whole of Judaism made his position still more
desperate.

Immediately after Paul's death the battle he had lost was turned
to victory. Facts brought about that liberation from the Law for
which he had contended with ideas. The destruction of Jerusalem
made an end of the primitive Christian Community which had
exercised authority over the Church. The divisive tendencies,
which gathered strength in Judaism after the catastrophe, set ago-
ing the process of division between Judaism and Christianity.
And the growing numerical superiority of the converts from
heathenism over those from Judaism worked in the same direction.

---

[1] See also *sup*. pp. 80, 114-116, 190, *sup*.

Thus the problem of the Law ceased to exist. The subject of controversy between Jewish and Gentile Christianity became Christological doctrine.

But if liberation from the Law was so rapidly and peacefully accomplished in the wake of the new state of affairs, the reason was that the theory was already prepared in the Pauline Epistles and the Pauline tradition. The original meaning of the Pauline freedom from the Law was as little understood by this new generation as was that of the eschatological mysticism from which it sprang. But it made its entry through the breach which the artillery of the Apostle of the Gentiles had opened for it.

In Paul, the first Christian thinker set himself against the authority of the Church, and shared the fate of those who have since made the same attempt. And both in this first case and later on it came about that the truth of reflection which had been opposed to the Church's doctrine afterwards became a commonplace of orthodox theology.

CHAPTER X

MYSTICISM AND RIGHTEOUSNESS BY FAITH

WHAT is the meaning of the doctrine of righteousness by faith, and in what relation does it stand to Mysticism? Is it independent of it, or does it hang together with it?

Our starting-point must be the observation that the righteousness meant belongs, strictly speaking, to the future. To be righteous means to acquire by keeping the commandments a claim to be pronounced righteous at the coming Judgment, and consequently to become a partaker in the Messianic glory.

For Paul, the place of keeping of the Law is taken by faith in the redemptive power of the death of Jesus Christ. His doctrine of righteousness by faith is, from this point of view, only a particular formulation of the fact of the incompatibility of Law and Eschatology, which Judaism refused to recognise, but which he had already expressed in the eschatological doctrine of redemption, and in the mystical doctrine of the dying and rising again with Christ.

This righteousness is therefore, properly speaking, a condition of the Messianic era, like the "resurrection state of existence."[1] As such it can only be considered as already attained as a consequence of the being-in-Christ, by means of which believers possess in advance the state of existence proper to the Messianic Kingdom. This righteousness is really the first effect of the being-in-Christ. From it comes all the rest. Because the believers, through the being-in-Christ, have become righteous men, they are already in the resurrection state of existence and in possession of the Spirit.

The tenets of the being risen with Christ and the possession of the Spirit therefore carry with them that of the righteousness-with-God as already attained. Had Paul wished to give it a special

---

[1] In accordance with this Paul speaks, in Rom. iii. 23, of lack of righteousness as being lack of the "glory of God" (ὑστεροῦνται τῆς δόξης τοῦ θεοῦ).

formulation it would have been most natural for him to derive it, like that of the possession of the Spirit and the resurrection state of existence, from the being-in-Christ. And there are in fact passages with the marks of its origin as thus conditioned.

Gal. ii. 17: "If, while we seek to be justified in Christ . . ."
Rom. viii. 1-2: "There is therefore now no condemnation for those who are in Christ Jesus. For the Law of the Spirit of Life in Christ has made thee free from the Law of Sin and Death."
2 Cor. v. 21: "Him who knew no sin, He has made to be sin for us, that we might be God's righteousness in Him."

If the function of faith was to be expressed, the formulation of the sequence would run thus: In consequence of believing in Christ we possess righteousness through being-in-Christ. And, in the Epistle to the Philippians, the doctrine once appears in this completeness.

Phil. iii. 8-9: "All this I count as dross in order that I might win Christ and be found in Him, not having my own righteousness, the righteousness of the Law, but that which comes through believing in Christ, the righteousness which is of God."

Generally, however, Paul is at pains to express himself as though the true righteousness was obtained by faith as such.

Rom. iii. 28: "We judge, then, that a man is justified by faith without the works of the Law."
Rom. iv. 5: "But to him who works not, but puts his faith in Him who justifies the ungodly, to him his faith is reckoned as righteousness."

That righteousness comes directly from faith cannot be meant by Paul in the strict sense, since it is in fact impossible. All the blessings of redemption which the believer possesses flow from the being-in-Christ, and from this only. Faith, in the abstract, has no effective significance: it becomes operative only through that being-in-Christ, beginning at baptism, to which it leads.

How comes Paul, then, to express himself differently from what he actually means, and to ascribe to faith itself what only comes into existence in the being-in-Christ to which faith leads? He is led to do so by considerations of linguistic and dialectic convenience.

The complete expression "Righteousness, in consequence of

faith, through the being-in-Christ" is too awkward to be constantly employed in the course of an argument. And the short and accurate "righteousness in Christ" is not well adapted to his dialectic purpose. For the righteousness which comes from the doing of the Law must be contrasted with another righteousness which also comes by doing. This antithetic 'doing' can only be provided by "believing".[1] For the being in Christ is always and only a state, not a 'doing'. Thus the expression "righteousness by faith," though really less accurate, makes a better antithesis to "righteousness by the Law" than the more accurate "righteousness in Christ." Not logical correctness, but dialectic convenience, has here been the deciding factor. Paul followed, it may be recalled, the same method when, in expounding his Mysticism, instead of speaking of fellowship in the corporeity of Christ he always spoke of being-in-Christ, because the shorter expression for the relation to Christ provided a better antithesis to the being-in-the-flesh.[2] Just as his mysticism becomes inexplicable when it is approached by way of the formula "in Christ," so it is with his view of righteousness when it is sought to understand the righteousness as coming directly from faith.

It is interesting to observe that the possession of the Spirit also, when it comes to be spoken of in the argument about the Law, is for dialectical reasons derived immediately from faith instead of from the being-in-Christ.

Gal. iii. 2: "Have you received the Spirit through the works of the Law, or through giving heed to the message of faith?"

Gal. iii. 5: "He who gives you the Spirit and works miracles through you, does He do this by the works of the Law or because you listened to faith?"

In the effort to represent faith as the "doing," which corresponds to obedience to the Law, Paul goes so far as to coin the phrase

---

[1] For the purposes of the present argument, it is a convenience to the writer of German that *Glaube* and *glauben* are—like πίστις, πιστεύειν—from the same root, and in the above sentence the force of the argument seems to me better given by using the gerundive of the verb than either of the nouns 'faith' or 'belief'. "Righteousness by faith" is too fully established in English Biblical versions and theological literature for it to be possible to break away from it entirely; but Paul's thought, as conceived by Dr. Schweitzer, would certainly be more clearly expressed by the formula "righteousness by believing."—TRANSLATOR.

[2] *Sup.* pp. 121-123.

"obedience unto faith,"[1] and to set the "Law of works" over against the "Law of faith."

Rom. i. 5: "Through whom we have received grace and Apostleship with a view to obedience unto faith among all Gentiles."

Rom. iii. 27: "What place is there for boasting? It is excluded. By what Law? By the Law of Works? No, but by the Law of Faith."

According to Rom. vi. 16, believers are servants of obedience with a view to righteousness. In Rom. x. 16 obedience to the Gospel is spoken of in the sense of belief in the Gospel.

Another reason which led Paul to the expression "righteousness by faith" was that it is required in the only passage from Scripture which he can cite in support of his doctrine. Let us try to imagine the position in which he found himself in trying to expound his doctrine of freedom from the Law. It can no doubt be derived with demonstrative clearness from the eschatological doctrine of redemption and the mystical doctrine of the dying and rising again with Christ. But what profits logical correctness when his opponents have Scripture on their side? And the Scripture is theirs to use in all its utterances save two. These two passages were Paul's brilliant discovery. One of them recounts that Abraham believed God and that this was reckoned to him for righteousness (Gen. xv. 6 = Gal. iii. 6; Rom. iv. 3).[2] With it Paul combines another, from Habakkuk, which he interprets as meaning, "He who is righteous by faith shall live " (Hab. ii. 4 = Gal. iii. 11; Rom. i. 17).

The Hebrew text has "The righteous shall live by his faithfulness (בֶּאֱמוּנָתוֹ)". Out of that the Septuagint makes "by my (God's) faithfulness" (ἐκ πίστεώς μου). By combining the original text and the Greek translation Paul arrives at ὁ δίκαιος ἐκ πίστεως ζήσεται, in which he takes πίστις not as faithfulness but as faith, separates "by faith" from the verb and combines it into the noun to form a single term. Thus arises the statement necessary to his argument, "The by-faith-righteous man shall live."

For Paul these two passages—Gen. xv. 6 and Hab. ii. 4— express the real meaning of the Scriptures. With them he invalidates all others. But in order to be able to use them he must

---

[1] At the close of the Epistle to the Romans (xvi. 26) this phrase occurs again. But it is not certain whether this verse is authentic. It is possible that it has been imitated from the beginning of the Epistle.

[2] Gen. xv. 6: "And he believed Jahwe, and He counted it to him for righteousness,"

formulate the doctrine of righteousness through being-in-Christ as the doctrine of righteousness by faith.

.   .   .   .

Paul twice develops the doctrine of righteousness by faith: once, briefly, in Gal. iii. 1-iv. 6, the other time at length in Rom. ii. 11-iv. 25. The two expositions differ from one another in a characteristic way. The earlier version is that of the Galatian Epistle. Its more original character appears in the fact that the doctrine of righteousness by faith has as yet not been detached from the eschatological doctrine of redemption and the mystical doctrine of the being-in-Christ, but shows its connection with both of them. In the Epistle to the Romans the attempt is made to present it, so far as possible, independently.

In the account in the Epistle to the Galatians the question, why the Law cannot produce righteousness and why Christ is the end of the Law and the beginning of faith-righteousness, is answered by reference to the eschatological doctrine of redemption. The Law cannot produce righteousness, because it was not designed to that end. It was given in order that men, through their servitude to it, might come to know the significance of the freedom brought by Christ. Coming as the Law does from the Angel-powers, it keeps men under their dominion. That it cannot offer any expectation of life is evident from the fact that Scripture (Hab. ii. 4) says only that the righteous-by-faith shall live.

The Law, since it is impossible of fulfilment, only makes sin manifest and thereby brings with it a curse.

Gal. iii. 10: "For as many as are of-the-works-of-the-Law stand under the curse."—Gal. iii. 19: "What purpose, then, does the Law serve? It was added because of trangressions until the seed should come to whom the promise was given, and was ordained through Angels."—Gal. iii. 22-24: "The Scripture has shut up all under sin, that the by-faith-in-Jesus-Christ promises might be given to believers. For before faith came we were all held prisoners under the Law, waiting for the faith which was to be revealed. Thus the Law was our pedagogue to bring us to Christ, that we might be justified by faith."

The promises of God to Abraham refer, according to Paul—and this he makes the basis of his argument!—not, according to their original meaning, to a historical period, but to the Messianic period. In so making them he was using a method of exegesis which was fully recognised by the Scribal learning of the time. Thus the Apocalypses of Ezra and Baruch are founded upon the idea that the prophecies of misfortune to Jerusalem refer to the earthly Jerusalem, the prophecies of future glory to the heavenly Jerusalem which was to appear in the Times of the End.[1] This view enables them to view the destruction of Jerusalem by Titus as the mere prelude to the Last Times. The earthly Jerusalem must perish in order to make way for the heavenly.

In this way the expression to "inherit the land" in Jesus' beatitude upon the meek (Mt. v. 4) means the same as to "possess the Kingdom of God." In this sense it is used already in Ps. xxxvii. and the Apocalypse of Enoch. Ps. xxxvii. 9: "For the wicked shall be rooted out, but those who wait patiently for Jahwe shall inherit the Land."—Ps. xxxvii. 11: "But those who are patient shall inherit the Land, and rejoice in the abundance of peace."—Enoch v. 7: "The Elect shall be given light, joy and peace, and they shall inherit the Land."

The promises relating to the Messianic period have, according to Paul, nothing to do with the Law, because they were in principle given to Abraham when he was not yet circumcised and there was as yet no Law.

With these exegetical arguments Paul comes at length by roundabout ways to the fundamental fact that the Messianic hope is not connected with the Law, because the earlier Prophets, from whom it took its rise, as yet knew nothing of the Law.

It was thus to an Abraham who showed his obedience through faith, not through the Law, that the promises were given. When he is well on in years and has no son, and God promises him that his seed shall be as numerous as the stars of heaven, he believes Him, and God reckons it to him as righteousness (Gen. xv. 3-6). It is only later (Gen. xvii. 1-14) that God concludes a covenant with him and enjoins upon him and his bodily posterity the rite of circumcision. Thus the righteousness for which the promises are to be fulfilled has nothing to do with the Law, and the Seed of Abraham for whom they are destined is not the bodily seed, the posterity which serves the Law. For whom then are they destined? The use of "seed" in the singular in the phrase "thy seed" shows, according to Paul, that they do not refer directly to a plurality of

---

[1] The heavenly Jerusalem is referred to in Apoc. Bar. iv. 1-6; 4 Ezra vii. 26, ix. 38-x. 49.

persons, but in the first place to a single person. Since they refer
to the Times of the End, the single person can be no other than
Christ (Gal. iii. 16). The 'great nation' must therefore be thought
of as included in Christ. It consists, in fact, of those who are in
Christ. In order to carry through the conception required by his
Scriptural argument Paul has recourse to the mystical doctrine of
the being-in-Christ. As those who are "in Christ," believers are
the true seed of Abraham (Gal. iii. 29), the Israel of God (Gal. vi.
16), and so the children of God (Gal. iii. 26).

Gal. iii. 28-29: "You are all one" (masc. sing.) "in Christ Jesus. But
if you are of Christ, you are Abraham's seed, heirs according to the
promise."

As the true People of God, believers are the children of the
heavenly Jerusalem, whereas the "Israelites after the flesh," with
whom God made the Covenant on Sinai, belong to the earthly
Jerusalem.

Gal. iv. 25-26: "The Mount Sinai in Arabia corresponds to the
Jerusalem that now is, for she is in bondage along with her children.
The Jerusalem which is above is free; and that Jerusalem is our mother."

Mount Sinai is the symbol of bondage, because Paul posits some kind
of relation, geographical or linguistic, which is no longer intelligible
to us, between Hagar and Sinai (Gal. iv. 24). The People of Israel,
which obeys the law given on Sinai, is therefore prefigured in the
Scriptures by the posterity of the bondwoman Hagar. That Paul makes
the citizens of the heavenly Jerusalem into its 'sons' is due to his applying the words of Isaiah (liv. 1)—which originally referred to Zion—
about the barren woman who later rejoices in a numerous seed, to the
heavenly Jerusalem. In 4 Ezra x. 7 the earthly Zion is spoken of as the
mother of the Children of Israel in the natural sense.

The heavenly Jerusalem also appears in Heb. xii. 22; Rev. iii. 12,
xxi. 2; xxi. 9-xxii. 5.

In order that the time referred to in the promise might come,
the end of the Law, the Law which had been interposed between
the prophecy and its fulfilment, must first take place. This end is
brought about by Jesus, through His dying on the Cross. By so
doing He makes void one of the provisions of the Law. For as one
who is hanged upon a tree He ought, according to the Law (Deut.
xxi. 23), to be accursed. But this is impossible on account of the
divine character of His Person. But if He has made void the Law

in one of its provisions, He has made it void altogether. For it stands or falls as a whole.[1]

In the Epistle to the Galatians, then, as should be carefully observed, it is not a question of an atonement made to God through Christ, but of a most skilfully planned foray made by Christ against the Angel-powers, by means of which He frees those who are languishing under the Law (Gal. iv. 5), and so brings about "the Coming of faith" (Gal. iii. 25).

Thus the doctrine of righteousness by faith is developed in the Epistle to the Galatians, with the aid of material drawn from the eschatological doctrine of the being-in-Christ, on strictly logical lines as a cosmico-historical speculation.

.   .   .   .   .   .

Since the presentation in the Epistle to the Romans (Rom. ii. 11-iv. 24) of the doctrine of righteousness by faith deliberately refrains from referring both to the eschatological doctrine of redemption and to the mystical doctrine of the being-in-Christ, it is obliged, in accounting for the failure of the Law, to dispense with all speculations about the Law and the dominion of the Angel-powers, and to find the explanation of the catastrophe as inherent in the nature of Law and in the nature of man.

That the Law (so runs the train of thought in Rom. iii. 9-20, iv. 15, v. 13, v. 20, and vii. 7-25) cannot effect righteousness is due to the conflict with the flesh. By the flesh all possibilities of good which belong to the Law are made ineffectual, and in fact turned into their opposites. In the flesh is sin. The Law forbids sin; but it has no power to kill it. All it can accomplish is to make sin manifest and active. And sin brings with it death, that is to say, the loss of a claim to life in the Messianic Kingdom. The result of the encounter of Law and flesh is therefore condemnation, death, and despair.

Rom. iii. 20: "By Law-works no flesh becomes justified before God, for through the Law comes only the knowledge of sin."

Rom. iv. 15: "The Law creates wrath. For where there is no Law there is no transgression." (Similarly Rom. v. 13 and v. 20.)

Rom. vii. 14: "We know that the Law is spiritual, but I am fleshly, sold under sin."—Rom. vii. 17-24: "For what I do, it is not I that do it, but the sin which has its dwelling in me. For I know that in me, that is

[1] On the invalidating of the Law by Jesus being hanged upon the tree (Gal. iii. 13) see pp. 72-73, sup.

in my flesh, no good thing dwells. For to will good is within my power, but not to carry it out. For it is not the good that I will, but the evil that I do not will, which I do. But if I do that which I do not will, it is no more I myself that do it, but the Sin which dwells in me. What I find about the Law, so far as I am concerned, is that when I will to do good I am only·able to do evil. In my inward man I assent with joy to the Law of God. But in my members is another law which is at war with the law of my reason and brings me prisoner under the Law of sin. Unhappy man that I am! Who shall deliver me out of the body of this death?"

With this failure of the Law in its encounter with the sinful flesh as a doctrine, Paul is able to say all possible good about the Law, without the negative final result ever being in doubt. Indeed he speaks of it in a way that might content the fiercest Judaism. He calls it 'good' (Rom. vii. 16), 'holy' (Rom. vii. 12), 'spiritual' (Rom. vii. 14), and 'divine' ("Law of God," Rom. vii. 22).

But does he not by these admissions abandon the theory of the Epistle to the Galatians, that the Law is derived from the Angel-powers? By no means. His thought is, precisely, that the Angel-powers, in order to get the Jewish People into their power, laid upon them a Law which it was impossible for them to fulfil. The good, the holy, the pneumatic, the divine, is unfulfillable by men. Therefore they gave men this as a Law, and thereby attained their end most perfectly.

That Paul in the Epistle to the Romans speaks only of the characteristics, not of the origin, of the Law does not therefore necessarily mean that he now takes a different view of the latter from that what he expressed four or five years before. Writing in an apologetic interest he avoids everything which could be used as material for attacks upon him, and goes as far as he can in ascribing worth to what was valued by his opponents. But, after all, the experience of the religious man with the Law leads to the same result as would be deduced from the true knowledge of its origin. So Paul sets forth the impossibility of righteousness by the Law as an experience which he himself had had, which was of general application and could be repeated by anyone who tried it.

In doing this he lets us see deep into his heart. There unrolls before us a terrible picture of what he had experienced with the Law. He had been a zealot for the Law, but the attitude of confidence in the Law had been denied him. His fate had been to experience sin through the Law.

That he was not alone among the Scribes of his time in such an experience we learn from the Apocalypses of Ezra and Baruch. In these writings also a deep consciousness of human sinfulness wrestles with the problem of the Law.

4 Ezra vii. 68-69: "For all who are born are deformed by godlessness, full of sin, laden with guilt. Far better were it for us if we had not to go after death into the Judgment."

4 Ezra vii. 118-120: "O Adam, what hast thou done! When thou didst sin, thy fall came not upon thyself only, but also upon us, thy seed. What profits it us that eternity is promised us if we shall have done the works of death?"

4 Ezra ix. 36-37: "We who have received the Law must be lost because of our sins, along with our hearts which received it. But the Law is not lost, but abides in its glory."

Apoc. Bar. xv. 5: "Man would not have understood My Judgment, if he had not received the Law, if I had not instructed him with understanding. But now, because he has consciously transgressed, shall he consciously also bear torment."

Apoc. Bar. xlviii. 42: "O Adam, what hast thou done to all those who are thy seed?"

Apoc. Bar. liv. 15: "Though Adam first sinned and brought upon all premature death, yet hath also every single one of those who are descended from him brought upon himself future torment."

The Apocalypses of Baruch and Ezra were under no necessity to enter on the problem how men who were not under the Law become conscious of their sinfulness. For them it was sufficient that the heathen were sinners. But for Paul it was necessary that through something corresponding to the Law they should experience the antagonism between the Law and the flesh, in order that they might be brought to desire the true righteousness. And thus he comes, at the beginning of the Epistle to the Romans (Rom.ii. 11-16), to set up the doctrine that for the Gentiles conscience plays the part of the Law, and having no Law they are a law unto themselves.

.   .   .   .   .   .

Since the Law can produce no righteousness, only the grace of God can come to man's aid, and that only by offering the possibility of another righteousness. The astonishing thing about the Epistle to the Galatians is that it develops the doctrine of the new righteousness wthout ever mentioning the forgiveness of sins or the atoning death of Christ. That does not mean that these at that time played no part in Paul's beliefs. But for the cosmico-historical speculations, in the light of which in this Epistle the problem of the impossibility of Law-righteousness and the consequent necessity for a means of redemption is posed and solved, the grace of God consists in His having caused Christ, by His death, to make an end of the rule of the Law. In the resulting state of freedom everything that belongs to redemption is implicitly given, and is appropriated by the believer through the being-in-Christ.

In the Epistle to the Romans the impossibility of Law-righteousness is developed by insisting on the personal consciousness of inescapable sinfulness. Consequently redemption must consist in the conscious assurance of the forgiveness of sins, which comes by God's grace through Christ.

In representing the righteousness which is a necessary qualification for the Kingdom as bestowed by God's grace, he is not announcing a new idea. From the time of the Prophets the conception that the mercy of God had a part to play in the bestowal of the glory of the Kingdom was at home in eschatology. The conception that men could become partakers in the Kingdom on the ground of a righteousness acquired by the keeping of the Law never held the field completely. For that was always difficult to reconcile with the grace of God, which in eschatology is thought of as bestowed irrevocably. Here again we find an instance of the essential incompatibility of eschatology and Law.

At one moment indeed it seemed as though the conception of righteousness by the Law would find a way of disposing of the grace of God. In the Psalms of Solomon, the triumph-song of the work-righteousness of the Pharisees, where the line is drawn so confidently between the righteous and sinners, God only needs to give the righteous a helping hand in so far as He gives them an opportunity to make atonement for their transgressions by the chastening which they receive from Him.

Ps. Sol. xiii. 10: "For the Lord spares His godly ones, and their transgressions He wipes out by chastening."

Ps. Sol. xviii. 4: "This chastening is applied to us as to a first-born son, that Thou mightest turn obedient souls from their unconscious errors."

This was at the time of Pompey's conquest of Jerusalem (63 B.C.). How completely different was the view of the Scribes who experienced the conquest of Jerusalem by Titus! (A.D. 70). It not only returned to the view of the Prophets, but went further along the same lines. In the Apocalypses of Baruch and Ezra it is hardly too much to say that the grace of God has to do everything. At the same time the number of the Elect is small, almost to the point of disappearance compared with that of the lost. For so has God determined from the beginning of the world.

4 Ezra vii. 132, 136-140: "I know that the Lord is now called the Plenteous-in-mercy, because . . . He is so rich in mercy towards the living, the dead, and those that are to be; and if He were not so the world and its inhabitants would never attain to the Life;[1] He is called kind, because if He did not in His kindness suffer sinners to get rid of their sins, the ten thousandth part of mankind could not attain to Life; He is called the Forgiver, because if He did not forgive those whom His word has created, and wipe out the multitude of their transgressions, there would perchance, out of numberless multitudes, only a very few survive."

4 Ezra viii. 31-32: "For we and our fathers have continued to live in the works of death, but Thou, just because we are sinners, art called the Merciful. For just because we have no works of righteousness wilt Thou, if it is Thy good pleasure to have mercy upon us, be called the Merciful."

4 Ezra viii. 1-3: "This world has the Most High created for many, but the world to come for but few. . . . Many are created but few are saved."

4 Ezra ix. 15: "The lost are more than the Elect, by as much as a flood is more than a raindrop."

4 Ezra ix. 22: "So let the multitude perish which is born for naught."

A few exceptional men will, according to the Apocalypses of Baruch and Ezra, be found righteous before God without needing to have recourse to His mercy, because a store of good works has been prepared for them by God from the beginning of the world. Apoc. Bar. xiv. 12-14: "For the righteous eagerly expect the end, and go fearlessly out of this life. Because they have a treasure of works with Thee, laid up in Thy storehouses, they can leave this world fearlessly and look forward, full of joyous confidence, to receive the world which Thou hast promised them."—4 Ezra viii. 33: "For the righteous who have many works laid up with Thee shall receive the reward, because of their own

---

[1] The Life in the Apocalypse of Ezra does not mean, as in Paul, life in the Messianic Kingdom but in the Final Kingdom. The Messianic Kingdom is for Ezra only the last phase of the natural world. Life in the sense of the resurrection state of existence only comes with the Final Kingdom.

works."—These good works were created by God along with Paradise and the heavenly Jerusalem (4 Ezra viii. 52).

Thus a small remnant of the ideal of righteousness by works is saved, so far as appearance goes, by the assumption of a special calling of God which makes it possible to some.

Since Paul regards the forgiveness of sins by God as the most essential thing in the bringing about of redemption, he follows the lines of thought which were familiar to at least certain circles among the Scribes of his time. But by interpreting the death of Jesus as an atoning death he is able to give a new definiteness to these ideas.

．   ．   ．   ．   ．   ．

From some mysterious hints which Jesus gave regarding the significance of His death it was known to His disciples that He looked upon it as an atoning sacrifice, making possible the forgiveness of the sins of those who were Elect to the Kingdom. The idea of the forgiveness of sins as having been obtained by the death of Jesus was therefore to primitive Christianity something self-evident, only that it did not retain the peculiar definiteness which it had in the thought of Jesus Himself.[1]

Paul is therefore standing on the same basis as primitive Christianity, and to a certain extent on that of the thought of Jesus, when in developing, in Rom. iii. 21-28, the doctrine of righteousness by faith, he gives to the death of Jesus the significance of the sin-offering of Lev. iv. 22-vi. 7, 11 (E.V.), and of the sin-offering on the Great Day of Atonement (Lev. xvi. 1-27), regarding it as a dying which wipes out sin and makes it possible for God to forgive. Attempts to deny the existence in this passage of the conception of a satisfaction offered by Christ to God, such as have been made by Albrecht Ritschl and others, are impossible to carry through.[2]

Rom. iii. 21-26: "But now apart from the Law, though witnessed to by the Law and the Prophets, is a righteousness of God made manifest, namely, a righteousness which is derived from God, through faith in Jesus Christ, for all who believe. For there is no distinction; all have sinned and come short of the glory of God, but now are freely made righteous by His grace, because of the redemption accomplished in

[1] On Jesus' conception of His death, and the change which it underwent in passing into primitive Christian belief, see pp. 57-62, *sup*.

[2] Albrecht RITSCHL, *Die christliche Lehre von der Rechtfertigung und Versöhnung* (3rd ed., 1888–1889).

Jesus Christ whom God has made the means of atonement [1] through faith in His blood, to give proof of His righteousness—because of the overlooking of sins in the past, in the long-suffering of God, to prove, I say, His righteousness at this present time; in order that He might be at the same time both just, and the justifier of him who is of the faith in Jesus."

Rom. v. 1-2: "Having been pronounced righteous on the ground of faith, we have peace with God through the Lord Jesus Christ, through whom we also, through faith, have access to the grace in which we stand, and have our boasting in the hope of the glory of God."

1 Cor. v. 7: "For our Passover is offered, namely, Christ."

Thus Paul illustrates the meaning of the death of Christ by means of a conception which was familiar to the religious thinking of Judaism, in the light of which primitive Christianity also was accustomed to see it, in consequence of the words of Jesus at the Lord's Supper. The most important thing for him is—and that is why Paul recurs to the idea of sacrifice—that in this way it is possible for him to give an intelligible form to the conception of a righteousness which results from the action of faith. For the idea of sacrifice involves the idea of the Sacrificial Community. Whoever in faith applies the atoning sacrifice of Christ to himself as having taken place for him along with others, is included among those for whom it was offered. And consequently he has a part in the forgiveness which has thus been obtained. He is one of the righteous by faith, like Abraham.

Having thus given to the conception of righteousness by faith an independent footing by his interpretation of the death of Jesus as a sin-offering, Paul feels himself able in the Epistle to the Romans (Rom. iv. 1-25) to dispense with the argument which derives the sonship to Abraham of believers (Gal. iii. 6-29) from their being the true seed of Abraham in virtue of their being-in-Christ, and makes believers Abraham's seed purely by their act of faith. As one who belonged to the non-Circumcision as well as to the Circumcision, Abraham was called to be the father of believers, whether

---

[1] "ἱλαστήριον is a substantivised adjective and means a thing in some way connected with atonement" (Hans LIETZMANN, *Kommentar zum Römerbrief*, 3rd ed., 1928, p. 49). In the Septuagint the lid of the Ark of the Covenant is called the ἱλαστήριον ἐπίθεμα (Exod. xxv. 17), or, in most passages, simply ἱλαστήριον.

The monument which Herod erected by way of atonement after violating the grave of David in the hope of finding gold and silver in it, is called by Josephus ἱλαστήριον μνῆμα (*Antiq.* xvi. 7. 1).

they be Jews or Gentiles (Rom. iv. 11-12). Alongside of the speculation about Abraham and Christ there appears also in the Epistle
to the Romans that about Adam and Christ which is in harmony
with his tendency to universal human sympathies. Adam is through
his sinning and dying the ancestor of those who are destined to
death; Christ is the ancestor of those who are to inherit life (Rom.
v. 12-21). This parallel is drawn as early as 1 Cor. xv. 22 and xv.
45-49, except that here the dying of Adam is not expressly derived
from his sinfulness, but, more generally, from his nature as an
earthly being. The first Adam is the psychic man, created out of
earthly materials; the second, Christ, is the 'pneumatic' (spiritual)
man, who comes from heaven. This conception of the second
Adam has, as we have seen above (p. 167), nothing whatever to do
with the Persian, Indian, or Hellenistic myths of the Primal Man.

    .   .   .   .   .   .

Did Paul, in the Epistle to the Romans, really succeed in providing the doctrine of righteousness by faith with proof drawn
from its own presuppositions, and thus setting it on an independent basis? Has he two independent conceptions of redemption,
one quasi-physical, the other intellectual?

For long it was assumed by scholars that the doctrine which
stood so much in the foreground in the Epistles to the Galatians
and Romans must be paramount in Paul's teaching. And this conclusion seemed the more obvious because we ourselves do not
think of redemption as something quasi-physical, but as consisting
in the intellectual appropriation of what Christ is for us. What
makes the quasi-physical redemption-doctrine of Paul's mysticism
so foreign to us is that it is a collective, cosmically-conditioned
event. The doctrine of righteousness by faith is, on the contrary,
individualistic and uncosmic. Redemption is for it something that
takes place between God, Christ, and the believer. Consequently
theology had understanding only for that redemption-doctrine of
Paul which has affinities with our own, and regarded the quasi-
physical doctrine, when at length this was brought into its purview,
as a curious subsidiary line of thought.[1] Consequently the attempt
is made, down to the present day, to see the being-in-Christ as
merely an allotropic form—to borrow a chemical analogy—of belief
in Christ, without allowing any doubts to be raised by the singu-
larly unsatisfactory results of this experiment in alchemy.

[1] See p. 17, *sup.*

By taking the doctrine of righteousness by faith as the starting-point, the understanding of the Pauline world of thought was made impossible. The interpreters modernised it unconsciously. And, moreover, they overlooked the fact that, however it may suit our taste to represent the results of Jesus' death as appropriated by the mind, there still clings to it something alien to our thought. The continuously renewed forgiveness of sins, which the religious have sought to find in it, both in the Reformation period and in modern times, is unknown to it and impossible to it. In it Christ's atoning death has reference only to sins committed in the old condition of existence, that is to say, before baptism (Rom. iii. 25). Paul's doctrine of righteousness by faith is nothing else than a particular formulation of the Early Christian conception of the possibility of repentance secured by the death of Jesus.

To derive the quasi-physical redemption-doctrine of the being-in-Christ Mysticism from the doctrine of righteousness by faith is from many points of view impossible. Accordingly the only question can be whether the latter doctrine can really stand independently on the basis of its own logic beside the former, or whether it merely offers in a peculiar presentation a result which was already present in the other.

There is a series of facts which suggest that the doctrine of the redemption, which is mentally appropriated through faith, is only a fragment from the more comprehensive mystical redemption-doctrine, which Paul has broken off and polished to give him the particular refraction which he requires.

What are these facts?

In the Epistle to the Galatians, where it lies before us in its simplest and most original form, the doctrine of the righteousness by faith is not yet independent, but is worked out with the aid of conceptions drawn from the eschatological doctrine of the being-in-Christ.

Always, whether in Galatians or in Romans, it only appears where the controversy over the Law has to be dealt with, and—very significantly—even then only where a Scriptural argument is to be based on the as yet uncircumcised Abraham. Only when it can find a point of attachment on this Scriptural argument does it come into prominence.

Another point, which tells strongly in favour of the doctrine of righteousness by faith being merely a fragment of a doctrine of redemption, is that Paul does not bring into connection with it the other blessings of redemption, the possession of the spirit, and the resurrection. Once Paul has left behind the discussion necessitated by his Scriptural argument, about faith-righteousness and Law-righteousness, it is of no more service to him. Neither in seeking a basis for ethics, nor in the doctrines of baptism and the Lord's Supper, does he have recourse to it in any way. In the doctrine of righteousness by faith, his thought is limited to the fact that the believer is justified by the atoning death of Jesus, without finding a way from that fact and the other facts of redemption. The doctrine of redemption can only be developed as a whole from the mystical doctrine of the being-in-Christ.

The question thus suggests itself, whether it was really from reflection on the atoning death of Jesus that Paul drew his conviction of the incompatibility of the Divine forgiveness of sins with the human endeavour to be so far as possible righteous before the Law, or whether that conviction was not a fixed datum from the mystical doctrine of the being-in-Christ, which he merely presents under the form of the doctrine of the atoning death of Jesus.

There is, as a matter of fact, nothing in the conception of the atoning death of Jesus which necessitates the negating of the Law. It is to be observed that in Gal. iii. 13, where the annulling of the Law is proved by the death of Jesus upon the Cross, this death is not regarded as in any way an atoning death, but simply as an act inimical to the Law. Logically Paul also, like the Apostles at Jerusalem and the rest of the believers, might have regarded the forgiveness of sins bestowed by God through Christ as something supplementary to the Law. Even if faith-righteousness, as filling up what is lacking in the attempted Law-righteousness, is put so high that the latter is reduced to insignificance, that does not justify the inference from the atoning death of Jesus that a concomitant endeavour after Law-righteousness is to be reprobated. In other words, Paul did not draw the idea of liberation from the Law out of the conception of the atoning death of Jesus, but, on the contrary, put that idea into it.

Whence, then, comes this conviction of the essential connection between liberation from the Law and forgiveness of sins?

From the mystical doctrine of the being-in-Christ.

That mysticism has its own doctrine of forgiveness of sins. This is in no way dependent on Jesus' death being an atoning death, but upon His death as such, and, moreover, in connection with the resurrection. This forgiveness of sins is brought about by the fact that Christ has come in the fleshly body, and by His dying and rising again has made the flesh, with all the guilt belonging to it, as though it were not. And the forgiveness is obtained, not by faith but by the believer's being freed, through his dying and rising again with Christ, not only from the being-in-the-flesh but also from the sin which is bound up with that state. It is not so much a matter of a forgiving of sin as of an annulling of sin, which in point of fact becomes the same thing as forgiving it. This forgiveness of sin is not appropriated by the believer, but takes place in the believer from the moment that he goes through the dying and rising again with Christ.

Rom. viii. 3-4: "What the Law could not do, because it was powerless on account of the flesh, God has done. By sending His Son in the likeness of sin-flesh, and to deal with sin, He has pronounced judgment upon the sin which is in the flesh, in order that the demands of the Law might be fulfilled in us who walk not according to the flesh but according to the spirit."

2 Cor. v. 17-19: "And so, if any man is in Christ, he is a new creation. Old things have passed away; behold, the new has come to be. This all comes from God, who has reconciled man with Himself, by not reckoning to them their transgressions."

2 Cor. v. 21: "Him who knew no sin, He made to be sin for us, that we might become the righteousness of God in Him."

It is a mistake to bring together, as is often done, the ideas of 2 Cor. v. 17-21 with those of Rom. iii. 21-26, as if the former referred, like the latter, to the atoning death. God here "makes Christ into sin" (2 Cor. v. 21), not by the atoning death but by causing Him to come in the sin-flesh which was to be destroyed by His death and resurrection. In all cases where, in connection with the dying of Jesus, the phrases "with Christ" or "in Christ" are used and the resurrection is mentioned, His death is thought of not so much as an atoning death as a dying shared by the believer.

An interesting example of this occurs in 2 Cor. v. 15: "One died for all; therefore all have died. And He died for all, that those who now live live not for themselves but for Him who died and rose again for them." This "One died for all" is not to be understood here in the sense of the atonement idea, but in that of the dying with Christ. The meaning is that in His dying all died, in order that henceforth, as having died with Him and risen with Him, they may live only to Him.

And the "died for all" does not mean that His death applies to all men. By 'all' only the sum of the Elect is to be understood.

The forgiveness of sins which comes about through the being-in-Christ is derived from both the death and resurrection of Jesus. And indeed the significance of the Resurrection is here so great that Paul can actually represent the forgiveness of sins as based upon it. Thus he writes to the Corinthians (1 Cor. xv. 17), "If Christ is not risen, your faith is foolish, for in that case you are still in your sins."

For modern feeling this doctrine of the forgiveness of sins as an annihilation of sin appears too objective and material. We do not easily reconcile ourselves to seeing a quasi-physical process take the place of an inward appropriation. But in point of fact this quasi-physical doctrine of the forgiveness of sins is irradiated with life, because the forgiveness of sins is in it an expression of the fundamental event of the dying and rising again with Christ.

Thus in Paul's writings there are two independent conceptions of the forgiveness of sins. According to the one, God forgives in consequence of the atoning death of Jesus; according to the other, He forgives, because through the dying and rising again with Christ He has caused the flesh and sin to be abolished together, so that those who have died and risen with Christ are, in the eyes of God, sinless beings. The former of these doctrines is traditional, the latter is peculiar to Paul, and is a consequence of the mystical being-in-Christ. Though he can express himself in both ways, his thinking follows by preference the lines of the latter, because in this the fact of forgiveness of sins falls into its due relation to the complex of facts involved in redemption. For it results, like them, from the fundamental event of the dying and rising again with Christ.

One of these facts is liberation from the Law. It is a fixed datum, derived from the mystical being-in-Christ, that those who have died and risen again with Christ are free both from sin and from the Law. Paul cannot help therefore associating these two certainties closely together. If he is unable henceforth to conceive the thought of forgiveness of sins without the thought of freedom from the Law, that is because he has experienced the forgiveness of sins in conjunction with the conception of dying and rising again with Christ. Had this not been the case, he would have been able, like others, to unite the forgiveness of sins bestowed by God, with the striving after a life in accordance with the Law. But, as it is, he finds himself compelled to express the incompatibility of the forgiveness of sins with the Law, even in his formulation of the traditional doctrine of the forgiveness of sins through the atoning death of Jesus.

It is probable that through his experience under the Law, the possibility of righteousness by the Law had already become more or less problematical to him, even though not to the extent represented in the Epistle to the Romans, where he gives to his former experience the definiteness and scope which it had taken on for him in the light of the solution that he had later discovered. But however intense the conflict which he carried about with him, and however clearly the belief in Jesus' Messiahship which took possession of him at Damascus, may have shown him the direction in which the solution lay, freedom from the Law and the incompatibility of the Law with the grace of God only became a certainty for him in the moment when he perceived them to be necessary consequences, both in fact and for thought, of the mystical dying and rising again with Christ.

When this first happened we do not know. We must assume that he had attained to this conviction at the latest immediately after the First Missionary Journey, at the end of which, according to the account in the Epistle to the Galatians, he went up to Jerusalem to fight the battle of the freedom of Gentile Christians from the Law. That the mystical doctrine of the being-in-Christ had been worked out at the time of the writing of the First Epistle to the Thessalonians, is shown by the occurrence in it of the concept "the dead in Christ" (1 Thess. iv. 16), as well as the general use of the formula "in Christ." [1]

Paul is therefore forced by his mysticism to recast the doctrine of the atoning death of Jesus, in the sense of inserting into it the doctrine of freedom from the Law. This is not possible by straightforward logic, because there is no argument against the validity of the Law to be derived directly from the atoning death of Jesus. All that can be done therefore is to bring the doctrine of freedom from the Law into close connection with the doctrine of the atoning death of Jesus by means of logical ingenuities. This Paul does by showing by the argument from Prophecy that the only valid righteousness is that which comes from faith alone, and that work-righteousness is incompatible with faith-righteousness. It is possible

---

[1] 1 Thess. i. 1 and ii. 14 (church in Christ), iv. 1 (exhort in Christ), v. 12 (preside in Christ), v. 18 (will of God in Christ).

for the idea of righteousness apart from works of the Law to be expounded by means of this ingenious reasoning; but it could never have arisen out of it. The doctrine of righteousness by faith is therefore a subsidiary crater, which has formed within the rim of the main crater—the mystical doctrine of redemption through the being-in-Christ.

That it is an unnatural construction of thought is clear from the fact that by means of it Paul arrives at the idea of a faith which rejects not only the works of the Law, but works in general. He thus closes the pathway to a theory of ethics. This is the price which he pays for the possibility of finding the doctrine of freedom from the Law in the doctrine of the atoning death of Jesus.

It is not, however, of importance to Paul that there is no logical route from the righteousness by faith to a theory of ethics, for in his mysticism ethics are brought in a natural way into connection with the idea of the forgiveness of sins and of redemption in general. There, ethics are just as natural a resultant phenomenon of the dying and rising again with Christ as is liberation from the flesh, sin and the Law, or the bestowal of the Spirit. It is an operative result of the forgiveness of sin, which God makes a reality by the destruction of the flesh and of sin. Since Paul habitually thinks of redemption on the lines of the mystical doctrine of the being-in-Christ, it does not matter to him that in the subsidiary doctrine of righteousness by faith he has shut off the road to ethics. What he wants this subsidiary doctrine for is to enable him, on the basis of the traditional conception of the atoning death of Christ, to conduct his controversy with the Law by means of the argument from Scripture. More he does not ask of it. But those who subsequently made his doctrine of justification by faith the centre of Christian belief, have had the tragic experience of finding that they were dealing with a conception of redemption, from which no ethic could logically be derived.

Since the close connection of freedom from the Law with the forgiveness of sins is originally made certain for him by the mystical being-in-Christ, it is on this point of view that he develops it when he wishes to give it its primary foundation. Thus in the Epistle to the Galatians, before going on to the doctrine of righteousness by faith, he sets forth freedom from the Law and the other righteousness that goes with it as a consequence of the being crucified and risen again with Christ (Gal. ii. 12-21). In the Epistle to the Romans an amazing thing happens, that, after the new righteousness has been presented at length as coming from faith in Christ's atoning sacrifice (Rom. iii. 1–v. 21), it is explained a second time, without any reference whatever to the previous exposition, as founded on the mystical dying and rising again with Christ (Rom. vi. 1–viii. 1). To the presence of these two independent expositions of the same question is due the confusing impression which the Epistle to the Romans always makes upon the reader.

For all these reasons it is obvious that the doctrine of righteousness by faith is something incomplete and unfitted to stand alone. But it was this fragment of a doctrine of redemption which proved to be the most influential of all Paul's teaching. In view of the formula there laid down he became the champion of the Divine sovereignty wherever in Christendom it might be threatened. Whenever faith was tempted to compromise with human thoughts and ordinances, and lost the living consciousness of sin and redemption, it was shaken into wakefulness again by Paul's doctrine of the true righteousness. And when a man of religious spirit came forward in defence of the purity of religious thought, he could always appeal to the affirmations with which Paul in his time had fought this fight.

For what does it matter that the logic of the doctrine of righteousness by faith is in itself disputable, and must become strange to later times? What is effectual in it is the conviction, striving to clothe itself in form, which Paul affirms in soul-shaking words as something which he had himself experienced, and which was constantly to be experienced anew in the hearts of men.

For this reason it has been a matter of moment for all times that the freedom from the Law, which has its foundation in the mystical being-in-Christ, was also formulated by Paul as righteousness by faith.

CHAPTER XI

MYSTICISM AND THE SACRAMENTS

WHAT were the sacraments as Paul found them in primitive Christianity, and what did he make of them?

The general view is to the effect that Baptism and the Lord's Supper were in the primitive Christian community some kind of symbolic ceremonies, and that it was first with Paul that they became real sacraments.

To this view theology attained through the obvious reflection that Judaism had no sacraments, as, indeed, it had no mysticism. Christianity cannot therefore have brought with it out of Judaism anything sacramental. Hellenism, on the other hand, thought along sacramental lines. It must therefore have been from this quarter that the sacraments were imported into Christianity, and this (so the theory goes) took place through Paul, because in his teaching Baptism and the Lord's Supper have already a clearly sacramental character.

The only escape from this view is by way of the reflection that Baptism and the Lord's Supper, in spite of the fact that Judaism does not think sacramentally, may nevertheless be sacraments based on Jewish ideas, provided that they are eschatological constructions. For in that case it would be very easily explicable why they already in Paul have sacramental character.

This alternative possibility has not been seriously considered by New Testament scholarship. That the eschatological belief could have brought forth sacraments out of itself appeared to it unthinkable. Bousset rejects the attempt in the preface to his *Kyrios Christos* as something absurd.

"Or will it be asserted in all seriousness that the sacrament is an original creation of the religion which took its rise from the preaching of Jesus, and was borrowed from it by the surrounding religious world?

That will scarcely be possible, unless with Albert Schweitzer—who, however, has a much keener sense of the problem in question than most of the scholars who reject Comparative Religion *a limine*—the desperate attempt is made to derive the Christian Sacrament from eschatology."[1]

Bousset therefore is prepared to undertake to offer proof that Paul derived both his mysticism and the sacramental view of Baptism and the Lord's Supper from Hellenism; as though this were not at least as desperate a project as that of deriving the sacraments from eschatology.

Now we have seen, earlier, that the mysticism of the being-in-Christ has nothing Hellenistic about it. And, that being so, it at once became questionable whether Paul can have taken the sacramental conception of baptism and the Lord's Supper from Hellenism. How can it be supposed that he is Hellenistic in his thinking about the sacraments when he is not Hellenistic in the rest of his thinking? Moreover, when the facts of his teaching are fairly apprehended, it is seen that his sacraments, though they present an outward analogy to those of the Mystery-religions, have no real affinity of thought with them, because they do not rest, as do the latter, upon symbol which enhances itself into reality.[2]

Since the attempt to explain the sacramental conception of Baptism and the Lord's Supper in Paul from the Mystery-religions is condemned in advance to failure, there remains no other course open than to derive their sacramental character from eschatology.

It is surprising that the possibilities of sacramental thought inherent in the eschatological belief were not observed long ago. What, after all, does "sacramental" mean? In the most general

---

[1] Wilhelm BOUSSET, *Kyrios Christos*, 1913. Preface, p. 14. On Bousset see pp. 29-33. He forgets that the movement from which Christianity took its rise did not begin with the preaching of Jesus, but with that of the Baptist. And the Baptist preached . . . baptism!

Johannes LEIPOLDT also in his valuable study, *Die urchristliche Taufe im Lichte der Religionsgeschichte* (78 pp.; Leipzig, 1928) fails to consider the possibility of eschatological sacraments, and so finds himself obliged to derive Christian Baptism and the Lord's Supper from the Hellenistic mysteries. On Paul's interpretation of baptism as a dying and rising again with Christ (Rom. vi. 3-6) he remarks: "Here is tangible proof that Paul makes use of the manner of thought and expression which is characteristic of the mysteries" (p. 62).

And the religious-historical imagination flourishes luxuriantly in Richard REITZENSTEIN, *Die Vorgeschichte der christlichen Taufe. Mit Beiträgen von* L· TROJE (399 pp.; Leipzig and Berlin, 1929).

[2] See above, pp. 18-21, *sup.*

sense it means that by partaking in some appointed contrivance, a ceremony thought of as having effectual powers, something related to a higher life is attained. If, as in Hellenistic thought and in our own, the conception of the higher life is dominated by the simple, timeless antithesis of material and spiritual, the sacrament consists in something spiritual being mediated by something material. Eschatological religious feeling apprehended the antithesis as between higher and lower, and also as between future and present. Is not in this the possibility given that, in the analogy of the Hellenistic redemption-cults, ceremonies might be given a sacramental value in the sense that by them assurance of that which is future is given in the present?

In proportion as the Jewish religion gave importance to the eschatological expectation it became a religion of redemption; in proportion as it became a religion of redemption it had need of the sacramental. The attainment of assurance of future deliverance acquires in it the same importance as the assurance of belonging to the Spiritual world had in Hellenistic religious life. That New Testament scholarship has not long since made this simple reflection, by which the eschatological expectation is brought into analogy with Hellenistic religious life, only shows how difficult it is for it to open its eyes to aspects of reality, which for any reason have been customarily overlooked.

That eschatology can give birth to conceptions of a sacramental character is shown by the idea, which plays a considerable part in it, of being marked out for salvation. In Ezekiel those who are to be spared in the day of visitation of Jerusalem are marked, by a man in a linen garment, commissioned thereto by God, with a sign upon their foreheads (Ez. ix. 4-11). In the Psalms of Solomon the godly are saved at the Divine Judgment, which precedes the coming of the Messiah, by bearing God's sign upon them, while the ungodly are marked out by the sign of destruction.

Ps. Sol. xv. 4-9: "The flame of fire and the wrath upon the ungodly shall not reach him (the godly),
When it goeth forth from the face of the Lord upon the ungodly.
For the godly bear God's sign upon them which saves them.
Hunger and sword and death abide far from the righteous,
For they flee away from the godly as the pursued flee in battle.
But they pursue after the godless and take hold upon them,
And they that do injustice escape not the Judgment of the Lord.

They are taken, as by warlike enemies,
For the sign of destruction is upon their foreheads." [1]

Now, if the eschatological expectation grows so intense that men
become convinced that they are destined to experience the Judgment and Coming of the Kingdom, a new question arises. Standing
thus at the point where the eschatology of expectation passes into
the eschatology of fact, they desire to know how they can acquire
beforehand the assurance of deliverance in the day of Judgment
and of possessing the coming glory. Anyone who preaches to them
the nearness of the End must satisfy this need. Therefore John,
when he comes with the proclamation that the Kingdom is at hand,
instead of launching out into descriptions of the coming events,
demands repentance, and marks out by baptism those who are
destined to find grace.

.   .   .   .   .   .

For those whom he baptizes the Baptist makes known that, while
he has baptized them with water, the Greater than he, who is to
come, will baptize them with the Spirit. In doing so he is not representing his baptism, as is constantly assumed, as a provisional,
merely symbolic act, merely pointing forward to that true Baptism,
but places it in a casual connection with the latter. He promises
those whom he baptizes that, in consequence of what he has now
done with a view to their repentance, they have received an initiatory consecration, which at the coming outpouring of the Spirit
will qualify them to receive the Spirit, and, as men endowed with
Spirit, to pass through the Judgment to the Kingdom. [2] In order
to emphasise in the strongest possible way the close connection
between the baptism and the outpouring of the Spirit, he represents this outpouring, which is to take place at the coming of the

---

[1] The idea of being marked with a sign, or sealed, in token of deliverance and
entrance into the Messianic Kingdom, continued to play an important part in
Christian eschatology. Paul gives to the possession of the Spirit the significance
of a sealing (2 Cor. i. 22), and glories in bearing on his body "the marks of Jesus"
(Gal. vi. 17). In the Epistle to the Ephesians also (i. 13, iv. 30) the possession of
the Spirit is thought of as a sealing against the day of redemption. In the Apocalypse the servants of God are sealed before the great persecution begins (Rev.
vii. 3). Those who have not the seal upon them are given over to torment (Rev.
ix. 4). Antichrist tempts men to take his sign upon their right hands and their
foreheads (Rev. xiii. 16, xx. 4). In the second Epistle of Clement there is mention
of those "who do not keep their seal" (2 Clem. vii. 6).

[2] See also p. 162, *sup*.

Greater than he, who is about to come, as a baptism, by the Greater one, with the Spirit. As we have seen, "He that is to come," the greater than John, is not the Messiah, but Elijah, who was expected to return to earth as the Messiah's forerunner. The Baptist therefore regards himself, strange as this may appear to us all, as the forerunner's forerunner.[1] He comes forward with his preaching of repentance and his baptism in order that Elijah, who was to come, and the expected Spirit, might find a multitude prepared and consecrated, ready to receive them.

As a plunging beneath the water this baptism of John was an act symbolical of the washing away of sin. But it is also more than that: it guarantees the efficacy of repentance as a preparation for the outpouring of the Spirit, and for the Judgment.

The occurrence of the Johannine baptism is therefore by no means so enigmatic as is usually supposed. It is an original creation, with a significance of its own, arising out of eschatological necessities. The only thing that is at all obscure about it is how the Baptist came to choose washing as the ceremonial sign. Was he led thereto simply by the natural significance of it and by the part which the idea of washing plays in the Prophets, or did Jewish, Essene or other, to us unknown, ceremonial washings contribute their influence? The latter assumption is wholly unnecessary.

The way in which in the Prophets a great purification with water is prescribed by God as a preparation for the Judgment makes it quite sufficiently clear how a man with a calling, in the Times of the End, might make it into a reality. Especially significant is the passage in Ezekiel (Ez. xxxvi. 25-26), where sprinkling with water and the bestowal of the Spirit are mentioned together.

Isa. i. 15-16: "Your hands are full of bloodguiltiness! Wash you, make you clean! Put away your evil doings."

Isa. iv. 3-4: "Those who are left in Zion and who remain in Jerusalem shall be called holy, everyone that is registered for Life in Jerusalem, when the Lord shall have washed away the filth of the daughters of Zion, and purged the bloodguiltiness of Jerusalem from the midst thereof by the spirit of Judgment."

Zach. xiii. 1: "In that day shall a spring be opened for the House of David and for the inhabitants of Jerusalem, for sin and for uncleanness."

Jer. iv. 14: "Wash thy heart, Jerusalem, that thou mayest be saved."

[1] See p. 162, *sup.*

Ezek. xxxvi. 25-26: "And I will sprinkle clean water upon you and ye shall be clean; from all your uncleanness and from all your idols will I cleanse you. And I will give you a new heart and put a new spirit within you."

The idea of baptism is therefore found by John in the same place where he finds the outpouring of the Spirit, namely, in the Prophets. And all the lustrations which have been or may be discovered by Comparative Religion cannot possibly contribute as much to the explanation of the occurrence of the Johannine baptism as these passages of the Prophets, because the near prevailing reference of the washing to the Coming Judgment, to the outpouring of the Spirit, and to Messianic Kingdom will necessarily be lacking in them. The question of the derivation of John's baptism is, however, comparatively unimportant, since in the complete originality of its significance it is not explicable by any other baptism.

Whether John was influenced by the Jewish proselyte-baptism must remain an open question. That the practice of baptizing proselytes was in existence earlier than the year A.D. 70 is very probable, although the scanty references to it are from a later period.[1] It is in fact just conceivable that it may have been adopted in Judaism at a time when baptism was practised by Christians. It is curious that Justin Martyr in his *Dialogue with Trypho* makes no reference to Jewish proselyte-baptism as an imitation of Christian baptism.

That a baptism, intended to secure to Jews forgiveness of sins and the reception of the Spirit, should have been suggested to John by the lustrations practised by Gentiles on their going over to Judaism is not easy to make intelligible. In any case, the significance of the Johannine baptism cannot possibly be derived from Jewish Proselyte-baptism.

Another reason why the baptism of John has no parallels in Comparative Religion is that it is the authoritative act of an individual man who felt himself endowed with plenary powers. Its efficacy was not in itself but in him who bestowed it.

That John himself regards his baptism as a sacrament which guarantees salvation at the Judgment is obvious from his utterance about the Pharisees and Sadducees who came to be baptized by him. His words (Mt. iii. 7), "Brood of vipers, who has warned you to flee from the wrath to come?" clearly shows that if he baptizes

---

[1] How little we know about Jewish proselyte-baptism may be seen in Johannes LEIPOLDT's study, *Die urchristliche Taufe im Lichte der Religionsgeschichte* (Leipzig, 1828), which on pages 1-25 brings together the available material.

them they will have the certainty of being acquitted at the Judgment. He only wonders, and is indignant, that they should have the clearness of vision to recognise his baptism as the effectual means of deliverance. But he does not refuse it to them.

For Jesus also the baptism of John is a ceremonial act which works supernaturally. When He is asked by the Priests and Levites to justify the authority which He takes upon Himself in the Temple, He puts to them the counter-question whether the baptism of John was from heaven, or of men.

The answer which he holds to be the right one, namely, from heaven, they cannot give, because in so doing they would bear witness against themselves that they had not paid due honour to an institution based on heavenly authority (Mk. xi. 28-33).

That baptism is to be regarded as an effectual means of obtaining the glories of the Messianic Kingdom is implied by Jesus when, in reply to the two disciples who had asked for the places upon His right hand and His left, He spoke of the undergoing of death, by which He was to reach His Messianic glory, as His baptism (Mk. x. 38-39).

The few statements which we possess in the two earliest Gospels in regard to John's baptism thus clearly show that it is an eschatological sacrament.

.   .   .   .   .   .

But how comes this baptism, which John administered in virtue of his special authority, to appear of itself, so to speak, without a command of Jesus in the Christian community? [1] The answer is that it arose as an eschatological sacrament.

The Christian community made out of it nothing different from what it had already been for John. It remained for it an act which guaranteed the efficacy of repentance, as a preparation for the outpouring of the Spirit and for salvation at the Judgment. What determined the taking over of baptism was doubtless that the primitive community was formed on Jewish soil, and doubtless mainly from adherents of the movement of belief in the Coming Kingdom which had originated with the adherents of John, who

[1] That tradition puts the commandment to baptize into the mouth of Jesus *after* His resurrection (Mt. xxviii. 19-20) shows that we have here to do with a later view. And this is confirmed by the fact that the baptismal command presupposes not baptism in the name of Christ, but of Father, Son, and Spirit.

afterwards came to believe on Jesus as Messiah. And the attitude of respect which Jesus took up towards John and his baptism may also have been of importance in connection with the arising of baptism in the Christian Community.

It is completely wrong to think of Early Christian baptism as a repetition, with similar significance, of the baptism of Jesus. This view finds no support whatever in the earlier passages about Christian baptism. Down to Ignatius the baptism of Jesus is never brought into any kind of connection with Christian baptism, and the connection which Ignatius finds between them does not mean that Christian baptism is a repetition of the baptism of Jesus.

Ignat. *Ad Eph.* xviii. 2: "Jesus was born and baptized in order that by His passion He might purify the water."

Justin does not bring the baptism of Jesus into connection with Christian baptism at all, not going beyond the thought that the wood of the Cross shows itself in the water of baptism a means of deliverance for believers, as the wood of the Ark did in the waters of the Flood for Noah and his family (*Dial.* cxxxviii.). Not before Irenaeus (*Adv. Haer.* iii. 9, 3) and Tertullian (*Adv. Judaeos* viii.) does Jesus by His baptism create Christian baptism.

The Christian Community therefore took over the eschatological sacrament of the Baptist. How did it come about that the ceremony, whose significance lay in the fact that it was performed by him, was now practised by others? The answer is that the place of his authority was taken by the authority of the Church.

The Gospel of John seeks to solve the enigma of the arising of John the Baptist's baptism in the Christian Community by making the disciples of Jesus during His lifetime administer water baptism (John iv. 1-2). This is a later expedient.

The streams of influence which transformed the eschatological sacrament taken over from the Baptist into Christian baptism set in from two directions. The eschatological expectation received a more definite content in the primitive Christian community through the belief in the Messiahship of Jesus. Accordingly baptism of the Spirit, looked forward to by the Baptist as a future effect of baptism, had now become a reality, as ecstatic manifestations in the baptized clearly show. Baptism with water is therefore at the same time baptism with the Spirit. Thus, through the facts of the case, the Johannine baptism as practised in the Christian Community became Christian baptism. Thenceforward this baptism with water, which is at the same time a baptism with the Spirit, was contrasted with the simple water-baptism of John, and the consciousness was lost that it stood originally in a casual connection with the latter.

This want of understanding of the true character of John's baptism is shown in the way the theory of Christian baptism, as a baptism of water and the Spirit, is developed in the later stratum of narrative in the Acts of the Apostles. Here it is assumed that believers at Ephesus possessed only the baptism by water, and had not so much as heard that there was a holy Spirit. They are then baptized anew by Paul and, in consequence of his laying-on of hands, receive the Spirit (Acts xix. 1-7). The artificial character of the theory shows itself in the answer of these disciples to the question about the nature of their former baptism, that they had been baptized "unto John's baptism." The baptism of John is thus exhibited, on the analogy of the baptism "unto Jesus," as a baptism "unto" John. It is equally inaccurate when Paul at his coming there teaches the inadequately baptized disciples that John only administered a baptism unto repentance, and that by the "One who was to come" he meant Jesus. It is hidden from the writer of Acts, as from present-day New Testament scholarship, that the baptism of John was a preparation for the outpouring of the Spirit, and that by "Him who is to Come" was meant, not the Messiah but Elijah. This narrative in Acts thus created the false point of view from which for centuries the preaching and the baptism of the Baptist was regarded.

That a Baptist movement continued alongside the Early Christian Church is not impossible, though not very probable. In any case, it is very doubtful whether we really have in Acts xix. 1-7 a record of such a survival of the Baptist movement.

Another improbability in the theory of this later stratum of narrative in Acts is that the Spirit was not given through baptism as such, but only by the laying-on of hands of the Apostles, with whom Paul is here equated (Acts xix. 6). Similarly the Samaritans, baptized by Philip in the name of Christ, only come into possession of the Spirit through the subsequent laying-on of hands by Peter and John (Acts viii. 12-17). The false theory of Christian baptism is thus bound up with an incorrect view of a laying-on of hands of the Apostles as supplementary to baptism.

The "tendency" of the narrative in Acts xix. 1-7 is thus to draw the line firmly between Johannine and Christian baptism, and at the same

time to place Paul, in virtue of the fact that his laying-on of hands
bestows the Spirit, in the ranks of the Apostles.

Against such theories as the depreciation of the Johannine baptism which is connected with them, the fact stands firm that the
baptism practised in the primitive Christian community was identical with the eschatological sacrament, preparatory to the outpouring
of the Spirit and deliverance from the Judgment, introduced by
John the Baptist, except that the bestowal of the Spirit is now contemporaneous with the baptism by water, and that baptism takes
place with the name of Jesus as the expected Messiah. "Repent
and be baptized every one of you with the name of Jesus Christ,
for the forgiveness of your sins; so shall ye receive the gift of the
holy Spirit"—so runs the exhortation of Peter in his speech at
Pentecost (Acts ii. 38).

The forgiveness of sins obtained in baptism refers only to sins
committed previous to baptism, and is thought of as guaranteeing
deliverance at the Coming Judgment.

This sacramental view of baptism was found by Paul already
present in primitive Christianity, and was taken over by him.

.   .   .   .   .   .

Jesus took up the Baptist's preaching of the nearness of the
Kingdom of God and carried it into Galilee. It would have seemed
natural for Him to take over also the baptism, by which believers
in Judaea had been consecrated in preparation for the bestowal of
the Spirit and deliverance at the Judgment.

Why did Jesus continue the preaching of the Baptist and not
also his baptism? That this question should never have been
thought worthy of investigation by scholars will always appear
unintelligible.

If Jesus denies to believers in Galilee the saving baptism of John,
He does not do so because it is bound up for Him with the authority
of the Baptist. For He Himself possesses full authority in matters
relating to the Kingdom of God, and could have baptized in the
same way as John with a view to the bestowal of the Spirit and
deliverance at the Judgment. He dispensed with it because he
held it to be unnecessary. His own presence has in itself sacramental significance. He who attaches himself to Him, the future
Messiah, and thereby enters into fellowship with Him, does not
need to be baptized in order to receive the Spirit and to be saved

at the Judgment. Such a man, without knowing it, belongs to the fellowship of the Messiah, and as such has the right to all the blessings to come.[1]

Since His authority is still greater than the Baptist's, Jesus does not need to bestow any special initiation in preparation for the Kingdom of God. Therefore He does not continue the Baptism of John, although he regards it as coming from heaven and as having saving virtue.

To the thought of the sacramental significance of His presence as communicating itself directly, He gives a special expression by distributing at the Lake of Gennesareth to the believers gathered about Him food from His own hand. He thereby consecrates them, without their being aware of it, to be His companions at the Messianic feast.[2]

The first suggestion of the Messianic feast of the Times of the End comes doubtless from a passage of Deutero-Isaiah, dating from the Exile.

Isa. lxv. 12-14: "Verily, my servants shall eat, but ye shall be hungry.
Verily, my servants shall drink, but ye shall be thirsty.
Verily, my servants shall rejoice, but ye shall stand shamefast.
Verily, my servants shall sing for joy of heart.
But ye shall cry out for sorrow of heart."

This idea is expanded in the late post-Exilic Apocalypse Isa. xxiv.-xxvii. As this work knows nothing of a Messianic Kingdom, but only a Kingdom of God, it speaks only of a feast prepared by God.—Isa. xxv. 6: "And Jahwe of Hosts will on this mountain prepare for all peoples a feast of fat things, of fat things full of marrow, of wines on the lees well refined."

[1] On the saving significance of fellowship with Jesus the unrecognised Messiah see pp. 105-109, *sup.*

[2] On the significance of the Feeding of the Multitude as a consecration to the Messianic Feast see above, p. 107. Cf. also Albert SCHWEITZER, *Geschichte der Leben-Jesu-Forschung*, 2nd and subsequent editions, p. 421.

Whether Jesus made this distribution on one occasion only and our Evangelists give duplicated reports of the same thing (Mk. vi. 34-44, 5000 fed; *ib.* viii. 1-9, 4000 fed), or whether He did it twice, cannot be determined with certainty. The former is the more probable.

That this not understood feast-sacrament at the Lake-side became a miraculous feeding of a multitude is the more easily to be explained because such an increase of food materials is related of the Prophet Elisha in 2 Kings iv. 42-44: "And there came a man from Baal-Shalisha and brought the man of God food of the first-fruits, twenty loaves of barley. . . . He commanded, 'Give the people to eat.' Then answered a servant, 'How can I set this before a hundred men?' But he said again, 'Give it to the people to eat, for thus saith Jahwe: Ye shall eat and shall leave thereof.' Then he set it before them, and they ate and left over, as Jahwe said."

In the Book of Enoch the Elect are the constant guests of the Son of Man at His feast.—Enoch lxii. 14-15: "The Lord of Spirits shall dwell above them, and they shall eat with that Son of Man, shall lie down and rise up to all eternity. The Righteous and the Elect shall raise themselves up from the earth, and cease to lower their eyes, and shall be clothed with the robe of glory."

According to the Apocalypse of Baruch the feast begins immediately upon the appearance of the Messiah.—Apoc. Bar. xxix. 3-8: "Then shall the Messiah begin to reveal Himself. And Behemoth also shall reveal himself out of his land, and Leviathan shall rise up out of the sea: the two monsters, which were created on the fifth day of creation and have continued until now, shall serve for food to all those who survive. And the earth shall bring forth her fruit ten-thousand-fold; and on one vine shall be ten thousand shoots, and a shoot shall bear a thousand bunches, and a bunch shall have a thousand grapes, and one grape shall yield a *kor* of wine.[1] And those that have hungered shall richly enjoy. And on that day they shall see further wonders. For winds shall go forth from Me, which morning by morning shall bear with them the odours of aromatic fruits; and at the end of the day, clouds which shall drop down a healing dew. And in that day the provision of manna shall again fall down from heaven, and those who have lived to see the things of the End shall eat of it in those years."

That Leviathan and Behemoth shall serve for food to the saints in the Last Times is presupposed also in Enoch lx. 24. And for them, too, will the trees of Paradise, which shall again appear upon earth, bear their fruit (Enoch xxv. 4-5, xxxii. 3-6; 4 Ezra vii. 123). In Ezekiel the inhabitants of the new Jerusalem are fed by the fruits of trees which ripen every month, which stand by the banks of the stream which flows from the Temple Spring, and by fishes from this miraculous water (Ez. xlvii. 7-12).

In the Apocalypse of John also the Messianic feast plays an important part. Rev. iii. 20: "Behold, I stand before the door and knock: he that heareth My voice and openeth the door, to him will I go in and feast with him, and he with Me."—Rev. vii. 16-17: "They shall not hunger any more nor thirst any more, neither shall the sun smite them nor any heat; for the Lamb which is in the midst of the throne shall shepherd them, and lead them to the well-springs of life."—Rev. xix. 7: "For the marriage of the Lamb is come."—Rev. xix. 9: "Blessed are they who are called to the Marriage-Feast of the Lamb."

---

[1] A similar saying about the miraculous fruitfulness of the vine in the Messianic Kingdom is, according to Irenaeus v. 33, 3, reported by Papias as derived from Jesus.

That the conception of the Messianic feast was present to the mind of Jesus is evident from the fact that He pictures the future blessedness as a sitting at meat with Abraham, Isaac, and Jacob in the Kingdom of God (Mt. viii. 11-12), and as a being invited to the Marriage-Feast of the King's Son (Mt. xxii. 1-14), and at the Last Supper with the disciples promises them that He will drink wine with Him 'new' in the Kingdom of His Father (Mk. xiv. 25).

.   .   .   .   .   .

The conception of the Messianic feast finds a place also in the Lord's Prayer, for in the fourth petition the correct translation refers not to daily bread but to the Messianic Feast.

In the Prayer which Jesus teaches the believers, what He causes them to ask for is, under various forms, nothing else than the content of the Kingdom—the hallowing of God's name, the rule of His will upon earth, forgiveness of sins—with the addition of a petition for deliverance from "Temptation," that is to say, from the pre-Messianic Tribulation. Is it suitable in this sequence of ideas that they should ask God at the same time for daily bread? This petition, coming in the midst of the others, seems entirely to break the connection. Moreover, it contradicts the immediately following direction of Jesus that the believers should take no thought for eating and drinking and the maintenance of life generally, but reject such thoughts as heathenish (Mt. vi. 25-34), being convinced that God knows and will supply all their needs, without their asking (Mt. vi. 8 and vi. 22). Leaving all else to take care of itself, they are to concern themselves about nothing but the Kingdom of God (Mt. vi. 33). That means that their prayers also should be directed only to these things. In order that they may not, like the heathen, ask for unnecessary things, Jesus teaches them this prayer for the Kingdom of God and its blessings (Mt. vi. 7-9). How then is it conceivable that, amid these petitions for the one thing needful, He should bring in one which gives expression to the forbidden anxiety about earthly needs?

Moreover, the text of the fourth petition is recalcitrant to the attempt to refer it to earthly bread. It runs τὸν ἄρτον ἡμῶν τὸν ἐπιούσιον δὸς ἡμῖν σήμερον (Mt. vi. 11). What is the meaning of the word ἐπιούσιος, which occurs here and nowhere else in Greek? The only possible thing is to take it as an adjectival formation from ἐπιέναι, and translate it by "at hand" or "coming," as in Acts (vii. 26) τῇ ἐπιούσῃ ἡμέρᾳ is translated by "on the coming—i.e. the following, day." [1] The fourth petition means "Our bread, the coming (future) bread, give us this day." [2]

It is only because the petition, if taken thus, has apparently no sense that ἐπιούσιος has been translated by "necessary." In order to give it this sense it is taken—which is linguistically impossible —as the adjectival formation from ἐπί and οὐσία. But in that case the hiatus would have been avoided and the form would have been ἐπούσιος. And what sense would this adjective have? οὐσία means 'essence'; in popular usage it means 'possessions'. But from neither of these can a natural meaning for the adjective be obtained. Accordingly, some translators have had the bright idea of taking οὐσία as existence and translating ἐπιούσιος as "necessary to existence." Against this there are the facts, first that an adjectival formation could not possibly have such a far-fetched sense, and secondly that, if existence is meant in the sense of the material needs of existence, the abstract philosophical concept of being, which οὐσία represents, is out of the question.

But all these philological ingenuities are unnecessary. The natural translation "Our bread, the Coming bread, give us to-day" makes sense of the fourth petition and, in fact, exactly the sense which is required to fit in with the remaining petitions. Like these it asks for one of the blessings of the Coming Kingdom of God; in this case, the food of the Kingdom. Bread stands for food in general, as the Hebrew word לֶחֶם constantly does. The petition therefore means: The future food which is destined for us, that is to say, the food of the Kingdom of God, give us even to-day. In other words: Let Thy Kingdom immediately come, in which we shall eat the food of the Messianic feast.

It is only when taken in this way that the σήμερον which closes the petition acquires a sense appropriate in itself, doing justice to its emphatic position at the end of the sentence. It forms an antithesis to the futurity of the bread, and asks for it to be given, "even to-day." Never could "to-day" stand for "daily." Luke, by giving "daily" (τὸ καθ᾽ ἡμέραν) instead of "to-day", shows that he no longer understands the sense of the phrase (Lk. xi. 3).

These elementary reflections on the meaning of the Lord's

---

[1] See also Acts xvi. 11, xx. 15, xxi. 18.

[2] The Gospel of the Hebrews had *mahar* ('to-morrow'). Jerome translates this correctly *panem crastinum, i.e.* "our bread of to-morrow."

Prayer and the natural translation of the text combine to show that the fourth petition is to be understood in the light of that antithesis between "then" and "now" which prevails throughout the eschatological beliefs, and refers to the coming of the Messianic feast.

.   .   .   .   .   .

It is this expectation of the Messianic feast which also explains Jesus' action at the Lake of Gennesareth. From the supplies actually present He gives everyone a morsel of food, not to satisfy his hunger, but only to let him receive food from the hand of the future Messiah, and so to consecrate him in preparation for the Messianic feast.

What He does here with a multitude He repeats, at the Last Supper, with the disciples (Mk. xiv. 22-25; Mt. xxvi. 26-29). During the meal He takes bread, gives thanks over it, and distributes to each of them. Similarly He takes the cup, gives thanks over it, and gives it to be passed to each in turn.

To what did Jesus' thanksgiving at the Last Supper refer? That He did not merely give thanks for food and drink, but offered up prayer and thanksgiving to God in prospect of the coming Kingdom of God and its feast, we are warranted in concluding, although the words are unfortunately not preserved, from the fact that in the Church celebration, which arose out of this meal, petition and thanksgiving were offered in prospect of the Kingdom of God and its blessings. This is evidenced by the prayers at the meal-celebration as recounted in the Didache (ix. and x.).

Did. ix. 4: "As this bread now broken was strewn abroad upon the mountains and gathered together became one, so may Thy people be brought together from the ends of the earth into Thy Kingdom."

Did. x. 3-7: "Thou, almighty Ruler, hast created all things for Thy name's sake; food and drink hast Thou given to man to enjoy, that they may thank Thee. But to us Thou hast given spiritual food and drink and eternal life through Thy Servant. Above all we thank Thee because Thou art mighty. To Thee be praise in eternity. Remember, Lord, Thy church, to redeem it from evil, and to perfect it in Thy love; and bring it, when it is sanctified, from the four winds together into Thy Kingdom. For Thine is the power and the glory for ever. May Grace come, and may this world perish. Hosanna to the God of David!

"If any is holy, let him come; if any is not, let him repent. Maranatha! Amen.

"Permit the prophets to give thanks as much as they will."

Even if we did not possess the Didache we should gather from Justin's *Dialogue with Trypho* something of the contents [1] of the thanksgiving at the "Lord's meal."

Dial. xli. 1: "The offering of flour, which according to tradition was made on behalf of the cleansed leper, was a prototype of the bread of the Eucharist, the celebration of which was ordained by Jesus Christ our Lord as a remembrance of the sufferings which He endured for men who are being purified in soul from all evil. He desired that we should give thanks to God, because He has created the world with all that is in it for the sake of men; and also that He has freed us from the sin in which we lived; and also that through Him (*i.e.* Jesus) whom He made capable of suffering He has completely gained the victory over the Powers and the Mighty." [2]

The offering in this way of petitions and thanksgiving for the Kingdom of God and its blessings can only be explained by supposing that the thanksgiving of Jesus at the last meal with His disciples had the same subject. And the same applies to the thanksgiving at the meal by the Lake of Galilee. The "miracle of the loaves and fishes" was in reality the first Eucharist.

The reference of the Last Supper to the Messianic feast finds expression also in the prospect which Jesus held out to His disciples of meeting Him again at this feast. For He closes the celebration with the words "I say unto you, I will drink no more of this fruit of the vine till the day when I shall drink it new with you in my Father's Kingdom" (Mt. xxvi. 29).[3] This can mean nothing else than that they will shortly be gathered with Him at the Messianic feast.

The Last Supper at Jerusalem was therefore in its essential nature the same as the celebration with the multitude at the Lake; a meal at which Jesus gives thanks in prospect of the Coming Kingdom and the Messianic feast, and then distributes to those present the food which has in this way been consecrated, thus recognising them as those who are to share with Him the Coming Messianic feast.

[1] TRANSLATOR'S Note.—*Herrenmahl*—it is necessary to use the literal translation since the author (p. 257, *inf.*) expressly deprecates the use of "Supper" in connection with the Early Church's rite as misleading.

[2] The Powers and the Mighty mean the Angels and Demons. On this concept in Justin see also *Dial.* xlix. 8. Compare p. 65, *sup.*

[3] In Mk. xiv. 25 there is no "with you." But the saying itself implies a reunion at the Messianic feast.

At the Last Supper, in addition to the Thanksgiving He speaks words which have reference to His approaching death. The bread He designates as His body, the wine as His blood of the Covenant, which is shed for many for the forgiveness of sins (Mk. xiv. 22-24; Mt. xxvi. 26-28). All that is clear in these words is the general fact that they have reference to His death. It is further obvious that in the saying about the cup there is an allusion to the words "this is the blood of the covenant which Jahwe has made with you" (Ex. xxiv. 8), spoken by Moses at the concluding of the Covenant at Sinai, during the sprinkling of the blood upon the people. But exactly in what sense Jesus describes the bread which they eat and the wine which they drink as His body and blood will always remain obscure.

But the essence of the celebration, for the Early Church, did not consist in the mysterious analogy of bread and wine with body and blood. If there is anything which is certain in the earliest accounts of the celebration of the "Lord's Meal" it is that the so-called "words of institution" were not repeated when the believers ate the bread and drank the wine. That is at once evident from the way in which Paul quotes them to the Corinthians as something which he has told them before, and must now repeat (1 Cor. xi. 23). That really does not look as though they were familiar to the church from its weekly Sunday celebration. In the instructions for celebration in the Didache, too, there is only mention of the prayer of thanksgiving, not of the repetition of the "words of institution."

Nor was it a command to repeat the act, any more than the "words of institution," which determined the Early Church to continue the celebration of the meal which Jesus held with His disciples. As is well known, the earliest witnesses, Matthew and Mark, know nothing of a command to repeat the eating and drinking such as is found in Luke (xxii. 19) [1] and Paul (1 Cor. xi. 24-25). It would therefore seem that the Last Supper must have been repeated by the believers as a "Lord's Meal" for some intrinsic reason, some necessity grounded in the nature of the celebration. [2]

·   ·   ·   ·   ·   ·

[1] Not, however, in all the earliest authorities.

[2] On the problem presented by deriving the Early Church celebration out o the last meal of Jesus with His disciples see Albert SCHWEITZER, *Das Abendmahls-problem auf Grund der wissenschaftlichen Forschung des neunzehnten Jahrhunderts und der historischen Berichte* (Tübingen, 1901: 62 pp.; 2nd (unaltered) edition, 1929).

How then did the Early Church come to repeat Jesus' last meal with His disciples, without a command to that effect, and without any allusion to the saying about the bread and wine being His body and blood?

In the first place, what exactly did it repeat?

The essential character of this historic Last Supper, as well as of the meal by the Lake of Gennesareth, consisted in its being a meal accompanied by thanksgiving which pointed forward to the Messianic feast, and at which Jesus distributed to those present food and drink. What it is possible to repeat in this action is not the distribution of food and wine by Jesus, the significance of which is dependent on its being done by Himself, but only the thanksgiving for the prospect of the Kingdom and the Messianic feast. The Early Church therefore repeated the Last Supper of Jesus with His disciples as a meal accompanied by thanksgiving which pointed forward to the Messianic feast. The reason for the repetition was the eschatological saying at the end about drinking wine new with His disciples in His Father's Kingdom. This became for the disciples a command to repeat the meal.

How did that come about?

In consequence of this saying the disciples expected that the risen Jesus would come to them as they sat at meat in the same room in which He had been present with them on that last evening, and would then journey into Galilee with them, where He would be manifested in glory as the Messiah. Therefore, instead of dispersing into Galilee they remained after His death in Jerusalem, meeting with the believers in this room and holding meals accompanied by thanksgiving in expectation of the appearing of Christ.

Far too little attention has been given by scholars to the question what the disciples of Jesus did between Easter and Pentecost. Pictures have been drawn in garish colours of their complete helplessness and their fear of the Jews. They are supposed to have remained hidden in Jerusalem, or to have fled to Galilee. But, according to Acts, they remained constantly in Jerusalem and, moreover, not in hiding, but as the heads of a community of some 120 believers, as we learn in connection with the choice of a successor, to fill the place of Judas (Acts i. 15). They had no need to hide, because they were not being persecuted. Unintelligible as this may seem to us, it was against Jesus only, not against His adherents, that the authorities in Jerusalem directed their enmity.

Not even the companion of Jesus who offered armed resistance at His arrest, cutting off an ear of the High Priest's servant, was taken into custody along with Him (Mt. xxvi. 51).

Why did these Galileans remain in Jerusalem instead of going to their own homes? It was a saying of Jesus which held them there as though under a spell. As they rose up from the Supper and started on the way to Gethsemane, He said to them, "When I have risen again I will go before you ($\pi\rho o\acute{a}\xi\omega\ \acute{v}\mu\hat{a}s$) into Galilee" (Mk. xiv. 28; Mt. xxvi. 32). This can mean nothing else than that He, who is risen, will journey at their head into Galilee, as He journeyed at their head from there to Jerusalem when He came to His passion. The words "I will go before you" ($\pi\rho o\acute{a}\xi\omega\ \acute{v}\mu\hat{a}s$, Mk. xiv. 28) in the prophecy of the going up after His resurrection, correspond to the words "and Jesus went before them" (Mk. x. 32, $\kappa a\grave{\iota}\ \mathring{\eta}v\ \pi\rho o\acute{a}\gamma\omega v\ a\mathring{v}\tau o\grave{v}s\ \acute{o}\ 'I\eta\sigma o\hat{v}s$) in the description of the journey to Jerusalem.[1] Jesus therefore did not expect to appear at once upon the clouds of heaven; He thinks of the sequence of events after His death as being that He, when risen, will immediately journey to Galilee with the disciples, there to be manifested in the glory of the Son of Man, and then on the clouds of heaven, surrounded by His angels, to begin His reign.

The promise of going at their head into Galilee was not fulfilled, any more than the expectation which the disciples drew from the last words spoken at the Supper, that He would immediately on His resurrection celebrate the Messianic feast. Jesus did indeed appear several times after His death to them and to other believers, as we know from Paul (1 Cor. xv. 5-7), but He did not celebrate the Messianic feast with them, nor go with them into Galilee.

Since the saying about the risen Jesus journeying with the disciples into Galilee was not fulfilled, the tradition has forced it into meaning something different from what it actually meant. It endeavours to dispose of it by putting it, in a different form, into the mouth of the angel at the tomb, and making it mean that the disciples are to go by themselves into Galilee where Jesus, who will already have gone there, will appear to them.

In Mk. xvi. 7 the angel says to the women at the tomb: "Go and tell the disciples and Peter that He is going before you into Galilee" ($\pi\rho o\acute{a}\gamma\epsilon\iota$ $\acute{v}\mu\hat{a}s$); "there shall ye see Him, as He said unto you." The local going

---

[1] Mk. x. 32: "And they were on the way going up to Jerusalem. And Jesus walked before them, and they were aghast, and as they followed they were afraid."

'before' them is here turned into a temporal. In Matthew the saying is given the new interpretation not only by the angel but also by the risen Jesus Himself (Mt. xxviii. 7 and 10).—Mt. xxviii. 10: "Then said Jesus to them (the women): Fear not, go and tell my brethren to go to Galilee, and there they shall see Me." In fulfilment of this so much corrected saying, Matthew makes the disciples really go to Galilee and there, not in Jerusalem, see the risen Jesus (Mt. xxviii. 16-20).

That the appearances of the risen Jesus took place at Jerusalem only, and that the disciples between the death of Jesus and Pentecost were in Jerusalem only, and not in Galilee, is put beyond doubt by the Acts of the Apostles in agreement with Luke. What Matthew and the Gospel of John have to tell us about appearances in Galilee is derived from secondary traditions, which arose in order to give some kind of fulfil-ment to the saying about Jesus going before them into Galilee. Mat-thew, moreover, makes Jesus appear to the disciples only in Galilee, whereas the Fourth Gospel narrates appearances in Judaea (Joh. xx. 19-29) as well as in Galilee (Joh. xxi. 1-23).

The secondary tradition also seeks to provide a fulfilment for the other unfulfilled expectation, which arose out of Jesus' last saying at the Supper. Hence arose the narratives in which the risen Jesus appears at a meal. The disciples at Emmaus recognise "at the breaking of bread" that the stranger is the risen Lord (Lk. xxiv. 13-35). At the ensuing appearance to the disciples at Jerusalem the risen Jesus asks for food, whereupon their doubt that it was He disappears (Lk. xxiv. 36-43). In the narrative of the appearance of Jesus at Gennesareth the risen Jesus is waiting for the disciples to disembark, with a meal pre-pared on the shore, and distributes to them bread and fish (Joh. xxi. 1-14).

According to the Gospel according to the Hebrews—the passage is preserved in Jerome, *De viris illustribus*, ii.—James the Just had sworn to eat no bread from the time when he had drunk the cup of the Lord until he saw Him risen from them that sleep. When the risen Jesus appears He causes a table [1] and a loaf to be brought, and gives James some of the bread which he has broken after thanksgiving, saying "My brother, eat thy bread, for the Son of Man is risen from among them that sleep." [2]

In the *Epistula Apostolorum*, a Coptic anti-Gnostic writing originating in Asia Minor about A.D. 160, which is also preserved in a variant form in Ethiopic, the Apostles narrate the conversation which they had with the

---

[1] Note by TRANSLATOR.—The German here has *Fisch*, but that is a mere mis-print for *Tisch*.

[2] There is a confusion here, inasmuch as James the Just, the brother of the Lord, had not drunk the cup, since he was not present at the Last Supper.

risen Jesus.[1] In the course of conversation they put to Him the question: "O Lord, is it again a necessary thing that we take the cup and drink?" He answers: "Yea, it is necessary, until the day when I shall come with those who have been killed for my sake" (viii. 12–ix. 1). Jesus then instructs them that His saying about drinking the cup new with them refers to His Coming in Messianic glory and is not fulfilled by His now appearing to them as risen from the dead. They must, therefore, in celebrating the supper, continue until then to drink the cup in expectation of that "drinking it new with Him." The meaning of the Lord's Supper as a feast of expectation, looking forward to fellowship with Jesus at the Messianic feast, is thus retained here with clear reference to Jesus saying at the Supper about drinking the wine new in the Kingdom of God.

The narratives in which the Risen Jesus Himself partakes of the meal might, of course, be understood as intended to prove the reality of His bodily existence. But those in which He only appears as the distributor of the food make it quite clear that the mention of a meal is connected with the original expectation of a meal at which the disciples should meet with Him again.

In Justin Martyr, too, the expectation of a meal of reunion still appears. In the *Dialogue with Trypho* (li. 2) he mentions, as an important point in the preaching of Jesus, that "He would come to Jerusalem again and would then eat and drink anew with His disciples."

That these two sayings of Jesus, about drinking the wine new in the Kingdom of God and journeying, after His resurrection, to Galilee, influenced the tradition in this way shows clearly what an important part they must have played in the expectation of the Apostles and of the primitive Christian Community. Jesus' disciples remain at Jerusalem because, in accordance with the last saying of Jesus at the Supper, they believe that after His resurrection He will celebrate such a meal anew with them, and then will journey with them into Galilee in order there to be manifested in His Messianic Glory. And these sayings did, in the main, bear the meaning which they attached to them.

. . . . . .

The saying about being reunited with Him at a meal is indeed understood by the disciples as meaning that the new meal was to

[1] Carl SCHMIDT, *Gespräche Jesu mit seinen Jüngern nach der Auferstehung (Epistula Apostolorum). Ein katholisch-apostolisches Sendschreiben des 2. Jahrhunderts*, Leipzig, 1919: 731 pp. (English readers should consult the Review by M. R. JAMES in the *J. Theol. Studies*, xxi. 334-338.)

be held in the very room where they were then assembled; and it was for that reason that they continued to meet there.

The Acts of the Apostles contains some details about the dwelling of the disciples in Jerusalem. They were at the house of the mother of John Mark. It was to this house that Peter went after the angel had liberated him from prison, and he had "come to himself" again (Acts xii. 11-12). Many believers were there assembled at prayer. The room in which they were was entered through an ante-room (Acts xii. 14, πυλών). The large room in which the disciples and believers met was an upper room (ὑπερῷον), that is to say, a room immediately under the flat roof, as we learn right at the beginning of Acts.

Acts i. 13-14: "When they had come in (to Jerusalem) after their return from witnessing the Ascension of Jesus, they went up to the upper room where they were accustomed to abide. . . . These all continued in one accord in prayer, with the women and Mary, the mother of Jesus, and with His brethren."—In Acts i. 15 the number of those assembled is given as 120.

It was in this room that the Apostles were assembled with the believers on the morning of the day of Pentecost (Acts ii. 1-2). Was this room, however, identical with that in which Jesus held the Last Supper? When He sent His two disciples into the city to prepare the Paschal meal for Him, He told them that a man carrying a pitcher of water would lead them to a large upper room with cushions (ἀνάγαιον μέγα ἐστρωμένον—ἀνάγαιον being identical with ὑπερῷον), where they were to prepare the meal (Mk. xiv. 13-15). That this large upper room is identical with that of Acts, and was therefore in the house of the mother of John Mark, can scarcely be doubted. This, by the way, lends further support to the early conjecture that the young man who followed Jesus and His companions that night, and escaped from the apparitors who seized him by leaving his linen garment in their hands, was John Mark himself (Mk. xiv. 51-52).[1]

In the place where Jesus had held with them the thanksgiving meal, and had held out to them the prospect of a reunion at the Messianic feast, the disciples wait His return for this feast, mean-

---

[1] On the theory of the identity of the house where Jesus held the Last Supper with the house of the mother of John Mark, mentioned in Acts xii. 12, see also Theodor ZAHN, *Einleitung in das Neue Testament*, 2nd ed., 1900, vol. ii. pp. 213, 242-245, 252.

while holding with the believers meals at which, in prospect of the Coming of the Kingdom and the Messianic feast, they offer thanksgiving as on that occasion they had heard Him doing. Of their own motion they repeat, in association with the first believers, as much as it is possible to repeat of their last meal with Jesus (the thanksgiving meal), and expect that the Lord will return to them during such a meal, and will make it into the Messianic feast.

Thus there arose, without a command from Jesus, out of an inner necessity, as a repetition with similar significance of the Last Supper of Jesus with His disciples, the Early Christian ceremonial meal.

How far Jewish cultus-feasts can be adduced in explanation of the occurrence of the Christian ceremonial meal cannot be determined with certainty. One that might be cited in this connection is the meal held on Friday evening in Jewish households, celebrating the beginning of the Sabbath (Kiddush for Sabbath), as known from the Mishna tractate "Berachoth" (chaps. vi.-viii.).[1] It shows a similarity with the Last Supper in so far as the cup which is handed round and the bread used in the meal are consecrated by thanksgiving to God as the Creator of the vine and the giver of bread, to which those present make response, in each case, with an Amen. It is probable that this meal was already known to Judaism in the time of Jesus, though we have no evidence about it going back to that generation. The thanksgiving at this meal makes reference, according to the present rite (see Lietzmann, p. 203), not only to bread and wine but to the creation of the world, the Sabbath, the Law, and the deliverance from Egypt.

A peculiar view regarding the origin of the Lord's Supper is expressed by Hans Lietzmann in his interesting study on the Eucharist and the Lord's Supper.[2] He brings the Early Christian celebration into connection with general religious feasts which, on the ground of Rabbinic notices, he thinks himself justified in assuming for the Judaism of the time of Jesus. Such meals in a community of friends (*chābūrā*) had been held by Jesus along with His disciples "in the sunny days of their journeyings through Galilee." After His death this custom was kept up in the Christian community. "The 'table-fellowship' (κοινωνία) which had been begun with the 'historic' Jesus was continued with the exalted

---

[1] On the form of this meal of the "Beginning of the Sabbath" see Hans LIETZMANN, *Messe und Herrenmahl* (263 pp.: Bonn, 1926), pp. 202-207.

[2] Hans LIETZMANN, *Messe und Herrenmahl*, pp. 197-263.

Jesus," the partakers looking forward jubilantly to the return of the Lord.[1]

This community meal is not therefore derived from the last meal of Jesus with His disciples, and is not inspired by what He did and said on that occasion. Alongside of this "Jerusalem form" of the community meal, the Pauline form found a place. This had reference to the historical tradition of Jesus' last meal, and is subsequently a memorial of the death of Christ. Along with His death were celebrated the resurrection and return of the Lord. This Pauline form was immediately felt to be "an analogon of the Hellenistic memorial feast to great men now dead," and also "as a sacrificial meal, in which reside elemental powers from Heaven," and it accordingly develops on these lines.[2] Paul held this conception of the Lord's Supper in consequence of a revelation made to him by Christ[3] (1 Cor. xi. 23). Within a short period the Pauline form of the celebration won the victory over the Jerusalem form.

The starting-point of this theory is the sound observation that the origin of the community meal is not to be explained by the "words of institution" of Jesus about bread and wine. But from what source of information does Lietzmann draw to his knowledge that Jesus was accustomed to hold religious meals with His disciples and other believers? The Evangelists tell us only of the Feeding of the Multitude and the Last Supper at Jerusalem. Lietzmann also overlooks the consideration that a religious meal held by Jesus and His followers would acquire a unique character from the fact that He, the future Messiah, uttered the thanksgiving and distributed the food. But if Lietzmann himself has to admit that "the eschatological elements of the expectation of the Parousia" is common to both forms, the Jerusalemite and the Pauline (p. 252), the most natural thing is to derive the primitive Christian celebration from that expectation of the Messianic feast, to which Jesus gave expression in His saying about drinking the wine new in the Kingdom of His Father, and in allusion to which he made the distribution of the food at the Lake of Gennesareth and at the Last Supper in Jerusalem. In that case it becomes unnecessary to make the artificial distinction, which has no support whatever from the evidence which has come down to us, between two different types of primitive Christian "Lord's Meal."

---

[1] LIETZMANN, p. 250.　　[2] Ibid. p. 251.　　[3] Ibid. pp. 252-253.

It is, however, possible and even probable that the Feeding of the Multitude and the Last Supper at Jerusalem are connected with Jewish religious meals, in the sense that Jesus found the custom in existence of holding meals at which thanksgiving was offered, not only for the food and drink, but also for religious blessings. Moreover, it would be the more natural that the Early Church should, of its own motion, begin to celebrate a meal which had reference to the last meal of Jesus and the Coming of the Kingdom, if religious meals accompanied by thanksgiving were not unfamiliar to the Jews of that time. But from the Jewish religious meal pure and simple, neither the two meals of Jesus with His disciples nor the "Lord's Meal" of the Early Church can be explained. These celebrations only become intelligible when it is recognised that for Jesus, as well as for the Early Church, this Jewish religious thanksgiving meal had become a mystical anticipatory celebration of the Messianic feast. That the thanksgiving in the Early Christian celebration is in some way dependent on an earlier one is made probable by the fact that, as the Didache shows (*Did.* ix. and x.), it makes reference not only to the Kingdom, but also to the creation of the world.

The Jewish Paschal meal played no part at all in the development of the Early Christian celebration. It is of course entirely probable that the Synoptics are right in representing the distribution by Jesus of the bread and wine to the disciples as taking place in the course of a Paschal meal, probably at the end of it. And it is natural to suppose that Jesus was thinking of Himself as the true Paschal Lamb when He spoke of the bread and wine as His body and blood. But the Passover did not continue to exercise an influence on the celebration of the meal by the primitive Christian community, Had the repetition of the meal been due to the influence of the Paschal meal, it could only have taken place on the historic day, not daily, as was the case.

And it is noteworthy that the idea of the Passover plays no part whatever in the prayers of thanksgiving at the "Lord's Meal."

What constitutes the essential character of the Early Christian meal is therefore not a reference to Jesus' saying about the bread and wine as His body and blood, but wholly and solely in the petition and thanksgiving for the Coming of the Kingdom. And since in the meantime the expectation of the Kingdom and of the Messianic feast has become bound up with the return of Jesus, the petitions and thanksgivings refer also to the latter. This is the new feature of the repeated celebration.

The thanksgiving is described by the word ἀγαλλίασις (rejoicing), which is also used for the jubilation at the Coming of the Kingdom. It is therefore an anticipation of that future rejoicing.

1 Peter iv. 13: "That at the revelation of His glory you may rejoice with exceeding joy (χαρῆτε ἀγαλλιώμενοι)."

Jude 24: "And can set you before His glory without defect in rejoicing (ἐν ἀγαλλιάσει)."

Rev. xix. 7: "Let us be glad and rejoice (ἀγαλλιῶμεν) and give honour to Him, for the marriage of the Lamb is come."

Acts ii. 46: "Breaking bread at home, they took their food with rejoicing (ἐν ἀγαλλιάσει)."

We get a hint of the petition for the Coming of Christ in the Aramaic exclamatory prayer *Maranatha* (מָרָנָא תָא—"Our Lord, Come!"). In the Didache it forms the close of the last thanksgiving at the celebration, in the formula (*Did.* x. 6): "Is any one holy, let him come; is any one not holy, let him repent. *Maranatha, Amen.*"

This *Maranatha* is also found in Paul, in the autograph greeting at the close of the First Epistle to the Corinthians; and it occurs in a phrase of which the content recalls the close of the prayer at the Lord's Meal in the Didache: "If any love not the Lord, let him be accursed. *Maranatha*" (1 Cor. xvi. 22).

In the Greek rendering (Ἀμὴν ἔρχου, κύριε Ἰησοῦ) the *Maranatha* forms the close of the Apocalypse of John (xxii. 20).

The Aramaic exclamatory prayer *Maranatha* thus comes from the celebration of the Supper as practised by the primitive community at Jerusalem. From it we can see how large a part the expectation of the Coming of Jesus played in those first celebrations of the "thanksgiving meal."

We asked at an earlier point, What did the disciples do between Easter and Pentecost? The answer is that day by day they waited with the other believers, holding with them the thanksgiving meal in the very room where Jesus had held the Last Supper with the disciples, expecting that the risen Jesus would return to them and, as Messiah, take His place at the feast. If they were inactive, it was not from fear of the Jews, but because the expectation of the Coming of Jesus fully occupied their minds and left no room for the thought of preaching Jesus. The significance of the Day of Pentecost is, that by the Spirit which then took possession of them they were forced to abandon this passive attitude and begin to proclaim the Messiahship of Jesus. The statement so often made, that Pentecost witnessed the founding of the Christian Church, is mistaken. The Church had been in existence since Easter. At Pentecost there were added to it, through the preaching of Peter, three thousand new members (Acts ii. 41). To the expectation of the Return of Jesus there was added on that day the preaching of belief in Him.

.   .   .   .   .   .

The Thanksgiving meal pointing forward to the Return of Jesus was the only kind of divine service held in the earliest times. There were no purely "Word-of-God-services."[1] All the praying, prophesying, preaching, and teaching took place within the framework of the thanksgiving at the celebration of the meal. All that we learn from Paul in 1 Cor. xiv. 1-40 about the activities of the spiritually endowed and the prophets took place in the course of this service. That Paul knows no other assembly of the church than that for the meal celebration is clear from the way he uses the term "Coming together" in the First Epistle to the Corinthians.

1 Cor. xi. 17: "And this, now that I am ordering matters, I cannot praise in you, that you come together not for good but for ill."

1 Cor. xi. 20: "When you come together to one place it is not possible to eat the Lord's Meal" (i.e. your meal is no proper Lord's Meal).[2]

1 Cor. xiv. 26: "When you come together, each one brings a psalm, or a teaching, or a revelation, or a speaking with tongues, or an interpretation."

1 Cor. xiv. 23: "If now the whole church comes together to one place, and all speak with tongues. . . ."

Only on the assumption that the holding of the meal was originally the form of divine service does the history of the earliest Christian worship become intelligible. It is quite clearly to be seen from Justin's account that at the morning celebration held every Sunday the reading of Scripture and preaching formed the introduction to the prayer and thanksgiving at the meal; and indeed we

---

[1] TRANSLATOR'S Note.—In German this is a technicality for a service of the form of the usual Protestant service, with prayer, reading of Scripture, and preaching.

[2] 1 Cor. xi. 20, συνερχομένων οὖν ὑμῶν ἐπὶ τὸ αὐτὸ οὐκ ἔστιν κυριακὸν δεῖπνον φαγεῖν.

see Paul endeavouring to secure a place in the thanksgiving for the instructive and edifying elements (1 Cor. xiv. 5, 19, 26).

Justin, 1 *Apol.* lxvii. "On the day which is called Sunday an assembly takes place of all who live either in towns or in the country. At this the memoirs of the Apostles or the writings of the Prophets are read aloud as long as is fitting. When the reader has ceased, he who presides gives in an address exhortation and encouragement to imitate all this good. Then we all rise up together and offer prayer. And as has already been mentioned, when we have ended the prayer, bread, wine, and water are brought, and he who presides offers prayer and thanksgiving with all his energy, and the people assent, saying, Amen. And then the food is distributed."

Every attempt to assume that the primitive Community had a "service of the Word of God" separate from the meal-celebration service ends in a fiasco; for to explain in this sense the statements which have come down to us about the earliest Christian cultus requires the most improbable hypotheses. It was only in the course of time that "word-of-God services" arose.

In those first weeks the "thanksgiving meal" was held every day, as the Acts of the Apostles tells us (Acts ii. 46).

It was considered essential that, so far as possible, all the believers living in one place should meet together for it. The view that it was held by small groups in separate houses is not correct. The first 120 believers met together for the breaking of bread in the room in which Jesus had held the Last Supper with His disciples.

Naturally these 120 partakers could not all "recline at table" together, for there would not have been room (even if, as is probable, the flat roof was also used), but this would not matter so long as all ate and drank together.

That the Corinthians met together "in one place" to celebrate the Lord's Supper we learn from Paul (1 Cor. xi. 20). And this is implied in Justin also. Here the thought that the whole community should eat of the same consecrated food is carried so far that the absent have their portions brought to them at their homes by the deacons (1 *Apol.* lxvii.). But when, after Pentecost, there were more than 3000 believers at Jerusalem, the meal must necessarily have been held in various rooms.

The celebration took place in the morning. It was at the hour when Jesus rose from the dead that His return was expected.

Accordingly the meal at which His return was looked forward to was held in the early hours. Exceptionally, however, any meal at any hour of the day might be given the character of the thanksgiving meal.

Hans Lietzmann, in his study *Messe und Herrenmahl*, assumes that the celebration originally took place in the evening, when the church met "after the dusty toil and the cares of the day were over" (p. 229). He does not succeed, however, in showing satisfactorily how it afterwards became transferred to the morning.

The morning hour is confirmed by the fact that it took place early on the day after the Sabbath, the day of the week on which Jesus arose. The celebration on the morning of the Sunday continued to be held after the daily celebration had gradually become impracticable. The return of Christ had at first been expected from day to day, later the conception narrowed to the day of the the week on which His resurrection had taken place. Accordingly, at the same hour on that day throughout the whole Church, every local church awaited that return with thanksgiving. Later on, Easter Day came especially to be looked upon as a possible day for His return. The embittered controversies over the date of Easter are to be connected with the feeling that at the Easter thanksgiving-meal the whole Church should be awaiting the coming of the Lord: Easter therefore ought to be held everywhere on the same day.

It is possible that the narrative of the outpouring of the Spirit at Pentecost (Acts ii. 1-47) contains the earliest evidence of the morning celebration. The fact that the believers were assembled on that morning in "the large upper room" is most naturally explained if they were met for the holding of the thanksgiving meal. The outburst of ecstatic speech is most naturally understood if the believers were in a state of excitement. Thus there is much to be said for the idea that the speaking with tongues began while they were rejoicing at the thanksgiving meal over the Coming of the Kingdom, and were praying earnestly for the return of Christ. If they were at the meal, too, the opinion of the hearers standing below, who thought the ecstatic speech was due to drunkenness, becomes intelligible.

Since the 120 believers at Pentecost were no doubt meeting, as at other times, in the house of the mother of John Mark, Peter must have preached his Pentecost sermon from the very room in which Jesus had held the Last Supper with His disciples.

Although it points back to the evening before the death of Jesus, the Early Christian celebration of the meal took place, as we have seen, in the morning, and was held on the Sunday, the day of the resurrection of Jesus, after the daily celebration was given up. This clearly shows that, notwithstanding the words about bread and wine being Christ's body and blood, it did not come into use as a memorial of the death of Jesus, but is concerned with His resurrection and return.

It so happens that there is no reference in Paul to the Sunday celebration of the "Lord's Meal." But that the day after the Sabbath already held a special position in his Churches is evident from the fact that in 1 Corinthians xvi. 2 he ordains that on that day believers are to set aside their gifts for the collection to be sent up to Jerusalem.

The "breaking of bread" on the Sunday is first mentioned in the "We-Source" of Acts. Paul took part in this with the believers at Troas when passing through on his way to Jerusalem (Acts xx. 7-11). The not entirely clear description of this meeting is most easily explained, if after the Sunday morning celebration the believers remained together all the night, and then at a second thanksgiving-meal waited for the morning, in which Paul was to continue his journey. In this way it would become intelligible that Paul, after raising the young man who had been over-come with sleep and fallen from the window, "breaks bread" and then continues a discourse with them until his departure at dawn.

The "breaking of bread" on every Sunday is prescribed in the Didache (xiv. 1), and is mentioned in Justin (1 *Apol.* lxvii.), about A.D. 150, with the explanation that Sunday was the day of the creation of light and of the resurrection of Jesus. That the celebration took place in the morning is so much a matter of course to both that they have no occasion to mention it. It is the Sunday morning meal celebration that Pliny has in view in his famous letter to Trajan (*Ep.* x. 96), about A.D. 113, when he reports that the Christians met on a particular day, before daybreak, to praise Christ in hymns as in some sense a God, and to bind themselves together by a 'sacrament'.

The earliest designation of the meal celebration which has come down to us is Paul's reference to it as the Lord's meal (1 Cor. xi. 20, κυριακὸν δεῖπνον). Whether the meal is so called because it arose out of that which Jesus held with the disciples, or because it points to the expectation of His coming to the feast of reunion, cannot be determined. In favour of the second hypothesis is the

fact that the Sunday was called, with allusion to the resurrection
of Jesus, the Lord's Day (ἡμέρα κυριακή).

In Acts (ii. 46, xx. 7) and, later, in the Didache (xiv. 1) the
meal is simply called the Breaking-of-bread, because the breaking
of bread, accompanied by thanksgiving, belongs to its traditional
form.

The designation Eucharist, which occurs in the Didache (ix. 1),
in Ignatius (*Ad Smyrn.* vii. 1; *Ad Philadel.* iv. 1), and in Justin
(1 *Apol.* lxvi.), doubtless originated in very early times. It is the
most accurate, since thanksgiving constitutes the essential character
of the celebration.

Ignatius (*Ad Smyrn.* viii. 2) implies that the term Agape (ἀγάπη)
was also used for the meal. This term signifies the intention of the
partakers to show that they are bound together in love with one
another and also with God and Christ. It is possible that this name
for the celebration is connected with the mystico-speculative conception of love in the Ignatian, Johannine, and Justinian theologies.

The Early Church's celebration is nowhere called the Supper;
and this term ought not to be applied to it. Anyone who uses it
shows that he still conceives the primitive Christian meal-celebration on the lines of the later 'Administration' form, in which Jesus'
"words of institution" about the bread and wine as His body and
blood make it into a ceremonial act, which logically should only
be performed once a year, on the evening of the Thursday before
Easter.

What is the general result as regards the meal-celebration which
Paul found in existence in the Primitive Church? That it was a
Thanksgiving-meal which looked backward to the last meal of
Jesus with His disciples, and forward to His return; and possesses
sacramental character, in the sense that those who take part in
it enter into table-fellowship (lit. "meal-fellowship") with Christ,
in prospect of being united with Him at the Messianic feast.

.   .   .   .   .   .

The unsatisfactory and confusing character of the accounts
hitherto given of the sacraments in Paul is due to their taking their
starting-point from a confused and inaccurate conception of the
Primitive Christian sacraments. They have not been able to distinguish accurately between what Paul found already in existence
and what he added of his own, but mix the two together in a confused whole. Once it is recognised that Paul took over Baptism

and "the Lord's Meal" from Primitive Christianity as eschato-logical sacraments, what he says about them can be quite easily understood.

That is at once apparent from the way in which his surprising parallel, between the Christian sacraments and God's deeds of deliverance for the Israelites on the way to the Promised Land, acquires a natural meaning. It now becomes intelligible how the passing through the Red Sea and the journeying beneath the pillar of cloud can become the prototype of Baptism, and the feeding with Manna and the giving to drink of the waters from the Rock similarly answer to the "Lord's Meal." [1]

I Cor. x. 1-12: "For I would not have you ignorant, brethren, that our fathers were all under the cloud and all went through the sea, and were all baptized unto Moses in the cloud and in the sea, and all ate the same spiritual food and drank the same spiritual drink. For they drank of the spiritual rock which went with them; and that rock was Christ. But with the majority of them God was not well pleased, for they were laid low in the wilderness.

"These things happened as an example to us, that we might not lust after evil, as some of them lusted. Become not worshippers of idols, as some of them did, of whom it is written: 'They lay down to eat and drink and stood up to dance.' Nor let us practise unchastity, as some of them did, and fell in one day to the number of three-and-twenty-thousand. And let us not tempt the Lord, as some of them did, and were slain by the serpents. Nor shall ye murmur as some of them murmured, and were slain by the destroyer. This happened to them for an example, and is written as a warning for us, upon whom the End of the Times is come. Therefore, let him that is confident of standing, take heed that he fall not."

For the exaltation of the water-giving Rock into a form of manifesta-tion of the pre-existent Christ the way had been prepared by the Book of the Wisdom of Solomon, which originated about 100 B.C. According to it all God's deeds of deliverance in freeing the Israelites from Egypt and on the journey to the Promised Land were wrought by the "Wisdom" of God, conceived as a distinct person. This Wisdom is the appointed protectress of the righteous and holy, and has revealed itself as such since the beginning of the world. It directed the course of Noah's ark (Wisd. x. 4); it was present in the cloud which went before the People; by it the waters of the Red Sea were caused to divide and the Rock to give forth water (Wisd. x. 17-19, xi. 4).

[1] On the equating of baptism and the Lord's Meal with God's deeds of de-liverance on the journey to the Promised Land see also pp. 20-22, *sup*.

For Philo, the contemporary of Paul, the water-giving rock is the Sophia and the Logos (Philo, *Legum allegoriae*, ii. 86, ed. Cohn-Wendland i. p. 107; *Quod deterius potiori insidiari soleat*, 115-118, ed. Cohn-Wendland i. pp. 284 f.).

That the rock followed the Israelites in their journeyings is a Rabbinic tradition on Numbers xxi. 16 (Tosefta Sukka iii. 11 ff. and Targum of the Pseudo-Jonathan on Num. xxi. 19).

Since Paul does not use the conception of the pre-existent Logos, but assumes the pre-existence of Christ, the Rock becomes for him a mode of manifestation of the pre-existent Christ. By means of the speculative interpretation of the Old Testament narrative the drinking from the Rock becomes in a very special sense the prototype to the drinking at the Lord's Meal.

The position in which the believers find themselves corresponds to that of the Israelites in their journeyings. The Israelites are the chosen race which was called to take possession of the Promised Land; believers are the Chosen Race who live at the End of the Times (1 Cor. x. 11) and are to be heirs of the Messianic Kingdom. These are, among all races of men, the two most privileged generations, because there is promised to them a blessedness of which they only can partake. The prerogative which is destined for them is assured to them by God by special provisions made by Himself. He enables the Israelites to reach the Promised Land by passing through the sea, journeying beneath the cloud, drinking of the water from the rock, and being fed with manna. Believers are prepared and strengthened with a view to inheriting the Kingdom by baptism and by the eating and drinking at the "Lord's Meal."

Here appears the distinction between the Hellenistic sacramental conception on the one hand, the Primitive Christian and Pauline on the other. For Primitive Christianity, and for Paul, it is a matter of provision for deliverance originating with God; for Hellenism, of ceremonies discovered by men, which by the symbolism set forth in them have the effect of creating a corresponding reality, provided they are carried out and made use of in the proper way.

For this reason Paul can do—what would be quite impossible to Hellenistic thought—he can treat supernatural historical events, which affected a plurality of men at once, as sacraments and make them types of Baptism and the Lord's Meal. The essential character, both of those ancient sacraments and these recent ones, is that they both have reference to expected historical events—the taking possession of the Promised Land and the Coming of the Kingdom —and guarantee the partaking in them. They thus cease to be properly comparable to the Hellenistic sacraments.

Once the eschatological character of the Pauline sacramental concept is understood, the parallel drawn between Baptism and the "Lord's Meal" on the one hand, and the baptism in the Red Sea and under the cloud and the eating of manna and drinking of the water from the rock on the other, ceases to be an obscurity which has to be excused as a product of Rabbinic ingenuity, and becomes thoroughly sound and natural.

Sound, too, is the application which Paul designs to make in thus citing the Old Testament parallels for Baptism and the Lord's Meal. He desires to correct the false confidence which was liable to arise from having been baptized and having partaken of the Lord's Meal. Now although the Israelites who came up out of Egypt were intended by God to take possession of the Promised Land, and were in so many ways consecrated thereto by the saving acts of God, they nevertheless forfeited the good that had been promised to them through idolatry, unchastity, tempting God, and murmuring against Him. As they failed to reach the Promised Land, so now will those who have been baptized and have partaken of the table of the Lord fail to attain the Messianic Kingdom if they sin in a similar way.

The great problem of the relation of the ethical to the sacramental which Hellenism cautiously avoids—when it does not rashly decide it in favour of the Sacramental—is here grasped by Paul with a sure hand, and solved by showing that the sacramental good is rendered invalid by unethical conduct. That he should come to such a conclusion is yet another sign that his mind is not moving on the lines of Hellenistic sacramental conceptions.

.   .   .   .   .   .

In the case of Baptism, it would have been natural to expect that, as the sacrament of the forgiveness of sins, it would have been brought by Paul into connection with his doctrine of righteousness by faith. This, however, he does not do. He never explains it as the appropriation, made by faith, of the forgiveness of sins which has been secured by Jesus' atoning sacrifice. That in itself would suffice to show that the doctrine of righteousness by faith is not the central point of his view of redemption.

The usual Primitive-Christian view of baptism as mediating the forgiveness of sins and the possession of the Spirit is for him something inadequate, which he can even treat with a certain irony. When he is rebuking the Corinthians for bringing law-suits before heathen courts and so doing wrong and robbing their brethren, and in connection with this reminding them that the unchaste, the worshippers of idols, thieves, drunkards, and blasphemers—such as many of themselves had formerly been!—are shut out from the Kingdom of God, he adds, "But you are washed clean, you are sanctified, you have been made righteous through the name of the Lord Jesus Christ and the Spirit of our God " (1 Cor. vi. 1-11). In this allusion to the change made in them by baptism he is not seeking to console them, but smiling ironically at their idea that now as baptized persons they have become, without any inner effort on their own part, entirely different from what they were before.

Why does Paul nowhere develop the thought that baptism brings about the forgiveness of sins and the possession of the spirit? Because, according to his view, in baptism that comprehensive redemption is obtained, of which the forgiveness of sins and the possession of the Spirit are only partial manifestations. With the change in cosmic conditions due to the death and resurrection of Jesus, and the higher conception of redemption which corresponds thereto, the effect of baptism has now become more profound than it previously was. If redemption now consists in having died and risen with Christ, the effect of baptism can be none other than that in it this dying and rising again has its inception.

Of all the traditional view of baptism the one thing which Paul retains is that it effects redemption. His fundamental conception of it coincides exactly with that of the Baptist. But the customary description of its effect, and the natural symbolism involved in the plunge beneath the water, have become for him meaningless. The conception of the sacrament is for him completely dominated by the conception of redemption, to which it is subordinated. If baptism possesses the power of effectually adding the believer to the number of those who are to be partakers in the Kingdom of God, its effect can, since Jesus' death and resurrection, only be understood as being the bringing into force of that union with Christ in His death and resurrection, which prepares the way for participating in the glory of Christ. It is on the basis of the mystical being-in-Christ, as the centre of his teaching, that Paul explains baptism.

Rom. vi. 3-5: "Do you not know that we, as many of us as were baptized into Jesus Christ, were baptized into His death? By baptism into His death we were buried with Him, in order that as Christ was raised from the dead through the glory of the Father we also might walk in a new condition of life. For if we have been implanted into the likeness of His death we shall also be implanted into the likeness of His resurrection."

Gal. iii. 27-28: "As many as were baptized into Christ (then) put on Christ. There is thus neither Jew nor Greek, neither bondman nor freeman, neither man nor woman; for ye all are One (Person) in Christ Jesus."

1 Cor. xii. 13: "For in one Spirit we were all baptized into one body, whether we be Jews or Gentiles, slaves or free, and were all given to drink of one Spirit."

Out of the outward "Christianising" of baptism by relating it to the name of Jesus as the expected Messiah, Paul makes an inward and spiritual Christianisation. It is, for him, powers that go forth from Christ which cause the redemptive event to take place in it. The implanting into the body of Christ is the thing that happens in it. In conformity with his conceptions of redemption Paul holds that baptism is a being buried and rising again with Christ. The symbolism of plunging beneath the water and rising out of it again is not made use of by him at all. So little is he concerned with the pictorial aspect of the rite that he can change the metaphor and describe baptism as a being given to drink of the Spirit (1 Cor. xii. 13), with the same freedom as it was possible for him to regard the passing through the Red Sea and the journeying beneath the cloud as a being baptized.

It is only by this deeper conception of what happens in baptism that it can be explained how, after the death of Jesus, it came to give the Spirit, which it had not previously done. What the ordinary view was content to affirm on the ground of experience, became manifest to Paul as a matter of cause and effect; because believers became in baptism risen-with-Christ, the Spirit was manifested in them as their new life-principle.

The forgiveness of sins is for Paul effected in baptism because, through the dying and rising again which takes place in it, the fleshly body and the sin which cleaves to it are abolished, and henceforth are as though they were not. Along with the flesh, sin is destroyed and does not count [1] any more. Baptism is thus not brought into connection with the conception of the forgiveness of sins, as this appears in the doctrine of the atoning death of Jesus, but only into that kind of connection with it which is valid for his mysticism.[2]

For the Baptist, baptism secures something future (forgiveness of sins at the Judgment, and partaking of the outpouring of the Spirit). In its external "Christianisation" in the Primitive-Christian Church it effected both something future (forgiveness of sins at the Judgment) and something present (the possession of the Spirit). In Paul's teaching present and future goods are combined in such a way that baptism is no longer an act in itself but the beginning of a process which will end with the coming of the Messianic glory. In this way he deepens and spiritualises its sacramental value without any detriment to the significance ordinarily ascribed to it.

Paul does not develop at length, or bring forward arguments in support of, his doctrine of the essential character of baptism. For him it is something which follows immediately from the knowledge of the true significance of the dying and rising again.

By the dying and rising again, which begins in Baptism, believers lay aside all that which in their natural existence distinguishes them from one another. They are no longer Jews or Greeks, men or women, slaves or freemen, but all together form a new humanity 'in Christ'. They ought, therefore, to attach no further importance to all that belongs to their natural existence, but must make it their whole concern to continue steadfastly in the being-in-Christ, and to walk as those who live no longer in the flesh but in the Spirit.

In setting forth this imposingly large and simple view of baptism Paul goes far beyond anything that Primitive Christianity affirmed about it. And yet, essentially, all that he has done is to grasp the new fullness of meaning which the death and resurrection of Jesus have given to that sacrament of redemption which the Baptist preached.

.   .   .   .   .   .

In writing to the Corinthians who were treating the "Lord's Meal" with a lack of ceremonial decency, each one eating provision which he had brought with him without caring whether the needy had anything at all, Paul calls the historic meal of Jesus with

---

[1] TRANSLATOR'S Note.—The German is *zählt nicht*, which can hardly be rendered otherwise than by the colloquial idiom.

[2] On the forgiveness of sins as an annihilation of sin by the being-in-Christ see above, pp. 222-223.

His disciples to their remembrance, with a view to making clear to them the solemn ceremonial character of the common meal. And because they accepted without scruple invitations to take part in heathen sacrificial feasts he explains to them the significance of the Lord's Meal, in order to show them that they could not be fellow-guests both of the Lord and of the demons.

1 Cor. xi. 20-34: "When you come together to one place it is not possible so to eat the Lord's Meal (*i.e.* your meal is no true Lord's Meal), for in eating each is in a hurry to take his own meal, and one is hungry and another drunken. Have you no houses in which to eat and drink? Or do you show contempt for the Church of God and put to shame those who have nothing?

"What shall I say to you? Shall I praise you? In this I praise you not.

"For I have received of the Lord that which I also delivered to you, that the Lord Jesus on the night in which He was betrayed took bread, gave thanks, brake it, and said: 'This is my body which is (given) for you; this do in remembrance of me.'

"Likewise also the cup after the meal, and said: 'This cup is the new Covenant in my blood, This do, as often as ye drink (it), in memory of me.' For so often as you eat this bread and drink this cup, you show forth the death of the Lord till He come. Whosoever, therefore, eateth the bread or drinketh the cup of the Lord unworthily, becomes guilty in connection with the body and blood of the Lord.

"Let each man examine himself, and so let him eat of the bread and drink of the cup. For he who eats and drinks eats and drinks judgment to himself, if he does not discern the body.

"Therefore many are weak and sickly among you, and not a few have fallen asleep. If we examined ourselves then we should not be judged. But if we are judged by the Lord we shall be chastened, that we may not be condemned with the world.

"Therefore, my brethren, when you come together to eat, wait for one another. If any is hungry let him eat at home that you may not come into judgment."

1 Cor. x. 14-22: "Therefore, my beloved, flee from idolatry. I speak to you as men of understanding. Judge for yourselves what I say.

"The cup of blessing which we bless, is it not union with the blood of Christ? The bread which we break, is it not union with the body of Christ. As it is one bread [1] so we are one body, for all have part in the one bread.[1]

---

[1] Both the German and the Greek admit of the translation "one loaf." In the Didache stress is laid on the grain which was originally scattered being gathered into one loaf.

"Consider the Israel which is after the flesh. Have not those who eat of the sacrifice union with the altar? What am I saying? That meat of idol sacrifice is anything? Or that the idol is anything? No, but what the heathen sacrifice, they sacrifice to the demons and not to God: I would not have you enter into union with demons. You cannot drink the cup of the Lord with the cup of demons. You cannot partake of the table of the Lord and the table of demons. Or shall we provoke the jealousy of the Lord? Are we stronger than He?"

.   .   .   .   .   .

In regard to the historic meal of Jesus with His disciples, we do not really learn anything new from Paul. For he himself has no clear consciousness of what the nature of the ceremony was, his conception of it being already wholly under the influence of the Church's Thanksgiving-meal. This is at once evident from the fact that at the giving of the bread and wine he makes Jesus say, not "for many," that is, for the many who are called to the King-dom, but "for you" which is inherently impossible. For in saying this the Lord would have been describing His death as of avail for the disciples only. But since Paul is looking past the historical ceremony to the Church ceremony, the disciples are for him the representatives of the believers at the future celebrations. It is to these believers that the "for you" addressed to the disciples refers. According to Mark and Matthew, Jesus represents His blood as shed for the still unspecified number of the Elect; for Paul these have become the believers. That clearly suggests a later point of view.

To this later point of view is also to be referred the identical form of the sayings about bread and wine. In Mark and Matthew it is only at the handing of the cup that Jesus speaks of the saving value of His death, whereas at the distribution of the bread He confines Himself to the statement that it is His body. In Paul's account, moreover, the "for you" is added to the saying about the body also.

The later conception is, further, fully and openly manifested in the fact that Paul makes Jesus enjoin the disciples to repeat the meal in memory of Him. This apparently self-evident presuppo-sition for the continuance of the celebration in the Church he projects back into the history, a bare decade and a half after the death of Jesus, at the same time ignoring completely the saying about drinking the wine new together with the disciples

in the Kingdom of God, from which the repetition of the ceremony arose. What a notable achievement for tradition it is, that
the two earliest Evangelists have not allowed any command of
repetition to intrude itself into the account of the last meal of Jesus
with His disciples; as also, that they allow the, to us curious, "for
many" to stand instead of the "for you," which was so natural
from a later standpoint; and, furthermore, have preserved the
eschatological saying at the close, in spite of its having remained
unfulfilled!

Since, in describing the historic meal, Paul has had an eye on
the Church's Meal-celebration, it escapes his notice that he has
represented the Lord as commanding the repetition of His own,
properly speaking, unrepeatable act of distribution, while He really
meant only the repetitions of the eating and drinking of the consecrated bread and wine accompanied by a similar thanksgiving. It
is characteristic of the interpenetration, in his account, of the historic celebration and the Church's Thanksgiving-meal, that it is not
obvious from his narrative exactly where the words of Jesus at the
historic meal end, and his own explanation to the Corinthian
church begins. In 1 Cor. xi. 25 the "you" is addressed by Jesus to
the disciples, in the following verse it means the believers taking
part in the celebration!

It has been disputed whether Paul, in saying "I have received from
the Lord that which I have delivered to you" (1 Cor. xi. 23, ἐγὼ γὰρ
παρέλαβον ἀπὸ τοῦ κυρίου, ὃ καὶ παρέδωκα ὑμῖν) means that he is repeating the words of Jesus at the historic meal, as preserved by tradition
and as known to him from the tradition, or whether he quotes them as a
revelation which had been made to him.

In the language of the Mysteries παραλαμβάνειν and παραδιδόναι
signify the reception and communication of the revelation received in
the Mysteries. If Paul could be supposed to be under the influence of
the Hellenistic mode of thought, his words would mean that he was
giving information to the Corinthians about the Last Supper derived
from a revelation which he had received. But since he did not live in a
world of Hellenistic conceptions, it is most probable that he means, in
accordance with Rabbinic linguistic usage, the receiving and passing on
of the tradition of these words of Jesus.

No doubt Paul claims in principle that his whole Gospel is based on
revelation coming from Christ (Gal. i. 11-12), and that "Christ after the
flesh" no longer means anything to him (2 Cor. v. 16). This theory,
however, he can hardly carry through on the question of the Lord's

Meal, since it is necessary for him here to be able to refer to the words spoken by Jesus at the Last Supper.[1]

According to Hans Lietzmann (*Messe und Herrenmahl*, pp. 254-256) Paul, who must have had his information about the Last Supper from the tradition of the Christian community, means by the assertion that he had "received it from the Lord" that the Lord had revealed to him the significance of the historic celebration for the community-meal. A detailed argument to show that Paul is referring only to tradition is offered by Gerhard Kittel (*Die Probleme des palästinischen Spätjudentums und des Urchristentums*, Stuttgart, 1926: 200 pp.; pp. 63-64).

.   .   .   .   .   .

In the course of his account of the historic celebration Paul makes clear his view of the significance of the Church's celebration. It coincides with the Primitive Christian view. The celebration was a thanksgiving meal which looks forward to the return of Christ. This eating and drinking is for Paul a proclaiming of the death of the Lord "until He come" (1 Cor. xi. 26). The only point in which he corrects the prevailing view is that thinking about this return of the Lord is to take as its starting-point the remembrance of His death. In doing so he is not really putting any new content into the celebration. He is only emphasising what follows from it naturally, but in such a way that it has a new effect.

Paul further assumes, in accordance with the Primitive Christian view, that partaking in the meal-celebration of the Christian community is an anticipation of the table-fellowship with Christ at the Messianic feast. It is in this sense that he calls the celebration a drinking of the cup of the Lord and a partaking of the table of the Lord (1 Cor. x. 21).

This conception of a meal of fellowship with the coming Christ, which he found in existence and took over, he now further develops in the sense that he gives the meal a reference to the already present fellowship with the dead and risen Christ. The Lord's Supper, like Baptism, is interpreted by him on the basis of the mystical being-in-Christ. But while in the case of Baptism the only fact which lends itself to his interpretation is that baptism takes place "into Christ," in the case of the Lord's Supper he can appeal to the fact that Jesus at the meal spoke of bread and wine as His body and His blood. In what sense Jesus meant this we do

[1] On further cases in which Paul has to have recourse to the tradition about Jesus see above, pp. 173-174.

not learn from Paul, since he has no more knowledge about it than the disciples. What he offers is an interpretation on the lines of his mysticism, according to which the words of Jesus mean that this eating and drinking signifies union [1] with Christ. In accordance with this the cup at the Thanksgiving-meal is the "communion [1] of the blood of Christ, and the bread is the communion of the body of Christ" (1 Cor. x. 16). He who eats the meal unworthily, that is to say, without consciousness of its significance, sins over the body and blood of the Lord and eats and drinks judgment, because he does not discern the body (1 Cor. xi. 27-32).

In the arguments which parallel the Lord's Meal with the idol-feasts the dominant idea is the simple Primitive Christian idea of uniting in a meal with Christ. That of the mystical union which Paul, with the aid of Jesus' words at the Supper about His body and His blood, imports into it only appears when, at the beginning (1 Cor. x. 16-17), he speaks of "communion with the blood and body of Christ" instead of simply, as, later on (1 Cor. x. 20-21), of the communion effected by drinking of the cup of the Lord and eating at the table of the Lord. The whole argument, however, depends on the idea of uniting in a meal.

It is impossible to understand why precisely this fact, that Paul puts heathen sacrificial meals parallel with the "Lord's Meal," has been hailed as one of the most convincing proofs that his thought moves in the world of conceptions proper to the Hellenistic Mysteries. For what is there about Mysteries here? Sacrificial meals were not Mysteries, whether for the heathen or the Christian Corinthians. The original idea, that through eating of the sacrifice fellowship (union) with the divinity to whom it was offered was effected, no longer obtained in the Greek world of Paul's time. The sacrifice had become a simple offering and the sacrificial meal an occasion for revelry. Except where it was a specific question of a sacrifice of atonement, sacrifice was no longer an expression of the need for redemption. It was precisely because the ordinary sacrifices had lost their religious significance for Hellenistic piety that it sought satisfaction in being initiated into the Mystery Cults.

The fact that Meal-fellowship with the divinity no longer played any part in contemporary Greek life is not got rid of by pointing out that it

---

[1] Translator's Note.—In both cases *Gemeinschaft*, for which 'fellowship' is here too vague a translation.

is known to us that in the second century A.D., as proved by discoveries among the papyri, in the Serapis cult invitations to sacrificial feasts were sent out in the form "Chairemon invites thee to a meal at the table of the Lord Serapis, in the Serapeum, to-morrow, the 15th, from 9 o'clock onwards" (*Oxy. P.* i. 110; similarly *Oxy. P.* xiv. 1755, *et al.*), or that, according to the story of the violation of Paulina by Decius Mundus in the Isis temple at Rome (Joseph. *Antiq.* xviii. 3, 4), invitations were issued for the Anubis-meal in the temple of Isis. The evidence here is of an Egyptian formula, which does not imply that at these meals the guests expected to enter into real fellowship (union) with the God. And there is still less reason for supposing that in the ordinary Greek sacrificial cult this conception obtained.

It is not, therefore, the case that Paul drew his conclusions regarding the significance of the Lord's Meal from the Hellenistic conceptions of meal-fellowship with the divinity, but exactly the other way round. From the fact that in the Lord's Meal meal-fellowship with the coming Christ is effected, he takes it to be indisputable that the proper sense of the idol-feast must be that by such eating fellowship with the demons, who were assumed to stand behind the idols, was brought about. And since he thus interprets the sacrificial feast in the analogy of the Lord's Meal, he cannot regard the feasting at them as innocent, but is compelled to point out to the Corinthians that they thereby come into close association with the demons, even though they may suppose that they are merely taking part in a friendly entertainment.

   .   .   .   .   .   .

In virtue of his mysticism Paul interprets Jesus' words at the Last Supper about the eating of the bread and wine as His body and blood as meaning that at the "Lord's Meal" the believer enters into fellowship (union) with the body and blood of Christ. It is not, for him, a question of eating and drinking elements which in some way are the body and blood of Christ. What happens in the "Lord's Meal" is that which is asserted in the mystical doctrine of the being-in-Christ. The eating and drinking effects union with the body of Christ in the same way that baptism does. This is, according to Paul, what Jesus meant when He spoke at the Supper of eating and drinking His body and blood. Paul's view can only be rightly understood when it is recognised that he takes as his starting-point the Primitive Christian conception of the "Lord's Meal " as an anticipation of the table-fellowship with Christ at the

Messianic feast, and that it is from this point of view that Paul interprets the words of Jesus at the Supper about eating and drinking His body and blood.

The bread and wine, for Paul, in no way are, or signify, the body and blood of Christ. No other material for him than the human body can, for him, ever become the body of Christ. The Body of Christ is for him always and only human bodies; the body of Christ, along with the bodies of the Elect who are "in Him."

In accordance with his attribution to Paul of Hellenistic conceptions, Hans Lietzmann interprets the union with Christ brought about by the eating and drinking as meaning that the Apostle supposes believers to eat and drink the bread and wine as the body and blood of Christ. "The believers eat the body of the Lord and thereby become *one* body with the Lord and with each other." "The elements become vehicles of the spirit (*Pneuma*), which is called down upon them in the ceremonial prayer."

Lietzmann overlooks the fact that Paul always associates the *Pneuma* with the spirit of man, never with non-human matter. It is not until we reach the Hellenistic theology of Ignatius and Justin that the Spirit enters into relationship with matter as such. When Paul speaks of pneumatic food and pneumatic drink, which was granted to the People of Israel during the wilderness wanderings (1 Cor. x. 3-4), he does not mean food and drink with which the Spirit had united, but food and drink which had been provided for them by a miracle wrought by the Spirit.

The old question whether Paul means by the body, against which a man must not sin at the "Lord's Meal," is the body of the crucified historical Jesus, or that of the risen Lord, is to be answered to the effect that he refers Jesus' words at the Supper to the mystical body, that is, to the extended corporeity of Christ, which includes the existences of believers. But if the reference is to the mystical body, how is it possible for him to speak not only of the body but also of the blood of Christ, as though the body in question was one in the natural state of existence? He does so because he is here bound by the wording of Jesus' saying at the Supper, and because these have in fact a meaning also for the Mystical Body. No doubt Christ Himself now exists only as a supernatural being. But the believers, who share His corporeity, are, until the beginning of the Messianic glory at His return, still going through the process of dying and rising again. Consequently the mystical corporeity of Christ, since it includes within itself both the exalted Christ and beings who are still in their earthly pilgrimage, is at once natural and supernatural. Dying and rising again are constantly taking place in it. If Jesus therefore speaks of bread and wine as His body and blood He is speaking, according to Paul, of the union in death and resurrection which in this Meal, as in baptism, becomes a reality.

Although he brings in the words of Jesus at the Supper in interpreting the Church's celebration, Paul shares completely the Primitive Christian view that the food taken at the "Lord's Meal" is consecrated, not by the application to it of Jesus' words of institution, but wholly and solely by the thanksgiving and the petition for the Coming of Christ which is associated with it. It is this thanksgiving and petition which constitutes the essence of the celebration. Paul indeed does not assume that the words of Jesus about the bread and wine are repeated at every celebration of the meal. The celebration by the Church which is presupposed in his reference is still so far an actual repast that it can degenerate into gormandising.

Thus Jesus' words about the bread and wine are not for Paul words of institution and consecration, but merely signify that the partakers of this Thanksgiving-meal become one body with one another and with the Lord.

Since his sacramental conception, like his mysticism, is dominated by the thought of the predestined close connection of the believers with one another and with Christ, Paul can describe the effect of the Lord's Meal, like that of Baptism, not only as fellowship (union) with Christ, but also as the unity of the believers with one another.

1 Cor. x. 17: "As it is one bread, so we, the many, are one body, for we are all partakers of the one bread."

1 Cor. xii. 13: "For in one spirit are we all baptized into one body."

In reference to baptism, he argues from the unity of the spirit which is received; in reference to the Lord's Meal, from the unity of the bread which is eaten, by which he does not mean that all eat of one loaf, but only that they all share bread which has been consecrated by the same thanksgiving.

The development given to the significance of the celebration by bringing in the words of Jesus about His body and blood consists in this—that for Primitive-Christian belief partaking of the "Lord's Meal" establishes table-fellowship with the future Christ, whereas Paul, in accordance with his mystical doctrine of the being-in-Christ, represents it as bringing about also that union which is to be experienced now in the present with the mystical body of Christ, a union which alone makes possible the future uniting with Christ at the Messianic feast.

.   .   .   .   .   .

By bringing in the words of Jesus about the bread and wine into the explanation of the essential character of the "Lord's Meal" Paul opens the way for the inevitable development of the Meal-celebration into a distribution-celebration. Since the Church's meal-celebration (like the historic Last Supper from which it is derived) arose out of, and draws its meaning from, an ardent eschatological expectation, its original significance became untenable in proportion as belief lost its eschatological character. The original conception of the essential nature of the Meal must necessarily, in course of time, give place to a different one. This new character was developed by Jesus' words, about the bread and wine as His body and blood, coming to constitute the central significance of the Church's celebration.

Once the necessary intensity of eschatological expectation had died down, and the view of the "Lord's Meal" as a thanksgiving-meal which looked forward to an early reunion with Christ at the Messianic feast had consequently become untenable, the Meal at once ceased to be a real meal, and the food and drink ceased to be thought of as consecrated to be holy food by the thanksgiving and petition for the coming Kingdom and the return of Christ. As the original meaning faded, the new meaning arrived at by going back to Jesus' sayings about the bread and wine found its way in—namely, that the bread and wine were (as they had not yet been in Paul's view) in some sense the flesh and blood of Christ. This substitution of the new for the old came about as something self-evident, since Jesus' mysterious sayings at the historic celebration were generally known from the Gospels, since Paul had already made use of them in interpreting the Church's "Lord's Meal," and since the old Thanksgiving-celebration still remained unaltered in the liturgy. New and Old thus continued side by side, until the old entirely lost its significance and in the course of generations withered and fell away.

Bread and wine become flesh and blood of Christ in Ignatius, in Justin Martyr, and in the Gospel of John. It is significant that in their writings (and in the whole of Greek theology) the word "flesh"takes the place of the word "body," for which alone there is evidence in the records of the words of Jesus at the Last Supper.

Ignatius, *Ad Rom.* vii. 3: "It is God's bread that I desire, that is the flesh (σάρξ) of Jesus Christ, who is of the Seed of David; and as drink will I have His blood which is imperishable love."

Ignatius, *Ad Philad.* iv.: "Give heed to celebrate only one Eucharist; for there is only one flesh of our Lord Jesus Christ and only one cup for uniting with His blood."

Ignatius, *Ad Eph.* xx.: "Breaking one bread that is a medicine of immortality, an antidote, not to die, but to live in Jesus Christ evermore."

Justin, *Dial.* lxx. 4: "In this prophecy he (Isaiah) speaks clearly " (Isa. xxxiii. 16-17) " of the bread which our Christ has given us in remembrance that He has become flesh for the sake of believers in Him, on whose behalf He also suffered; in this prophecy he speaks clearly, on the one hand, of the cup which he has given us in the Eucharist in remembrance of His blood. And this too is revealed in this prophecy " (Isa. xxxiii. 17) " that we shall see Jesus as a King surrounded with glory." [1]

Justin, 1 *Apol.* lxvi.: "For we do not take it (the Eucharist) as common bread or as common wine; but, as Jesus Christ, our Redeemer, when He, through God's Logos became flesh, took upon Him flesh and blood for our salvation, so we have been taught that this food, consecrated by a word of prayer which proceeded from Him (δι᾽ εὐχῆς λόγου τοῦ παρ' αὐτοῦ) [2] with thanksgiving, by which our flesh and blood is nourished by transformation, is the flesh and blood of that Jesus who became flesh. For the Apostles in the Memoirs derived from them, which are called Gospels, have delivered to us that the following injunction had been given to them, that Jesus took bread, gave thanks, and said, 'Do this in remembrance of me; this is my body.' And likewise that He took the cup, gave thanks, and said 'This is my blood,' and He shared it among them only."

Joh. vi. 53-56: "Then said Jesus unto them, 'Verily, verily, unless ye eat the flesh of the Son of Man and drink His blood ye have no life in you. Whoso eateth my flesh and drinketh my blood hath eternal life, and I will raise him up at the last day. For my flesh is food indeed, and my blood is drink indeed. He that eateth my flesh and drinketh my blood, abideth in me, and I in him'."

---

[1] Isa. xxxiii. 16-17 (LXX.): "Bread shall be given to him, and his water is sure. A King with glory ye shall see."

[2] This untranslatable passage has also been rendered "by a prayer about the Logos, who goes forth from Him."

In speaking of the flesh and blood of Christ, instead, like Paul and in accordance with the historic words of Jesus, of the body and blood of Christ, Ignatius, Justin, and the Gospel of John are obeying an inner necessity of their conception of the "Lord's Meal." They are interpreting Jesus' words at the Last Supper on the basis of the Logos doctrine. According to Greek thought and usage the Logos unites not with the body but with the flesh.

The beginning of the Hellenisation of Christianity consists in the adoption of a Hellenistic conception of resurrection in place of the Late-Jewish. It was a conception which ran counter to Paul's saying that flesh and blood cannot inherit the Kingdom of God. Hellenistic thought could not so conceive of the resurrection required by the Christian hope as to suppose the soul, thought of as corporeal, to become naked in death and to assume at the resurrection a heavenly corporeity. Corporeal immortality comes about, according to it, through the spirit working upon the material of the flesh in such a way as to impart to it imperishability. For this type of thought the great thing which has happened in redemption is, that flesh and spirit, which have hitherto been unrelated to each other, have been made capable of uniting. This happened for the first time in the Person of Jesus. From it begins the process by which all flesh, so far as it is called thereto, by this unification of flesh and spirit (ἕνωσις σαρκινή τε καὶ πνευματική, as Ignatius says in *Ad Magn.* xiii. 2) is prepared for the resurrection.

The difference thus introduced into the conception of the bodily resurrection never came to expression in the first Christian generations. The Christian-Hellenistic view took the place of the Late-Jewish Christian unobserved. The Church was solely concerned to maintain, against Gnosticism, the corporeal resurrection as such, and so preserve continuity with the Primitive Christian belief. This firm hold on the corporeal resurrection shows that the Christian belief in immortality was originally closely connected with eschatology, and had reference to the expected participation in the Messianic Kingdom.

The appearance of the word "flesh" instead of the previous "body" is a sign that Hellenistic Christian thought has taken the place of Late-Jewish Christian in Sacramental doctrine as well as in Christology.

According to the Greek view bread and wine become in the Eucharist flesh and blood of Jesus in the following way. The Logos-

Spirit which was left in the world by Jesus after His death, and through Him has become capable of uniting with matter, becomes one with this bread and wine in the same way that it became one with the flesh of Jesus. The bread and wine in the "Lord's Meal" carry on that union of Logos-Spirit and matter which began with Jesus, and which is the effective means of redemption, and they do so in a form which is assimilable by men and prepares their flesh for the resurrection. As a unity of matter and Logos-Spirit, the bread and wine at the "Lord's Meal" are essentially the same as the flesh and blood of Jesus, and can therefore be so described.

But Ignatius, Justin, and the Gospel of John are at one with Paul in not representing the bread and wine as changed into the body and blood of the historic Jesus. For the Greek doctrine they are a continuation of His corporeity, by means of which the baptized believer enters into union with Him. What we have here, therefore, is an interpretation of Jesus' words at the Supper in the light of the idea of a union with Christ which is based on the mystical unification of flesh and spirit. It thus forms the pendant to the interpretation which Paul gives on the basis of the mystical union with Christ in His dying and rising again. In both cases Jesus' words at the Supper are understood only as stating what happens when the believers eat and drink the bread and wine; they are not yet thought of as a formula of consecration, to be repeated at every celebration, which makes the bread and wine into the body and blood of Christ. Both for Justin and Ignatius the bread and wine are consecrated only by the thanksgiving, which is offered as a continuation of the thanksgiving of Jesus at the Last Supper. The celebration in the form of a meal, which is implied by both of them, as yet knew nothing of a repetition of Jesus' saying about the bread and wine as His body and blood.

It is not Jesus' saying about the bread and wine, but His prayer for the Coming of the Kingdom, which has a place in the early form of celebration. From the time when prayer in a fixed form of words took its place alongside of the free thanksgivings and petitions of the 'prophets' and those who had "spiritual gifts" the Lord's Prayer must have been given a place in the "Lord's Meal," even if this was not so from the first. This is evidenced by the fact that it appears as early as the Didache (viii. 2-3), with the addition of the doxology ("For Thine is the power and the glory for ever"), whereas the Lord's Prayer, as taught by Jesus to His disciples, closed, according both to Matthew and to Luke, with the prayer for preservation from the Temptation (Mt. vi. 9-15; Lk. xi. 2-4). From this it appears that from the earliest times it was repeated before the Christian community, the audience responding with the doxology and an Amen. Of such responses to prayer we have evidence from Paul (1 Cor. xiv. 16), and later from Justin (1 *Apol.* lxv.). Since in the earlier period the Thanksgiving-meal was the only form of service, this shows that the Lord's Prayer must have taken its place very early, if not actually from the first, in the thanksgiving at the "Lord's Meal," to which, as a petition for the Kingdom, it is logically appropriate.

According to the liturgy of the Eucharist, as known to us from the fifth mystagogic catechesis of Bishop Cyril of Jerusalem (middle of 4th century A.D.), the Lord's Prayer concluded the thanksgiving before the eating.

Thus in Ignatius and Justin the celebration still follows the lines of the old Thanksgiving-meal, except that the bread and wine, since in accordance with Jesus' words at the Supper and the essential nature of the celebration they are to bring about union with Jesus Christ, are now thought of as continuing His bodily existence. The Pauline—eschatological—conception of the partaking of the body of Christ has been displaced by a Hellenistic conception.

How closely the old and the new are connected together may be seen from the passage quoted above from Justin's *Dialogue with Trypho* (lxx. 4), where he cites a passage of Isaiah (xxxiii. 16-17) in which he sees both a prophecy of the Eucharist as a giving to eat and drink of the flesh and blood of Christ, and a prophecy of the manifestation of Jesus in His Messianic glory.[1] That shows clearly that the connection between the expectation of the return of Christ and the Meal-celebration was still present to his mind.

It was only through the Logos-Christology that the conception of the bread and wine as the flesh and blood of Christ became possible. It is generally overlooked that the Logos doctrine is the solution not only of the Christological problem, but of the problem of the Sacraments also. Its usefulness in this latter respect contributed as much to its establishment as did the value which it had for Christology. At the time when the Christian faith was obliged, in consequence of the weakening of the eschatological hope, to find a new orientation, the questions of the character of the historic manifestation of Jesus Christ and that of the significance and method of

---

[1] On this passage from Isaiah see above, p. 273.

working of the sacraments were closely interwoven, and needed to be solved together.

The assertion that bread and wine became in the Eucharist the body and blood of Jesus Christ was opposed as an innovation, as we learn from Ignatius.

Ignat. *Ad Smyrn.* vii.: "From the Eucharist and the Prayer (those who do not teach rightly) hold themselves aloof, because they do not recognise that the Eucharist is the flesh of our Redeemer Jesus Christ, which suffered for our sins and which the Father in His goodness raised again. Those who speak against the gift of God shall perish in their contention. It had been better for them if they had had love, in order that they also might arise."

But these conservative believers, who were averse from the Logos-Christology and the Logos-interpretation of the Sacraments, were defending a hopeless position. Progress won the day, because Greek thought (and indeed the faith itself, since it could no longer live entirely in eschatology) was obliged to seek a new logical connection between the fact of the resurrection of Christ and the hope of the resurrection of believers, to take the place of that which had previously been supplied by eschatology.

How closely the new view is still connected with the old is evident when we find that, according to Ignatius, bread and wine only take on the character of body and blood of Christ when the Eucharist is celebrated in the true Church, the mark of which is the bishop. It is only in this circle, in which Christ and the believers are united with one another in love, that the powers are at work which make the eating and drinking of bread and wine bring about union with the body and blood of Christ. The conception of the Church as the predestined whole formed by the union of the believers with one another and with Christ, which underlies the eschatological Christ-mysticism of Paul and his eschatological conception of union with Christ in baptism and the Lord's Supper, is still just as much in force in the new Greek Christ-and-Sacrament-mysticism. It is on the basis of this that Ignatius says that only in the Church are believers "in love."

What, then, was the course of the development of the Primitive Christian Meal-celebration through Paul to Ignatius, Justin, and the Johannine Gospel? The starting-point is that the "Lord's

Meal" signifies union (uniting in a meal), with the returning Christ. This future union is conceived by the Pauline and the Greek doctrine as already present, and they explain it on the basis of the mystical being-in-Christ with the aid of Jesus' words about the bread and wine at the Last Supper. They thus give a further development to the sacramental interpretation of the Meal-celebration, which was already present in principle in the Primitive-Christian idea of "meal-fellowship" with Christ at the "Lord's Meal."

In proportion as the Eucharist becomes, in accordance with the Greek view, an eating and drinking of the flesh and blood of Christ, it ceases to be a real meal and becomes of necessity more and more a purely "distribution-celebration." In the course of this development the identity of Eucharist and Agape was broken up. By the Agape is now meant a fellowship-meal, in which the food partaken of is no longer thought of as the flesh and blood of Christ.

Hans Lietzmann holds that Agape and Eucharist were from the beginning separate celebrations.[1] The Agape was, he thinks, originally the Christianised Jewish religious meal, which arose without any reference to the Last Supper of Jesus with His disciples. The Eucharist proper was a Pauline ceremony, dominated by the reference to Jesus' words about the bread and wine as His body and blood, which later became combined with the religious meal at which men ate to satisfy hunger, and was developed into a particular fact within that meal. Later, the Eucharist was separated from the Agape and transferred to the morning meeting for worship.

Here the original separateness of Agape and Eucharist is asserted, in order to support the assumption that during the first generation of Primitive Christianity there was a Pauline and a Jerusalem type of Meal-celebration. The evidence of Ignatius, who uses Agape (*Ad Smyrn.* viii. 2) and Eucharist (*Ad Smyrn.* vii. 1; *Ad Philad.* iv. 1) as designations of one and the same celebration, stands in the way of any attempt of this kind.

For the separation of a distribution-celebration from the cultus-meal the way is prepared even in Paul's teaching. For he is the first to give Jesus' words about the bread and wine a significance for the community-celebration. And he is the first, by his command that the believers, in order not to endanger the sacredness of the meal,

[1] On Hans LIETZMANN's *Messe und Herrenmahl* see pp. 249-250, *sup.*

are to satisfy their hunger at home, to make the actual meal into the semblance of a meal.

He also, by making the future fellowship with the Coming Messiah which was celebrated in the "Lord's Meal" into a present one by his mystical doctrine of the dying and rising again with Christ, and thereby deepening it and making it more inward, prepares the way for another development. This was, that at the appropriate time the Greek sacramental conception of the Meal-celebration, and the union with Christ which was brought about in it, forced its way into the obsolescent Primitive Christian Eschatological view and began to usurp its place. Later, the old was so completely ousted by the new that for centuries the very memory of the original character of Baptism and the "Lord's Meal" was lost, and historical scholarship obstinately refused to admit the possibility of even considering the idea of "eschatological sacraments."

.   .   .   .   .   .

By interpreting baptism and the "Lord's Meal" on the basis of the mystical dying and rising again with Christ, Paul gives them at the same time a significance, with reference to the resurrection, which in the Primitive Christian view they had not had. In so doing he prepared the way for the conception which later became dominant—the conception implied in Ignatius' designation of the Eucharist as the "medicine of immortality" (Ign. *Ad Eph.* xx.). This conception was not first invented by Ignatius, nor was it foisted upon Christianity from Greek sources. It is a logical development of the Primitive Christian conception of the "Lord's Meal," and only continues what had been begun by Paul.

In order to understand this development we must make clear to ourselves that, for Primitive Christianity and for Paul, there were two separate blessednesses (the Messianic and the eternal), and that the sacraments have reference only to the former.[1] Because this simple distinction, which is constantly suggested by the early texts, was not perceived, the attempt to trace the early history of the sacraments was necessarily a groping in the dark.

The sacraments refer solely to the obtaining of the Messianic blessedness ; indeed they are only there for the sake of the Elect of that generation of men on whom, in Paul's phrase, the End of the Times is come (1 Cor. x. 11).

[1] On the distinction of a Messianic and an eternal blessedness see pp. 90-94, *sup.*

To the question whether the sacraments are necessary to the obtaining of blessedness or no, Paul—better off in this than later theologians—can give a clear pronouncement. They are necessary only for the men of the last generation who desire to make real their election to participation in the Messianic Kingdom, that is to say, to share with the Messiah the supernatural state of being. But simply to attain to resurrection at the general resurrection of the dead and to enter into eternal blessedness, sacraments are not necessary. This blessedness is obtained through election in itself and through the "walk well-pleasing unto God" which attests it. The question how the Elect of former generations, without having a knowledge of Christ and being baptized, can nevertheless be redeemed, does not exist for Paul. The redemption wrought by Christ and appropriated through faith and baptism, does not arise for them. It is not for the whole of mankind, but only for the last generation, that Jesus came and died in order to procure for the Elect in it the attainment of the Messianic glory. The working of the sacraments cannot extend more widely than that of the dying and rising again of Christ.

A special case arises in regard to the Elect of the last generation who have received no knowledge of Jesus. In this case, even though they belong to the privileged generation "on whom the End of the Times has come," participation in the Messianic Kingdom is for them impossible. There remains for them only, like the generations which lived before Christ's coming, the eternal blessedness.[1] It is for that reason that Paul is so determined upon carrying the knowledge of the Gospel to the ends of the earth before the return of Christ.[2]

.   .   .   .   .

The Primitive Christian Sacraments were thought of, essentially, only as guaranteeing the Messianic glory itself, it being assumed as a matter of course that the believer would survive to this time, believed to be so near at hand. It may have been that originally the conception obtained that whoever was baptized and took part in the celebration of the "Lord's Meal" thereby acquired the certainty of not dying before the beginning of the Messianic Kingdom. If he did actually die before it, that only proved that the Messianic blessedness was not appointed for him.[3]

---

[1] See p. 133, *sup.*   [2] See pp. 158 and 181-186, *sup.*

[3] On the problem of the death of believers before the return of Christ and its solution by Paul see pp. 91-94, 112-115, *sup.*

In interpreting Baptism and the "Lord's Meal" by the mystical being-in-Christ Paul attributes to them *implicite* the power of bringing about the resurrection at the return of the Lord. In so doing he makes of them something different from what they were for the Primitive-Christian view.

The development of the Christian belief would certainly sooner or later have given rise to the conception of the resurrection of believers at the return of Jesus, and would have connected it with the sacrament, in order to secure for the baptized dead the possibility of participation in the Messianic Kingdom. The introduction of this resurrection idea became necessary, if, in view of the increasing number of dying before the return of Jesus, the faith and the sacraments were not to lose their meaning. And the possibility of this development was an immediate consequence of the Primitive-Christian view of Baptism and the "Lord's Meal" as giving the believers the right to participate in the Messianic Kingdom, and therefore also to obtain the resurrection state of existence which was a necessary presupposition for participating in the Kingdom. All that was further necessary was to accept the tenet that this effect of the sacraments was available also for those who had died in the meantime. But natural as it seemed to venture on this step, it proved in practice difficult to take. What was the conception which could provide a basis for the view that the sacraments put the dead on the same footing as the living? Here it proved to be Paul who was first to take the necessary step in thought, because the mystical being-in-Christ provided him with the required conception. Since his mystical doctrine caused him to see in baptism the beginning of a dying and rising again with Christ, which caused the natural man to enter at once on the process of dying and rising again, he took it as self-evident that, in consequence of the sacraments, those who had meanwhile died were rendered capable, in exactly the same way as the survivors, of participating in the glory of Christ. His significance consists, therefore, not only in his being the first to assert the resurrection of believers in preparation for the Messianic glory, but also in his giving to this idea so complete a basis in his mysticism and connecting it so closely with the sacraments. A result which Primitive Christian belief, left to itself, might have reached by uncertain gropings was here offered to it by a thinker as a piece of clearly articulated knowledge.

It is only when it is recognised that baptism and the Lord's

Meal have reference only to the Messianic glory that it becomes intelligible why Paul makes the consequence of falling from baptismal grace and of unworthy participation in the "Lord's Meal," not eternal damnation, but simply dying. He who is not in Christ dies at the beginning of the Messianic Kingdom, if not before, and is then, like the members of former generations, a prey to death until the General Resurrection and the Judgment, at which it will be decided whether he is only to forfeit the Messianic glory but to attain to eternal blessedness, or whether he is to lose this also. Therefore Paul, in rebuking the Corinthians, reminds them that the Israelites, although they were all baptized in the Sea and under the Cloud and given Manna to eat and water out of the Rock to drink, nevertheless died in the wilderness and did not inherit the Promised Land, because they forfeited the glory which had been promised to them by their subsequent transgressions. They themselves, who have been baptized and had the privilege of partaking of the "Lord's Meal," are to learn from this, that in case of similar conduct sentence of death will similarly be passed upon them. Instead of entering into the Messianic Kingdom, they will fall a prey to that death which the loss of participation in the Messianic Kingdom entails (1 Cor. x. 1-13).[1] The parallel between the sacraments of the wilderness journey and Baptism and the "Lord's Meal" is therefore much appropriate than it is usually taken to be, since in both cases loss of the sacramental grace entails the same fate.

It now also becomes intelligible how Paul comes to connect the cases of sickness and death in the Church at Corinth with the unworthy celebration of the "Lord's Meal," and to give the explanation that by such judgments the Lord purposed to turn the church to repentance, in order that, at the Coming Judgment, they should not need to be condemned with the world (1 Cor. xi. 29-32).[2] By not realising that the Meal brings them into a union of dying and rising again with the Body of Christ, they do despite to their being-in-Christ and run the risk of ending it. If this happens, then they, as no longer being-in-Christ, are men destined to death, whereas they still believe themselves, in consequence of their baptism and

---

[1] On 1 Cor. x. 1-13 see pp. 20-22 and 258-260, *sup.*

[2] By this Judgment can only be meant the Judgment which is to take place at the return of Christ, at which it will be decided whether this church is to have part in the Messianic glory, or, along with the children of the world, to fall temporarily under the dominion of death, until their final fate is decided at a general resurrection of the dead.

their partaking of the Lord's Meal, to be among those who at the return of Christ will be changed into the resurrection-state of existence, or, should they be among those who have died meantime, to rise at once, as those who have died in Christ, to take part in the Messianic Kingdom. Therefore the Lord, by these cases of sickness and death, is bringing it home to them that a dying which will lose them the glory of the Messianic Kingdom may be their fate if they do not use the "Lord's Meal" as an opportunity for strengthening their union with Christ.

Paul, by his mystical doctrine of union with Christ, had made the sacraments into guarantees of resurrection to the Messianic glory; he must therefore warn them, with all earnestness, that the cessation of that being-in-Christ which is bestowed in Baptism and maintained by the Lord's Meal necessarily entails the dying which the loss of the Messianic glory brings in its train, whether this dying happens now, before the return of Jesus, or at that return, when the mass of the non-elect will be delivered over to death. The doctrine of the being-in-Christ, by means of which he widens the significance of the sacraments, at the same time enables him to define the limits of their effectual working, and thus to combat the setting of a false confidence upon them.

    .   .   .   .   .   .

The test case for the right understanding of the Pauline sacraments is the explanation of the enigmatic baptism for the dead.

1 Cor. xv. 29: "If the dead do not rise at all, why do men have themselves baptized for the dead?"

No parallel for this baptism for the dead can be produced from the Hellenistic Mystery-religions. Reitzenstein, it is true, asserts that he can regard the Christian baptism for the dead "only as the adaptation of a heathen Mystery-usage to Christian conceptions and ordinances."[1] But he is not in a position to produce, in support of his opinion, passages from Hellenistic literature which really speak of a baptism for the dead.

In the Second Book of Maccabees (xii. 39-45) Judas Maccabaeus causes an atoning sacrifice to be offered in Jerusalem for the Jews fallen in battle, who had sinned in wearing heathen amulets.

Plato in the *Republic* (ii. 7) makes the ironic suggestion that, calling on

---

[1] R. REITZENSTEIN, *Die hellenistischen Mysterienreligionen*, 3rd ed., 1927, p. 233.

the names of Orpheus and other poets, atonement should be made for
the transgressions of both the living and the dead by sacrifices and games
called Sacral.

(Plato, *Rep.* ii. 7, ὡς ἄρα λύσεις τε καὶ καθαρμοὶ ἀδικημάτων διὰ θυσιῶν
καὶ παιδιᾶς ἡδονῶν εἰσὶ μὲν ἔτι ζῶσιν, εἰσὶ δὲ καὶ τελευτήσασιν, ἃς δὴ
τελετὰς καλοῦσιν, αἳ τῶν ἐκεῖ κακῶν ἀπολύουσιν ἡμᾶς, μὴ θύσαντας δὲ δεινὰ
περιμένει.)

A confirmation of this statement is found in an Orphic fragment, according to which the Orphics offered purifying sacrifices and held mystic
celebrations in order to obtain forgiveness for their godless ancestors.

(O. Kern, *Orph. Fragm.* (1922), p. 245, ἄνθρωποι δὲ τελήέσσας ἑκατόμβας
πέμψουσιν πάσῃσι ἐν ὥραις ἀμφιέτῃσιν ὄργιά τ᾽ ἐκτελέσουσι λύσιν προ-
γόνων ἀθεμίστων μαιόμενοι.)

In both cases what is in view is not individual action, in which individuals cause themselves to be received into the initiate community,
but collective arrangements made by a community, which are intended
to benefit the dead as well as the living. That in both cases atoning
sacrifices are mentioned, makes it probable that the reference is to
ceremonies which stood in close connection with the idea of atoning
sacrifice. It is evident that Plato so understood it, in view of the whole
wording of his arguments.

This is the sum of what can be brought in the way of Hellenistic
citations for the explanation of 1 Cor. xv. 29. The usage cited by Reitzenstein from admittedly late Mandaean sources of pouring water upon the
dying [1] is not apposite here any more than the Egyptian baptism of the
dead. A baptism of the dead is not a baptism for the dead.

Even if passages about a baptism for the dead could be found
in Hellenistic literature, it would not thereby be proved that the
usage attested by Paul is derived from Hellenism and is to be explained from it. Hellenistic Baptism always has to do with the rebirth to immortality, Christian baptism only with participation in
the Messianic glory by means of the resurrection. It is not, according to the Pauline view, in order to enable a dead man to obtain
immortality as such, that anyone needs to be baptized for him.
In the general resurrection of the dead he will at once enter
the eternal life, provided he is elect thereto and has not made
his calling ineffectual by a godless life. The reason which, for
Hellenistic conceptions, might give rise to baptism for the dead,
does not exist for Paul's view. The baptism for the dead which he

---

[1] R. REITZENSTEIN, *Das mandaische Buch des Herrn der Grösse und die Evan-
gelienüberlieferung*, Heidelberg, 1919, pp. 87 f.

implies answers to a need which could only arise out of the eschatological expectations of Primitive Christianity, and is only explicable on the basis of the quasi-physical conception of the being-in-Christ.

According to the Pauline view representative baptism is only applicable in cases where the dead person belongs to the last generation of mankind. Such persons, had they known Christ and believed in Him, and consequently been baptized "into Him," would have acquired the possibility of partaking in the Messianic glory. In order to restore to them what they had lost by their premature death, others caused themselves to be baptized on their behalf. This procedure is rational only if a relation of corporeal union subsists between the living and the dead. In view of this quasi-physical union it is conceivable that the unbaptized dead might have part in the being-in-Christ of their baptized relatives, provided that the latter, by being baptized on their behalf as well as on their own, make known their desire to take them up into their baptism and thus make them capable of taking part in the resurrection at the return of Jesus. We have seen that Paul assumes a similar projection of the being-in-Christ, thought of as quasi-physical, into the natural corporeal union of one human being with another, when he asserts that the unbelieving husband is sanctified in the believing wife, the unbelieving wife in the believing husband, and the child in the believing parents (1 Cor. vii. 14).[1] This corporeal unity is not ended by death. Therefore the believing husband, who causes himself to be baptized for his dead wife, may expect that she will in consequence, as being now with him "in-Christ," have part in the resurrection which takes place immediately upon the return of Christ, instead of having to wait, like the rest of the dead, for the general resurrection at the end of the Messianic Kingdom; and, similarly, wives would be baptized for their husbands and children for their parents.

Thus in the eschatologico-sacramental view of Baptism, and in the eschatological mysticism of the quasi-physical "being-in Christ," conceptions are present which make the undergoing of baptism for the dead appear possible and rational. The position is not that Paul had to make the best of a misuse of Baptism among the Corinthians, drawn from the heathen Mystery-religions, but rather that it was only in consequence of his teaching about the being-in-

[1] See above, pp. 127-129.

Christ and his view of the effect of baptism that baptism for the dead could arise.

The practice of baptism for the dead did not maintain itself in the Church because it was wholly bound up with the eschatologico-Pauline view of baptism, and it became obsolete along with it. Only among the Gnostics was it practised later (Epiphanius, *Haer.* xxviii. 6, 4; Tertullian, *De Resurrectione*, xlviii.; *Adv. Marc.* v. 10). To what extent this was the case we do not know.

What happened to the Christian sacraments at the moment when the eschatological concept of redemption, with which they were so closely bound up, became untenable? They necessarily then took on a new and much more general significance. Instead of, as originally, guaranteeing participation in the Messianic glory, they now bring about immortality pure and simple. This development was made possible by Paul, for it was he who by interpreting Baptism and the "Lord's Meal" on the basis of the mystical being-in-Christ first made them sacraments of resurrection. And if the special function of the sacraments was to guarantee partaking in the Messianic glory they must also possess the power of causing those who had died in the meantime to arise to this end. And once the dying of believers becomes the rule the distinction between the Messianic and the eternal blessedness is lost. The conception of the privileged generation of the Last Times, which was alone destined to share the Messianic glory, is rendered obsolete by the dying out of the contemporaries of Jesus and the Apostles, and the arising of a new generation. Henceforth there is no distinction; under like conditions men are destined to the like blessedness. All are now prepared to have to pass through death and resurrection in order to attain blessedness. And for them all the expectation is both of partaking in the Kingdom and of the eternal blessedness. The Messianic and the eternal blessedness now form a unity. The Messianic Kingdom passes into the Kingdom of God. Consequently the sacraments no longer mediate to a particular generation the resurrection to a Messianic glory reserved for it alone, but bestow immortality as such, and are valid for all future generations. This transformation took place unobserved in consequence of the passing over of the eschatological concept of redemption into a more general one.

Once again it is Ignatius, Justin, and the Gospel of John who mark the definite stage of evolution. As they make the bread and wine become the body and blood of Christ, so now they give to the Sacraments the function of mediating immortality as such. And this they explain by the influence of the Logos-Spirit. By uniting, in baptism, with the water and so taking possession of the man it brings about rebirth to the new life. In the Eucharist the Spirit-Logos makes the bread and wine vehicles of the Logos in continuance of the existence of Jesus Christ, and renders those who partake of this food and this drink capable of attaining the immortality which is bound up with the possession of the Logos-Spirit.

Now that redemption consists in eternal life as such, it has become similar to that arrived at by the personal piety of Hellenism. A specifically Christian element is retained only in the emphasis laid on the resurrection of the flesh. In the idea that the whole human personality is to enter upon immortality the influence of its different origin still survives, the original conception being that of participation in a Kingdom, not as in Hellenism of the return of the spiritual being to spiritual existence.

As in Paul's teaching, so also in Ignatius, Justin, and the Gospel of John, the resurrection is effected by the mystical union with Christ which is brought about by the sacraments. The only difference is that the mystical partaking in the Logos-Spirit of Christ has taken the place of the mystical dying and rising again with Christ. Baptism consequently no longer brings about a state of having already risen again, but as in the Greek Mysteries a new birth.

Ignatius, Justin, and the Fourth Evangelist do not therefore, in their conception of the sacraments, create anything essentially new, however surprisingly new their formulae may sound in some respects, but simply develop further, in accordance with the needs of the time, something which began with Paul.

.   .   .   .   .   .

As soon as the two different blessednesses cease to be distinguished there at once arises problems concerning the redemption effected by Christ and the significance of the sacraments, which before had no existence. For a conception according to which Christ died only for the Elect of the last generation, and in which the sacraments apply to them only, everything is simple. For the Elect of pre-Christian generations an eternal blessedness is appointed, for the attainment of which they need neither the redeeming death of Christ, nor belief in Him, nor the sacraments. It is as a kind of prelude to this blessedness that the Elect of the last generation obtain also the Messianic glory, for which the redeeming death of Christ, faith in Him, and the sacraments are necessary.

But now, in consequence of the delay of the second coming of Christ, the place of this "last generation" is taken by the successive Christian generations. Had these been able simply to enter on the rights of that supposed "last generation," all would have been easy. But this was scarcely possible. And the reason it is not possible is that now, when there is only one blessedness in question, the dilemma inevitably arises that either the pre-Christian generations must be denied this blessedness altogether; or they must be admitted to possess it on the same terms as the generations subsequent to the contemporaries of Jesus.

Faced with this dilemma Christian doctrine could not but admit that the Elect who lived before Jesus were destined to the same blessedness as those who lived after Him. And in support of this it could cite, as Justin does (*Dial.* cxx. 5-6), the saying of Jesus that Abraham, Isaac, and Jacob would sit at table in the Messianic Kingdom (Mt. viii. 11).

The assertion that the righteous from among both Jews and Gentiles, even though they lived before Jesus and consequently knew nothing of Him, would also share the blessedness of the believers in Christ, is often found in Justin.

1 *Apol.* xlvi. "Those who lived according to the Logos are Christians, even though they may have been accounted ungodly, as among the Greeks, Socrates, Heraclitus, and others, and among the non-Greeks, Abraham, Ananias, Azarias, Elijah, and many others."—*Dial.* xxvi. 1: "The heathen, if they believe on Him (Christ) and repent of their sins, shall inherit along with the Patriarchs, the Prophets, and all the righteous of the race of Jacob."—*Dial.* xlv. 4: "He who does that which is universally, eternally, and by nature good is well-pleasing to God, and will therefore be saved through our Christ at the resurrection, like the earlier righteous, such as Noah, Enoch, Jacob, and the like, and shall be included in the number of those, who have recognised the Son of God in our Christ. . . ." (See also *Dial.* lxvii. 6 and lxxx. 1.)

With the giving up of the distinction of the Messianic and the eternal blessedness Christian doctrine naturally returns to the view held in the eschatology of Daniel, Enoch, and Jesus, who all know of only one and the same blessedness for the Elect of all generations, namely, that of being in the Kingdom of God, and who represent the Son of Man as holding judgment upon the risen of all generations.

Now Christian doctrine represents the blessedness of Christians as won through the death and resurrection of Jesus and as appropriated by faith in Him. If, then, it is obliged to come to the conclusion that the same blessedness is appointed for the pre-Christian righteous as for Christian believers, it finds itself in the curious situation of having to assert that the righteous who did not know Christ appropriate to themselves the results of His death without its being possible for them to supply the belief which is man's necessary part. And if the sacraments are taken into account the matter becomes still more complicated. For those pre-Christian righteous obtain without sacraments what Christian believers can only attain through Baptism and the Eucharist!

Of all the theologians only one ventured to admit the predicament and to find a way of escape. This was the author of the prophetic writing known as the Shepherd of Hermas (*Hermae Pastor*), which originated at Rome A.D. 150, who faced the problems which confronted the Christian faith of his time in a large and simple spirit. In the vision of the building of a Tower, the stones for which are brought up out of the deep through the water, it is revealed to Hermas—who in his youth had been sold as a slave and sent to Rome (*Vis.* i. 1)—that the Apostles and Teachers who had died had brought to the Elect in the underworld the knowledge of Christ and of baptism, by which means they were incorporated into the Church and enabled to obtain Life (*Sim.* ix. 16, 1-7). The number of the pre-Christian righteous who in this way enter into blessedness is, however, held by Hermas to be very small (*Sim.* ix. 15, 4).

Hermae Past., Sim. ix. 16, 1-7: "Wherefore, Lord, came these stones out of the deep, and were laid into the building (of the Tower), if they were vehicles of this spirit?"

"They must necessarily rise up through the water in order to obtain life; for they could not enter into the Kingdom of God otherwise than by putting off the mortality of the (former) life. Thus these dead also have received the sealing of the Son of God (and have entered into the Kingdom of God). For before a man bears the name of the Son of God he is dead; but so soon as he has received the sealing he puts off mortality and puts on life. The sealing is the water: into the water they plunge as dead, and they rise up as living. To them, too, came the message about this sealing; and they availed themselves of it, in order that they might attain to the Kingdom of God."

"Wherefore, Lord, came these forty stones up out of the deep along with these, although they already had the seal?"

"Because the Apostles and Teachers, the preachers of the name of the Son of God, after they had fallen asleep in the power and faith of the Son of God, preached also to those who had fallen asleep aforetime, and gave them the seal of the message. They plunged into the water with them and rose up again out of it, but these were living when they plunged beneath it and living when they rose out of it; but those who fell asleep aforetime plunged beneath it as dead, and came up again as living. Through the former the latter have here obtained life, and ac-knowledged the name of the Son of God; therefore also they rose up with the others, and were along with them built into the structure of that Tower and, though unhewn, became part of the building; for they had fallen asleep in righteousness and great purity, only this sealing they had not received."

The few Elect of pre-Christian times, "who had fallen asleep in righteousness and great purity," thus receive from the Apostles in the underworld the knowledge of Christ and of the necessity of baptism, and by coming in contact with water in a way appointed by God they are baptized. In this way the conditions of obtaining blessedness are fulfilled.

Since Hermas, no theologian has had the courage to tackle the problem and solve it in this gallant fashion. All of them carefully evade the problem of the necessity of the sacraments and of the extension of the results of the death of Jesus to pre-Christian humanity. They make, for example, the pre-Christian genera-tions attain to blessedness through Christ, between His death and resurrection, preaching to the spirits in the lower world, as is already assumed in the First Epistle of Peter (iii. 19-20). But the problem is not only whether they receive the knowledge of Jesus and become believers, but rather how without a real act of faith and without sacraments they can enter into blessedness.

For the time of the eschatological belief none of these problems existed. So long as eschatology holds the field, dogmatics can pro-ceed logically. Afterwards, it finds itself obliged to set up assertions about the death of Jesus and the sacraments which are historically incorrect and full of inconsistencies. Whereas, for example, Jesus gives His death its significance with reference to the entering of the Elect of the last generation into the Kingdom of God, the later dogmatic must give it a reference to the whole of humanity. And when, in accordance with this, it finds itself forced to the assertion that the sacraments bring about eternal blessedness, it is deflecting them from their original significance, and finds itself confronted with the problem of the universal necessity of the sacraments, from which there is no escape.

After the eschatological sacramental conception had become obsolete, only assertions with regard to the sacraments were possible, but no self-consistent doctrine in regard to them. This is merely an expression of the fact that the sacraments continued to subsist beyond the time in which they could have their original meaning and for which they were, properly speaking, valid, and now have attributed to them a new meaning which cannot be brought wholly into agreement with the original meaning, and in itself is incapable of being thought out clearly and without contradictions. This has been the position of the doctrine of faith from the time of Ignatius and Justin down to the present day.

Since the world conditions have changed, we can do no other than to think our own thoughts about the redemptive significance of the death of Jesus and all that is connected with it, basing our thoughts, so far as possible, on the original and Primitive-Christian doctrine. But if we undertake this task, as we needs must, we ought to make clear to ourselves what we are doing. We ought not to bemuse ourselves with the belief that we are simply taking over the whole of the dogmatic conceptions of Jesus and of Primitive Christianity, seeing that this is, in fact, impossible. And we ought not to regard the obscurities and contradictions, in which we find ourselves involved, as originally attaching to Christian doctrine; we ought to be clearly conscious that they arise from the transformation of the historical and Primitive-Christian concepts into concepts necessary to adapt them to a later situation. Instead of simply being able to take over traditional material as we find it, we must, exactly, as did Ignatius and Justin, recast it by a creative act of the Spirit.

From this point of view the recognition of the original eschatological orientation of the Christian faith has a truly liberating value. For it compels us to admit that we "can do no other" than to build both upon the tradition and upon the spirit.

And nowhere does the difference between the Primitive-Christian faith and our own come more convincingly to light than in the fact that Paul is able to think out the Primitive-Christian conception of the redemption through Jesus Christ and the significance of the sacraments with absolutely clear and self-consistent logic.

Since modern scholarship has hitherto been blind to the specifically eschatological character of his sacramental conception with all its concomitant advantages, it never even became aware of the peculiarly advantageous position which he enjoyed in respect of consistency as compared with all later theologians.

CHAPTER XII

MYSTICISM AND ETHICS

FOR the Baptist, for Jesus, and for the Primitive-Christian community the whole of Ethics falls under the concept of repentance (μετάνοια). By this they understand a change of mind, consisting in penitence for the past and the determination to live henceforward, liberated from everything earthly, in expectation of the Messianic Kingdom. Ethical conduct after baptism is regarded as the fruit of repentance.

Matt. iii. 2 (the Baptist's preaching): "Repent, for the Kingdom of Heaven is at hand."—Mt. iii. 8: "Bring forth fruits worthy of repentance."

Matt. iv. 17: "From that time forward Jesus began to preach and to say, Repent, for the Kingdom of Heaven is at hand."

Acts ii. 38: "Peter said to them, Repent and be baptized every one of you in the name of Jesus Christ."—Acts xxvi. 20: ". . . to repent and be converted to God, and to bring forth fruits worthy of repentance."

But for Paul ethics is no longer repentance. The word occurs in only a few passages of his writings and never in a context where he is expounding his ethic.

2 Cor. vii. 9-10: "Now I am glad, not that you have been grieved (by my letter), but that you have been grieved into repenting. For to be grieved in accordance with God's purpose produces a repentance unto salvation, a repentance not to be repented of."—2 Cor. xii. 21: ". . . and I shall have to bewail many who have sinned before and have not repented of the uncleanness and unchastity and lasciviousness which they have committed."—Rom. ii. 4: "Knowest thou not that God's goodness urges thee to repentance."

Repentance for Paul is only the ethical act leading up to baptism; the freedom from earthliness and sinfulness, which the baptized man is to maintain, is more than repentance. In it he translates into act the state of having died and risen again with Christ and of walking in a condition of existence which is no longer earthly. Ethics, like the sacraments, is included within the sphere of the mystical dying and rising again with Christ, and is to be interpreted from this point of view. By means of the mystical doctrine of the being-in-Christ, the ethic of expectation directed towards the Kingdom of God, which was based on belief in the Messiahship of Jesus, was transformed into the Christian ethic, that is to say, the ethic produced by Christ in the believers who attach themselves to Him.

Primitive Christianity, under the impression of the prophecy of Joel, thinks of the Spirit only as the power bestowed on believers by a promised Divine miracle, of being in communication with the super-earthly world by means of the receiving and announcing of revelations. Paul brings the possession of the Spirit into connection with the dying and rising again with Christ.[1] As one who is already raised from the dead, the believer, according to him, receives the Spirit of the glorified Christ as the life-principle of the supernatural state of existence on which he has now entered. Thus, for the mystical doctrine of the being-in-Christ, ethics is nothing else than the Spirit's working. In setting forth this view Paul makes an end of that impoverishment of the doctrine of the Spirit which began with Joel, and returns to the view of the earlier Prophets, according to which the Spirit bestows upon man a new mind and a new heart.

Ethics for Paul is not a matter of fruits of repentance but of fruits of the Spirit (Gal. v. 22).

Of his two doctrines of righteousness, it is only with the mystical being-in-Christ that Paul brings his ethic into connection; he never makes any attempt to derive it from the righteousness by faith. In order to be able to deny the value of law-works with sufficient emphasis he commits himself to the inherently irrational general assertion that faith has no need of and no desire for works. To give ethics, from this point of view, any real foundation is impossible for him.[2] It only remained open to him to set up an ethic independent of faith-righteousness. He might have made use for this purpose of the natural demand that the righteousness obtained without

---

[1] On the Primitive-Christian and the Pauline doctrines of the Spirit see pp. 165-167, *sup.*

[2] On the impossibility of deriving ethics in any natural way from the doctrine of righteousness by faith see pp. 224-225, *sup.*

works must manifest itself in works. But it would have been difficult to offer proof that it is capable of doing this, or that it carries
in itself any impulse in that direction. It would have been necessary
to show how the man who previously was inherently incapable
of producing good works received through the act of justification
the capacity to do so. That capacity can only be bestowed upon him
through Christ; but according to the doctrine of faith-righteousness, all that Christ does to believers is to cause them to be justified.

In the doctrine of justification by faith, redemption and ethics
are like two roads, one of which leads up to one side of a ravine,
and the other leads onwards from the opposite side—but there is
no bridge by which to pass from one side to the other. But Paul
is here in the favourable position, as compared with the Reformers,
of not having to make desperate efforts to procure the unprocur-
able material necessary to build this bridge. For in the mystical
being-in-Christ he possesses a concept of redemption from which
ethics directly results as a natural function of the redeemed state.
In this concept there is a logical foundation for the paradox, that
the man before redemption was incapable of good works, but
afterwards not only can but must bring them forth; since it is
Christ who brings them forth in him.

The fact that the mystical doctrine of the dying and rising again
with Christ can thus be transmitted directly into an ethic without
leaving any unresolved difficulties might give rise to the impression
that it was simply a metaphorical thought-form which had grown
up out of ethical considerations. For this reason it used to be
customary to designate it not as the mystical, but as the ethical,
teaching of Paul. As such it still figures in H. J. Holtzmann's
Neutestamentliche Theologie (1897).[1] But in reality the dying and
rising again with Christ is not a metaphorical but a quasi-physical
conception. It results from the eschatological view of redemption,
when this is understood in the light of the fact of Jesus' death and
resurrection. From this concept, in itself quasi-physical, ethics
follow directly.

Once this relationship between the quasi-physical and the ethical
is understood it gives to the Pauline system of thought a new large-
ness, restfulness, and simplicity. The unmediated transitions by
which quasi-physical speculative and ethical arguments pass into
one another—look at Rom. v.-viii.!—no longer makes the impres-

---

[1] On the earlier view of Paul's mysticism see pp. 17-18, *sup.*

sion of something chaotic. The apparent medley is due to the quasi-physical mysticism shimmering with the colours of ethic. There is here in reality a unity, unique in religious thinking, of cosmic philosophy, doctrine of redemption, and ethics. The ethics result from the unique character of the condition of the world here pre-supposed. Since with the dying and rising again of Christ the super-earthly world has already begun to be, the believers who through the being-in-Christ already belong to it, can already exercise the temper of mind appropriate to their liberation from the natural world.

Paul's ethic is therefore nothing else than the mysticism of the being-in-Christ, conceived from the point of view of will. Its greatness lies in the fact that it is wholly supernatural, without thereby becoming unnatural.

Jesus in His demand for ethical perfection takes as His starting-point the natural constitution of man, whose proper function is to submit himself to the will of God. This Paul does not do. His teaching about conscience as the natural instinct for the good, which becomes to the heathen an inner law (Rom. ii. 14-16), is only the expedient to enable him to assert universal sinfulness among the heathen on the same basis as among the Jews. It is not made use of in connection with ethics any more than the "inward man" of Rom. vii. 22, who approves the ethical require-ments of the Law. The demands which Paul's view of ethics sets up presuppose not the natural man but the "new creation" en-dowed with the Spirit, who has come into existence in the dying and rising again with Christ.

The desperate battle between the inward man and the fleshly man, which Paul describes in Rom. vii., is therefore not a post-baptismal but a pre-baptismal experience. He who is "in Christ" is, through the dying and rising again with Him and the possession of the Spirit, lord over the flesh. He has "crucified the flesh with its affections and lusts" (Gal. v. 24), and can now "walk in the Spirit" (Gal. v. 25). Of himself Paul says that he "buffets his body and keeps it in subjection" (1 Cor. ix. 27).

How the new comes into the place of the old, and how the Spirit unites with that natural "inward man" which resists sin (Rom. vii. 22), we are not told by Paul. The inward man, which as we learn from 2 Cor. iv. 16 is renewed amid sufferings from day to day, is no longer the natural man but the new man who has come into existence through the dying and rising again with Christ. To those who are in Christ the psychology of the natural man no longer applies. The Spirit has taken possession of them. Instead of the natural mind ($\nu o \hat{v} \varsigma$) they possess the "mind of Christ" (I Cor. ii. 16). By what psychological process this comes about, Paul does not explain.

Although Paul's ethical demands are in essence not different from Jesus' absolute ethic of unworldliness, he nevertheless cannot appeal to Jesus' words in support of it. He is himself, indeed, conscious of expressing this same thing as quite a different thing. In place of an ethic preached by Jesus Christ, it is for him, in view of the altered world-conditions, to substitute an ethic brought into being by Jesus in the believer. Those who continue to preach an ethic based only on the words of the historic Jesus are guilty of an unpardonable anachronism. They are leaving out of account the enablement towards the good, which God has since then bestowed upon believers through the death and resurrection of Jesus, and the consequent gift of the Spirit. Accordingly Paul does not derive his ethic by tradition from Jesus, but develops it solely from the character of the new state of existence which results from the dying and rising again with Christ and the bestowal of the Spirit.

.   .   .   .   .   .

The great danger for all mysticism is that of becoming supra-ethical, that is to say, of making the spirituality associated with the being-in-eternity an end in itself. This valuation of the spiritual in and for itself is found among the Brahmans, the Buddhists, and in Hegel. And the mysticism of Hellenistic personal religion is, it might almost be said, without ethical interests. Its efforts are directed only towards attaining for the individual man, through initiation, the assurance of immortality. It does not urge the man, born again to new life, to live as a new person an ethical life in the world. How difficult it is for the intellectual mysticism of the being-in-God to reach an ethic is seen in Spinoza. Even in Christian Mysticism, whether medieval or modern, it is often the semblance of ethics rather than ethics itself which is preserved. There is always the danger that the mystic will experience the eternal as absolute impassivity, and will consequently cease to regard the ethical existence as the highest manifestation of spirituality.

In Paul's teaching, however, ethics comes to its full rights. He is never tempted to give to the thought, that those who are in

Christ are already supernatural beings, the special complexion that they are now exalted above what is held in the natural world to be good and evil. However much Gnosis there may be in his conception of redemption, he is far enough from the devalorisation of the ethical which took place in the later Gnosticism.

There is a touch of Gnosticism in Paul's convictions that the being-in-Christ signifies, in every respect, liberty.

2 Cor. iii. 17: "Where the Spirit of the Lord is, there is liberty."

It is from the consciousness of this liberty that Paul holds, contrary to the text of Scripture, that the Jewish Law is only a temporary embodiment of the ethical, the validity of which has been annulled by the death and resurrection of Christ.

It is in this consciousness of liberty, too, that he feels himself raised above the meticulous anxieties of the people at Corinth, who regarded the meat which came from idol sacrifices as in itself dangerous, and from fear of accidentally eating such meat, would accept no invitations from the heathen friends and would buy no meat in the market (1 Cor. viii. 1-13, x. 23-33). As one who has become a free man in Christ he refuses to draw distinctions between days that are holy and days that are not, and between clean and unclean meats, such as formed a subject of controversy in certain churches (Rom. xiv. 1-xv. 2).

This conception of liberty, however, is limited by considerations of ethical expediency. Only where it is necessary in the interests of the Gospel does he insist on maintaining the freedom which his knowledge gives. If his liberty causes offence to others he is willing to give it up, if there are ethical grounds for doing so.

In cases connected with the Law it is necessary to maintain this liberty with determination. Any yielding in this question would signify a surrender of the only true valuation of the being-in-Christ.

Gal. ii. 4-5: ". . . on account of false brethren who had wormed their way in in order to spy upon our liberty, which we have in Christ, to the end that they might enslave us, to whom we did not give way for a moment by submitting to them, in order that the liberty of the Gospel might be kept for you."

Gal. v. 1: "For freedom hath Christ set us free. Therefore stand firm and do not let the yoke of bondage be again laid upon you."

Gal. v. 13: "To freedom are ye called, brethren."

In all other cases Paul requires that the free man shall, from ethical motives, not insist upon his freedom, but shall make concessions to him who is not yet free.

In the question of the meat offered to idols, he recommends consideration for the opinion of those who have not yet attained to the knowledge "that the earth is the Lord's, and the fullness thereof," as the Psalmist says (1 Cor. x. 26 = Ps. xxiv. 1), and that therefore all meat except that eaten at the idol feasts has nothing to do with the demons, even though it were brought from the idol's altar to the market, and thence to the table at which the Christians sit as guests. It is not the act in itself, but the conviction in which it is done which decides, for Paul, whether it is good or evil. But if one who is convinced that the eating of meat from idol altars is a matter of indifference by his example leads another to treat it, against his convictions, as a matter of no importance, he, by his knowledge, is destroying the weaker brother, and sinning against Christ, by wounding the weak conscience (1 Cor. viii. 10-12). Better eat no meat for evermore than put a stumbling-block in the way of a brother (1 Cor. viii. 13).

1 Cor. vi. 12: "All things are lawful, but not all things are expedient." 1 Cor. x. 23: "All things are lawful, but not all things are expedient; all things are lawful, but not all things are edifying."

It is in the same spirit that Paul decides the question how a man should behave towards those who distinguish between clean and unclean meats. As it is not here a case, as it might be with the fear of eating meat from idol altars, of scruples which might have some kind of connection with belief in Jesus, he ought in logic simply to dismiss them as unjustifiable. But on ethical grounds he makes concessions.

Abstinence from flesh meat was taught by the Orphics and Pythagoraeans. It is possible that they were led to do this under Indian influences, to which no doubt are to be traced back also the conception of transmigration of souls in Plato. For in ancient European thought there are no grounds for refusing flesh meat or for the rise of the idea of transmigration.

Abstinence from wine and all intoxicating liquor is in the Semitic Orient a sign of being dedicated to God, the Jewish Nazirites being a case in point (Num. vi. 1-31). While the Orphics and Pythagoraeans only confined themselves to vegetable food, the Neo-Pythagoraeans abstained

from the use both of flesh meat and of wine (Diog. Laert. viii. 38).
Similar asceticism was practised by Philo's Therapeutae (*De Vita Contemplativa*, 37), and probably also by the Essenes.[1] It is worthy of note
that Hegesippus reports this also of James 'the Just', the brother of the
Lord (Euseb. *Hist. Eccl.* ii. 23, 5). That even in Primitive Christianity
this asceticism endeavoured to combine itself with the belief in Jesus
we learn from Paul. But as it is not possible to decide against whom
the arguments of Rom. xiv. 1-xv. 6 are directed, it remains doubtful
whether this happened in Rome or in the Eastern churches. The propaganda for this religious asceticism was not destined to any permanent
success in Christianity.

In the prominence given to freedom Paul goes extraordinarily
far. It would have seemed the most natural thing to forbid believers
to force these weaker brethren to give up their convictions. Instead
of that he demands of the man who knows that all things in themselves are clean that he should submit to limitations on his eating
and drinking, in order to avoid hurting the consciences of the
weak.

Rom. xiv. 20-xv. 1: "All things are, indeed, clean; but yet it is of evil
if a man eats with offence. It is good neither to eat meat nor to drink
wine, nor to do anything else which causes offence to thy brother. The
faith which you have, have for thyself before God. Blessed is he who has
no conscientious scruples about what he judges right. All that is not of
faith is of sin. So we who are strong are under obligation to take up the
burden of the infirmities of the weak, and not to live to please ourselves."

How far such deference to the weak might ultimately lead, Paul
does not trouble to enquire. He is not setting up permanent principles for the practical guidance of human society, but thinking only
of the period bounded by the return of Christ. His efforts are
directed only towards determining what conduct the man who has
knowledge must adopt, in order to use his Gnosis in the Spirit of
Christ. The true "Gnostic" is for him the man who allows his
knowledge to be ruled by love.

1 Cor. viii. 1: "Knowledge puffs up, but love edifies."

.   .   .   .   .   .

Strictly speaking, it ought to have been a difficult question for
Paul, how those who have died and risen with Christ can, in the

---

[1] The genuineness of Philo's *De Vita Contemplativa* is disputed.

new state of existence in which they now are, sin at all. For again and again he asserts that for those who have died and risen again the flesh and sin have been completely done away with. But this supra-mundane condition is only so far an accomplished fact that the baptized ought to be conscious that the limitations of the natural existence no longer apply to them, and that they ought not therefore to attribute to them an importance which they no longer possess. Really, and in principle, they are a new creation because the powers of death and resurrection, to the working of which they are subjected by their union with Christ, have begun their work in them. But at the same time this fact is only in process of being realised. Here ethics come into play.

The believer, by his will, should progressively make into a reality his death to the flesh and sin, and his being ruled in his thinking and acting by the new life-principles of the Spirit. He will show by his ethical conduct how far the dying and rising again with Christ has proceeded in him. Since there are among the Corinthians factions and contentions, they are, in Paul's estimation, so backward that he holds them to be no real "pneumatics," that is to say, spirit-ruled men. They are for him "in their nonage in Christ," and, as such, still fleshly (1 Cor. iii. 1-3).

On two occasions Paul expounds his ethic as the putting into operation of the dying and rising again with Christ ; once, briefly, in the Epistle to the Galatians (v. 13-vi. 10), the other time at greater length in the Epistle to the Romans (v. 1-viii. 17).

In the former he enumerates the works of the flesh and of the Spirit, and summons the Galatians to action appropriate to their deadness of the flesh and their life in the Spirit.

Gal. v. 16: "But I say to you, walk in the Spirit, and ye will not fulfil the desires of the flesh."

Gal. v. 19-25: "The works of the flesh are manifest, such as these: fornication, uncleanness, lasciviousness, idolatry, sorcery, enmity, strife, jealousy, anger, factions, divisions, envy, drunkenness, revellings and the like; of which I have told you before that they who do such things shall not inherit the Kingdom of God. But the fruit of the Spirit is love, joy, peace, long-suffering, kindness, goodness, faithfulness, gentleness, chastity; against such things there is no Law. For they who belong to Christ Jesus have crucified the flesh with its desires and lusts. If we have life by the Spirit, let us also walk in the Spirit."

Gal. vi. 7-8: "Be not deceived; God is not mocked. What a man sows that shall he also reap. He who sows to the flesh will of the flesh reap corruption; he who sows to the spirit will of the spirit reap eternal life."

In the Epistle to the Romans Paul develops his mysticism and his ethics side by side. And in this exposition the unity of active and passive ethics is admirably shown. For the only profound ethic is one which is able, on the basis of one and the same conception, to give an ethical interpretation to all that a man experiences and suffers as well as to all that he does. The great weakness of the utilitarian ethic is at all times that it can relate itself only to man's action and not to that which he undergoes, although for his full development both must be taken into account. It is only in so far as a man is purified and liberated from the world by that which he experiences and endures, that he becomes capable of truly ethical action. In the ethic of the dying and rising again with Christ passive and active ethics are interwoven as in no other. The being "not as the world" in action is the expression of the being made free from the world, through suffering and dying with Christ. This constitutes the greatness and originality of Paul's ethics. And therefore these chapters of the Epistle to the Romans are among the most fundamental and impressive passages which have ever been written about ethics.

The essential character of the ethical, as it arises out of the mysticism of the dying and rising again with Christ, is formulated by Paul in many and various ways, as sanctification, giving up the service of sin, living for God, bringing forth fruit for God, serving the Spirit.

1 Thess. iv. 3: "This is God's will—your sanctification."

Rom. vi. 6: "Knowing this, that our old man has been crucified with (Him), that the body of sin might be destroyed and that we should no longer be slaves to sin."—Rom. vi. 11: "Therefore reckon yourselves also to be dead for sin, but alive for God in Christ Jesus."—Rom. vi. 13: "Offer yourselves to God as men alive from the dead, and your members as weapons of righteousness to God."—Rom. viii. 5: "Those who are after the flesh set their minds on the things of the flesh; but those who are after the Spirit, on the things of the Spirit."—Rom. viii. 12-14: "So, then, brethren, we are not debtors to the flesh, to live after the flesh, for if you live after the flesh you must die. But if through the Spirit you make dead the things of the body, you will live. For as many of you as have for your motive power the Spirit of God, you are sons of God." —Rom. xii. 1: "So I exhort you, brethren, by the mercy of God, that you offer your bodies a living, holy sacrifice, well-pleasing to God, for that is your rational worship."

1 Cor. vi. 20: "Glorify God in your body."

.   .   .   .   .   .

Cases occur where Paul has to meet the objections which can be brought from the point of view of ethics against his doctrines of righteousness by faith and of freedom from the Law. If the objection is raised, that his doctrine of God's grace as the sole source of righteousness does not give man a sufficient motive to work his way clear of sin, he answers, on the basis of his mysticism, that he who has died to sin can no longer live therein (Rom. vi. 1-2). That liberation from the Law is not liberty to sin, he proves by pointing out that by the Spirit a man is immediately placed under the new, more perfect Law of Christ, which is the Law of Love.

Gal. v. 13-14: "To liberty are ye called, brethren, but not (to use) liberty as an encouragement to the flesh, but by love ye are to serve one another. For the whole Law is fulfilled in the one word, 'Thou shalt love thy neighbour as thyself'."—Gal. v. 18: "If your motive power is the Spirit, you are not under the Law."—Gal. vi. 2: "Bear ye one another's burdens, and so shall ye fulfil the Law of Christ."

Rom. viii. 2: "The Law of the Spirit of the life in Christ Jesus has made thee free from the law of sin and death."—Rom. viii. 4: "That the just requirements of the Law might be fulfilled in us, who walk not after the flesh but after the spirit."—Rom. xiii. 8-10: "Be in debt to no man—except for the debt of loving one another. He who loves his neighbour has fulfilled the Law. For the commandments 'Thou shalt not commit adultery, thou shalt not kill, thou shalt not steal, thou shalt not covet' and all the other commandments are summed up in this saying, 'Thou shalt love thy neighbour as thyself.' Love works no ill to the neighbour: therefore love is the fulfilling of the Law."

Paul's thought is not merely that the law of the Spirit is substituted for the Law of Moses, but rather that it is only those who are no longer mere natural men who can properly fulfil the ethical demands of this Law. The tragic thing was that this "pneumatic" and holy law (Rom. vii. 12, 14) laid upon the natural man demands which only the "pneumatic man" could fulfil. For only the pneumatic man is capable of love, which is the only real fulfilling of the Law. And Love is a gift of the Spirit.

Whether Paul actually knew the saying of Jesus about love as including in itself all the commandments of the Law (Mk. xii. 28-33) cannot be determined with certainty. It is probable that he did, but he has no occasion to quote it. For him it is only a prophecy of the time when love should become, through the Spirit, a reality.

Love is for him the highest of the "fruits of the Spirit"; he places it first among these in the Epistle to the Galatians (v. 22). And why it is so he explains in the First Epistle to the Corinthians (1 Cor. xiii.). After writing at length (1 Cor. xii. 1-30) on the variety of the gifts bestowed upon individual men through the Spirit and giving to each its meed of praise, he ends with the exhortation to strive after the greatest of these, that is, the gifts which chiefly and most directly serve to edification. Among these highest gifts he places love highest of all. From their disputes as to whether prophesying, or ecstatic speech, the working of miracles, knowledge, the gift of teaching, or the power of healing was the most important, he turns believers to the way of love, "the more excellent way" which leads out beyond all these. Speaking with tongues, prophesying, knowledge, faith, and action have only a value when the spiritual gift which is to be sought by all, and which is obtainable by all, is present.

1 Cor. xii. 31-xiii. 6: "Strive after the higher gifts; and yet show I unto you a more excellent way.

"Though I speak with tongues, both of men and angels, and have not love, I am a sounding brass or a tinkling cymbal. And though I have prophesyings and know all mysteries and all knowledge, and though I have all faith, so that I could remove mountains, and have not love, I am nothing.[1] And though I give away all my goods and deliver up my body to be burned, and have not love, it profiteth me nothing.

"Love is long-suffering; love is kind; love envies not; it does not boast; is not puffed-up; does nought unseemly; seeks not its own; does not allow itself to be provoked; does not bear malice; has no pleasure (in seeing) ill-doing, but rejoices with the truth; bears all things, believes all things, hopes all things, endures all things."

[1] The faith which can remove mountains is spoken of also by Jesus. Mt. xvii. 20: "If ye have faith as a grain of mustard seed, ye shall say to this mountain, 'Remove hence to yonder place,' and it shall remove."—Mt. xxi. 21: "If ye have faith and doubt not, ye shall not only be able to do that which was done with the fig-tree, but ye shall also be able to say to this mountain, 'Be thou removed and cast into the sea, and it shall be done.'" Whether Paul's expression was influenced by knowledge of this saying of Jesus, or whether both allude to a popular proverb, we cannot determine.

Love is the highest among spiritual gifts because it is the only one which is eternal. Prophecy and speaking with tongues are for the period between Jesus' death and His return. In the Messianic Kingdom they will cease, because there will be no more need of them. Nor will knowledge such as is now given by the Spirit continue, for it is a partial thing, which will give place to that which is complete. In God Himself there is place neither for faith nor hope, there is only love. Thus love is the only thing which has been from all eternity and will continue to be to all eternity. It is therefore greater even than faith and hope, although redemption is dependent on these. It is the pre-eternal thing which man can possess here and now in its true essence.

1 Cor. xiii. 8-10: "Love has no end. Prophesyings—they shall be no more; speaking with tongues—it shall cease; knowledge—it shall be no more. For our knowledge is a partial thing and our prophesying a partial thing. But when that which is complete is come, that which is partial shall be no more."

1 Cor. xiii. 13: "But now remain faith, hope, love, these three. But the greatest among them is love."

1 Cor. xiv. 1: "Pursue after love, and strive after the gifts of the Spirit."

The enumeration of faith, hope, love together cannot be meant in the sense that faith and hope have the same kind of permanence as love. For that would destroy the whole logic of the passage. Moreover, faith and hope are left without an object from the moment when the Messianic glory becomes a fact. Paul's purpose must be simply to place together the three manifestations of the Spirit, in which all others are included.

The trinity of faith, hope, love occurs as early as the First Epistle to the Thessalonians. Paul praises the Thessalonians for their work of faith, their labour of love, and their steadfastness in hope (1 Thess. i. 3), and exhorts them to put on the breastplate of faith and love and the helmet of hope (1 Thess. v. 8).

R. Reitzenstein cannot of course admit that Paul thought of this trinity for himself, but is obliged to maintain that he received it in some way from Hellenism. He is supposed to have obtained it from the four-membered Hellenistic formula, Faith, Eros, Gnosis, and Hope by "striking out" the Gnosis. By this omission of Gnosis he is supposed to be polemising against a Hellenistic formula on Hellenistic soil! (See Richard Reitzenstein, "Die Formel Glaube, Liebe, Hoffnung, bei Paulus," in *Nachrichten der K. Gesellschaft der Wissenschaften zu Göttingen :* Philologisch-historische Klasse, 1916, pp. 367-416; and *Hellenistische*

Mysterienreligionen, 3rd ed. pp. 393-391.) How then is it to be explained
that this trinity is alluded to by him as early as 1 Thessalonians?

Love is for Paul something metaphysical, and nevertheless
directly ethical. It is the love of God, that is to say, the love which
is in God, which through the Holy Spirit is shed abroad in the
hearts of men (Rom. v. 5). In the benediction at the end of the
Second Epistle to the Corinthians Paul's wish for the believers is
that the love of God may be with them all (2 Cor. xiii. 14). Love
is the true knowledge, in which God and the believers are mutually
known to one another.

1 Cor. viii. 1-3: "Knowledge puffs up, but love builds up. If a man
prides himself on possessing knowledge of anything, he has not yet true
knowledge. But he who has love to God, he is known by God."

This being known by God, that is to say, the being acknowledged by God as belonging to Him, plays a great part in Paul's
thought.

1 Cor. xiii. 12: "Then shall I know even as I am known."—Gal. iv.
9: "But now knowing God, or rather, being known by Him."

This conception has nothing to do with the Hellenistic mystical
theory of becoming one with God through knowledge, even
though phrases connected with the latter can be cited which have
some affinity with those of Paul. For Paul's conception is directly
derived from the eschatological idea of predestination. In the love
which passes from the one to the other, God acknowledges the
elect man as belonging to Him, and the elect man also receives
knowledge of this belonging. Since the highest manifestation of
the Spirit is love, the Elect are made aware by the Spirit that they
are God's children (Rom. viii. 15-16).

As a metaphysical concept, love, in Paul's teaching, is nothing
else than a particular form of expression of the unity which subsists between God and Christ and the Elect. Therefore it is always
the same love, whether it is manifested in God, in Christ, or in
the Elect. When Paul speaks of the love of Christ (Rom. viii. 35),
he means the same as when he speaks of the love of God which is
in Christ Jesus (Rom. viii. 39). It is even possible for him to wish
for the Corinthians that the love of God may be with them (2 Cor.
xiii. 14), and that his own love may be with them! (1 Cor. xvi. 24).

If in so many Pauline passages it remains uncertain whether

by the love of God and love of Christ is meant the love felt by God and Christ or the love felt for them, this ambiguity is not a mere consequence of linguistic inadequacy; it belongs to Paul's thought. Love is for him not a ray which flashes from one point to another point, but one which is constantly vibrating to and fro. Love to God and Christ is always at the same time love proceeding from God and Christ, which works effectually in the Elect who love. Since love is thus the highest manifestation of the being-in-Christ, love, for Paul, belongs to the essence of faith.

Gal. v. 6: "In Christ neither is circumcision anything nor uncircumcision, but faith which expresses itself in love."

.   .   .   .   .   .

This mystico-speculative ethic is marked by an admirable naturalness and fervour. The beatitudes of the Sermon on the Mount are alive in it. The moving exhortation to let all things be done in love (1 Cor. xvi. 14) finds expression in striking phrases.

Ethical sayings of Paul.

1 Thess. v. 14-22: "Admonish the disorderly, encourage the faint-hearted, help the weak, have patience with all. See that none renders to anyone evil for evil, but be always seeking to do good to one another and to all. Rejoice always. Pray without ceasing. Be thankful for everything. For this is the will of God in Christ Jesus for you. . . . Test all things; hold fast the good. Avoid evil in every form."

Gal. v. 13: "Serve one another in love."—Gal. v. 26-vi. 1: "Let us not be eager for vain reputation, not competing with one another, not envious towards one another. Brethren, even if a man be overtaken by[1] a fault, ye that are spiritual set him right in the spirit of gentleness, and let each look to himself, lest he also be tempted."

Rom. xii. 9-21: "Let love be without hypocrisy. Hate evil; cleave to the good. Be closely united with one another in brotherly love, vie with one another in showing courtesy. In zeal be unremitting, in the spirit be fervent. Serve the Lord diligently. Rejoice in hope. In affliction be steadfast. Persevere in prayer. Share with the saints in their need; ply hospitality diligently. Bless those that persecute you; bless, not curse. Rejoice with the rejoicing; weep with the weeping. Be in agreement with each other. Be not ambitious, but rather stoop to the level of lowliness. Be not conceited about your wisdom. Do not repay any man evil for evil. Set your mind on good towards all men. If it is possible, so far as it depends on you, live at peace with all men. Do not vindicate your rights, beloved, but leave it to the Wrath. For it is written, 'Vengeance

---

[1] TRANSLATOR'S Note.—So the German R.V., "be overtaken in any trespass."

is mine, saith the Lord, I will repay' (Deut. xxxii. 35). Nay rather, 'If your enemy is hungry, feed him; if he is thirsty, give him to drink; for in so doing thou wilt heap coals of fire on his head' (Prov. xxv. 21-22). Be not overcome by evil, but overcome evil by good."

Rom. xiv. 13: "Let us therefore not judge each other any more; but exercise your judgment rather in avoiding the putting of stumbling-blocks in your brother's way."

.   .   .   .   .   .

The ethical utterances of Paul, and the way in which he bases them on the doctrine of love, show some remarkable affinities with the ethical ideas of the later Stoicism as known to us from the writings of Seneca, Epictetus, and Marcus Aurelius. This is to be explained from the fact that in the Late-Stoicism also an ethical mysticism is present. From the beginning Stoicism is marked by its struggle to reach a theory of ethics. It is from the pressure of ethical needs that the later Stoic abandons the rigid conception of the Divine as the primal necessity which rules the world, and comes in the end to recognise in the course of events the rule of a Divine will which is determined by rational and ethical ends. To this Divine will it is the duty of the thinking man to surrender himself, in order that it may work effectually in his actions. The affinity of this ethic with that of Paul is therefore to be explained from the fact that the Stoic-pantheistic mysticism of the being-in-God leads to ethical demands similar to those of the Pauline being-in-Christ, even though in depth and living energy it is much inferior. The resemblance is a question of a mere analogy.

When it is asserted, as is often done, that Paul shows, in the gnomic sayings in which he embodies his ethic, the influence of the wandering philosophical lecturers of his time, the answer is that he is much more likely to have been influenced by the Jewish proverbial literature, from which he has adopted some of his sayings. Thus the saying about love to enemies in the Epistle to the Romans (xii. 20) is derived from the Proverbs of Solomon (xxv. 21-22). How far the Jewish gnomic writers were themselves influenced by Greek literature is another question.

That Paul's ethical ideas recall in many points those of Chinese thinkers, such as Kungtse (Confucius, sixth century B.C.), Mengtse (Mencius, fourth century B.C.), and especially Mitse (fifth century B.C.), is to be explained in the same way as the affinities with Late-Stoicism. For in the Chinese thinkers the same thing happened as in Stoicism. Laotse (sixth century B.C.) and Tschuangtse (fourth century B.C.) and others did not attain to any living ethic, because they did not conceive of the primal will which rules all things as ethical. But alongside of them Kungtse, Mitse, Mengtse, and others reached a living ethic by the same path as the Late-Stoicism—and long afterwards, the Rationalism of the eighteenth century: they assume the existence of a world-will which works rationally and ethically, to which a man ought to surrender himself, and they arrive accordingly at the inculcation of love in a way which shows a certain analogy to Paul's teaching.

But, fundamentally, Paul's ethic is comparable to no other, save that of Jesus. It is born, like that of Jesus, of the eschatological expectation. It presupposes, like it, a conception of love which is not to be explained by any general relation of God to the world and man, but is derived from the special association, in a united whole, of God, the Messiah, and the Elect, which is to realise itself in the Times of the End.

Yet although Paul's impressive ethic of love is identical in content with that of Jesus, he has not simply taken over the latter as it stands, but repeats it with a new explanation. For he must necessarily bring it into accord with the new stage in redemption, which has come about through Christ's death and resurrection. The facts compel him, as in the case of the formulation of redemption, so also in that of ethics, to take his place alongside of Jesus as an originator. It thus comes about that we have the ethic of love in two successive versions; in that of Jesus as the simple ethic of preparing for the Kingdom of God by being other than the world; and in that of Paul as the mystical ethic of being other than the world through having died and risen again with Christ, and through the possession of the Spirit.

It was a tremendous achievement, this of Paul's, in bringing ethics into connection with the possession of the Spirit and explaining love as the highest manifestation of the Spirit. What inward greatness and what power of thought it implies, that he who, like other believers, knew what it was to be overwhelmed by the sensible manifestations of the Spirit, and like them prized this experience as a supernatural power bestowed on man, nevertheless saw in it something relative and secondary, and recognised with such certainty of conviction love as the truly essential manifestation of the eternal in the temporal.

By preserving this ethical spirituality amid the enthusiastic expectation of the glory of Christ, and laying down in such forceful words the ethical character of the belief in Christ, Paul shows himself the true disciple of Jesus. He has therein accomplished something essential to the preservation of the spirit of Jesus' message and work—something which is overlooked by those who are content simply to repeat His ethical sayings. Paul, alone of all the believers of this early period, recognised the faith in Jesus Christ essentially, and with all that it implies, must place itself under the absolute authority of the ethical, and must draw its warmth from the flame of love.

.   .   .   .   .   .

Paul's ethic, because it is eschatological, is dominated by the idea of judgment and reward. Again and again he exhorts the believers to continue steadfastly in the good, because eternal life at the coming of Christ is promised to them as a consequence. In view of the Coming Judgment they are to avoid all judgments upon each other, and leave everything in the hands of Him who knows the hearts of men, and can bring even that which is hidden to light.

1 Thess. iii. 13: "That your hearts may be unblamable in holiness before God our Father at the coming of our Lord Jesus Christ with all His saints."—2 Cor. v. 10: "For we must all be made manifest before the judgment-seat of Christ, that each may receive for the things done in the body, according to what he has done, whether it be good or evil." —Rom. ii. 6-8: "Who shall reward every man according to his works, to those who by perseverance in well-doing have sought glory and honour and immortality, eternal life; but to the contentious, who followed not truth but unrighteousness, wrath and anger."

1 Cor. iv. 5: "Therefore judge nothing before the time, before the Lord comes, who shall bring to light that which is hidden in darkness, and shall lay bare the purposes of the heart: then shall each receive his praise from God."

It is interesting that, according to Paul, personal conduct and works done for the cause of Christ are judged separately. In the First Epistle to the Corinthians he takes for granted that, in the day when all things shall be tested in the furnace of God, one whose work for Christ, because it was not rightly done, will not stand the test, may nevertheless find grace on account of his personal conduct. Whether he expects such clemency for those whom he threatens with the Judgment, because their contention for the Law and circumcision have jeopardised the redemption of so many, must remain doubtful.[1]

1 Cor. iii. 15: "If his work is destroyed by the fire he shall be punished. But he himself shall be saved, though as one who has passed through the fire."

How natural the idea of reward is to Paul appears from the fact that in Philippians ii. 4-11 he cites the humility of Christ, along with the exaltation which He thereby earned, as an example. Christ's humility consisted in renouncing the divine glory, which He possessed as a pre-existent being, in order, in obedience to His Father's will, to enter into human existence and suffer death. This humbling of Himself was rewarded by God's exalting Him to be ruler over all existence, in heaven, upon earth, and beneath the earth; thus bestowing upon Him a rank which, divine as He was, He did not previously possess.

In another passage Paul cites Christ's coming into the world as an ethical example, where he encourages the Corinthians to give generously to the collection for the Jerusalem church by pointing to Christ's becoming poor in order that his followers might become rich.

2 Cor. viii. 9: "You know the grace of our Lord Jesus Christ, how for your sakes He became poor, in order that you through His poverty might become rich."

.   .   .   .   .   .

Paul's ethic, since it is oriented to the expectation of the end of the natural world, might be expected to be ascetic; and it in fact is so, though not by any means in the degree which might be expected.

In principle, no doubt, Paul's point of view is that a man should make himself free from all earthly things, in order to be the better prepared for that which is to come. Thus, with direct allusion to the coming trials of the Times of the End (1 Cor. vii. 26) and the destruction of the world (1 Cor. vii. 29, 31), he holds up celibacy as the ideal (1 Cor. vii. 1, 7, 26, 38). He points out that the unmarried can give themselves entirely to caring for the things of the Lord and for their own sanctification, whereas the married

---

[1] Gal. i. 9, v. 10; 2 Cor. xi. 15. See p. 157, *sup.*

are drawn aside from this by their care for one another (1 Cor. vii. 32-34). But he is not rigorous in his application of the ascetic principle, whether in the question of marriage, or that of property, or any other. His spirituality raises him above outward asceticism. He maintains the principle that a man should be as free as possible from earthly cares in order that his thoughts may be directed wholly to the Lord (1 Cor. vii. 32); but the essential thing for him is the spiritual liberation from the earthly, not the outward. He therefore lays no special stress upon remoulding the daily life of the believer in consequence of the expectation of the imminent end of the world. It does not occur to him to make the experiment of giving up personal property, or to object to work as showing an untimely care for earthly things. He would much rather that daily life should go on in its usual way, except that believers should have an inward freedom from it. That is the meaning of the saying that those who have wives should be as those who have none, and those who weep as though they weep not, those who rejoice as though they rejoiced not, those who buy as though they possessed not, those who have to do with the world as though they did not use it (1 Cor. vii. 29-31). By substituting for renunciation of the earthly inner freedom from it, Paul cuts across the Early Christian world-negation in the same way as Buddha does with that of Brahmanism.

His own self-discipline leads to the same attitude. Disorderliness and idleness are in his view a spiritual danger. Therefore, in spite of his thoughts being concentrated on the end of the world, he commends work because he sees it to be desirable in the interests of the spiritual life of the community. And from the way in which he does this it is evident, too, that in his view work has also a value in itself, because it confers material independence, which belongs for him to the idea of an ethical personality.

1 Thess. iv. 11-12: "Be ambitious of living quietly, attending to your own affairs and working at your handicraft as I enjoined upon you, that your conduct may be respected by those without, and that you may be independent of anyone else."

Because his churches consisted of workers it was possible for them to collect means for the support of the saints in Judaea. The satisfaction which this gave him appears clearly in the words in which he commends this collection to the Corinthians. As a reward

for their gifts he holds out to them the prospect of making, by
God's blessing, a competency, which will enable them always to
make contributions for good works.

2 Cor. ix. 7: " 'God loves a cheerful giver' (Prov. xxii. 8). And God
has the power to pour out upon you richly all grace, that you may always
have a sufficiency, and, beyond that, the wherewithal to give to every
good work."

Paul is thus already far removed from Jesus' prohibition of
having any care for earthly things! The way in which he brings
back the ethical value of work has in it something prophetic. Led
by his own inner intuition, he propounds an idea, to which Christianity was later obliged under the pressure of facts to give its assent,
namely, that the world was not coming to an end, but was to go on.

Another significant point, to which far too little attention has
been paid, is that Paul pictures the glory of the Messianic Kingdom
not as repose but as action. The whole period of the Messiah's
reign is filled by a succession of victories over the God-opposing
powers. In the moment when, by defeating the last of these
enemies, death, he has brought all things into subjection to Himself, He will deliver up the rule of His Father and thereby put an
end to the Messianic Kingdom (1 Cor. xv. 24-28). That the Elect
will aid Him in this overcoming of evil we learn from the fact
that they are to judge the angels (1 Cor. vi. 3). The Messianic
blessedness consists therefore for Paul in the comradeship of the
Elect with the Messiah in His struggle against the evil powers.

With the ascription of an ethical value to action, a similar attitude towards order is naturally associated. Indiscipline is numbered
by Paul among the vices; opposition to all disorder he makes a
duty. He himself gives precise directions regarding the conduct
of the spiritually-gifted at public worship, "that everything may
be done with seemliness and order" (1 Cor. xiv. 40), supporting
this injunction with the reminder that "God is not a God of disorder but of peace" (1 Cor. xiv. 33). He constantly enjoins respect
for those who bear rule in the churches and a peaceable temper in
all circumstances.

Gal. v. 20: "Idolatry, sorcery, enmities, strife, jealousy, wrath,
factiousness, divisions, schisms."—1 Cor. iii. 3: "You are still fleshly!
For when there is jealousy and strife among you are you not fleshly and
walking after the manner of men?"

1 Thess. v. 14: "Rebuke the disorderly."—1 Thess. v. 12-13: "We beseech you, brethren, acknowledge those who work among you, and are over you in the Lord, and admonish you, and esteem them in very special measure, in love, for their work's sake. Be at peace with them."

Phil. ii. 2-4: "Make my joy complete by being of the same mind, in the same love, one soul, one mind, doing nothing from party spirit or vanity, but in all humility each looking up to the other, each man seeking not his own advantage but that of others."

.   .   .   .   .   .

It is in consequence of Paul's estimation of order as an ethical good that he gives such surprisingly high commendation to its natural guardian, authority. Jesus' saying about giving to the Emperor what belonged to him, and to God what was His (Mk. xii. 13-17), was meant ironically. He evaded the trap set for Him in the question whether the Emperor's taxes ought to be paid by this answer, which derived its real meaning, not understood by His hearers, from the conviction that there would soon be no Emperor. For Jesus rulers are not those charged with the maintenance of order; they are the mighty, those who are not humble, those who do not serve; as was for eschatology the natural way of regarding them.

Matt. xx. 25: "You know that those who rule over the nations keep them in subjection, and their great ones tyrannise over them."

But for Paul the power of the mighty has the meaning that they, by God's commission, have the duty of preserving order and doing justice. They are therefore to be obeyed, not only from fear but from an inner conviction of this mission of theirs.

Rom. xiii. 1-7: "Let everyone be obedient to the authorities which are set over him. For there is no authority that is not from God, and the existing authorities are appointed by God. He therefore who resists the authorities resists the ordinances of God, and those who resist draw down judgment upon themselves. For rulers are not a terror to well-doing but to ill-doing. Dost thou desire to have no fear of authority? Do good and thou shalt have praise from it. For it is God's servant for your sake, for good. But if thou dost ill, then fear; for authority bears not the sword for nought. It is God's servant, an avenger for the execution of the sentence of Wrath upon him that does evil. Therefore it is needful to subject yourselves to it, not alone on account of the Wrath, but for conscience sake. Therefore pay your taxes, for (the authorities) are God's officials, constantly occupied with their work. Give to each his due: taxes to whom taxes are due, customs to whom customs, fear to whom fear, honour to whom honour is due."

How does Paul come to ascribe this remarkably high ethical value to earthly governments? Its parallel can only be found in antiquity in the consciousness of their office among the great Stoic Emperors, who felt themselves to be truly the servants of the State for the realisation of good. This Late-Stoic conception of rulership was at that time in process of growing up. It was put into practice in the rule of Trajan (98–117). It is documented in the Correspondence of Trajan with Pliny the Younger, who from A.D. 111–113 was governor of Bithynia. But from the point of view of the subject this ethical valuation of rulership was expressed by no other writer of antiquity, except the Jew, Paul. Neither Socrates, Plato, nor Aristotle carry the idea of obedience to authority so far. Not even Reitzenstein can discover any parallels in Hellenistic literature to Rom. xiii. 1-7.

Paul did not derive his view from the Late-Stoicism, in which it was at that time not yet worked out, but takes it over from Judaism and gives it a further development. Post-Exilic Judaism, living as it did constantly under foreign rule, had no real national consciousness, but only a racial religious consciousness. Foreign domination had become a natural idea to it, and it was prepared to accept it, provided that it made for order and prosperity and did not interfere with religion. Of this loyalty based on religion we have documentary evidence down to the fixation of the Rabbinic tradition. It was shown also in the fact that sacrifices were offered for the Emperor in the Temple at Jerusalem, and petitions, as we learn from Philo, were offered on his behalf in the synagogues.

Proverbs xxiv. 21: "My son, fear God and the king; and have thou nothing to do with disturbers of the peace."
Wisdom of Solomon vi. 3: "Because there was given to you (the kings) dominion from the Lord, and sovereignty from the Most High; Who shall examine your works and search your counsels."
Pirke Aboth iii. 2: "Pray for the prosperity of the government, since but for the fear of it one man would swallow the other alive."

For the eschatological view the ruling powers belong to the God-opposing world-power. But there persists along with this the original view that their power comes, properly speaking, from

God. They, however, misuse their power and so become deserving of Judgment. A preparation for this idea, which is current in the Apocalypses of Enoch and Baruch, is found in the Wisdom of Solomon, which originated about 100 B.C.·

Wisdom vi. 4-5: "Because ye, though servants of His (God's) government, did not judge aright, nor observe the Law, nor walk according to the Will of God; terribly and swiftly will He come upon you, because a sudden judgment shall be held upon those in high places."

Enoch xlvi. 5: "He (the Son of Man) shall throw down the kings from their thrones and out of their kingdoms, because they did not exalt Him or praise Him, or gratefully acknowledge whence their sovereignty was bestowed upon them."

Apoc. Bar. lxxxii. 4: "And we look upon the extent of their (the nations') dominion though they do iniquity, and yet they shall be but as a drop."—Apoc. Bar. lxxxii. 9: "And we observe their boastful might, though they deny the goodness of God, who has given it them; and yet shall they perish like a cloud that passes away."

Paul too, in virtue of his eschatological beliefs, cannot but hold that all dominion belonging to the world-power has incurred judgment because, although set up by God, it has become hostile to God. He does not expect that any particular earthly ruler will receive commendation from Christ at His return on account of the good which, according to the Epistle to the Romans, they accomplish in the service of God. But so long as they are actually ruling they are held by him to be those who have their office from God and exercise it by His commission. Paul is here maintaining a fiction. Just as, in spite of the nearness of the end of the world, he does not in fact repudiate private property, but only calls on the possessor to behave as though he possessed it not; so he suffers worldly dominion to continue, as though it were really acting as it were from God. Since its rejection in act would unfailingly lead to disorders, it is to be treated by believers, for the short time during which it is still to exist, as being that which it is in principle, though it is not so empirically.

Because the fiction is useful for the short time during which earthly authority will still exist, Paul carries it out consistently. He leaves out of account that this authority has so many times wrongfully imprisoned him himself and has three times had him beaten with rods (2 Cor. xi. 23, 25); that, in the time of the Emperor Caius (37-41), it abandoned the Jews of Alexandria for months at a time in the years 38 and 39 to the mercies of the mob; that the same Emperor in the year 40 proposed to set up his statue in the Temple at Jerusalem and was only prevented from committing this sacrilege by the firmness of the governor, Petronius; that in the reign of his successor, Claudius (41–54), the Jews were expelled from Rome (Acts xviii. 1-2); that under less enlightened governors than Petronius the land of Judaea was subjected to severe oppression. But as though these, and so many other misdeeds of rulers great and small, did not exist, Paul declares authority to be God's righteous servant, because obedience to it is necessary to the maintenance of order. In support of this attitude he might have cited the fact that the Roman governors, as we know from Josephus, had put an end to the brigandage which was devastating Judaea; that an edict of Claudius put an end to the deprivation of legal rights under which the Jews of Alexandria had suffered; that whatever justice was maintained in the world was the work of Roman authority, and that its representative at Corinth, Gallio, the brother of Seneca, had refused to condemn him when the Jews brought accusation against him (Acts xviii. 12-16).

The references of the poor Jewish tent-maker of Tarsus to authority in the days of the Roman Empire constitute the highest praise that authority has ever received. But it is not a purely empiric judgment, but a Jewish theory which he holds to, in face of all possible criticism, from an inner necessity. Paul does not speak as one who champions the cause of the Roman rule, or earthly authority in general, because he expects advantage from it for the future of the world, but as one who is already loosed from the world, and yet for the time in which it is still to continue finds it desirable that governmental authority should be maintained.

This, however, he might have expressed in measured language. The fact that he expresses himself so enthusiastically is, in any case, difficult to explain. Perhaps he found it necessary to oppose a disorderly tendency, of which he had been informed, in the place to which his Epistle was addressed, for it is not quite certain that the last chapters were addressed to Rome. Or it may have been important for him to make known the law-abiding attitude of the Christian believers, in face of calumnies which were actually in circulation, or which there was reason to fear. Perhaps, after all, it was pure zeal for order as such which inspired these vigorous phrases.

That all earthly power falls for Paul under the conception of a relative and temporary, not a permanent and absolute, good is evident from the fact that he is indignant at the idea of believers in Christ bringing cases before the Civil Courts.

1 Cor. vi. 1-3: "Can any of you really have the audacity, when he has a matter against another, to submit it to the judgment of the righteous and not of the saints? Do you not know that the saints shall judge the world? And if the world is to be judged by you, are you incapable of judging petty law-cases? Do you not know that we are to judge Angels? How much more the things of ordinary life."—1 Cor. vi. 6-7: "Brother goes to law with brother, and that before unbelievers. To begin with, it is in itself unseemly that you should go to law with one another at all. Why do you not rather put up with injustice?"

Paul thus forbids believers to bring cases against one another before secular courts, and indeed to seek to vindicate their legal rights in ordinary human fashion. For those who belong to the coming Messianic world have no more need of earthly justice. The righteousness in which they seek to live is, for them, the peace which goes forth from the God of peace. In this they leave behind them all earthly relationships, except that they are to render obedience to the authorities in matters pertaining to the external order.

Like Paul, the authors of the First Epistle of Peter and of the First Epistle to Timothy, Clement of Rome, Polycarp, and Justin Martyr all acknowledge heathen governmental authority as a Divinely-willed institution. In doing this they are carrying on the Jewish tradition; and in this the author of 1 Timothy, Clement of Rome, Polycarp, and Justin are certainly also influenced by Paul's attitude.

1 Peter ii. 13-17: "Be subject to every human institution (Greek and German, lit. "creation") for the Lord's sake, whether to the king as the supreme authority, or to the governors as appointed by him for the punishment of evil-doers and the reward of those who do well, for so is the will of God that by well-doing you should put to silence the ignorance of foolish men; as free, yet not using freedom as a cloak for evil, but as servants of God. Honour all; love the brotherhood; fear God; honour the king."

1 Tim. ii. 1-2: "Thus I exhort you first of all to make supplication, prayer, intercession, and thanksgiving for all men; for kings and for all who are in high places, that we may live an undisturbed and quiet life in all piety and seemliness."

1 Clem. lxi. 1: "Thou, O Lord, hast given them authority to rule, by

Thy exceeding great and ineffable might, in order that we, knowing the glory and honour which Thou hast given them, might render obedience to them without doing anything contrary to Thy will. Grant ûnto them, Lord, health, peace, unity, and to be firmly established, that they may wield without offence the authority which thou hast bestowed upon them."

Polycarp, *Ad Philipp.* xii. 3: "Pray also for kings and potentates and princes, and for those who persecute and hate you. . . ."

Justin, 1 *Apol.* xvii.: "For that reason we pray indeed to God only, but in other matters we render to you cheerful obedience, acknowledging you as kings and rulers of men, and we pray that, along with your authority as rulers, you may be found in possession also of wisdom and understanding."

From this ethical valuation of earthly authority there followed the possibility of Christianity and the Imperium Romanum continuing to exist side by side. But the possibility was tragically destroyed by the authorities' demanding from believers the worship of the Emperor as divine. By this demand the continuance of the ascription of ethical value to governmental authority was rendered impossible for Christianity, and a life-and-death struggle between Church and State was begun. In the course of the struggle the unethical estimate of the State, which eschatology had brought into Christianity from the first, became firmly established. In the Apocalypse of John, as in the teaching of Jesus, the rulers are simply tyrants. In proportion as the Church attained to independence and power, it felt itself called to organise God's rule upon earth, and could only recognise earthly governmental authority so far as this entered into its service.

In contrast to the Roman Church, the Reformers later, and following in their footsteps modern thinkers, have again arrived at an ethical valuation of the State, in support of which they appeal to Paul. Thus his statement about the ethical character and Divine origin of secular government, have, after remaining without influence for centuries, again acquired a historical significance. No doubt they are now understood in a much more comprehensive sense than that in which they were originally meant. Paul is willing, from religious and ethical motives, to recognise, for the short remainder of its existence, a State which is destined to pass away. Modern thought, on the other hand, attributes to the State the possibility of being a vehicle of religious and ethical development.

In the philosophy of Fichte and Hegel, and in the rationalistic Protestantism of their time and the following period, this belief is treated as something self-evident. Since then, however, especially in consequence of the blow which the ethical idea of the State received in the World-war, this view has more and more been obliged to fight for its existence.

    .   .   .   .   .   .

Seen in the light of his ethic, Paul is a figure to provoke admiration. For he is the embodiment of what he taught.

His requirement, that a man should work in order to be independent, he fulfilled before the eyes of his converts. As a preacher of the Gospel he had indeed the right to be maintained by the churches. And this right he in principle maintained, taking the ground that he who serves as a soldier "wars not at his own charges"; that he who plants a vineyard is entitled to eat of the fruit of it; he who feeds a flock lives on its milk; he who serves in the Temple receives his food there; and he who serves the altar has a share of the offerings (1 Cor. ix. 4-7, 13). He even appeals to an ordinance of the Lord.

1 Cor. ix. 14: "For thus the Lord ordained, that those who preach the Gospel should live by the Gospel."

The most natural explanation of this statement is that Paul is referring to a historical Saying of Jesus which he can take for granted as being well known.[1] That the reference is to something which happened in the past, and not to an injunction derived from the glorified Christ, is made probable by the aorist διέταξεν, 'ordained'.[2] And indeed a saying of this tenor is found in the discourse at the sending forth of the disciples. Mt. x. 9-10: "Provide not for yourselves gold, or silver, or money in your purse, no wallet for your journey, no second coat, or shoes, or staff; for he who works earns his keep."

Paul even ventures to interpret the Scriptural command not to muzzle the ox which treads out the corn on the threshing-floor, so that while working he can snatch a mouthful, as not referring to oxen, but to the servants of the Gospel who have a right to the thresher's share.

1 Cor. ix. 9-10: "In the Law of Moses it is written, 'Thou shalt not muzzle the ox that threshes' (Deut. xxv. 4). Is God concerned for oxen?

---

[1] See pp. 173-174, *sup.* [2] TRANSLATOR'S Note.—Not as A.V., "hath ordained."

For our sakes it is written: that the plougher may plough and the thresher thresh in the hope of having their share."

Of course Paul's exegesis is here at fault. It is part of the greatness of the legislation of Deuteronomy, that in this and so many other ordinances it does imply that God concerns Himself about the animal creation.[1]

But although the Apostles at Jerusalem and James the Lord's brother made use of this Apostolic right, Paul himself abstained from doing so, in order to be completely independent, and to be a burden to none. By the work of his own hands, in the making of tent-cloth, as we learn from Acts xviii. 1-3, he earned his livelihood.

If in the course of his travels he chances to come into the position of needing help from others, he takes it only from those churches which offer it to him of their own free will, and of whom he knows that they will not presume upon having thus contributed to his support. In this way he accepts a contribution from the Philippians at the beginning of his work in Greece, and again during his imprisonment. The Corinthians he never allowed to help him, because they were capable of making him feel his dependence.

1 Thess. ii. 9-10: "No doubt you still remember, brethren, our toil and labour. Day and night we worked, in order to be a burden to none, while we were preaching the Gospel to you."

1 Cor. ix. 12: "But we have made no use of this right, but bear all burdens, in order to cause no hindrance to the Gospel of Christ. . . . But I have never availed myself of any such privilege."—1 Cor. ix. 15: "For it were better for me to die, than that any man should be able to make my boasting vain."

1 Cor. iv. 11: "To this hour we hunger and thirst, we go naked, we are beaten, we are homeless, and we toil over our handicraft."

Phil. iv. 11-16: "I have learnt, in whatever condition I am, to be content with it. I can bear humiliation; I can bear prosperity. I have become thoroughly accustomed to all these things; to be full and to be hungry, to have abundance, to be in penury. I can do all things in Christ, who makes me strong. But you have done well, in sharing with me of your means, in my affliction. You yourselves know, you men of Philippi, that in the time of the beginning of the Gospel, when I started from Macedonia, no church had any relation of giving and receiving

---

[1] TRANSLATOR'S NOTE.—This comment becomes particularly interesting in the light of the author's own view, as set forth in pp. 256-257 of *Civilisation and Ethics* (E. Tr., 1929).

with me except yourselves. For no less than twice you sent means to Thessalonica for my support."

2 Cor. xi. 8-10: "Other churches have I laid under contribution, taking my service-pay [1] from them while serving among you. And when I was with you and fell into want I laid no burden upon any. For the brethren who came from Macedonia helped me in my necessities. In every respect I avoided being a burden to you, and shall continue to avoid it. As the truth of Christ is in me, no man in the regions of Achaia shall rob me of this boast."

In this determined clinging to his material independence Paul shows something of the mentality of the modern man. In antiquity men, of whatever race, thought of it as the most natural thing in the world to accept support from those for whom they were conscious of being of some significance, or doing some service. It was, indeed, only in the eighteenth century that this mentality was got rid of.

In order to keep himself entirely free for the service of the Gospel Paul abstained from marrying, though he claimed the same right to do so as the other Apostles and the brethren of the Lord (1 Cor. ix. 5). As an athlete submits himself to all kinds of self-denial in order to win an earthly crown, so will he do in order to win a heavenly (1 Cor. ix. 25). He treats his body hard, and leads it prisoner, that he may not, while preaching to others, himself prove to be base metal (1 Cor. ix. 27).

.   .   .   .   .   .

Jesus' saying that whosoever will be great shall be the servant of all (Mt. xx. 26), is not indeed handed down by Paul's pen, but it is exemplified in his life. He feels himself to be the bondman of Christ, a steward of the mysteries of God, whose one concern is to be found faithful (1 Cor. iv. 1-2). As a recruiting officer he goes about urging men, on Christ's behalf, to accept the atonement with God which has been made in Him (2 Cor. v. 20-21). For Christ's sake he makes himself a slave to men (2 Cor. iv. 5), conciliates them, humbles himself among them, and endures whatever burdens they lay upon him. What he had to go through and to suffer in all this he twice recounts to the Corinthians in moving words. This is the illustration to his saying about love, which

---

[1] TRANSLATOR'S NOTE.—The German plays on the military metaphor with "*Sold*" and "*Dienst*," as the Greek (ὀψώνιον, διακονία) probably also does.

"beareth all things, believeth all things, hopeth all things, endureth all things" (1 Cor. xiii. 7).

1 Cor. ix. 19-23: "As one who had made himself free from all things, I have sold myself into slavery to all, that I might save the more. To the Jews I became as a Jew, that I might gain the Jews; to those who are under the Law as one under the Law, though I am not myself under the Law, that I might gain those that are under the Law; to those who are without the Law, I became as without the Law—though I am not without law towards God, but under law to Christ—that I may gain those who are without the Law. To the weak I became weak, in order to gain the weak. I have become all things to all men, if by any means I might save some. And all this I do for the Gospel's sake."

2 Cor. vi. 3-10: "To no man do we give offence in anything, that no discredit may be brought upon our office. But in all things we show ourselves servants to God, in much endurance, in afflictions, in necessities, in distresses, in stripes, in imprisonments, in tumults, in labours, in night vigils, in fastings, in integrity, in knowledge, in long-suffering, in kindness, in love unfeigned, in proclaiming truth, in the power of God, through the weapons of righteousness, those for the right hand as well as those for the left, amid honour and dishonour, amid good repute and ill, as leading astray yet leading to righteousness, as unknown yet recognised, as dying—and behold we live, as chastened yet not killed, as troubled yet always joyful, as poor yet making many rich, as those who have nothing and yet possess all things."

Repaying reviling with blessing, patiently enduring amid persecution, answering abuse with conciliatory speech (1 Cor. iv. 12-13), this servant of the new Covenant (2 Cor. iii. 6) holds tirelessly on his way. He feels himself responsible that the knowledge of Christ shall sound forth to the ends of the earth within the short time that remained before His return.[1]

This love and this feeling of responsibility came to him from his having died with Christ. Since Christ has died for all, those for whom He died and who have now died with Him ought no longer to live for themselves, but must live for Him. "The love of Christ constraineth them" (2 Cor. v. 14-15).

.   .   .   .   .   .

Paul does not take as a standard for others all that he demands of himself. Although he holds celibacy to be in principle the only state suited to the time, and himself orders his life accordingly, he

---

[1] See pp. 183-186, *sup.*

is full of consideration for those who are not capable of doing so, and counsels them to marry, with the excusatory explanation that all have not received the same gifts from God, but one this gift, and another that (1 Cor. vii. 7).

He goes as far as he possibly can in commending the conduct of others. Indeed, he is prepared to make much out of little. How grateful he is to his churches for the smallest kindness which they may have shown him! If there is any cause for praise he usually rises into a genuine epistolary rhetoric of the elaborate kind customary in antiquity.

The newly converted Thessalonians are already an example to all his believers in Macedonia and Achaia. The news of their faith has been spread abroad everywhere (1 Thess. i. 7-9). He knows not how he is to thank God for all the joy which they have given him (1 Thess. iii. 9). About love he has no need to write to them, for therein they have been taught by God Himself (1 Thess. iv. 9).

How earnestly he thanks the Galatians for not despising him on account of his bodily infirmities when he visited them first! They had received him like an Angel from Heaven! They would have plucked out their eyes to give them to him! (Gal. iv. 13-15).

The Corinthians, whom he has immediately after to rebuke for their divisions and on so many other counts, he praises at the outset of the Epistle as having become rich in all things in Christ, in knowledge of every kind, so that the testimony of Jesus is firmly established among them, and they are lacking in no gift (1 Cor. i. 5-7). In order to stir them up to contribute to the collection for the Church at Jerusalem he begs them to be as forward in giving as they are in all else; in faith, in speech, in knowledge, in zeal of every kind, and in love to him! (2 Cor. viii. 7).

The gift sent him by the Philippians during his imprisonment assumes for him the significance of a fragrant, well-pleasing sacrifice offered to God (Phil. iv. 18).

In his judgment of others Paul is very mild. The conduct of Epaphroditus, who had brought him the gift from Philippi, had afterwards fallen ill, and the moment he was recovered desired to return home instead of, as had been intended, remaining with Paul to look after him, is presented by him in the most favourable light. He himself is sending him back as soon as possible, because those at home had heard of his illness, and might, as Epaphroditus himself feared, be concerned about him (Phil. ii. 25-30). He thus provides beforehand against the messenger's being blamed for not having remained with him.

In the case of the violent letter which he wrote to the Corinthians with tears, to force them into repudiating the opponents who were stirring them up against him, after this matter is finished with, he says he has only sent the letter in order to show them how intense his love for them is, and to put their obedience to the proof. Even the fact that they so soon restored the mischief-maker to favour he declares himself to approve, in order that Satan may not take occasion by the disunion between the Apostle and his church (2 Cor. ii. 4-11). He does not triumph over their submission, but praises and consoles them: "You have done everything to show yourselves pure in the matter" (2 Cor. vii. 11).

But when it is a question of practical action he can be uncompromising. Since John Mark had deserted him and Barnabas and the cause of the Gospel on the First Missionary Journey, in Pamphylia (Acts xiii. 13), he refuses to take him as a companion on the Second Journey, and separates on this score from Barnabas, who wishes to take his cousin with them again (Acts xv. 37-39). And when it is a question of the truth of the Gospel, Paul can take his stand against even the original Apostles at Jerusalem.

But firmness is not easy to him; he has to force himself to it. His conciliatoriness sometimes betrays him into concessions which endanger men's respect for him. At Corinth he is thought of as the man who talks big in his letters, but in face-to-face debate shows himself weak and yielding (2 Cor. x. 1, 10-11). In the way he conducts his case it is easy to see that he is not by nature a fighter, but was forced by circumstances to become so. On occasion he can be vehement. Writing to the Corinthians, who think he has not the courage to meet them in debate, he asks them whether he is to come with a rod, or in love and in the spirit of gentleness (1 Cor. iv. 21), and promises them that the Christ who speaks in him shall not be weak, but strong (2 Cor. xiii. 3-4). But gentleness keeps breaking through. How beautifully he depicts at the close of the Second Epistle to the Corinthians the temper in which he desires to meet them on his return, beseeching them, on their side, to do everything they possibly can for peace!

2 Cor. xiii. 7-10: "We pray to God that you may do no evil, not that we might be approved, but just that you might do good, even though we were put in the wrong. For we can do nothing against the truth,

but only for the truth. For we rejoice when we are weak and you are strong. This we pray for, even your perfecting. Therefore I write these things to you while still absent, in order that when present I may not need to deal sharply; according to the power which the Lord hath given me, which is for building up and not for breaking down."

Out of the zealot Paul, the love of Christ has made a gentle-minded man who only fights with reluctance, always preserves his magnanimity, and has no petty readiness to take offence or desire for self-vindication. In the midst of a vehement argument he suddenly lets us hear the voice of his heart and of the love of Christ.

1 Cor. iv. 14-15: "I write this, not to put you to shame, but to admonish you as my beloved children. For though you may have ten thousand masters in Christ you have not many fathers."

2 Cor. vii. 2-4: "Bear with me. I have wronged no man, corrupted no man, overreached no man. I speak not for your condemnation. Have I not told you before that you are in our hearts, to die together and to live together? I am full of confidence towards you, full of boasting over you. I am abundantly comforted, I overflow with joy amid all my affliction."

Gal. iv. 19-20: "My children, of whom I am again in travail, till Christ take form in you; I would that I were now with you and could change my voice, for I am distressed about you."

Was Paul the zealot even then at heart a diffident man—for the two things often go together—or was it through the love of Christ that he lost his original self-confidence? In any case, he thinks of himself not as confident, but rather as diffident.

1 Cor. ii. 3: "I was with you in weakness, fearfulness, and great diffidence."

He fears that in the matter of the collection for Jerusalem his good faith may be suspected, if his own companion Titus is alone concerned with it. He therefore sends a universally respected believer with him to Corinth to act as trustee for the churches. This brother had already been officially appointed by the churches to be Paul's companion on the "collection" journey (2 Cor. viii. 16-22).

2 Cor. viii. 20-21: "For we are guarding against any man's being suspicious of us in the matter of this bounty which we are administering. For we are anxious to have things right not only in the sight of the Lord but of men also."

How carefully Paul chooses his words in the lines devoted to the arrangements for the collection (2 Cor. viii. 1-15), so that it may not seem as though he were ordering or using pressure! And how he wraps up these careful words in commendations!

2 Cor. viii. 8: "I say this not by way of commandment, but by the zeal of others I am testing the genuineness of your love."[1]—2 Cor. viii. 10: "And here I am only expressing my opinion, for this is expedient for you, for you have been forward about the matter since last year, not only in act but in will."

How humble is his attitude in the Epistle to the Romans! He even excuses himself for taking upon himself to write to a church whose faith is spoken of in the whole world (Rom. i. 8), as though it had any need of his wisdom.

Rom. xv. 14-15: "For I am convinced about you, brethren, that you are already filled with goodness, abounding in all knowledge, and capable of admonishing each other."

But from natural temperament, and because he desires to serve, Paul makes no effort to secure the respect due to him by taking up a carefully planned and impressive attitude. With the outward technique of association with men he does not concern himself. He does not act from calculation, but relies entirely upon the spiritual power which goes forth from him. The quiet saying with which he pricks the bubble of the Corinthian conceit, that the Kingdom of God is not a matter of words, but of power (1 Cor. iv. 20), and that other saying that, though he still walks in the flesh, he does not war after the manner of the flesh (2 Cor. x. 3), give the keynote of his own conduct.

. . . . . .

Behind this humble attitude lies a tremendous self-consciousness. Paul is possessed by the thought that God has called him to a unique work for Christ, and that Christ's spirit manifests itself in his thought, speech, and action. So that it is possible for him to pass without transition from sayings embodying this self-consciousness to sayings expressive of humility. But this self-consciousness is in reality unaccompanied by pride, however proud

---

[1] TRANSLATOR'S NOTE.—The German here follows the extreme succinctness of the Greek. The meaning would in both cases be fairly represented by paraphrasing "I have mentioned the zeal of others by way of inciting you to prove the genuineness of your love."

his phrases may sometimes sound. It is not a consciousness of power, but of a tremendous responsibility.

Had his right to teach as an Apostle not been called in question, and had it not been necessary for him to claim the necessary authority to oppose the pernicious doctrine of the necessity of the Law and circumcision, Paul's self-consciousness might have remained in the background. But, things being as they were, he was compelled to speak of himself and to 'boast'. He does this, according to circumstances, with deep earnestness or with a lofty irony. The last four chapters of the Second Epistle to the Corinthians are a continuous 'boasting'.

Gal. i. 1: "Paul, an Apostle, not of men nor through men but through Jesus Christ and God the Father."

1 Cor. xv. 9-10: "For I am the least of the Apostles and am not worthy to be called an Apostle, because I persecuted the Church of God. But through God's grace I am what I am; and His grace toward me has not been in vain, for I have laboured more than they all—yet not I, but the grace of God which is in me."

2 Cor. xi. 16: "Let no man think me beside myself; but if you must so think of me, do so, provided I may boast myself a little."—2 Cor. xii. 11-13: "Now if I have taken leave of my senses, it is you who have compelled me to do so. For you ought to have cared for my reputation. For in nothing am I behind the super-Apostles, although I am nothing. The signs of an Apostle were wrought in me among you, by endurance of every kind of hardship, by signs and wonders and putting forth of power. Wherein have you been at a disadvantage compared with other churches, except that I have not been burdensome to you? Forgive me this wrong!"

2 Cor. x. 8: "Even though I should boast very freely in respect of the authority which the Lord has given me—for your edification not for your destruction—I should not be shamed in my boasting."

1 Cor. iii. 9: "We are fellow-workers with God, for you are God's tilth and God's masonry."

2 Cor. ii. 14-15: "But thanks to God who at all times makes us to triumph in Christ and makes the savour of His knowledge manifest through us in all places. For we are a sweet savour to God, among those who are being saved, and among those that are perishing."—2 Cor. ii. 17: "But, as of sincerity, as from God in the sight of God, we speak in Christ."—2 Cor. iii. 4-6: "Such confidence have we through Christ toward God, not as though we had of ourselves any power to think anything as from ourselves—our enabling comes from God, who has

made us fitted to be servants of a new Covenant, a Covenant not of the letter but of the Spirit."

2 Cor. x. 1: "I, Paul, myself exhort you by the meekness and gentleness of Christ, I who when face to face with you am humble, but when distant full of courage."

2 Cor. x. 17-18: "He who boasts, let him boast in the Lord, for it is not the man who commends himself who is approved, but he whom the Lord commends."

Paul's self-consciousness rests as its ultimate basis upon the greatness of the sufferings which he has passed through. That he has had more to endure in the service of Christ than all others, gives him the assurance that he stands nearer to Christ than they do. Because he has experienced in himself in special measure the dying of Christ, he has a right to the conviction that he is in special measure the vehicle of Christ's Spirit and of His power. Therefore his own weakness is for him the subject of his highest boasting.[1]

2 Cor. xi. 30: "If there must be any boasting I will rather boast of my weakness."

2 Cor. xii. 9: "I like best to boast in my weakness, that the power of Christ may descend upon me."

That Paul often speaks in the plural has nothing to do with his self-consciousness. He may have fallen into it from wishing to suggest to the churches that his travelling companions, whom they had been accustomed to see constantly at his side, were speaking and writing along with him. And the use of the plural by individuals is not unknown in ancient literature.

There is something almost metaphysical in the self-consciousness with which Paul asserts his spiritual presence among the believers at Corinth, when they assemble to judge the man who has married the wife of his (dead) father. Here the conception really seems to be present that his spirit, present in their midst as an organ of the Spirit of Christ, will force upon them the decision which is to be taken in Christ.

1 Cor. v. 3-5: "I, absent in body, but present in spirit, have already as one present, given sentence, that he who has committed such a trespass—after you, in the name of the Lord Jesus, have been assembled, and my spirit with you, with the power of our Lord Jesus—that this

---

[1] In regard to the connection between suffering and self-consciousness in Paul see also p. 159, *sup.*

man should be delivered over to Satan for the destruction of the flesh, in order that the Spirit may be saved in the day of the Lord Jesus." [1]

.   .   .   .   .   .

In a manner which is almost offensive to modern taste Paul, in numerous passages, holds himself up as a moral example. The spirit in which he does it, however, forbids the idea of any kind of self-exaltation. Since he is conscious of desiring to realise in his own conduct the being-in-Christ, and the sincerity, peaceableness, and humility of the Spirit of Christ, he beseeches those to whom he has brought the Gospel to strive after this in like manner, and he is happy when he observes such endeavour in them. And, having the right thereto, he cites himself as an example to them of selflessness in imitation of the example which Christ, by His coming into the world and His dying, has given to His followers.

1 Thess. i. 6: "You have become imitators of me and of the Lord by receiving the word amid much affliction with the joy of the Holy Spirit."

1 Cor. iv. 16-17: "I exhort you, be imitators of me. For this reason I have sent you Timothy, my beloved and believing son in the Lord, who will remind you of my ways in Christ, as I teach everywhere in every church."

1 Cor. x. 33-xi. 1: "As I also in all things seek to please all men, and have not thought of my own advantage, but of that of the many, that they might be saved. Be imitators of me, as I of Christ."

Phil. iii. 17: "Be imitators of me, brethren, and watch those who walk as I have given you an example."

Phil. iv. 9: "What you have learned and had delivered to you and heard and seen in me, that do, and the God of peace be with you."

.   .   .   .   .   .

Except in cases where he feels it to be his duty to impose his own enlightened will upon others, Paul's self-consciousness does not take the form of desiring to subject others to himself. He knows indeed that he has the right to exact obedience, because he is greater than the others in knowledge and in self-devotion. But he

---

[1] By the "day of the Lord Jesus" nothing else than His return can be meant. It is therefore implied that this sinner will find mercy in the day of the Judgment held by the Messiah, and will enter into the Messianic Kingdom. The delivering over "to Satan" can therefore only mean that he is delivered to him for the infliction of suffering. In the fleshly sufferings which he is to experience, he is to make atonement for his transgression. But how is this to be reconciled with the fact that precisely those who are most devoted to Christ have to endure sufferings caused by Satan, as was the case with Paul himself?

will carry out his rule in the spirit of gentleness and peace. Indeed he shrinks from giving commands, and substitutes, where he can, counsel and request. The passage dealing with marrying and not marrying (1 Cor. vii.), and with the arrangements for the collection for the Judaean church (2 Cor. viii.-ix.), bear witness to this endeavour on his part. An admirable example of the exercise of this tact in Christ is the letter to Philemon, which exhibits the lofty charm of Paul's personality in a unique degree. Paul is sending back to Philemon his runaway slave Onesimus, whom he has converted during his imprisonment.[1] As an Apostle, to whom, moreover, Philemon owes his own conversion, he would have had the right to require him to take Onesimus back into favour. He prefers, however, to beg him to do so.

Philem. 8-12: "Although I know myself in Christ to be fully entitled to prescribe to thee what thy duty is, yet for love's sake I prefer to entreat. I, Paul, of venerable age and now also the prisoner of Jesus Christ, beseech thee for my child whom I have begotten in my bonds, Onesimus, formerly of little value to thee, but now become valuable both to thee and to me.[2] I am sending him back, and I send thee my heart with him."

Paul would willingly have kept Onesimus with him as his attendant, and to this, he feels, he would have had a right, since Philemon as his convert ought to be willing to put himself at his disposal, and Paul would only be taking the slave instead of the master.

Philem. 13-14: "Gladly would I have kept him by me, that he might serve me in thy stead, in my bondage for the Gospel. But I could do nothing without thy consent, that the kindness from thee might not be as of necessity, but of free will."

In order that Philemon may at once take the slave back into favour, Paul declares himself ready to make good the material loss which his running away may have caused—it is possible that a theft, as the cause of the running away, may be in question—out

---

[1] The running away of slaves is referred to in Jesus Sirach in his proverbs, written down about 180 B.C. Sirach xxx. 39-40: "Hast thou a slave? Treat him like a brother, and rage not against thy (own) life-blood. If thou treat him ill and he run away, how shalt thou get possession of him (again)?"

On Paul's attitude towards slavery see pp. 194-195, *sup.*

[2] TRANSLATOR'S NOTE.—The Greek, it may be recalled, plays on the root-meaning of the name Onesimus (='helpful', 'profitable').

of his own pocket, though he gracefully suggests that this should
not be necessary since Philemon owes him much more, namely, his
salvation, because of his conversion through him. This debt, however, he will not reckon against the other, though he would have
had the right to do so.

Philem. 17-21: "If thou feel thyself closely attached to me receive
him as myself. If he has caused thee any loss, or owes thee anything,
write it down to my account. I, Paul, write this with my own hand: I will
pay it. I will not say unto thee that thou owest me thine own self. Nay,
my brother, I would fain have joy of thee in the Lord; ease my heart in
Christ. I write in confidence of thy compliance. Indeed I know that
thou wilt do more than I ask."

There is another fine touch. Paul hopes to be freed before long
. . . and ascribes this to the prayers of Philemon and the believers
who are with him. At the same time he lays on him the duty—it
is the only command expressed as such in the letter—of providing
hospitality for him at his coming.

Philem. 22: "Prepare at once a lodging for me; for I hope through
your prayers to be speedily given back to you."

If we possessed no other writing of Paul's than these few lines
to Philemon we should still know a good deal about him.

. . . . . .

Paul is the only man of Primitive-Christian times whom we
really know, and he is a man of a profound and admirable humanity.

Although he lives in the expectation of the imminent end of the
world, an expectation in view of which all earthly things lose their
significance and value, he does not in consequence become an
ascetic zealot. For an external abandonment of the things of the
world he substitutes an inner freedom from them. As though he
had an intuition that it might be the fate of Christianity to have
to make terms with the continuance of the natural world, he reaches
by his spirituality that attitude towards earthly things by means of
which Christianity must henceforth maintain its place in the world.
Though living and thinking in his own day, he is at the same time
preparing the future.

And since, in virtue of his spirituality, he moves within the
narrow bounds of eschatology as a free man, he does not suffer it
to rob him of his direct humanity, which only becomes the more

profound. With tremendous certainty and precision he goes in all things straight to the spiritually essential. In the most natural way the mystical dying with Christ and rising with Him is transmitted into a living ethic. The problem of the relation between redemption and ethics finds in his teaching a complete solution. Ethic is for him the necessary outward expression of the translation from the earthly world to the super-earthly, which has already taken place in the being-in-Christ. And, further, that the man who has undergone this translation has placed himself under the direction of the Spirit of Christ, and so has become Man in the highest sense of the word.

By his eschatological mysticism Paul gives his ethic a relation to the Person of Christ, and makes the conception of the Spirit an ethical conception. By his eschatological thought he grasps ethics as life in the Spirit of Christ, and thereby creates a Christian ethic valid for all time to come.

Side by side with Paul's achievement as a thinker must be set his achievement as a man. Having a personality at once simple and profound, he avoids an abstract and unnatural ideal of perfection, and makes perfection consist in the complete adjustment of spiritual with natural reality. So long as the earthly world with all its circumstances still subsists, what we have to do is so to live in it in the spirit of unworldliness that truth and peace already make their influence felt in it. That is the ideal of Paul's ethic, to live with the eyes fixed upon eternity, while standing firmly upon the solid ground of reality. He gives to the enthusiastic conception of the Good a practical direction, without thereby robbing it of its originality and power.

He proves the truth of his ethic by his way of living it. Alike in suffering and in action he shows himself a human being, who by the Spirit of Christ has been purified and led up to a higher humanity. Though his work lies in the world, he ventures to live the unworldly life, and to rely only on the power which is at his disposal, because of that which he, in the Spirit of Christ, has inwardly become.

As one who truly thought, served, worked, and ruled in the Spirit of Christ he has earned the right to say to the men of all periods: "Be imitators of me, as I am of Christ."

CHAPTER XIII

THE HELLENIZATION OF PAUL'S MYSTICISM BY IGNATIUS
AND THE JOHANNINE THEOLOGY

PAUL did not Hellenize Christianity; but he prepared the way for its Hellenization.

What is meant by this?

Paul took over no Hellenistic conceptions. His mystical doctrine of union with Christ and his sacramental doctrine are entirely built up out of eschatological ideas. But in this mysticism, and in the conception of the sacraments which was associated with it, the Christian faith received a form in which it was capable of being Hellenized.

The more fully the problem of the Hellenization of Christianity is studied the more astonishing becomes the transformation which the Christian faith underwent in the course of a few decades. What, one asks, had Greek religious thought, characterised as it was in all its longing for immortality by its demand for logic and its tendency to spiritualisation, to do with the Jewish expectation of a super-earthly world-kingdom and its king? How could Jesus, as the claimant to this throne, become for Hellenistic piety a redeemer? And this at a time when through the manifest disappointment of that expectation He might seem to have lost all significance!

The Primitive-Christian faith as such, that is to say, the belief in the early coming of the Kingdom, in the Messiahship of Jesus, in His atoning death and subsequent resurrection, and in the saving effect of baptism as understood by the Primitive-Christian community, is not Hellenizable. The process of the historical development at the beginning of Christianity was that the belief in Jesus and in redemption through the sacraments continued even after the belief in the Coming of the Kingdom, of which it was originally a part, had lost its hold. But the part could only continue to exist by becoming a whole with a life of its own. That this could come about in the way in which it did was due to Paul.

It must, no doubt, be assumed that the faith in Jesus Christ would have succeeded, under the pressure of necessity and in virtue of the religious and ethical power which was in it, in maintaining itself in the world after the dying down of the eschatological hope, even apart from Paul. But that this process went forward so smoothly, and especially that this faith, faced with the necessity of becoming independent, was able to give itself a logical expression in Greek thought-forms, was due to the development which it underwent at Paul's hands. In Paul's teaching the redemption, originally conceived of as the inheriting of the Messianic Kingdom, was so closely bound up with the Person of Christ that it was able to survive for coming generations, as the power of the Messianic hope progressively declined, simply as redemption through Christ.

In Primitive-Christian belief the thought of redemption was only bound up with Christ in that He was the Lord of the Messianic Kingdom, and that by His death was rendered possible the forgiveness of sins which was a necessary condition of obtaining the Kingdom. The significance of Jesus for redemption was thus entirely dependent on the validity of the eschatological beliefs, and seemed destined to share their decay. But, for Paul, the connection of redemption with Jesus, although it was still logically conditioned by eschatology, was a much closer one. Belief in Christ becomes union with Him. By that step redemption was brought into a relation with the Person of Christ, in such a way that its coming about and its character was conditioned by Him in much larger measure than in Primitive-Christian belief. And another point in which Paul's work was preparatory was, that for him redemption was no longer thought of simply as assurance of participation in the Kingdom, but as resurrection to participation in the Kingdom. The idea of resurrection became bound up with that of union with Christ, and is explained as a consequence of that union. In this way the belief in redemption by Christ acquired the capacity to maintain itself, when the eschatological expectation died away, as belief in the resurrection through Christ. By the pronouncement that the "dead in Christ" will arise at once upon the return of Christ (1 Thess. iv. 16) Paul, although he himself still thinks entirely along eschatological lines, became the father of the Hellenistic religion of the immortality brought by Christ. He also helped to prepare for this future Hellenization by explaining the sacraments on the basis of the concept of union with Christ, thus connecting them with the hope of resurrection.[1] The idea that the sacraments effect a redemption which looks forward to a coming Kingdom is explained by Paul on the basis of the mystical being-in-Christ, in the sense that they bestow the power of rising again to take part in the Messianic Kingdom, and not only of rising at the resurrection which was to follow at its close. He thus lays the foundation of the concept of the Lord's Supper as a food conferring immortality, into which it developed in the teaching of Ignatius.

Into the un-Hellenizable belief in Christ as the bringer of the Messianic Kingdom Paul thus inserts the derivative belief in resurrection through the being-in-Christ. And this belief in the Messiah as the bringer of the resurrection, and in the sacraments as guaranteeing the being-in-Christ and, consequently, the resurrection, is Hellenizable. In it the Greek world found a logically explicable certainty of immortality, and a conception of "mysteries" which indicates this immortality with certainty. Eschatological Mysticism thus created the concept of the redemption effected by Jesus, a concept which was susceptible of Hellenization.

.   .   .   .   .   .

The Hellenization of Christianity took place unobserved. The belief in Christ as the bringer of the resurrection developed along lines of Hellenistic reasoning without coming into conflict with the eschatological expectation, which surrounded it like an outer integument which was later to drop away. It is, moreover, not a fact that this belief first began to be Hellenized at the moment when the weakening of the eschatological hope became apparent. The theologians of Asia Minor, at the end of the first and beginning of the second century A.D., who effected the Hellenization of the belief in resurrection, began upon this task at a time when the expectation of the return of Jesus and the Coming of the Messianic Kingdom still possessed, as the existing evidence shows, a large measure of importance for them.

Ignatius, in his Epistle to the Ephesians (about A.D. 110), holds that "the last Times (ἔσχατοι καιροί) have come" (*Ad Eph.* xi. 1).[2]

For Polycarp, the Bishop of Smyrna, who wrote about the same time

---

[1] See pp. 281-282, *sup.*

[2] The Apocalypse of John closed with the words, "Surely I come quickly. Amen. Come, Lord Jesus!" (Rev. xxii. 20).—In the Epistle of Barnabas, doubtless to be dated about the end of the first century, we read: "Near is the day on which for the wicked all is lost; near is the Lord and His reward" (Ep. Barn. xxi. 3).

to the Philippians, the resurrection still signifies being associated with Christ in ruling in the Messianic Kingdom (Polyc. *Ad Phil.* v. 2).

Papias, Bishop of Phrygia, who lived about A.D. 150, was so far influenced in his beliefs by eschatology that Eusebius (*Hist. Eccl.* iii. 39) later depreciates him on account of his Chiliasm.[1]

That for Justin, who by his Logos doctrine is connected with the Asia Minor theology, the expectation of the return of Christ was still, about the middle of the second century A.D., a living element in Christian doctrine, is obvious from the efforts which he makes in the *Dialogue with Trypho* to find everywhere in the Jewish Prophets predictions of a two-fold coming of Christ (once in earthly humility, and once in Messianic glory). What eschatology means for him is evidenced in his saying to Trypho: "You have only a short time now in which to attach yourself to us; after the return of Christ your remorse and weeping will be of no avail, for He will not listen to you" (*Dial.* xxviii. 2).

Justin is a Chiliast. He expects that the Elect will live for a thousand years with Christ in the New Jerusalem. "But I and Christians in general, if they hold the true faith in all things, know that there is a resurrection of the flesh, and that a thousand-year period will come in the restored, adorned, and greater Jerusalem of which the Prophets Ezekiel, Isaiah, and the rest speak" (*Dial.* lxxx. 5. See also *Dial.* cxxxix. 4-5). In support of his view about the thousand-year kingdom Justin appeals to the Apocalypse of John (*Dial.* lxxxi. 4 = Rev. xx. 4-6), without having realised that, according to the latter, only the Elect who have believed in Christ will be associated with Him in the thousand-year kingdom, whereas, according to Justin's own beliefs, those also who lived before Christ will share in the same resurrection as those who have believed in Christ, and will also participate in the thousand-year kingdom.

What a strong hold the eschatological expectation still had in the Church in Asia Minor about the middle of the second century A.D. is shown by the rise of Montanism. This enthusiastic movement, which began in Mysia, was determined to give to the belief in the immediate nearness of the Kingdom the same importance as it had had in Primitive Christianity.

That the delay of the return of the Lord awakened doubts as to the certainty of the Coming of the Messianic Kingdom we know from some of the New Testament Epistles. The writer of the Epistle to the Hebrews is obliged to exhort believers not to give up hope, but to remain steadfast to the end (Heb. vi. 11-12, x. 23, 35, xii. 12-14).

The Second Epistle of Peter points out, as against the mockers who asserted that the return of Christ would not take place at all, that God's

---

[1] A saying about the miraculous fruitfulness of the vine in the Messianic age is quoted by Papias as from Jesus. (See p. 85, *sup.*)

reckoning of time is not like man's, for a thousand years are in His sight as a single day. If he still delayed the Coming of Christ it was from long-suffering, to give men further time for repentance (2 Pet. iii. 4-9).

According to the Epistle of Jude the attitude of the scorners in regard to the delay of redemption is the sign that it is near at hand, since, according to the words of the Apostles, there should come in the last time mockers (Jude 17-23).

Justin, too, has to admit that not all believers still live in the expectation of the New Jerusalem. "But that, on the other hand, even among Christians of a pure and pious temper, many do not share this view I have already indicated" (*Dial.* lxxx. 2). The earlier passage in the Dialogue to which Justin here refers is missing.

In general, therefore, it must be concluded, up to near the middle of the second century, at least in the Church in Asia Minor, of which we know something from Ignatius, Polycarp, and Papias, the eschatological hope still formed a living element in Christian belief. The fact that in the thanksgiving prayers at the Eucharist, as known to us from the Didache (*Did.* 9 and 10), the expectation of the Kingdom and of the return of Christ was expressed every Sunday with the earlier fervour, no doubt contributed much, in spite of the doubt aroused by the delay, to keeping alive this hope.

But for the explanation of the evolution of Christian belief it does not matter whether it can be exactly determined how much or how little of living eschatological expectation still survived at a given time. The Hellenization of the belief in the resurrection brought by Christ naturally began much earlier than the general enfeeblement of the eschatological hope. The belief in the coming of the Messianic Kingdom is a matter of expectation pure and simple. The certainty of the resurrection as a consequence of the union with Christ is, on the other hand, capable of being logically thought out.

It is therefore at this point, where development is possible, that the work of thought directed to providing a reasonable basis for the Christian hope naturally began. For if the certainty of the resurrection can be logically made good, the partaking in the Messianic Kingdom is thereby guaranteed.

The question is therefore not how long the eschatological expectation still continued to retain some significance, but how long it continued to retain so much significance that the logical formulation of the belief in the resurrection, consequent on union with

Christ, continued to be conditioned by it. This relationship is only to be observed in Paul. Only in his teaching is the certainty of the resurrection to the Messianic Kingdom based on the thought, that because with the resurrection of Jesus the Messianic world-period (that is, the resurrection period) has already begun, believers have already died and risen again with Christ and thus have the guarantee of sharing the resurrection state of existence at the return of Christ. For the representatives of a reasoned faith, who followed after Paul, this argument in support of the certainty of the resurrection is no longer possible. Their eschatological expectation, however much alive, no longer possesses the temperature necessary to enable it to be cast in the mould of eschatological mysticism. Such fervency of belief is only reached where the resurrection of Jesus is so directly conceived as the beginning of the resurrection, that the believer can feel sure he is actually in process of being changed into the resurrection state of existence. From the moment when believers have no longer the consciousness of being the single generation "upon which the End of the Times has come" (1 Cor. x. 11), and which alone is to share in the Messianic Kingdom, the intensification of the eschatological expectation into the eschatological mysticism of the dying and rising with Christ is no longer possible. The resurrection through Christ, if it is not to be simply asserted in dependence on the Pauline formulae, must be worked out in the thought-forms of a new uneschatological logic. This uneschatological formulation was necessarily of a Hellenistic character.

That the Christian faith of the earliest times had no need to be either eschatological or Hellenistic, but was a self-determined and self-sufficing world-view, is a desperate expedient introduced by Albrecht Ritschl, by which it was hoped to subjugate the problems of the earlier history of Dogma. As a matter of fact, the circumstances of Paul's day and the following period were such that his doctrine of the being-in-Christ, and the consequent certainty of the resurrection at the Return of Christ, must have lost their hold if they had not undergone a new intellectual interpretation by Hellenistic thought.

The man to whom it fell to renew the mystical doctrine of the being-in-Christ in a thought-form appropriate to the time was Ignatius.

.   .   .   .   .   .

About the turn of the century, that is to say, a generation after Paul's death, his thoughts had authoritative weight in the churches of Asia Minor. This appears from the Epistles which Ignatius, on his journey to Rome, where he was martyred, wrote to Polycarp, to the Ephesians, the Magnesians, the Trallians, the Romans, the Philadelphians, and the Smyrnaeans, and also from the contemporary letter of Polycarp to the Philippians. Indeed the Roman bishop Clement, writing to the Corinthians about A.D. 90, already shows acquaintance with Paul. He reminds this church how the blessed Paul had written to them, and shows himself well acquainted with the contents of that Epistle (1 Clem. xlvii.); he uses the formula "in Christ"; he regards governmental authority as instituted by God, as Paul does in the Epistle to the Romans (1 Clem. lxi.).

But Ignatius and Polycarp are dominated in a much higher degree by Paul's thought. They live in his Epistles.

In *Ad Eph.* xviii. 1 Ignatius alludes, in the question "Where is the wise?" to 1 Cor. i. 20; in *Ad Eph.* xix. 1 he speaks, with allusion to 1 Cor. ii. 8, to the ignorance of the princes of the world with regard to the death of Jesus; in *Ad Magn.* x. 2 he commands, in allusion to 1 Cor. v. 6-8, that the old leaven shall be put away; in *Ad Smyrn.* iv. 2 he mentions Christ as the bestower of strength, using the same word that Paul uses in Phil. iv. 13; in the letter to Polycarp (v. 1-2) he deals with the problem of marriage and celibacy on the lines of 1 Cor. vii. and Eph. v. 25-29.

In his Epistle to the Philippians Polycarp reminds the Church (Polyc. *Ad Phil.* iii. 2) of the Epistles (*sic*) which Paul had written to them; with allusion to 1 Cor. vi. 2 he admonishes them (*Ad Phil.* xi. 2) that the saints shall judge the world, "as Paul teaches."

Ignatius, like Polycarp, constantly uses the formula "in Jesus Christ." —Ignat. *Ad Eph.* viii. 2: "Ye do all things in Jesus Christ"; *Ad Eph.* x. 3: "Continue in Jesus Christ"; *Ad Eph.* xi. 1: "to be found in Christ Jesus"; *Ad Magn.* vi. 3: "Love one another in Jesus Christ"; *Ad Magn.* x. 2: "to be salted in Him (Jesus Christ)"; *Ad Magn.* xii. 2: "You bear Jesus Christ in you"; *Ad Trall.* xiii. 2: "Fare ye well, in Jesus Christ"; *Ad Rom.* i. 1: "In bonds in Jesus Christ"; *Ad Rom.* ii. 2: "To sing praise to the Father in Christ Jesus"; *Ad Philad.* v. 1: "Bound in Christ"; *Ad Philad.* x. 1: "The compassion which you feel in Christ Jesus"; *Ad Philad.* x. 2: "Happy in Jesus Christ"; *Ad Philad.* xi. 2: "Farewell, in Christ Jesus."—Polyc. *Ad. Phil.* i. 1: "Made joyful in our Lord Jesus Christ"; Polyc. *Ad Phil.* xiv. 1: "Farewell, in the Lord Jesus Christ."

[1] 1 Clem. xlviii., "Righteousness in Christ".—1 Clem. xlix., "Love in Christ."

Moreover, the way in which Ignatius repeatedly speaks of faith and love as a unity (*Ad Eph.* xiv. 1; *Ad Magn.* i. 2; *Ad Trall.* viii. 1; *Ad Smyrn.* vi. 1) is only to be understood in the light of the Pauline conception of "faith which worketh by love" (Gal. v. 6).

Thus Ignatius and Polycarp show themselves, both by direct mention of Paul and by reminiscences of thought and language, to be most closely dependent on him. But their references to him show a remarkable limitation. They never quote the sayings which are characteristic of the logic of the Pauline mysticism! They never argue from the conception that believers have already died and risen again with Christ!

Ignatius and Polycarp thus take over from Paul only the general formula of his mysticism, not its real content. Historical theology has hitherto been helpless in face of this enigma. It could not attain to any clearness about the relation of Ignatius to Paul, because it was still in the dark as regards Paul himself. If it assumed that Paul's ideas are in any way of a Hellenistic character, Ignatius' attitude is unintelligible. Once it is recognised, however, that Paul's thought is conditioned by eschatology in a way only conceivable in Paul's period, it becomes quite naturally explicable why Ignatius cannot take it over, and why, familiar though he is with Paul's Epistles, he has to content himself with adopting in quite a general way that view of redemption, as something experienced through union with Christ, which Paul intended to convey by the formula "in Christ." The empty form which he thus takes over, he was obliged to fill, in accordance with the needs of his time, with a Hellenistic content. He does so by the doctrine of the union of flesh and Spirit which comes to pass, in the Church, through fellowship with Christ, and which is the guarantee of the resurrection.

Since Paul's mysticism also represents the resurrection as a working of the Spirit, the teaching of Ignatius looks at first sight like a simplification of Pauline doctrine, arrived at by omitting the concept of the dying and rising again with Christ. It thus becomes intelligible how Ignatius can feel himself to be the continuator of Paul's teaching, quite unaware that, for the original logic of Paul's mysticism, he has substituted a different one.

In reality, the concept of the Spirit, and of the connection between the possession of the Spirit and the resurrection, is in the two cases entirely different.

For Paul, the believer possesses the Spirit in consequence of his dying and rising again with Christ; for Ignatius he comes into possession of the Spirit as a natural man. The idea that in the union with Christ the resurrection has already begun is displaced by the simpler one that it is prepared for by the Spirit. The doctrine of the necessary connection of the resurrection with the possession of the Spirit is, so to speak, the curtain behind which the unperceived transformation of the eschatological mysticism into the Hellenistic took place.

One thing that indicates that it is not a case of a mere simplification, but of a real alteration of the Pauline doctrine, is that Ignatius cannot take over the Pauline antithesis of flesh and Spirit. For Paul, the way in which the resurrection is prepared for is, that through the dying and rising again with Christ the flesh is done away with, and the Spirit uniting with the psychic corporeity makes this capable of being, at the return of Christ, at once clothed upon with the body of glory.[1] For Paul a union of flesh and Spirit is unthinkable; Ignatius, on the contrary, must necessarily maintain it. Against the Gnostic spiritualistic conception of immortality as a return of the spiritual to the primal source of the spiritual, Ignatius is concerned to defend the belief in the bodily resurrection, which had been taken over by Christianity from the Late-Jewish eschatology. The only possibility of making a bodily resurrection conceivable on the lines of Hellenistic thought consists in developing the view that through the inworking of the Spirit the flesh is made capable of immortality.[2] Thus, in order to maintain the original eschatologico-Christian conception of the resurrection which Paul also shared, Ignatius is obliged, against Paul, to conceive of the flesh as something capable of being glorified, not as something doomed by its nature to perish, something which consequently cannot be thought of in connection with the resurrection. This view is for Ignatius so entirely natural that he substitutes it for the Pauline quite unconsciously.

For Paul, therefore, the Spirit unites with the spiritual part of man's personality; for Ignatius, with his fleshly corporeity.

By wrapping up his Hellenistic conception of flesh and Spirit in the formulae of the Pauline mysticism, Ignatius arrives at affirmations which sound Pauline, but are, for Paul's premises, unthinkable.

[1] On Paul's conception of death and resurrection see pp. 132-134, *sup.*
[2] On the transformation of the Late-Jewish conception of the bodily resurrection into the Hellenistic-Christian see p. 274, *sup.*

Ignat. *Ad Eph.* viii. 2: "Even what you do in the flesh is spiritual, for you do all in Christ Jesus."—*Ad Eph.* x. 3: "Abide in Christ, both fleshly and spiritually."—*Ad Trall.* viii. 1: "Strengthen yourselves anew in the faith, which is the flesh of the Lord, and in love, which is the blood of Jesus Christ."

The Hellenization of Christianity by Ignatius and by the Asia Minor theology consists, therefore, in taking over the Pauline mysticism of "being-in-Christ" as the proper formulation of the Christian doctrine of redemption, but giving it for content, not the eschatological conception of the dying and rising again with Christ, but the Hellenistic conception of the union of flesh and Spirit (ἕνωσις σαρκική τε καὶ πνευματική, *Ad. Magn.* xiii. 2).

By this conception of the union of flesh and spirit it explains (1) the uniting of the Divine with the human in the person of Jesus; (2) the bringing about of redemption by Him; (3) the mediation of redemption through the sacraments.

In the Person of Christ, Spirit enters into union with flesh for the first time. Thus is created the possibility that the flesh, which has hitherto not been able to do so, receives into itself immortality-producing powers, and becomes capable of resurrection. For this Hellenistic mode of thought the redemptive act of Jesus consists in His coming into the world as a unity of flesh and Spirit, and thereby providing the possibility of that union of flesh and Spirit which leads to the resurrection of the Elect. No doubt Ignatius also speaks of the redemptive significance of the death on the Cross and the resurrection. The death and resurrection of Jesus, however, for him only make manifest that redemption which, as a consequence of the mode of Christ's incarnation, comes about as a kind of natural process. For Paul the death and resurrection of Jesus effect redemption, because He is the future Messiah and dies as such. His dying is an atoning sacrifice for the Elect, and, at the same time (since death possesses no power over Him, as a pre-existent being and the future Messiah), has for its necessary consequence His resurrection and the beginning of the resurrection-period.

For Paul, therefore, Jesus creates the possibility of the resurrection by bringing in the resurrection-period; for Ignatius He does it by fulfilling in His own person the conditions necessary to resurrection, which have hitherto not been present. The difference goes deep. Outwardly, however, the two conceptions are held together by the fact that in both the Spirit of Jesus is the guarantor of the resurrection.

. . . . . .

Just as the basis of redemption is entirely different, although Ignatius believes himself to be simply repeating the thoughts of Paul, so also is the manner of its mediation by the sacraments. For Paul, the believer shares through the sacraments the experience of Christ. In them he enters into union with Him in His dying and rising again.

While for Paul the Lord's Meal is overshadowed by Baptism, in the Hellenistic mysticism of Ignatius the relationship is reversed, Baptism becoming, as it were, only an introduction to the Eucharist. For in the Eucharist is made manifest, for Ignatius, the act of conveyance and appropriation of redemption. In the bread and wine the becoming-one of matter and spirit is effected in the same way as in the corporeity of Jesus. They continue the existence of the Redeemer in a form capable of appropriation.[1]

As for Paul, so with Ignatius, the mystical doctrine of the being-in-Christ has its roots in the conception of the pre-existent Church.[2] If, for Paul, the dying and rising again, which the Elect experience together and with Christ, is nothing else than the working out of their predestined solidarity with one another and with Christ; for Ignatius, the same is true of their partaking in the unity of flesh and Spirit which comes to pass in the Person of Jesus. It is only where the pre-existent Church comes into the matter that this redemptive miracle, which begins with Jesus, is carried on in the sacraments.

Not every community which professes to be Christian belongs to the true Church. This is only to be found where, by holding fast to the doctrinal tradition and to the episcopal organisation, the connection with the Apostolic Church originating from Jesus is maintained, and belief in the miracle of the becoming-one of flesh and Spirit is present.

In order to have the right faith in the becoming-one of flesh and Spirit, it is essential to have the right conception of the Person of Christ. The Gnostic-Docetic doctrine represents the Spirit as

---

[1] On Baptism and Eucharist in Ignatius see pp. 273-278, *sup*.

[2] On the conception of the pre-existent Community of the Saints as the germ-cell of Paul's mysticism see pp. 101-105; on the way in which the mysticism of the becoming-one of the flesh and spirit is conditioned by the concept of the pre-existent Church see also p. 277, *sup*.

only temporarily (from Jesus' baptism to His death) entering into connection with the fleshly body of Jesus. Consequently belief in the resurrection of the flesh is impossible to it. These heretical teachers, therefore, adopt the expedient of making redemption consist in the return of the spiritual to the primal source of the spiritual. But according to the teaching received by tradition from the Apostles it is man as such, who, becoming immortal, is to enter the glory of God. This view of redemption is only conceivable when it is held that the connection of the Spirit with the flesh in Jesus was an organic and permanent one. Only if there subsisted, from His birth onwards, a unity of flesh and Spirit arising in a fleshly body which was immortal, had He created the conditions of a true redemption, that is to say, the possibility of the resurrection of a fleshly corporeity. This is the sense in which Polycarp says (*Ad Phil.* vii. 2): "Everyone who does not confess that Christ has come in the flesh (ἐν σαρκὶ ἐληλυθέναι) is an Antichrist." And that is why the "speaking in the spirit" is not to be accepted as coming from God, unless the spirit in question makes the correct confession in regard to the Person of Christ.

1 Joh. iv. 1-3: "Beloved, believe not every spirit, but test the spirits, whether they be from God. For many false prophets have gone forth into the world. Hereby shall ye recognise the spirit of God; every spirit which confesses that Jesus Christ has come in the flesh (ἐν σαρκὶ ἐληλυθέναι) is of God; and every spirit which does not (so) confess Christ is not of God. And this is the nature of the Antichrist, of whom you have heard that he was coming; and who now is in the world." [1]

As, for Paul, the believer, by taking upon him the Law and circumcision, is "abolished out of Christ" (Gal. v. 4), so it is in the Hellenistic theology with one who holds an inadequate conception of the union of flesh and spirit in the Person of Jesus.

This Hellenistic theology, therefore, can no longer acknowledge that Jesus Himself expected through His death and resurrection to become the Messiah, or that He obtains this honour through dying and rising again, as Paul taught. The futuristic view of Messiahship has its roots in eschatological thought, and, like the Pauline Mysticism, becomes impossible in proportion as eschatological thought becomes simply eschatological expectation.

Of the Church as the sphere within which the becoming-one of flesh and Spirit is realised, the essential characteristic is love. For

---

[1] On this criterion of the true Spirit see also pp. 174-175, *sup.*

Ignatius, as for Paul, love is a metaphysical concept. In love the Elect are united with one another and with Christ, and through Him with God. In some sense also, the uniting of the Spirit with the material of flesh, and the consequent exaltation of the flesh to immortality, is a manifestation of love. The being-in-Christ becomes for Ignatius a being-in-love.

The Church is thus, for Ignatius, a metaphysical conception, which has its roots in the idea of the pre-existent Church and in the metaphysical view of love. Paul's eschatologico-speculative conception of the Church is Hellenized and further developed.

It looks like an intermediate step between Pauline and Ignatian speculation when the Epistle to the Ephesians interprets the saying "And the twain shall be one flesh" (Gen. ii. 24) as a mystery which is to be interpreted as referring to the unity between Christ and the Church (Eph. v. 31-32). Here, too, it seems to be assumed that love is a kind of metaphysical entity. Behind the mystery of the quasi-physical unity of Christ with the Church there begins to become visible the becoming-one of flesh and Spirit.

Only within the sphere of the true Church can the uniting of Spirit with flesh take place. Only within it does the Spirit unite with the water of baptism and the bread and wine at the Eucharist to bring about the immortality of the flesh in believers!

Ignat. *Ad Philad.* 4: "Be very careful to celebrate only one Eucharist. For there is only one flesh of our Lord Jesus Christ, and only one Cup for the becoming-one with His blood, and only one altar, as there is only one bishop in association with the presbytery and the deacons, my fellow-servants, in order that whatever you do may be done according to God."

Ad Smyrn. viii. 1-2: "That Eucharist is to be considered valid which takes place under the bishop, or under one appointed by him . . . without the bishop it is not permissible to baptize or to hold the Agape."

Ad Magn. xiii. 2: "Be subject to the bishop and to one another, as Jesus Christ was to His father according to the flesh, and the Apostles to Christ and to the Father and to the Spirit, that there may be unity of flesh and of Spirit." [1]

It is a further consequence of the transformation of the concept of being-in-Christ that Ignatius' mysticism is no longer so exclusively Christ-mysticism as Paul's.

---

[1] TRANSLATOR'S Note.—Not here "between flesh and Spirit," the Greek being ἵνα ἕνωσις ᾖ σαρκική τε καὶ πνευματική.

Whereas Paul thinks of the believer, up to the beginning of the eternal blessedness, as only "in-Christ," not at the same time "in-God," in Ignatius the thought is beginning to come in that "being-in-Christ" mediates "being-in-God." [1]

The concept of rebirth has not yet been reached by Ignatius. But the way is already left open for it, since Paul's conception of the new state of existence as an anticipatory resurrection has already been abandoned.[2]

The Logos Christology is already known to Ignatius. He calls Christ God's Son, "who is His Logos, proceeding forth from silence, who in all things was well-pleasing to Him who sent Him" (*Ad Magn.* viii. 2). But he works out the mysticism of the being-in-Christ without laying any stress on the idea that the Spirit which works in the sacraments is identical with the Logos or goes forth from Him. This is doubtless because he is still so far under the influence of Paul that he confines himself to the conception of the Spirit as found in Paul. In fact, the Christian Hellenistic doctrine of redemption has in itself nothing to do with the Logos doctrine. The mystical doctrine of union with Christ, as based on the idea of the becoming-one of flesh and Spirit, is a self-contained, self-sufficing cycle of ideas which arises out of the Hellenistic interpretation of the Pauline mysticism independently of the identification of the Logos with the pre-existent Messiah. The subsequent combination with it of the concept of Christ as the organ of the Logos does not alter its essential character. The widely held view that the concept of redemption held by the Greek Church was the creation of the Logos theology is therefore not in accordance with the facts.

It is worth noticing that Paul himself might quite conceivably have carried out the identification of Christ with the Logos. For one who, like him, is so dominated by the idea of the pre-existent Christ that he sees Him in the rock which gave water in the desert, and whose conception of the Spirit is such that he thinks of the manna and the water in the desert as given by the Spirit, the application of the Logos concept to Christ and the Spirit is a further step which might easily have been taken. The way was opened for the Logos doctrine by the Jewish conception of the activities of Wisdom and of the Word of God. How

---

[1] On the problem of the "being-in-Christ" and of "being-in-God" see pp. 4-13, *sup*.

[2] On the absence of the concept of rebirth in eschatological Mysticism, and its presence in Hellenistic, see pp. 13-15, 120, 138, *sup*.

easy it was to take this road is shown by Philo. And how close Paul came to it is evident from his saying, "One Lord, Jesus Christ, through whom all things are, and we through Him" (1 Cor. viii. 6). But he does not take this road, because his thinking is eschatologically conditioned. How the rank assigned to Christ and to the working of the Spirit can be brought into relation with Greek conceptions is not a matter in which he is interested, because his only concern is to explain the scope and significance which the death and resurrection of Christ possess for redemption, as events in which the supernatural world-era and the resurrection of the dead begin.

It was only in the moment when the Christian Faith no longer *thought* eschatologically, though it still cherished the eschatological hope, that the Logos conception acquired significance for it. The possibility of adopting it is closely connected with the development of the mystical doctrine of the becoming-one of flesh and Spirit.

. . . . . .

Justin and the Gospel of John carry forward the work of Ignatius by inserting the Hellenistic union-with-Christ mysticism into the doctrine of Jesus Christ as the organ of the Logos.

Justin's contribution, so far as it can be judged from the polemical and apologetic writings, which are all that have come down to us, is not very important. He is chiefly concerned to show that the Logos spoke from the Patriarchs, Prophets, and Greek sages, and was, in general, the power by means of which God worked in the world. But this Logos had first been fully, and in perfect union with a human personality, manifested in Christ.

Dial. lxi. 1: "Before all creatures, God, as a beginning, begot out of Himself a rational power which is called by the Holy Spirit sometimes Glory of the Lord, sometimes Son, sometimes Wisdom, sometimes Angel, sometimes God, sometimes Lord and Logos . . . . For all attributes belong to it, because it serves the Father's will, and because it has been begotten out of the Father by His will." (See also *Dial.* cxiii. 4-5.)

The unification of flesh and Spirit is assumed by Justin, but not expressly set forth. Baptism he describes as the bath of regeneration and of the forgiveness of sins (*Dial.* cxxxviii. 2, 1 *Apol.* lxi.).

The Pauline interpretation of Baptism as a dying and rising again with Christ is as impossible of acceptance by Justin as by Ignatius. He is obliged to explain its efficacy as due to the action of the Spirit which unites with the water. How, precisely, he thinks of this happening we are not told.

But in some way, he holds, Baptism possesses its efficacy in consequence of the death of Jesus. A view having some affinity with his is suggested by the saying of Ignatius, that Jesus Christ was born and baptized in order that through His sufferings He might purify the water (*Ad Eph.* xviii. 2).

As regards the Eucharist, Justin holds that the Logos unites with the elements, consecrated by the thanksgiving, in the same way as with the flesh and blood of the Logos-Christ when He became flesh, and that this food and drink nourishes the flesh and blood of believers "by a transformation" ($\kappa\alpha\tau\grave{\alpha}$ $\mu\epsilon\tau\alpha\beta\omicron\lambda\acute{\eta}\nu$, 1 *Apol.* lxvi.).[1]

It is remarkable that Justin in the Dialogue never enters more fully into the significance of the Eucharist, but is content to speak of it simply as the true sacrifice, well-pleasing to God.

Justin is already considerably further from Paul than Ignatius was. The formula "in Christ" no longer plays any part for him at all. The interpretation of the Church as the precinct, within which alone the becoming-one of Spirit and flesh can take place, does not find expression in his writing. Only fragments, therefore, of the system of Hellenized Christianity sketched out by Ignatius are to be met with in Justin. This is certainly in part due to the fact that we know his teaching only from writings, in which he is endeavouring to make the Christian faith intelligible to the Jews as the fulfilment of Old Testament prophecy, and to the heathen as the true ethical philosophy. What his own teaching essentially is we do not know. He does not, however, appear to have been a speculative thinker of the greatness and originality of an Ignatius. Compared to the latter, there is something unformed about him, though, curiously enough, it is uncertain whether he is to be numbered among the pioneers or the epigoni.

．　　　．　　　．　　　．　　　．　　　．

The Hellenistic conception of redemption through union with Christ is set forth with admirable completeness in the Gospel of John. The literary enigma of this writing is insoluble. We shall never know who its author really was, nor how he came to make John, the disciple of the Lord, the authority for his narrative (Joh. xxi. 24). But it is quite clear why he writes, and why he makes Jesus speak and act as he does: it is to show the historic Jesus preaching the mystical doctrine of redemption through being-in-the-"Logos-Christ."

[1] See p. 273, *sup.*

For the Hellenistic mysticism of the being-in-Christ finds itself in exactly the same position as the eschatological; it cannot appeal in support of its doctrine of redemption to the preaching of the historic Jesus. That is why Ignatius is driven to place his ideas under the aegis of Paul's authority; and Justin, to extract proof of his from the Old Testament by the exercise of unheard-of ingenuities of exegesis. For ethics alone can they appeal to Jesus.

Paul ventured to claim openly that his knowledge was not limited to the preaching of Jesus. He demanded that it should be accepted as a revelation made to him by the glorified Christ. This appeal to the glorified Christ could not, however, enforce acceptance even in Primitive Christianity. Since the Apostles at Jerusalem had the authority of the historic Jesus behind them, Paul could not hold his own with them. The Hellenistic mysticism perceived the necessity of being able to appeal to the preaching of Jesus, since it is unable to read its own interpretation into His parables and His discussions with the Scribes. As it nevertheless regards itself as possessing the truth about redemption, it is forced to the assumption that the tradition about Jesus is incomplete. A great unknowi:, therefore, probably about the beginning of the second century, claimed the right to supply in appropriate fashion the missing material, and write a Gospel in which Jesus appears as the Logos-Christ and preaches redemption through the working of the Spirit which was to be experienced by union with Himself. The extra material, beyond that of the ordinary tradition, is explained as the report of a disciple of Jesus who remembered mysterious hints in the discourses of the Lord, which the others, not understanding their import, had not noted. This making known of discourses and actions of the Messiah-Jesus as the organ of the Logos, which had been overlooked in the Jewish Christian tradition, is carried out in the Gospel of John on a perfectly thought-out plan.

The redemption preached by the Logos-Christ is the same as that which is developed in the Letters of Ignatius. It is based on the obtaining of immortality through being 'in' the Bringer of immortality. The condition attained through the being-in-Christ is thought of as a rebirth.

The being-in-Christ is also a being-in-God. The Logos-Christ prays to God for those who are "in us" (Joh. xvii. 21), that is to say, in Him and the Father.

The characterisation of the new condition as rebirth and the

extension of the being-in-Christ to a being-in-God together constitute the fundamental difference between the Hellenistic and the
eschatological mysticism of the being-in-Christ.

The union with Christ goes back to a pre-temporal, predestined
"belonging" to Him. Whereas in the Ignatian mysticism the thought
of predestination is only brought into play in so far as it is involved
in the conception of the pre-existent Church. The Gospel of John
makes a point of working it out with the utmost sharpness of
definition. Two classes of men are distinguished—those who are
"from above," and so have the capacity to understand the message of Him who is the organ of the Logos and to be saved by
Him, and those who are "of the world." Only of those whom
God has given Him does the Logos-Christ make mention in His
prayer. He expressly refrains from praying for the world (Joh.
xvii. 9).

It is worthy of note that the Gospel of John regards the Jewish
people as such, with the exception of a few individuals, as hostile
to the Logos. Of concern for the fate of Israel, such as is shown
by Jesus and Paul, the Johannine Christ knows nothing. He simply
states that the Jews who possess the prophecies about Him are
so blinded that they fail to find in them that which they contain
(Joh. v. 45-47).

The general attitude in the Gospel of John is the same as in Justin's
Dialogue with Trypho. It reflects the struggle with which Christianity
freed itself from the Judaism which began, after the destruction of
Jerusalem, to close itself against the outside world.

We have two notices which shed light upon the relations between
Judaism and Christianity in that period. In consequence of having in
A.D. 62, before the arrival of the Governor Albinus, caused James the
Just, the brother of the Lord, to be stoned, the High Priest Ananus,
according to Josephus (*Antiq.* xx. 9), made enemies precisely among the
stricter Jews, and, owing to the accusation which they brought against
him in this matter before Albinus and King Agrippa, was immediately
deposed from his office.

In the second Jewish insurrection (132–135), Barkochba, as Justin
records in his Apology (1 *Apol.* xxxi.), caused Christians to be delivered to
the most terrible tortures, if they refused to deny and blaspheme Jesus
Christ.

As in the Ignatian mysticism, so in the Johannine, love is the
mysterious power which binds the Elect to one another and to

Christ. To be 'in-love' signifies, according to the preaching of the Logos-Christ, not only to exercise love in the ethical sense, but above all to continue steadfast in the true fellowship of the Elect, and through it to remain united to Christ and God (Joh. xv. 9-10, 12). Similarly in the First Epistle of John 'love' has at once an ethical and a metaphysical significance.

1 Joh. iv. 7-8: "Beloved, let us love one another, for love is from God; and every one who loves is begotten of God and knows God. He who loves not, has not known God, for God is love."

.   .   .   .   .   .

Like Paul and Ignatius, the Gospel of John represents the being-in-Christ as brought about in the sacraments.

There are, no doubt, in the preaching of the Logos-Christ sayings which sound as though redemption was obtained simply by faith in Him.

Joh. iii. 36: "He who believes on the Son has eternal life."—Joh. viii. 51: "If any man keep my word, he shall never see death, to eternity." —Joh. xi. 25-26: "I am the resurrection and the life. He who believes in Me shall live, even though he die. And he who lives and believes in Me shall never die."

In other sayings, however, the Logos-Christ points in the clearest words to baptism and the Eucharist, and declares that the rebirth from water and the Spirit, and the eating and drinking of the flesh and blood of the Son of Man, are necessary to salvation. This interweaving of the sacraments into the preaching of the redemptive power of belief in the Logos-Christ forms the great enigma of the discourses of the Johannine Christ.

The solution is that the Logos-Christ demands belief in Himself not merely as the Logos become flesh, but also as the Bringer of the sacraments. The Gospel of John represents the Hellenistic mystical doctrine of redemption through the being-in-Christ as having been preached by Jesus. This doctrine is, like that of Ignatius and that of Paul, from which it is derived, of a sacramental character. The Logos-Christ therefore, who makes it known, must also speak of Baptism and the Eucharist as institutions necessary to salvation. He preaches, accordingly, a faith in Jesus Christ which includes faith in the sacraments which are derived from Him.

On what lines does he do this? According to the Hellenistic

mysticism the efficacy of the sacraments is due to the Spirit, who unites with the baptismal water and the elements of the Eucharist in a way capable of being appropriated by the believer. It is only since Pentecost, however, that there has been 'spirit' in the world, that is to say, since the death and resurrection of Jesus. In accordance with this view, the Logos-Christ can only "institute" Baptism and the Eucharist in the sense that, by constant allusions He directs the attention of His hearers to the fact that something indispensable to redemption is going to happen in connection with water and the elements as soon as, after His exaltation, the Spirit begins its work in the world. The Johannine Christ therefore predicts the sacraments as something which His hearers cannot yet understand. Once the Spirit has enlightened them, and has begun to work in the baptismal water and the bread and wine, they will understand what He meant.

So long as the Logos-Christ walks upon earth, all the power of the Logos-spirit is concentrated in Him and only works directly from Him. The Logos-Christ proclaims the truth, performs significant miracles, and manifests His life-giving power by restoring to the dead their natural life, but after His exaltation the Spirit which works in Baptism and the Eucharist receives the power of communicating to men eternal life.

So long as the Logos-Christ lives on earth, the Spirit in Him is comparable to water which flows through a deep-banked channel without watering the country round. After His death the Spirit flows through it in the sacraments as in a network of runnels.

The theory that during the lifetime of Jesus there is as yet no Spirit is carried through in the Gospel of John with strict logic. In His farewell discourses Jesus repeatedly impresses upon His disciples that after His departure the Spirit will come to them as the Comforter, and will lead them into all truth. Through Him they will understand all things which are now obscure to them. Whereas up to then the Logos had spoken of things to come in parables through the lips of Jesus, the Spirit will then take these "things to come," namely, the sacraments, and make them intelligible as something now present. The promise which is made in the preaching of the Logos-Christ of a coming perfect knowledge remains enigmatic, so long as it is not recognised that what is referred to in the promise is insight into the mystery of the sacraments, which will carry on and will begin to complete the activity of the Logos-Christ. Whenever the Spirit is promised, the sacraments are to be understood along with the Spirit, and wherever the prospect of the sacrament is held out, the coming of the Spirit is implied.

John vii. 39: "There was as yet no Spirit, because Jesus was not yet glorified."

John xvi. 7: "It is good for you that I go away, for if I go not away the Comforter will not come to you. But if I go, I will send Him to you."

John xvi. 12-13: "I have yet many things to say to you, but you cannot bear them now. But when He is come, the Spirit of truth, He will lead you into all the truth."

Since the Spirit is nothing else than the Logos, no longer limited by His historical manifestation in Jesus Christ, Jesus describes the coming of the Spirit as being also His personal Coming-again to His own. And it is only when He is again present with them as the Spirit that their being-in-Him can begin. So long as He walks among them as a human person they listen to His discourses, but they cannot be "in Him." It is not until after the death of Jesus Christ that there can be a being-in-Christ; in that respect the Hellenistic mysticism is entirely at one with the Pauline. In His discourses the Logos-Christ never makes the statement that His disciples are already "in Him"; He only exhorts them again and again to be in Him. So long as He lives, all they can do is to believe on Him. His sayings about being-in-Him, since they refer to something which is necessarily future, are just as enigmatic to them as the references to the sacraments. It cannot indeed be otherwise. In the Gospel of John, as in Paul's teaching, a being-in-Christ first comes about through the Sacraments. It should be noted that the Logos Christ first speaks of the "being-in-Him" in connection with eating and drinking the flesh and blood of the Son of Man (Joh. vi. 56); and the second time in connection with the promise of the Spirit (Joh. xiv.-xvii). It is only through the Spirit and the Sacraments that the "being-from-God" becomes a being-in-Christ and a being-in-God, by which the assurance of the resurrection is given.

John vi. 56: "He who eateth My flesh, and drinketh My blood, abideth in Me, and I in Him."

That the being-in-Christ first begins with the Coming of the Spirit is expressed in the first Epistle of John with all clearness.—1 Joh. iv. 13: "Hereby know we that we abide in Him, and He in us, because He has given us of His Spirit."

The concept of the Mystical Body of Christ cannot be retained in connection with the Hellenistic Mysticism of the being-in-Christ. Being through and through eschatologically conditioned, it is incapable of being Hellenized.[1] Thus it comes about that the being-in-Christ is understood in the Gospel of John exclusively as a being-in-the-Spirit, whereas for Paul the being-in-the-Spirit is only a form of manifestation of the union with the Mystical Body of Christ.

.   .   .   .   .   .

Until the Spirit that goes forth from Him who is the organ of the Logos after His exaltation begins to work in the world, there is only a baptism with water, which has no special significance. The Gospel of John expressly states that Jesus did not baptize (Joh. iv. 2).

Jesus points forward, both by word and deed, to baptism with water which shall be at the same time a baptism of the Spirit, as He does in general to the future miracle of redemption. According to the Early Christian use of the argument from prophecy, as we find it in Paul (1 Cor. x. 1-12; Gal. iv. 21-31), and especially in Justin's *Dialogue with Trypho*, not only utterances, but also events, have a significance with reference to the expected future. Following this line of thought the Gospel of John represents the future sacraments as being made known by Jesus not only in His sayings, but by His miracles. In almost all the miracles, except those which reveal Jesus in a general way as the bringer of the resurrection, water plays a part.

That there is no "birth from above" and no receiving of the Spirit without water being associated with it, is set forth by Jesus in His conversation with Nicodemus.

John iii. 5: "Verily, verily, I say unto thee, that unless a man be born of water and the Spirit he cannot enter into the kingdom of heaven."

It is the baptismal water that the Logos-Christ means when He speaks to the Samaritan woman, whom He asked to give Him water from the well, about the water of life which He will give,

---

[1] On the mystical Body of Christ see pp. 116-118, *sup.*

and which will become in the man who drinks it a well of water springing up into life eternal (Joh. iv. 14).

At the Marriage at Cana, when He judges that His time for manifestation has come, He changes the water in the Jewish vessels of purification into wine (Joh. ii. 1-11).

He heals the sick man at the Pool of Bethzatha, who was waiting for someone to carry him down to the water, in the very moment when the water was set in movement and possessed healing power. This man in his waiting attitude symbolises the hope of the truly healing water of baptism, which is to go forth from Jerusalem. The help which he receives from Jesus shows that it is through Jesus that this hope will be fulfilled.

Immediately after the miracle of the Feeding of the Multitude, which points forward to the Eucharist, Jesus walks upon the water set in commotion by the wind, thus showing that water is obedient to the Logos-Spirit, and that He, as the wind which "bloweth whither it listeth" (Joh. iii. 8), will in the future descend upon the water (Joh. vi. 16-21).

The man born blind at Jerusalem He heals by putting spittle upon his eyes and telling him to go and wash in the Pool of Siloam (Joh. ix. 1-11). The "waters of Shiloah that go softly," of which Isaiah spoke (viii. 5-6), which came forth out of the Temple hill, are, like the moving water of the Pool of Bethzatha, a prophecy of the truly healing water of baptism, which, after the death of Jesus, will go forth from Jerusalem.

The Logos-Christ, however, does not confine Himself to prophesying by speech and action the coming of Baptism, but also indicates in what way water is to receive, through His death, the property of communicating the Spirit and so giving life. The Gospel of John thus offers an expansion of the saying of Ignatius, that Christ by His suffering has purified water (*Ad Eph.* xviii. 2).

This revelation, that Baptism arises from the death of Christ, is contained in the words which the Logos-Christ speaks in Jerusalem at the Feast of Tabernacles.

John vii. 37-39: "On the last day, the great day of the Feast, Jesus stood up and cried: 'If any one thirst let him come unto Me and drink; whosoever believeth on Me, as the Scripture saith, Out of His body shall flow rivers of living water.' But this He said of the Spirit which those who believe on Him were to receive; for the Spirit was not yet present, because Jesus was not yet glorified."

In this utterance the Johannine Jesus makes known, citing a passage of Scripture in support, that men must believe on Him, not only as the organ of the Logos, but also as the creator of Baptism with living water.

The explanation of this saying given by the Evangelist makes it clear that this water of life will only come into existence after the death of Jesus, when the Spirit can bring to bear its efficacious action through the baptismal water.

The Scripture passage cited by Jesus is not to be found in the Old Testament. It is true that Ezekiel (xlvii. 1-12) speaks of the miraculous waters, which in the new Jerusalem will stream forth from the Temple, which are to 'heal' the salt water of the Dead Sea and water the roots of the miraculous trees whose fruits, ripening every month, are to be for nourishment. It is to this passage that the Revelation of John refers when it makes Him who sits upon the throne promise to the thirsty water from the well-spring of life (Rev. xxi. 6, xxii. 17), and pictures the water of life as breaking forth from the throne of God and the Lamb (Rev. xxii. 1-2). But of living water flowing forth from the body of the Messiah there is no mention, either in Ezekiel or anywhere else in the Old Testament. To suppose that the Gospel of John is quoting from an Old Testament apocryphal book otherwise unknown to us is a mere arbitrary hypothesis. It no doubt is the passage in Ezekiel which is meant, but the Logos-Christ claims liberty to give a version of it which reveals its true meaning. The temple of the new Jerusalem, from which the water is to flow forth, is Himself. This He asserted in speaking to the Jews who, after the Cleansing of the Temple, demanded a sign from Him. He offers, if they break down the Temple, to build it up in three days, by which He meant (as the Evangelist explains) the Temple of His body, with allusion to His death and resurrection (Joh. ii. 18-22). The true temple of God, that is to say, the abiding-place in which He really dwells, can only, according to the Logos theory, be the body of the Logos-Christ, just as for Justin Martyr the bread and wine of the Eucharist with which the Spirit unites are the true sacrifice. The water of life which flows forth from the Temple is therefore, according to the true sense of the passage in Ezekiel, the water of baptism which, beginning from the dying and rising again in Jerusalem of the Logos-Christ, is to go forth into the whole world. Thus the Logos-Christ can affirm that the Scripture prophesies that "Streams of living water shall flow forth out of His body." By doing so He makes an end of the literal, unspiritual Jewish expositions of the promise about the miraculous Spring in the Temple, and prepares His followers for the miracle at His death, in which it was truly fulfilled.

358 THE MYSTICISM OF ST. PAUL CH.

At the lance-thrust there flowed forth from His body blood and water, which is unintelligible, because experience shows that from a dead body (since the blood in it is no longer under pressure) there is no emanation of fluid from wounds. The miracle is still further heightened by the statement that it was not watery blood, but blood and water separately, which flowed out (Joh. xix. 34). To this occurrence the Gospel of John attaches such significance that it attests its truth in the most solemn fashion:

John xix. 34-35: "One of the soldiers pierced His side with a spear, and forthwith came there out blood and water. And he that saw it has testified to it, and his testimony is true, and he knows that he says what is true, that you might believe."

From the material of the body of Him who was the Logos-organ there remain, therefore, water and blood on earth; that is to say, water and blood which have the capacity to be united with the Spirit. This shows that the existence of the Logos-bearer is continued upon earth in the water of Baptism and the wine of the Eucharist. The Logos-bearer did not simply enter into the world as a Person who was to return to Heaven, but also as water and blood, which continue to be present in the world. And there has also remained behind in the world His Spirit. To believe in Jesus Christ as the Son of God means, further, to live in the conviction that this triad, which He has left behind Him in the world, continues His redemptive life among men, and mediates to them eternal life. To this Spirit-revealed truth the passage about the three witnesses in the First Epistle of John refers, upon which light is thrown by the prophecy of Jesus at the Feast of Tabernacles and by the miracle of the spear-thrust, while it, in turn, throws light upon these passages.

1 John v. 5-8: "Who is he that overcometh the world but he that believeth that Jesus is the Son of God? This is he that came by water and by blood, Jesus Christ. Not with[1] the water alone, but with the water and the blood. And it is the Spirit that beareth witness, because the Spirit is the truth. So there are three who bear witness, the Spirit and the water and the blood. And these three agree in one."

It is quite wrong to understand the "water," in which Jesus Christ has come, of the water of baptism. According to the view taken in the Gospel of John, the baptism of Jesus did not constitute

---

[1] TRANSLATOR'S NOTE.—Greek "in"; not so translated here, but referred to in the next paragraph.

a significant experience for Himself, nor an outstanding event of His Coming into the world, but only as a means of making known to the Baptist that he can thenceforth preach Jesus as Him who is to baptize with the Holy Spirit, that is to say, as Him from whom the union of the Spirit with water takes its beginning. The coming of Jesus in or with the water can therefore only mean His presence as Spirit in the baptismal water.[1]

In the Synoptists the saying of the Baptist about the Greater than he who should baptize with the Holy Spirit remains not fulfilled, since Jesus did not baptize. The Gospel of John makes the Baptist's saying true, in the deeper sense that it does apply to Jesus as Him who by His death and glorification brings about the Coming of the Spirit in baptism.

Paul's conception that baptism is a dying and rising again with Christ cannot be retained by the Gospel of John any more than by Ignatius.

.   .   .   .   .   .

The Gospel of John also explains the way in which baptism with water and the Spirit made its beginnings in the Christian community. It represents the disciples as, from the first, even in the lifetime of Jesus, administering the simple baptism with water in the same way as the disciples of the Baptist (Joh. iii. 22-26, iv. 1-2). The use of baptism was thus, according to this Gospel, customary in the circle of Jesus. It does not, therefore, need to explain how baptism originated in the Christian Church, but only how the water-baptism, which was already in use, passed into baptism with water and with the Spirit. A baptism with water, which at the same time bestows the Spirit, only becomes possible after the death of Jesus, and when performed by men who possess the Spirit—such men in fact as the Apostles. . .

But how was it possible for them to receive the Spirit, otherwise than by baptism with water and the Spirit? The axiom of the Johannine sacramental mysticism, that the Spirit does not communicate Himself directly, but only in conjunction with water, admits of no exception.[2] The disciples can therefore possess the

---

[1] It was only in later times that Christian baptism was represented as derived from the baptism of Jesus. On the question of finding the explanation of Christian baptism in the baptism of Jesus see p. 234, *sup*.

[2] According to the saying of Jesus to Nicodemus (Joh. iii. 5) all rebirth takes place from water and Spirit.

Spirit and consequently begin to administer water-and-Spirit-baptism, only if they have already been baptized by one who is a vehicle of the Spirit. They must therefore have received the baptism of water and spirit from Jesus. And this is in point of fact the view of the Johannine Gospel.

What is the meaning of the fact that this Gospel replaces the account of the Lord's Supper by an account of the foot-washing which took place at this last meal (Joh. xiii. 4-17)? Jesus Himself gives the disciples two explanations of His action. He interprets it as an act of humility which they are to repeat; but He also explains it to Peter as a washing by which He makes them clean, and gives them a part in Himself—a washing, the meaning of which they cannot know yet, but will only understand later.

John xiii. 7-8: "Jesus answered and said to him, What I do thou knowest not now but thou shalt recognise hereafter. Peter said to Him, 'Never shalt Thou wash my feet.' Jesus answered him, 'If I wash thee not thou hast no part in me'."

What is the mystical meaning of this washing of the disciples, which thus stands behind the ethical? Exegetes have hitherto not grasped it rightly, although the saying about only understanding it later, and the inherently so logical Johannine theory of baptism, ought to have put them on the right track.

The foot-washing is the baptism of the disciples by Jesus, that is to say, the first stage of the rite. Since the Spirit who unites with the water will only be present after the death and glorification of Jesus, Jesus cannot, so long as He walks on earth among them, communicate to them the Spirit. On the other hand, they could not have received the Spirit if they had not previously been baptized by a bearer of the Spirit, that is to say, by Himself. The only escape from this dilemma was to have the baptism of the disciples "with water and with the Spirit" carried out in two stages: on the last night of His earthly existence Jesus, in the foot-washing, baptizes them with water; after His resurrection He breathes the Holy Spirit into them.

John xx. 21-23: "Then said Jesus unto them again, Peace be with you; as my Father hath sent me, even so send I you. And after these words He breathed upon them and said to them, Receive the Holy Spirit. If you forgive any their sins, they are forgiven to them; and if you retain the sins of any, they are retained."

Having in this way become vehicles of the Spirit, the disciples have the power, in their turn, of administering "baptism with water and the Spirit" to others.

At the moment when Jesus washes their feet the disciples do not understand the scope and significance of His action. But when they afterwards receive the Spirit, who is to guide them into all truth, it becomes obvious to them that they had to be brought into contact with the water by the hand of Jesus in order that they might have part in Him.

The Gospel of John thus deals with the fundamental question, which has been cautiously avoided by theologians of later times, when and how the Apostles, who began the administration of Christian baptism, themselves received Christian baptism, and solves it in accordance with its own theory of the nature of baptism. Under the pressure of this theory it is obliged to invalidate the tradition of the outpouring of the Spirit at Pentecost. It cannot admit that the disciples received the Spirit without baptismal preparation, not to speak of receiving it along with a multitude of other believers! (Acts ii. 1-4).

The Gospel of John is already so churchly in its views that, for it, all Spirit present in believers must be derived ultimately from the Apostles, who, in turn, received it from the Lord. It is by the receiving of the Spirit that they are equipped for the Apostolic office. The moment that He communicates to them the Spirit, the glorified Christ sends them forth, as His Father had sent Him forth (Joh. xx. 21), and gives them power to forgive and to retain sins (Joh. xx. 23). Here, too, we have a correction of the Synoptic tradition. It is for the Gospel of John unthinkable that the disciples already in the lifetime of Jesus, without having been enlightened by the Spirit in the requisite manner, should possess this authority.

For Paul, the beginning of baptism with water and the Spirit, and the receiving of Christian Baptism by the disciples, do not constitute a problem which has to be solved by historical conjecture. The case is, for him, quite a different one, because according to his view the receiving of the Spirit is in consequence of the dying and rising again with Christ in baptism. Immediately the death and resurrection of Jesus have taken place Baptism administered in His name, for the forgiveness of sins and as a pledge of belonging to the Messianic Kingdom, directly brings about the dying and rising again with Christ, from which the possession of the Spirit results. The water is in no sense a vehicle of the Spirit. It is also not essential that the man who administers baptism should be a vehicle of the Spirit. Thus, for Paul too, baptism with water becomes, in consequence of the death and resurrection of Jesus, baptism with water and with the Spirit, but in a quite different and much simpler way than in the later view, which is carried to its logical conclusion in the Gospel of John.

From the moment of the foot-washing the disciples are consecrated to the receiving of the Spirit. Jesus therefore now begins, in the hours which remain before His arrest, to prepare them for the mysterious event which awaits them. He now speaks to them of the Coming of the Spirit and of their being in Himself and in the Father. In His public discourses these mysteries of redemption had been only glimpsed as by a flash of lightning from behind dark clouds.

When the significance of the foot-washing is understood we have an explanation of the otherwise unintelligible fact, that all the previous preaching of the Johannine Christ is only a prologue to the discourses between the Last Supper and His arrest.

.   .   .   .   .   .

The miracle of the Feeding of the Multitude at the lake-side points forward to the future Eucharistic meal. By miraculously increasing the bread, Jesus consecrates bread to the use which it is to have in the sacrament. At the Lake of Gennesareth bread is indicated as the vehicle of the redemptive miracle, which carries on the existence of the Logos-bearer in the same way as water and blood are indicated by the miracle of the spear-thrust.

The future bread of life is meant in all those passages in which Jesus speaks of bread and the grain out of which bread is made. In this way is to be explained the obscure conversation with the disciples at Jacob's Well. The disciples, returning from the town with provisions, offer Him earthly food (Joh. iv. 8, 31), just as, a little before, the Samaritan woman wished to give Him earthly water. Just as He had refused this and begun to speak of the water of life, so He refuses the disciples' food, that He may teach them about the true food assigned to Him by His Father, this food being to accomplish that whereunto His Father had sent Him (Joh. iv. 34). He goes on abruptly to speak of the harvest which is at hand, and makes known to the disciples that a harvest "into eternal life" is coming, at which the reaper will not be the same as the sower. They are to reap what He has sown.

John iv. 34-38: "My food is to do the will of Him that sent me and to accomplish His work. Say ye not that there are yet four months before the coming of the harvest? Behold I say unto you, lift up your eyes and look upon the fields, for they are white already to harvest. Already the reaper receiveth wages and gathers fruit into life eternal that the sower may rejoice at the same time as the reaper. For herein is the saying true, that the sower is one and the reaper is another. I have sent you to reap what ye have not laboured upon; others have laboured, and you have entered into their labours."

Hitherto exegesis has laboured in vain to extract a meaning from this medley of sayings! This only becomes possible when we realise that Jesus in these obscure utterances is speaking of the bread of life after previously having spoken of the water of life. He points His disciples to the fact that He is not one who takes food, but who gives it—who in accordance with the Will of God is calling into existence by His death a food that supports eternal life.[1] Only as a consequence of His death and resurrection can it come about that the Spirit unites with the bread, and makes it a food of immortality. The harvest from which the bread of life comes grows out of His body which He gives to the earth as seed-corn. He Himself, therefore, will not be present at this harvest, but only disciples. In consequence of this harvest they will possess the bread of the Eucharist as His flesh, which is the food that bestows eternal life.

That this discourse only becomes intelligible when the true facts to which it points are known, is not a matter of importance to the Johannine Christ. His discourses are not meant to be understood, but to direct attention to that which is still future.

At His entry into Jerusalem, Jesus speaks of the corn of wheat which, by its dying in the earth, brings forth much fruit.

John xii. 23-24: "The hour is come that the Son of Man should be glorified. Verily, verily, I say unto you that unless a corn of wheat fall into the ground and die it abideth alone. But if it die, it shall bring forth much fruit."

Here, too, what is meant is not the fruit of His death in general, but the living bread of the Eucharist which is made out of the

[1] The food which Jesus speaks of as His own food (Joh. iv. 32-34) is therefore not a food for His own support, as the disciples misunderstood Him, but a food which enables those who eat it to obtain immortality, a food first made possible by His death. The will of God, to do which is His own food (Joh. iv. 34), is that He should die, and thereby bring into existence the food of immortality, which is offered to believers at the Eucharist.

harvest which arises from this corn of wheat, which in dying so miraculously multiplies itself.

The sacramental stands for so much, in the Johannine mysticism of union with Christ, that the main significance of the death of Jesus is, according to it, the provision of the sacraments.

With perfect clearness Jesus makes known in His discourse about the Feeding of the Multitude that the living food, the true Manna, arises out of His flesh which is offered for the world.

John vi. 47-50: "Verily, verily, I say unto you, He that believeth hath eternal life. I am the bread of life. Your fathers ate Manna in the wilderness, and have died; such is the bread that comes down from Heaven, that a man shall eat of it and shall not die."

John vi. 51: "And in truth the bread, which I shall give for the life of the world, is my flesh."

John vi. 53-56: "Verily, verily I say unto you, Unless you eat the flesh and drink the blood of the Son of Man, you have not life in you. He who eateth my flesh and drinketh my blood hath eternal life, and I will raise him up at the last day. For my flesh is food indeed, and my blood is drink indeed. He who eateth my flesh and drinketh my blood abideth in me and I in him."

Here, too, it is not the purpose of the discourse to be understood. Its aim is solely to direct attention to the miracle which is to happen in connection with bread in the future. It does not matter, therefore, that it should offend the multitude. But to help those who already believe in Him to overcome the offence, Jesus points out to them that the prospect which He has held out in such enigmatic assertions is connected with His glorification and with the coming of the Spirit.

John vi. 61-63: "Jesus, knowing in Himself that His disciples murmured at this, said to them, Does this offend you? What if you shall see the Son of Man rising up where He was before? It is the Spirit that makes alive, the flesh profits nothing. The words which I have spoken to you are Spirit and Life." [1]

The solution of the enigma by the reference to the Spirit, from whom alone life proceeds, consists in the fact that it is the Spirit who unites with the bread and wine of the Eucharist and makes

[1] By the "disciples" are meant here, as the context shows (Joh. vi. 66-70), not the Twelve, but the disciples in the wider sense.

them into the flesh and blood of the Son of Man, which bestow
the possibility of resurrection. Justin's explanation about the food
and drink of the Eucharist, which through the Logos became flesh
and blood of the incarnate Jesus, and by a transformation nourish
the flesh and blood of men (1 *Apol.* lxvi.), and the Ignatian concepts
of the becoming-one of Spirit and flesh (*Ad Magn.* xiii. 2) and of
the bread of God, which is the flesh of Jesus Christ (*Ad Rom.* vii.
3)—these are the contemporary and, therefore, the only reliable
explanations of the part played by the Spirit in the sacramental
doctrine of the Johannine Gospel.[1]

Exegesis has not yet worked its way to the recognition of this truth.
It is constantly endeavouring to make the Logos-Christ speak 'spiritually' (in the modern sense), and to interpret the references to the Spirit
as meaning that it is the purely 'spiritual' union with Christ which is
really alone in view here, and that the sacramental is only a symbol of
this. The attempt is constantly made to deduce from the phrase in
which the discourse about the flesh and blood of the Son of Man ends,
that the writer's intention is to put into the mouth of Jesus the realistic
view of the sacraments which was current in many circles in the contemporary Church, in order finally to oppose to it, also through the
mouth of Jesus, a 'spiritual' view intended to take the place of the other.
The incentive to such attempts is found in the statement, "The words
which I have spoken to you are Spirit and life" (Joh. vi. 63), which is
taken to mean that all the foregoing discourse is to be understood
spiritually. In reality, however, the Johannine Jesus only means by that
saying that the foregoing conveys spirit-given knowledge about the
way of obtaining life such as the believers will themselves possess when
once they have received the Spirit.

In the saying about the Spirit who alone gives life, the Logos-
Christ is not taking back anything that He has previously said, but
merely explaining how it comes about that the bread and wine of
the Eucharist are the flesh and blood of the Son of Man. They are
so because, as in Justin, the Spirit, who in consequence of the
death and resurrection of Jesus has acquired the capacity to unite
with those elements, forms a unity with them in the same way as
the Logos does with the flesh and blood of Jesus Christ. The elements thus carry on the redemptive becoming-one of the Logos-

[1] In regard to Justin's explanation of the bread and wine as the flesh and blood
of Christ see pp. 273-276; on the Ignatian view of the becoming-one of flesh
and Spirit see pp. 342-343, *sup.*

Spirit with matter, which took place in the Person of Jesus Christ, in a form capable of appropriation by believers. Through them the immortality of the flesh, which was first brought into the world in the Person of Jesus, can be obtained.

Since the Spirit who makes the bread and wine into the flesh and blood of Christ has His being in the world only after, and in consequence of, the death and resurrection of Jesus, it is for the author of the Fourth Gospel unthinkable that Jesus Himself at that last meal with the disciples should have given them bread and wine as His body and blood. The absence of an account of the Last Supper is therefore due to the fact that what the Synoptists narrate cannot, according to his theory of the sacraments, have happened. The report of the Last Supper of Jesus with His disciples, is for him an erroneous tradition, which he deliberately sets himself to invalidate.

He is strengthened in his conviction that this report can only be due to a Jewish misunderstanding by the fact that the Synoptists represent Jesus as making this distribution of bread and wine in the course of a Paschal meal. How is it possible that the Logos-Christ, who is in all things exalted above the Jewish Law, should have celebrated a Jewish Feast with His disciples? The Pauline view, that the Christ was "after the flesh" subject to the Law and lived accordingly, no longer exists for the Logos doctrine. According to it Jesus Christ is, in all that He says and does, the negation of that Law of which the Jews had so unspiritual a conception, and cannot therefore take part in legal usages—to do so would have been for Him an inconceivable humiliation!

As for Justin, so also for the author of the Fourth Gospel, everything Jewish has in the last resort only the significance of a signpost pointing to the Logos-Christ. The Paschal lamb is a prophecy of Him as the Lamb which bears the sin of the world. This He fulfils. Therefore in the Johannine Gospel the statement that Jesus before His death celebrated the Paschal meal with His disciples must give place to the statement that He suffered on the Cross on the day on which the Paschal lamb was killed (Joh. xiii. 1-2, xviii. 28).

Paul's mystical doctrine of the union with Christ does not need to come to terms with the tradition of the doings and sayings of Jesus, because it simply takes an independent place alongside of the latter, as being derived from a direct revelation of the Spirit.

The Hellenized mystical doctrine of union with Christ, on the other hand, claiming as it does to be the proper understanding of the teaching of Jesus, is forced to choose between history as required by its own logic, and history as embodied in the tradition. Since, for it, its doctrine of redemption through union with Christ is the truth which must be maintained without capitulation, it can only accept the tradition in so far as it can be brought into harmony with the doctrine.

The Pauline Mysticism does violence to the facts of the natural world; the Johannine to those of history.[1]

.   .   .   .   .   .

Since the Logos-Christ is conscious of having come into the world and of being about to undergo death in order to bring in the era in which resurrection will be mediated by the sacraments, He prepares His hearers to expect that they will see still greater works than those which He has done during His earthly existence.

John v. 20-21: "For the Father loves the Son and shows Him all things that He himself does. And He will show them greater works than these that you may marvel. For as the Father raises the dead and makes them alive, even so the Son makes alive whom He will."

In these words the Johannine Jesus is alluding to the "making-alive" which the Holy Spirit is to effect in the sacraments. During His earthly life He only performs the miracle of raising the dead to natural life in order to show that He possesses power over death. As the Spirit working in the sacraments, He will make multitudes of believers partakers of eternal life.

Since it is the believers who institute baptism and the Eucharist, the Johannine Christ can go so far as to say that they, in consequence of His departure to the Father (through which the Spirit comes with the world), will do greater works than He, the Logos, while dwelling among them in His human Person.

John xiv. 12: "He who believes on Me, the works that I do shall he do also, because I go to my Father."

The Pauline view that the redemptive activity of the glorified Christ is immeasurably greater than in the days of His flesh, is also present in the Hellenized being-in-Christ mysticism, the only difference being that the Christ after the flesh is not so unimportant

---

[1] TRANSLATOR'S NOTE.—The German is *vergewaltigt*.

for it as for the eschatological. This is due to the fact that in the Christian-Hellenistic conception of the world the natural and supernatural eras are not sharply divided in the same way as in the eschatological view. The Hellenistic view makes the supernatural period begin with the appearing of the Logos instead of, as in Paul's view, only with the death and resurrection of Jesus. It is an outcome of this that for the Johannine view of the problem of the Law, as envisaged by Paul, is non-existent. For the Law is not abolished only by, and at, the death and resurrection of Jesus; from the moment of the appearance of the Logos-Christ it has become meaningless. He is not, as for Paul (Gal. iv. 4-5), made subject to the Law in order that He might redeem those who are under the Law, but stands, along with those who are His, outside of the Law, which is only a prophecy of Him.

With the coming of the Logos both redemption and judgment begin. As the bringer of immortality, He effects a division among men. On some He bestows life, others He delivers over to death. This judgment is carried into effect in the sacraments. Christ's return as the Spirit who works in the Sacraments is thus already a return for judgment. It is with intention that the Gospel of John makes Jesus so speak in His farewell discourses that His words seem to refer, now to His return in the Spirit, now to His return at the end of the world.

How much living eschatological expectation the Johannine Gospel still presupposes is hard to make out. Certainly a visible Coming of the Son of Man and a general resurrection for judgment is expected.

John v. 26-27: "For as the Father has life in Himself, so also has He given to the Son to have life in Himself. And He has given Him authority to hold a judgment also, because He is the Son of Man. Wonder not at this, for the hour is coming at which all those who are in the graves shall hear His voice, and shall come forth, those that have done good to the resurrection of life, those that have done evil to the resurrection of judgment."

When one remembers how lively the eschatological expectation still is which finds expression in scattered sayings of Ignatius[1] and Justin[2], one is inclined to think that the Johannine teaching must have had a much stronger eschatological background than it would appear from the discourses of the Logos-Christ to have had. But

[1] See pp. 336-337, *sup.*   [2] See pp. 337-338, *sup.*

these after all only aim at showing the way in which the Logos-Christ brings eternal life into the world and bestows it, through the union with Him which is brought about in the sacraments, upon His followers. The expectation of the times of the end which must have accompanied these ideas and conceptions is only glimpsed, as it were, incidentally.

But however lively this hope may have been, it was nevertheless not comparable with the Pauline, because the logic of the Johannine being-in-Christ Mysticism is no longer of an eschatological, but of a Hellenistic, character.

.   .   .   .   .   .

The process of the Hellenization of Christianity was therefore of the following kind. The Asia Minor theology of about the end of the first and beginning of the second century A.D. adopted the Pauline mystical teaching about redemption through union with Christ, in the form of a doctrine of redemption through receiving the Spirit of Christ in the sacraments, and translated it out of the world of eschatological conceptions into that of Hellenistic thought. Thus, within the framework of the eschatological expectation, was set up a universally intelligible, logical, Hellenistic doctrine of a resurrection to eternal life, brought by Jesus Christ and to be obtained through the sacraments. This doctrine continued to dominate the theology of the Greek Church from that time forward.

The Christian faith has no need to take over conceptions from the Hellenistic religions of the surrounding world, in order to transform itself into a mystical doctrine of union with Christ. For this development had already been effected, in genuinely Primitive-Christian thought-forms, in the teaching of Paul. From Hellenism it took over only the apparatus of concepts necessary to make the bodily resurrection, and its attainment through union with Christ, intelligible on the lines of Greek metaphysic. Here the Logos-doctrine came to its aid. By means of this it converted the Jewish conception of the Messiah into the Greek conception of the Bringer of eternal life.

The view adopted in Adolf Harnack's History of Dogma, that the earliest dogmatic constructions were not influenced by the religious ideas of the Hellenistic Orient, but by Greek philosophy, is therefore justified.

Harnack was not able to carry it through completely because he, in common with previous scholarship generally, possessed no satisfactory explanation for the teaching of Paul. It thus remained possible to assume that in Paul's teaching religious concepts of the Greek Orient had found their way into Christianity. It was at this point that students of Comparative Religion set themselves in the last decades of the nineteenth century to make a breach in Harnack's theory. They started out from the consideration, in itself justified, that it would border on the miraculous if Christianity, transferred, as it was, from the Jewish to the Hellenistic world immediately after it arose, had entirely escaped the influence of the Hellenistic Mystery-religions. The explanation of the Pauline Mysticism from Hellenism offered itself as something absolutely self-evident, the more so as its doctrine of union with the dead and risen Christ and its sacramental mysticism seemd to present obvious affinities with the mysticism of the mystery-religions. Here there began the assault upon this fort which lay in so obviously exposed a zone.

The confidence of victory in which the forces of Comparative Religion indulged prevented them from becoming conscious of the very curious position into which they had brought themselves. For, even supposing that they had succeeded in taking this particular fort, they would have had no hope whatever of capturing the whole fortress or even the other forts of the outer ring. For it was only in the case of Paul that there was any possibility of maintaining the hypothesis of the taking over of religious conceptions from Oriental Hellenism. In the case of Ignatius, of Justin, and generally of all the Christian Hellenistic thinkers who followed Paul, it was obvious that they took over from Hellenism only formative elements, not content, as was indeed manifest from the fact that Comparative Religion left them severely alone. So it came to this, that two successive Hellenizations of Christianity had to be assumed. The first was that of Paul, who introduced new ideas into it and gave it a new character, the second that of Ignatius and his successors, which consisted merely in the attempt to express Paul's ideas in the thought-forms of Greek philosophy. So it was only at one moment and in a single personality that Christianity was receptive of the ideas of the Greek mystery-religions! And the Hellenistic thinkers who later repudiated these ideas had nevertheless, so far as they had been already taken over by Paul, adopted them without a qualm; and, moreover, as though they had not been already Hellenistic, Hellenized them all over again! According, therefore, to the exponents of Comparative Religion, Ignatius, Justin, and the creator of the Johannine theology must have been smitten with blindness.

The eschatological theory of Paul's mysticism thus signifies the relief of the beleaguered fort and the defeat of Reitzenstein's attack upon Harnack. The theory that it was not Hellenistic-Oriental beliefs but Greek philosophy which influenced the formation of Christian dogma has no longer a weak point to invite attack.

That is not to say, however, that ideas from the Hellenistic Mystery-religions exerted no influence upon Christianity. But so far as they did this in the decisive early period, the influence is observable only in particulars, and never affects the formation of the fundamental conceptions of Christ and redemption. It is only later that, alongside of an already formed theology, numerous conceptions and usages were adopted into Christianity, which were derived from the world of Hellenistic religious ideas.

The correctness of the eschatological interpretation of Paul's Mysticism is proved not only by the fact that it explains the texts in a much more natural way than previous interpretations, at the same time bringing clearness into Paul's relation to Jesus and to Primitive Christianity; but also by the fact that it alone makes it intelligible why Ignatius and the Asia Minor theology do not simply take over the Pauline conceptions, but simplify them and give them a different form. And, on the other hand, it is only by the demonstration that the Ignatian and Johannine form of the doctrine of the mystical union with Christ is Hellenized Paulinism, that the eschatological character of the latter is fully established.

How impossible it is to arrive at a clear view of the relations between Paul and Hellenized Christianity until the above explanation is arrived at is evident from the fact that, down to the present time, the most diverse opinions of the relation of the Johannine theology to the Pauline are found side by side. No doubt the historical criticism of the nineteenth century, as embodied in Ferdinand Christian Baur and Heinrich Julius Holtzmann, had pointed out the difference between the Pauline and the Johannine world of thought, and had shown that the former was the earlier and that the latter was dependent on it. But they were unable to secure their gains completely, because they regarded the Pauline teaching as in part Hellenistic, and therefore could not say quite definitely what was the cause of the "difference amid resemblance" of the two. Consequently the right understanding at which they had arrived did not hold its ground. Scholars busied themselves in making attempt after attempt to place the Johannine doctrine alongside of the Pauline as being independent of it, or even to make it the earlier of the two, or again, to obliterate the difference between them. What lapses scholarship is capable of is shown by Adolf Deissmann, who, as though Baur and Holtzmann had never lived, commits himself to the statement "The most imposing monument of a genuine and thorough understanding of the Pauline mysticism is furnished by the Gospel and Epistles of John.[1] One might as well say that Beethoven was the best interpreter of J. S. Bach!

To all this confusion the recognition that the Johannine mysticism is a Hellenization of the Pauline puts an end. By it the resemblances and differences are alike explained. The solution of the Pauline problem is both that of the Johannine problem and of the problem of the formation of Early Christian doctrine generally.

The significance of Paul in the process of the Hellenization of Christianity is thus twofold. His mysticism makes the Hellenization possible. But, in addition to that, it so prepares the way that the process can go on without the taking over of Hellenistic ideas of a kind foreign to its nature. For in the doctrine of the mystical union with Christ the Christian faith presents itself in a Hellenizable form. At the same time it already possesses such a consistency and completeness that it cannot take up into itself any further conceptions, but simply Hellenizes itself in the sense that it learns to understand and express itself in Greek thought-forms. The miracle that the Gospel of Jesus in entering the world of Hellenistic-Oriental thought is able to maintain itself against the syncretistic tendencies of the time is in part the work of Paul.

.   .   .   .   .   .

What is the exact relation of the Pauline and the Hellenized union-with-Christ mysticism as regards their content?

The Hellenized mysticism has the advantage over the Pauline of being simpler. By giving up the conception of dying and rising again with Christ, which has its roots in eschatology, it has become a logical doctrine, immediately apprehensible by Greek thought, of the redemptive work of the Spirit of Christ.

Moreover, in consequence of this simplicity, it becomes extra-

[1] Adolf DEISSMANN, *Paulus*, 2nd ed., 1925, p. 123.

ordinarily capable of undergoing various transformations, and thus enables it to take a form adapted to the most various periods. A 'spiritually' interpreted Johannine mysticism dominates the religious thought of modern times.

Nevertheless the original doctrine, for all the apparent complexity and strangeness which it owes to its eschatological root, conceals within it a greater value than the derivative one. In a quite general sense the Pauline mysticism is superior to the Ignatian-Johannine, in that it expresses the relation with Christ experienced by a great personality, whereas the Ignatian-Johannine is the outcome of a theory. The Pauline Mysticism possesses an immediacy which the other lacks. Its conceptions grip, even if its logic remains foreign to us. In the more complex mysticism there pulsates a warmer life than in the simplified.

This is manifest from the fact that it is richer on the ethical side. The eschatological mysticism can be translated entire, without leaving anything over, into an ethic of life in the power of Christ. In the Ignatian-Johannine this is not to the same extent the case. Hellenized Mysticism has not the same direct interest in ethics that the Pauline has. The combination of the ethical with the metaphysical in it is of such a character that the metaphysical is the dominant partner. No doubt for Paul also love is a metaphysical entity; but he nevertheless succeeds in finding complete expression for his ethical personality in the ethic which he derives from his mysticism. Ignatius, who, both as a man and a thinker, is doubtless the greatest figure in the post-Pauline generation, so far as we know it, does not succeed in doing this in the same measure. Although his mysticism is a mysticism of love, his ethic stands alongside it rather than within it. How poor are his Epistles, compared with Paul's, in ethical sayings which have a kindling fire in them! Even in the discourses of the Johannine Christ the ethical note sounds curiously muted out of the metaphysic of love.

In the further progress of development it became more and more apparent how difficult it was for Greek theology to secure a proper place for ethics in the metaphysical doctrine of redemption. It tends to develop into a purely logical speculation upon the obtaining of immortality through the working of the spirit upon matter. For ethics it has recourse to the repetition of ethical sayings of Jesus, which, moreover, it mixes with Greek philosophical ethics. It is the tragedy of the doctrine of the being-in-Christ in its

Christian Hellenistic form, that in it ethics has to struggle for its existence.

As in ethics, so in spirituality, the Pauline Mysticism shows itself superior to the Ignatian-Johannine. This is due to the difference in the conception of Spirit. For Paul, the Spirit unites with the spirit of man, that is to say, with the psychic side of man's nature, and works through it. In the Ignatian-Johannine Mysticism the union is with the material side of man's nature, and also with matter itself, as such. For this is required by the Hellenistic logic, which must explain the bodily resurrection, and the mediation of this by the sacraments, as caused by the working of the Spirit upon the flesh, because the Late-Jewish eschatological concept of the resurrection has been ousted by the Hellenistic. A material concept of the Spirit has taken the place of the purely spiritual.

From this difference in the nature of the Spirit is to be explained why it is that in Paul's Mysticism the sacramental does not play quite the same part as in the Hellenized Mysticism, although it takes an equally important place. Paul's Mysticism is sacramental, but without a metaphysic of the sacraments. Though what happens in Baptism is realistically conceived in this theory, it is nevertheless a personal spiritual experience, because the spirit which is thereby received unites with the psychic side of man's nature. In Hellenized mysticism the receiving of the spirit through the sacraments is thought of rather as an event which takes place outside of the personality. The magical sacramental ideas, which notwithstanding his realistic theory of the effect of Baptism and the Lord's Meal are not found in Paul, begin to develop.

The Pauline mysticism is also richer than the Hellenistic, in virtue of the part played in it by the idea of dying and rising again with Christ. This idea gives an ethical warmth and glow to the mystical union with Christ, and preserves to the conception of Baptism and the Lord's Meal its inwardness. It makes of the union with Christ something to be constantly experienced and verified in life. It has thus a deep significance, that for Paul the Spirit is in believers in consequence of the dying and rising again with Christ.

In giving up the conception of the dying and rising again with Christ the Hellenized mysticism abandoned a part of the inner life of the idea of union with Christ.

Thus the simplification which the union-with-Christ Mysticism

underwent in the process of Hellenization signifies at the same
time a loss of ethical and spiritual values. With the Hellenization
of Christianity begins its impoverishment.

This impoverishment was increased by the fact that the Hellenization took place in the course of the struggle with Gnosticism.
In order to meet this enemy to best advantage Christian doctrine
aimed at allowing the greatest possible simplicity and logical consistency. It allows only those religious ideas to make their influence
felt which will fit into the system which was being formulated to
oppose Gnosticism. All others, however valuable they might be
in themselves, signify for it a deadweight and a danger. It ceases
therefore to occupy itself with the fundamental religious problems
which have a place with Paul and with intellectual religion in
general, because Gnosticism had made them its special preserve.
Instead of fighting it out along this line, Christianity leaves these
problems alone. Except in the positions which it had marked out
for defence, Christianity declines all combat.

From the impoverishment which it underwent in the process
of Hellenization and in the struggle with Gnosticism Christianity
has hardly recovered to this day.

CHAPTER XIV

PAUL vindicated for all time the rights of thought in Christianity. Above belief which drew its authority from tradition, he set the knowledge which came from the Spirit of Christ. There lives in him an unbounded and undeviating reverence for truth. He will consent only to a limitation of liberty laid on him by the law of love, not to one imposed by doctrinal authority.

Moreover, he is no mere revolutionary. He takes the faith of the Primitive-Christian community as his starting-point: only he will not consent to halt where it comes to an end, but claims the right to think out his thoughts about Christ to their conclusion, without caring whether the truths which he thereby reaches have ever come within the purview of the faith held by the Christian community and been recognised by it.

The result of this first appearance of thought in Christianity is calculated to justify, for all periods, the confidence that faith has nothing to fear from thinking, even when the latter disturbs its peace and raises a debate which appears to promise no good results for the religious life. How strongly the faith of the Primitive-Christian community resisted the thinking of Paul! And yet it was the raising, by the Apostle of the Gentiles, of the belief in Jesus Christ to a reasoned faith which provided a solution of the problem set to the Christianity of the next generation by the non-fulfilment of the eschatological hope. The idea which looked so dangerous to the leaders of the Primitive Church enabled the Gospel of Jesus after its rejection by Judaism to find entrance and understanding in the Greek world. It is the thoughts of the Apostle of the Gentiles, who was opposed by the faith of his own time, which have again and again acted as a power of renewal in the faith of subsequent periods. Thus it appears, from the course of this first conflict of Christian thought with Christian faith, that the thought proved an investment for the future which brought profit to the faith of later generations, as has proved to be the case again and again in the history of Christianity.

It has also a significance for all future times that the Symphony of Christianity began with a tremendous dissonance between faith and thought, which later resolved itself into a harmony. Christianity can only become the living truth for successive generations if thinkers constantly arise within it who, in the Spirit of Jesus, make belief in Him capable of intellectual apprehension in the thought-forms of the world-view proper to their time. When Christianity becomes a traditional belief which claims to be simply taken over by the individual, it loses its relationship to the spiritual life of the time and the capacity of assuming a new form adapted to a new world-view. If the debate between tradition and thought falls silent, Christian truth suffers, and with it Christian intellectual integrity. This is why it is so deeply significant that Paul undertakes as an entirely obvious duty to think out Christianity in its whole scope and its whole depth by the use of the materials provided by the eschatological world-view of his time. The sayings "Quench not the Spirit" and "Where the Spirit of the Lord is, there is liberty," which owe their place in the records of the origin of Christianity to him, carry the significance that thinking Christianity is to have its rights within believing Christianity, and that the Little-faiths will never succeed in suppressing loyalty to truth. Never must Christianity lay aside the large simplicity with which Paul claims thought also as having its origin in God. Never must the spring-like freshness of Pauline Christianity die out from amid our own.

Paul is the patron-saint of thought in Christianity. And all those who think to serve the faith in Jesus by destroying freedom of thought would do well to keep out of his way.

.   .   .   .   .   .

But it is not merely that Paul was the first to champion the rights of thought in Christianity; he has also shown it, for all time, the way it was to go. His great achievement was to grasp, as the thing essential to being a Christian, the experience of union with Christ. Out of the depths of the expectation of the Messiah and of the Messianic world this thought wells up to him, a thought to which expression had already been given by Jesus when He spoke of the mystery of the consecration of believers through fellowship with the unrecognised future Messiah who was dwelling among them. By penetrating to the depths of the temporarily conditioned, Paul wins his way to a spiritual result of permanent value. Strange as his thoughts are to us in the way they arise out of, and have their form moulded by, the eschatological world-view which for us is so completely obsolete, they nevertheless carry a directly convincing power in virtue of their spiritual truth which transcends all time and has value for all times. So we too should claim the right to conceive the idea of union with Jesus on the lines of our own world-view, making it our sole concern to reach the depth of the truly living and spiritual truth.

For Christianity is a Christ-Mysticism, that is to say, a "belonging together" with Christ as our Lord, grasped in thought and realised in experience. By simply designating Jesus "our Lord" Paul raises Him above all the temporally conditioned conceptions in which the mystery of His personality might be grasped, and sets Him forth as the spiritual Being who transcends all human definitions, to whom we have to surrender ourselves in order to experience in Him the true law of our existence and our being.

All attempts to rob Christianity of the character of Christ-Mysticism are nothing more or less than a useless resistance to that spirit of knowledge and truth, which finds expression in the teaching of the first and greatest of all Christian thinkers. Just as Philosophy, after all its aberrations, has always to return to the primary truth that every genuinely profound and living world-view is of a mystical character, in the sense that it consists of some kind of conscious and willing surrender to the mysterious and infinite will-to-live, from which we are; so thought of, an essentially Christian character cannot do other than conceive this surrender to God, as Paul conceived it long ago, as coming to pass in union with the being of Jesus Christ.

God-mysticism, in the sense of a direct becoming-one with the infinite creative will of God, is impossible of realisation. All attempts to extract living religion from pure Monistic God-mysticism are foredoomed to failure, whether they are undertaken by the Stoics, by Spinoza, by Indian or by Chinese thought. They know the direction, but they do not find the way. From the becoming-one with the infinite essence of the being of the Universal Will-to-be there can result nothing but a passive determination of man's being, an absorption into God, a sinking into the ocean of the Infinite.

Pure God-mysticism remains a dead thing. The becoming-one of the finite will with the Infinite acquires a content only when it is experienced both as quiescence in it and at the same time as a 'being-taken-possession-of' by the will of love, which in us comes to consciousness of itself, and strives in us to become act. Mysticism only takes the road to life when it passes through the antithesis of God's will of love with His infinite enigmatic creative will, and transcends it. Since human thinking cannot comprehend the eternal in its true nature, it is bound to arrive at Dualism and be forced to overcome it, in order to adjust itself to the eternal. It must, no doubt, face all the enigmas of existence which present themselves to thought and harass it, but in the last resort it must leave the incomprehensible uncomprehended, and take the path of seeking to be certified of God as the Will of Love, and finding in it both inner peace and springs of action.

The Messianic eschatological world-view is an overcoming of Dualism, arrived at by bold and vigorous thinking, through the victorious arising, within the belief in the infinitely enigmatic Creator God, of a belief in the God of Love. All religious mysticism must, indeed, take up into itself some kind of Messianic belief, if it is to receive the breath of life. Thus the Messianic-eschatological mysticism of Paul is an expression of essential religious mysticism which has forced its way to living truth. In Jesus Christ, God is manifested as Will of Love. In union with Christ, union with God is realised in the only form attainable by us.

That Paul is prevented by his eschatological world-view from equating Christ-mysticism with God-mysticism has a deep significance. For all intellectual apprehension God-mysticism remains always something imperfect, and incapable of being perfected. Paul, by confining himself to seeing sonship to God realised in the union with Christ, without trying to make this sonship to God intelligible as a being-in-God, is a guiding light to lead Christianity back from all divagations into the course which it ought to follow. Like a lighthouse that throws its beam upon the ocean of the eternal, the Pauline mysticism stands firm, based upon the firm foundation of the historical manifestation of Jesus Christ.

.   .   .   .   .   .

Wherein consists, in the ultimate analysis, the specific character of the Pauline Mysticism?

The fact of being thought out by the aid of the conceptual apparatus of the eschatological world-view constitutes only its outward character, not its inner. This inner character is determined by the fact that Paul has thought out his conception of redemption through Christ within the sphere of belief in the Kingdom of God. In Paul's mysticism the death of Jesus has its significance for believers, not in itself, but as the event in which the realisation of the Kingdom of God begins. For him, believers are redeemed by entering already, through the union with Christ, by means of a mystical dying and rising again with Him during the continuance of the natural world-era into a supernatural state of existence, this state being that which they are to possess in the Kingdom of God. Through Christ we are removed out of this world and transferred into the state of existence proper to the Kingdom of God, notwithstanding the fact that it has not yet appeared. This is the fundamental idea of the concept of redemption, which Paul worked out by the aid of the thought-forms of the eschatological world-view.

Since the transformation of the world into the Kingdom of God begins for Paul with the death of Christ, the Primitive-Christian belief which looked to a redemption only to be realised in the future is changed into the belief in a redemption which is already present, even though it is only to be completely realised in the future. A faith of the present arises within the faith of the future. Paul connects the expectation of the Kingdom and of the redemption to be realised in it with the coming and the death of Jesus, in such a way that belief in redemption and in the Coming of the Kingdom becomes independent of whether the Kingdom comes quickly or is delayed. Without giving up eschatology, he already stands above it.

That he thinks out his concept of redemption through Christ within the sphere of the Kingdom brought in by Him, is the Primitive-Christian element in the teaching of Paul. In the Gospel preached by Jesus and in the belief of the Primitive-Christian community, redemption consists in the Coming of the Kingdom and of the Messiah.

Paul takes the belief in Jesus as the coming Messiah, in which these beliefs are comprehended, and thinks it out so thoroughly that it becomes freed from its temporal limitations and becomes valid for all time. He thus solves in a definitive fashion that pressing problem of the Christian faith of all times, namely, that although Jesus Christ has come His Kingdom is still delayed. He does not admit that, because God has tried us by not causing them to coincide temporally, the two events are no longer to be connected practically in Christian belief; but he makes Christian belief capable of holding together in thought, in their original integral connection, these two realities which have become separated in time. Thus, in Paul's mysticism, Primitive Christian belief has taken a form in which its essential feature, the inner connection between the conception of redemption through Christ and a living belief in the Kingdom of God, can become a possession of the faith of all times.

What Paul thus firmly grasped was later lost hold of. When Christianity became Hellenised there grew up a conception of redemption through Christ which no longer stood within that of the Kingdom of God, but alongside of it. Redemption is now explained as brought about by the appearance of Christ in itself, no longer by his Coming as the bringer of the Kingdom of God. And thus it has continued through the centuries. Never again do the belief in redemption through Christ and that in the Kingdom of God form a living unity. In Catholicism and in the Protestantism of the Reformers, both of which had their structure determined by the form which Christianity had taken in the process of being Hellenised, Christian doctrine is dominated by the idea of a redemption based upon the atoning death of Jesus for the forgiveness of sins, alongside of which the belief in the Kingdom of God maintains a not very vigorous existence. No doubt this belief from time to time makes a struggle to regain the position of importance which it had lost. A succession of the several shocks which the Church has had to endure have been due to the extinct volcano of the Primitive-Christian belief in the Kingdom of God again becoming active. Even in the Reformation period a movement for the renewal of belief in the Kingdom of God is also found, but it was not able to enforce its claims, in spite of the impression which it made on Luther.

It was because the Catholicism and the Protestantism of the Reformation period did not possess the belief in and the desire for the Kingdom of God in its original strength, that they were unable to exert a transforming influence upon the circumstances of their time.

With the growth of toleration in post-Reformation Protestantism there arose a religious movement which was evangelical, in the sense that it desired to go back directly to the teaching of Jesus and found itself entirely on that. In it, for the first time for centuries, belief in the Kingdom of God developed without hindrance. Previously, all such movements had come into conflict with the Church, and in that conflict had either lost their original character or been suppressed.

The movement for rational progress which was active in contemporary thought came into friendly contact with the belief in the Kingdom of God, and received from it intellectual, ethical, and religious ideals, which strengthened it for the mighty work of reform by which, between the end of the seventeenth century and the early part of the nineteenth, it changed existing conditions into those of the modern world. In this pietist movement, therefore, the belief in the Kingdom of God attained a position of powerful influence.

The weakness of this Kingdom-of-God religious movement was that it proved unable to make a place, in its belief in the Kingdom of God, for any living concept of redemption through Christ. The concept of redemption remains as undeveloped in it as the belief in the Kingdom of God did in the redemption religion of Catholicism and the Reformers. Consequently the modern Kingdom-of-God belief is an incomplete Christianity, because the personal experience of redemption through Christ does not receive its rights in it.

And similarly, because of its undeveloped belief in the Kingdom of God, the redemption-religion of the present day is an incomplete Christianity, though this is not so obvious in it as in the Kingdom-of-God religious belief. For since it gives the central place to the personal experience of redemption through Christ, it safeguards the inwardness of religion. In another respect also this redemption-religion is in a more advantageous position than the Kingdom-of-God religion. Since it has less to do with the intellectual and spiritual life of the time than the former it is less affected by the decline of that life. To-day the Kingdom-of-God religion is compelled to recognise that the ethical thought and the will to social, spiritual, and religious progress, with which for generations it has been accustomed to ally itself, have lost their vigour, and that it has been attributing a belief in the Kingdom of God to a humanity which, in the chaotic circumstances in which it finds itself, has no longer the insight or the strength to devote itself to truly spiritual ideals.

Thus modern Kingdom-of-God religion has to-day lost its

power and influence, and has had to find itself looked down upon as "Protestantism with a tincture of sociology." [1] An epigonic theology, which has adapted itself to the ideas of the time, plumes itself on representing Christianity, by aid of a modernised Reformation scholasticism, as little more than a doctrine of redemption through Christ, while allowing the belief in the Kingdom of God only to state itself in dogmatic formulae which no longer have behind them any living conviction. It confines itself to the Pauline doctrine, understood in a thoroughly un-Pauline way, of justification by faith (which itself is only a fragment of a doctrine of redemption, owing its prominence to the controversy about the Law, not Paul's real doctrine of redemption), and proceeds, by the aid of ingenuous arguments, to erect into a principle the one-sidedness from which Christianity has suffered since its Hellenisation. The belief in the Kingdom of God which lies at the heart of the Gospel of Jesus, and gives its warmth and glow to the religious life of Primitive Christianity, seems destined in the Christianity of to-day to become, if possible, even weaker than it has been for centuries.

Behind the arguments of the epigonic theology, which by its one-sided renewal of the redemption-religion of the Reformers believes itself to be doing service to Christ and to our time, there lurks the admission that, faced with the difficulties of holding in our day a living faith in the Kingdom of God, and at the same time connecting it with its own conception of redemption, which is not based on the idea of the Kingdom of God, it has been forced to capitulate.

In an undertaking which would rob of meaning and value both the religious life which responded to Christ's preaching and that of Primitive Christianity, this theology can appeal only to a Paul whom it has adapted to its own purpose, not to the Paul of reality. The path which Paul as the creator of Christ-mysticism has pointed out to all later times as the sole true path is quite a different one. He bids us return to fundamental Christianity, and to hold a profound belief in redemption through Christ as an integral part of a living belief in the Kingdom of God. In spite of all dogmatic

[1] TRANSLATOR'S NOTE.—This is the best I can do for *Kultur-protestantismus* used contemptuously, *Kultur* being in German much more nearly equivalent to 'civilisation' than to the 'culture' with which it is often confused. The Kingdom-of-God religion corresponds generally to "Religious philanthropy," the redemption-religion to "Old-fashioned Evangelicalism."

innovations, present or future, it will always remain the true ideal, that our faith should return to the richness and vitality of the Primitive-Christian faith. To this Paul gave perfect expression in his Christ-mysticism. As the uniquely great teacher of all times, he lays on us the task of striving to make more profound both our belief in redemption through Christ and our belief in the Kingdom of God, and to become constantly more strongly established in both.

The renewing of Christianity which must come will be a return to the immediacy and intensity of the faith of Early Christianity. No doubt a reintegration of Primitive-Christian faith as such is impossible, because it was embodied in temporally conditioned conceptions to which it is impossible for us to return. But the spiritual essence of them we can make ours. This we can do in proportion as we toilfully win for ourselves a living faith in the Kingdom of God, and realise ourselves within this as men redeemed by Christ.

The great weakness of all doctrines of redemption since the Primitive Christian is that they represent a man as wholly concerned with his own individual redemption, and not equally with the coming of the Kingdom of God. The one thing needful is that we should work for the establishment of a Christianity, which does not permit those who allow their lives to be determined by Christ to be "of little faith" in regard to the future of the world. However much circumstances may suggest to them this want of faith, Christianity must compel them to realise that to be a Christian means to be possessed and dominated by a hope of the Kingdom of God, and a will to work for it, which bids defiance to external reality. Until this comes about Christianity will stand before the world like a wood in the barrenness of winter.

A change has come over our belief in the Kingdom of God. We no longer look for a transformation of the natural circumstances of the world; we take the continuance of the evil and suffering, which belong to the nature of things, as something appointed by God for us to bear. Our hope of the Kingdom is directed to the essential and spiritual meaning of it, and we believe in that as a miracle wrought by the Spirit in making men obedient to the will of God. But we must cherish in our hearts this belief in the coming of the Kingdom through the miracle of the Spirit with the same ardour with which the Primitive Christianity cherished its hope of the translation of the world into the supernatural condition. Christianity cannot get away from the fact that God has laid upon it the task of spiritualising its faith. Our concern must be to see that the strength of our faith is not impaired by this transformation. It is time for our Christianity to examine itself and see whether we really still have faith in the Kingdom of God, or whether we merely retain it as a matter of traditional phraseology. There is a deep sense in which we may apply to the theological preoccupations of our day the saying of Jesus, "Seek ye first the Kingdom of God and His righteousness, and all these things shall be added unto you."

But whenever Christian faith attempts the task of bringing the significance of the appearance of Jesus and the nature of the redemption brought by Him into living relation with belief in the Kingdom of God, it finds Paul before him as the pioneer of such a Christianity. In his words there speaks the voice of a Primitive Christianity which will never pass away.

Great has been the work as a reforming influence which Paul, by his doctrine of justification by faith alone, has accomplished in opposition to the spirit of work-righteousness in Christianity. Still greater will be the work which he will do when his mystical doctrine of being redeemed into the Kingdom of God, through union with Christ, begins to bring quietly to bear upon us the power which lies within it.

.   .   .   .   .   .

Much as it needs to be emphasised, as against all false spiritualising and symbolical interpretations of Paul's mystical doctrine of redemption, that it is thought of on the lines of a natural process, it is equally certain that the quasi-natural process takes on, as it were of itself, spiritual and ethical significance. As radium by its very nature is in a constant state of emanation, so Pauline mysticism is constantly being transmuted from the natural to the spiritual and ethical. The spiritual and ethical significance shine through the naturalistic conception in a marvellous way. This shows that the naturalistic-eschatological constitutes only the outward character of his mysticism, whereas its inner essence is determined by the close connection of the concept of redemption with the belief in the Kingdom of God, which retains its significance even when the concept of the Kingdom of God is transformed from the natural into the spiritual. That is why Paul's teaching about the dying and rising with Christ, which are to be experienced in the circumstances of our lives and in all our thinking and willing, are just as true for our world-view of to-day as they were for his.

By his doctrine of the Spirit he has himself thrown a bridge from his world-view to ours. While the faith of his contemporaries was being dazzled by the outward phenomena of the possession of the Spirit, he grasped the concept of the Spirit as the manifestation of all the radiations which pass from the super-earthly into the earthly. Of these radiations he estimates the value not according to their degree of visibility, but according to the influence which they exert. Thus he values highest the unsensational ethical guid-ance of the Spirit, and recognises love as the gift in which what in its essential nature is eternal becomes reality within the temporal.

Paul's doctrine of the Spirit therefore results in the metaphysical side of redemption, as a participation in eternal life during the time of our earthly existence, appearing as something spiritual and ethical. The metaphysical and the spiritual-ethical are for Paul identical, in the sense that the spiritual-ethical bears the meta-physical within it. This conception of the unity of the eternal and the ethical, which had its origin in the eschatological world-view, contains a permanent truth. Our thought finds itself at home with it as completely as if it had been a modern synthesis.

The distinctive characteristic of the Pauline doctrine of redemp-tion is that it arose out of profound thought and, at the same time, out of direct experience. The profound thought is primary, because it carries within it an impulse to realisation in experience.

The experience which Paul sets before us as the gateway to the eternal is the dying and rising again with Christ. What deep signifi-cance lies in the fact that he does not speak of the method of the new life's beginning as a rebirth! He seems deliberately to pass by this term, already coined in the language which he spoke and wrote, and lying ready to his hand. He does so because it is impossible to fit it into the eschatological doctrine of redemption. If the Elect who belong to the Kingdom of God are already in the resurrection state of existence, their redemption, conceived of as anticipatory participation in the Kingdom while still in their natural being, must consist in their undergoing, through the union with Christ, a hidden dying and rising again, by which they become new men raised above the world and their own natural being, and are translated into the state of existence proper to the Kingdom of God. This conception of redemption, with its naturalistic realism, due to its embodiment in the thought-forms of the eschatological world-view, at the same time carries within it an intensely spiritual realism. Whereas the idea of rebirth remains a metaphor, imported into primitive Christian beliefs out of another world of thought, the conception of dying and rising again with Christ was born out of Christianity itself, and becomes for every man who seeks new life in Christ a truth continually renewed, at once primitive and permanent.

Paul powerfully urges men, by the self-revelations in which he lays bare his inner life to them, to embark upon an experience like his own. From the point of view of a later fully formulated theology his doctrine is incorrectly stated. He has not been sufficiently careful to express himself in such a way as to exclude the misunderstanding that a man, through union with Jesus Christ, redeems himself— to exclude it, that is, with the decisiveness which a later religious thought, having lost its hold on simplicity, might consider desirable. It is the prerogative of the mystic to think truth in its living vigour, unconcerned about formal correctitude.

Paul's mystical doctrine of redemption has not been taken up into Church dogma. It has preferred to adopt the concept of the sacrificial death of Jesus, basing itself on the formulation of this thought which it has received in the Pauline doctrine of justification by faith. Mysticism can never become dogma. But, on the other hand, dogma can never remain living without a surrounding aura of mysticism. Therefore Paul's mystical doctrine of redemption is for us a precious possession, without which we cannot form the right conception either of Christianity or of our individual state as Christians. It is truth which a man who has been taken possession of by Christ urges his brethren to verify in experience.

There are hosts of sayings in Paul's Epistles which offer us guidance through life, familiar sayings which we know so well, yet ever new sayings because they reveal themselves to those who accept their guidance in ever new significance. The conception of dying and rising again with Christ brings us into an inner controversy with our own existence, which extends itself in ever-widening circles. From it we receive an interpretation of all that happens to us. It does not permit us to slip through life regardless of external events, but bids us seek in them the appointed way of passing from natural being to being in the Spirit. If we want to "live a quiet life," it attacks us with the question whether the being possessed by

Christ is living itself out in us, or whether it is merely a distant echo on the horizon of our lives.

He who has fallen under the power of the conception of dying and rising again with Christ advances into an ever deeper consciousness of sin, and attains in the struggle to die from sin a quiet certitude of the forgiveness of sin. That is what Paul promises to those who, like himself, are determined to make the being-redeemed-through-Christ not a matter of word only, but of deed.

How penetratingly true is the lesson he teaches, that we cannot possess the Spirit of Christ as mere natural men, but only in so far as the dying with Christ has become reality in us!

.   .   .   .   .   .

Paul does not urge those who have been redeemed by Christ to withdraw from the world; he bids them take their place in it, that they may make use of the powers derived from their being in the Kingdom of God. His extraordinary realism preserves him from all extravagance. Inasmuch as the conception of dying and rising again with Christ has its roots in the belief in the Kingdom of God, the world-negation which it involves does not urge to asceticism or to withdrawal from the world. Consequently this religious ethic, which, moreover, arose out of the world-view incident to an expectation of the imminent end of the world is, for all its glowing ardour, sound and natural. Out of a deep necessity, and with an amazing naturalness, it makes the experience of redemption through union with Christ become actual as a manifestation of the Spirit of the being-in the Kingdom of God.

Our religion must renew itself by contact with Paul's Kingdom-of-God religion. As modern men we are in danger of confining ourselves to Kingdom-of-God propaganda and external Kingdom-of-God work. Modern Kingdom-of-God religion calls on men to do Kingdom-of-God work, as though anyone could do anything for the Kingdom of God who does not bear the Kingdom of God within him. Thus, with the best intentions, we are constantly in danger of giving our allegiance to an externalised Kingdom-of-God belief.

Paul's Kingdom-of-God belief does not take into account the possibility of a development of this natural world into the Kingdom of God. But though he gives up this world he nevertheless expects the redeemed man to manifest in it the Spirit of the Kingdom of God which is in him. Purely from inner necessity, not with a view to success, there arises an activity which is determined by the Kingdom of God. As a star, by the inner law of the light which is in it, shines over a dark world, even when there is no prospect of heralding a morning which is to dawn upon it, so the Elect must radiate the light of the Kingdom in the world. This manifestation of the Kingdom of God from inner necessity must be the core and kernel of the matter; to this any work deliberately directed to the realisation of the Kingdom is merely the outer envelope. We have constantly to remember the inexorable law, that we can only bring so much of the Kingdom of God into the world as we possess within us.

Contact with Paul's Kingdom-of-God religion is a means of giving our own this inward character. Steeled by it our religion becomes independent of welcome from the spirit of the age, or of seeing outward success. No doubt, as men who have left behind them the eschatological world-view, we cannot do otherwise than desire the transformation of the conditions of human society in the direction of the Kingdom of God, and work to that end. The Spirit of God, that speaks to us out of the non-fulfilment of the eschatological expectation of the Kingdom of God, demands it of us. But our belief in the Kingdom of God must remain Primitive Christian, in the sense that we expect its realisation not from deliberate organised measures, but from a growing power of the Spirit of God. For we also know that the manifestation, arising out of an inner necessity, of the Spirit of the Kingdom of God, of which we became partakers in the dying and rising again with Christ, is the true way of working for the Kingdom of God, without which all others are in vain.

.   .   .   .   .   .

What is the significance, for our faith and for our religious life, of the fact that the Gospel of Paul is different from the Gospel of Jesus? Is the alternative "Jesus or Paul" a real alternative, or should the phrase run, for us, "Jesus and Paul"?

It is doubtless a fact in the history of Christian belief that for centuries, in a certain sense, the Gospel of Paul stood in the way of the Gospel of Jesus. How did this result come about?

The attitude which Paul himself takes up towards the Gospel of Jesus is that he does not repeat it in the words of Jesus, and does not appeal to its authority. But in doing so he does not aim at invalidating it, but only at carrying it on in the proper way. He

preaches the Gospel of the Kingdom of God and of Jesus as the
Coming Messiah in the form which it must necessarily take in
consequence of the death of Jesus having already occurred, and
of the assigning to this death of the significance of the initial event
of the Coming of the Kingdom.[1] In the mystical redemption-
doctrine of Paul the Primitive-Christian faith discharges the task
which it had been set of bringing the belief in the expected Kingdom, and the redemption which goes with the Kingdom, into logical
connection with the belief that the Jesus who had died was the
Coming Messiah. This is, according to Paul, necessary in order
to bring home to the believer that in the union with Christ he has
already attained the state of existence proper to the Kingdom of
God, and is therefore a redeemed man, even though the Kingdom
is not yet present; and also that, as being in this state of existence,
he is freed from the domination of the Law. At the same time this
belief in the redemption already obtained through the death of
Jesus, when thus connected with the expectation of the Kingdom,
helped him to rise superior to the delay of the return of Christ
and of the appearing of the Kingdom.

It was facts and problems, with which it was necessary for the
Christian faith to deal in the period subsequent to the death of
Jesus, that made it impossible for Paul to preach the Gospel of
Jesus in exactly the same form as Jesus Himself did.

These facts and problems continued on into the following period,
so that it was not possible for the generations immediately subsequent to Paul simply to return to the Gospel of Jesus; they had to
recast His doctrine of redemption in the light of those facts and
problems, whether they did so in their own thought-forms or called
to their aid those of Paul.

The Asia Minor theology, which succeeded to the Primitive-
Christian eschatological, took over from Paul the concept of redemption through union with Christ, and recast it in Hellenistic material
as the mystical doctrine of participation in the working of the Spirit
upon the flesh, which began in the appearance of Jesus and guarantees the resurrection.[2]

Christian theology could not simply continue to steer the course
set by the Gospel of Jesus, as is obvious from the difficulties which
confront it in the attempt to establish a Christian ethic. Why did

[1] See above, pp. 113-115.
[2] See above, pp. 340-369.

it not simply set up the ethic of Jesus as the Christian ethic? Because logically it could not do so. Jesus preached the ethic of preparedness for a Kingdom which was expected to come immediately. Hellenised Christianity no longer lived in such an expectation. Therefore it could not take over the ethic of Jesus on the same basis as it had in His teaching. It was equally unable to take over Paul's ethic of the dying and rising again with Christ and of the life in the Spirit, because it no longer retained in its mysticism the eschatological conception of dying and rising again with Christ, and because the Hellenistic metaphysical conception of Spirit was no longer ethical in the same measure as Paul's eschatological conception was.[1]

It was not possible therefore for the theology of the early centuries to have recourse to Paul's ethic in the same way as they did to his doctrine of redemption. From its own conception of redemption it was unable to adduce any ethic whatever. Thus it came to set forth as Christian an ethic on a rational basis borrowed from the Greek popular philosophy, interspersed with sayings of Jesus. This was the procedure of Justin, of the great Alexandrians, and of the Greek Church teachers in general.

Whereas Eastern theology drew its life from the Hellenised Pauline mysticism, Western theology was forced by circumstances to fall back upon the Pauline doctrine of justification—it was obliged to do so because it had not the presuppositions necessary to enable it to make the Hellenised Pauline Mysticism permanently its own, and because it was equally unable to take over Paul's mysticism in its original eschatological form.

The doctrine of justification it made its own by simplifying its logic, and also by bringing it into harmony with its conception of the Church as mediating the benefits obtained by the atoning death of Jesus, and also with the natural ethical requirements of its religious life.

At the Reformation this Pauline doctrine of justification rose up and cast off the fetters which the Church had laid upon it. In this way there arose in Western Christianity a movement which professed an absolute allegiance to Paul's teaching.

The fateful thing is that the Greek, the Catholic, and the Protestant theologies all contain the Gospel of Paul in a form which does not continue the Gospel of Jesus, but displaces it. The true

[1] See above, pp. 341-343 and 373-375.

continuation of the Gospel of Jesus is found only in the authentic Primitive-Christian eschatological Paulinism. This alone is the Gospel of Jesus in the form appropriate to the time subsequent to His death. So soon as Paulinism is made into any kind of doctrine of redemption, in which the concept of redemption is no longer attached to the belief in the Kingdom of God, it naturally comes into opposition with the Gospel of Jesus, which is wholly orientated to the Kingdom of God.

The Hellenised Pauline mysticism gives up the Pauline connection between the belief in redemption and the belief in the Kingdom of God, by substituting for the Pauline eschatological concept of dying and rising again with Christ, as a means of attaining the state of existence proper to the Messianic Kingdom, the concept of participation in the working of the Spirit upon the flesh which began with the incarnation of Christ. Consequently it ceases to have any connection with Jesus' simple Gospel of the Kingdom of God. It is shut off from it by Hellenised Paulinism as though by a wall.

In Western Catholicism and in the doctrine of the Reformers the import of Jesus' teaching is impaired by that of Paul, in the sense that the doctrine of justification by faith, which took shape in the conflict with the Law, does not bring the concept of redemption into the connection with the Kingdom of God, which is essential to it in Paul's thought, but founds it on the fact of the death of Christ in itself, supplemented by the idea of sacrificial offering.

Thus in Eastern Christianity the Paul who was looked up to was unauthentic, and in Western Christianity, incomplete, with the result that for centuries the personal religion which springs from belief in the Kingdom of God has been held in abeyance by the personal religion which is dominated by the idea of redemption.

The Protestantism of the Reformers experienced this antagonism in tragic fashion. As a movement which sought the fundamental in religion it strove to return to a living Kingdom-of-God religion. As a doctrinal theology, however, it was unable to clear the narrows of the Pauline doctrine of justification by faith, into which it had come in trying to escape from the restricted Paulinism of the Catholic doctrine of redemption. In Luther's powerful mind, which could never be completely held within the bonds of any logical system, the elemental Gospel of Jesus breaks through alongside of the doctrine of justification by faith. In the end, however,

he came to rate the Hellenised Gospel of Jesus according to the
Fourth Evangelist higher than the authentic version of the Synop-
tics, because the former was easier to bring into harmony with his
Paulinism!

The difficulty of uniting ethics with a doctrine of redemption,
which (because it contains no Kingdom-of-God belief), was not
itself ethical, was very strongly felt in the Protestantism of the
Reformers and their immediate successors.[1] The conflicts which
broke out in it and shook it to its core were all ultimately traceable
to the fact that it cannot combine the doctrine of redemption with
ethics in any natural way.

The Kingdom-of-God belief, which has arisen in modern Protestantism, is not capable of being combined with a redemption-
doctrine of the Pauline type, but necessarily tends to wish to displace the Gospel of Paul in favour of the Gospel of Jesus.

An unauthentic Gospel of Jesus here comes into conflict with
an unauthentic Gospel of Paul! For in the attempt to give itself a
historical basis this Kingdom-of-God religion modernises both the
Person of Jesus and His message. It brings on the stage a Jesus who
is dominated by modern ideas of development, and whose aim is
to lay the foundation-stone of a Spiritual Kingdom of God which,
from small beginnings, is to spread over the whole world. Between
such conceptions of Jesus and of the Kingdom of God, and Paul's
doctrine of redemption, there is no road.

On the other hand, the pseudo-historical Paul, to whom
scientific theology for decades professed allegiance, moved even
further away from Jesus than did the unauthentic Paul of the
Church. The complicated Paulinism, at which the historico-critical
theology of the nineteenth century arrived, cannot be thought of
as any kind of continuation of the modernised Gospel of Jesus.
And the explanation of Paul's teaching, from the point of view of
historical theology, was finally obliged to maintain that Paul had
apostatised from Jesus and fallen under the influence of the Greek
mystery-religions!

But it is only the unauthentic Gospel of Jesus and the unauthentic Gospel of Paul which stand on this kind of relationship to one
another. Once both are understood in the light of the eschatological expectation of the Kingdom of God, out of which they arose,
the alternative "Jesus or Paul" becomes meaningless, and the

[1] See on this above, pp. 220, 225, 294-295.

modern depreciation of Paul has to be given up. For at once the integral connection between them becomes obvious, inasmuch as Paul shares Jesus' conception of the Kingdom of God, his doctrine of the redemptive significance of the death of Jesus is founded on that expectation of the Kingdom of God which is common to them both, and in his Christ-mysticism he is only developing further the concept of the redemptive significance of the fellowship of the believers with the future Messiah, which is already present in the preaching of Jesus.[1] From a truly historical point of view the teaching of Paul does not diverge from that of Jesus, but contains it within it.

Thus when our belief attains to clearness, and relates itself to the true Jesus and the true Paul, we find that for it too they belong together. It thenceforth neither permits an unauthentic or incomplete Paul to obscure for our religious life the fundamental Gospel of Jesus, nor does it continue to cherish the delusion that it must free itself from Paul in order really to give allegiance to the Gospel of Jesus. Henceforward Paul is for it, as he so often designated himself, the "minister of Jesus Christ."

It is no more possible for us than it was for Primitive Christianity and the generations between simply to set up the Gospel of Jesus as the Christian Faith. We, too, have to come to terms with the facts and problems of the period subsequent to the death of Jesus. Our faith, like that of Primitive Christianity, must grasp the appearance and the dying of Jesus as the beginning of the realisation of the Kingdom of God, must become certified of the future redemption as being already present, and must rise superior to the fact that the substitution of the Kingdom of God for the Kingdom of the world is still delayed. To believe in the Gospel of Jesus means for us to let the belief in the Kingdom of God which He preached become a living reality within the belief in Him and in the redemption experienced in Him. Paul, in his Christ-mysticism, was the first to accomplish this: is it reasonable for us to neglect the gains which he has secured, and attempt to reach the same result in our own strength and by independent thought?

However much confidence we rightly or wrongly feel in ourselves, if we have any real appreciation of unique greatness we cannot fail to come under the attraction of the powerful thinking and deep personal religion, in which Jesus' Gospel of the Kingdom

[1] See above, pp. 102-110.

of God first became the religion of belief in Him and in the Kingdom of God. No other road is available to us than that which Paul opened up. It is only by way of Christ-mysticism that we can have the experience of belief in the Kingdom of God and in redemption through Jesus Christ as a living possession.

This Christ-Mysticism Paul thought out within the framework of the eschatological world-view, with such depth and living power that, so far as its spiritual content is concerned, it remains valid for all aftertimes. As a fugue of Bach's belongs in form to the eighteenth century, but in its essence is pure musical truth, so does the Christ-mysticism of all times find itself again in the Pauline as its primal form.

If the Christian faith of any particular period desired to free itself from Paul in order to adopt the Gospel of Jesus to its own thought-forms, it would not be necessary to take any special measure to bring it back to the allegiance which it had cast off. For just in the measure in which it had attained by its own efforts to religious convictions of permanent value, it would also have returned to Paul. If a preacher passes through the stage of desiring to preach Jesus only, to the exclusion of Paul, there is no need to try to turn him from his purpose. Just in the measure in which he communicates truth about Jesus, which he has known in experience, he will be preaching in his own words Paul's doctrine of redemptive union with Christ.

Paul is so great that his authority has no need to be imposed upon anyone. All honest, accurate, and living thought about Jesus inevitably finds in his its centre.

Thus the Christian faith of to-day, like that of past and future centuries, is in some way or other determined by that of Paul. Let us hope the authentic and complete Paul will be expressed in it. May there never happen again, as in the past, the tragic error by which an unauthentic or an incomplete Gospel of Paul perverts Jesus' Gospel of the Kingdom of God from coming to its rights! If the Gospel of Paul, the primal Christian mystic, strikes the keynote of our faith, the Gospel of Jesus will sound forth clear and true.

Mysticism is not something which can be imported from without into the Gospel of Jesus. For that Gospel is itself not a mere proclaiming of the Kingdom of God; it promises in mysterious sayings the attainment of the Kingdom of God, and the redemption which is bound up with it, to those who are in fellowship with Jesus as the future Lord of the Kingdom. Thus Paul's mystical doctrine of redemption has its roots in the Gospel of Jesus. In Paul's doctrine of dying and rising again with Christ the sayings live again in which Jesus adjures His followers to suffer and die with Him, to save their lives by losing them with Him. What else does Paul do than to give to those sayings of Jesus the meaning which they bear for all those who have ever desired to belong to Him?

In the same way the ethic of the Gospel of Jesus lives on in that of Paul. Jesus' ethic of preparedness for the Kingdom of God becomes, for Paul, the ethic of redemption into the state of existence proper to the Kingdom of God—a redemption known in experience through fellowship with Jesus. By means of the concept of a redemption through Christ which has already become reality, the ethic of the expectation of the Kingdom is transformed into the ethic of its verification. It leaves behind its dependence on the eschatological expectation, and becomes bound up with the assurance that with Christ the realisation of the Kingdom has begun. In the only possible logical way, Paul's thought transforms the ethic of Jesus into the ethic of the Kingdom of God which Jesus brought, and in doing so it retains all the directness and force of the ethic of the Sermon on the Mount. Jesus' great commandment of Love shines forth in all its splendour in Paul's hymn of that Love which is greater than Faith and Hope, as well as in the precepts which he gives for daily life.

In the hearts in which Paul's mysticism of union with Christ is alive there is an unquenchable yearning for the Kingdom of God, but also consolation for the fact that we do not see its fulfilment.

Three things make up the power of Paul's thought. There belong to it a depth and reality, which lay their spell upon us; the ardour of the early days of the Christian faith kindles our own; a direct experience of Christ as the Lord of the Kingdom of God speaks from it, exciting us to follow the same path.

Paul leads us out upon that path of true redemption, and hands us over, prisoners, to Christ.

INDEX OF REFERENCES

1. OLD TESTAMENT, WITH APOCRYPHA, ETC.

3. OTHER LITERATURE

INDEX OF NAMES

INDEX OF SUBJECTS